TIBET

AND THE TIBETANS

TIBET

AND THE TIBETANS

BY

GRAHAM SANDBERG

GYAN

ISBN : 978-81-212-1537-4(HB)

First Published, 1906

Published, 2018

Published by

GYAN

Gyan Publishing House
5, Ansari Road
Daryaganj, New Delhi-110002
Phone: 011-47034999, 9811692060
www.gyanbooks.com
E-mail: books@gyanbooks.com

Printed at: G. Print Process, Delhi.

PREFACE.

In the following pages have been epitomized the results of many years of personal investigation into Tibetan mysteries. The unique physical features, the geology, the botany, the zoology of the country, also the characteristics, occupations, religion, and literature of the inhabitants, are the subjects mainly treated of. Much of the matter included here had been put in type before the conclusion of the recent political Mission to Tibet. However, few new facts concerning Tibet were revealed by this Mission. It is, moreover, a testimony to the fulness of the information brought back in previous years by the secret native agents of the Transfrontier Survey, that our own description of Lhasa in these pages (derived mainly from the private reports of these agents) tallies in most particulars with the accounts of the city as now described by the English visitors of 1904. Only, the native explorers in question seem on the whole to have been a little more exact in their narratives than the English visitors.

GRAHAM SANDBERG.

London:
January, 1905.

NOTE.

When death overtook Mr. Sandberg, this book was almost ready for publication. The bulk of the work—280 pages—had already been revised in proof by him; and had he been spared for a few weeks longer, he would have seen his book go forth into the world as another testimony to the ripe scholarship that he had strenuously gathered through years of toil. Unhappily it was not to be. In March of this year he was taken away, and his book was denied the finishing touches of the master's hand. At the request of Mrs. Sandberg, I have accordingly revised the remaining sheets and added a list of contents.

The career that was thus cut short was one of singular devotion to learning and religion. In 1870 Samuel Louis Graham Sandberg graduated at Trinity College, Dublin. Called to the Bar in 1874, he practised for some years on the Northern Circuit, while at the same time eagerly carrying on literary studies. His sympathies were extraordinarily wide, interesting him alike in science, natural history, literature, and philology. In 1879 he took orders, and in 1886 he entered upon a chaplaincy in India. Here, as chaplain at Dinapur, Dacca, Jhansi, Cuttack, Subathu, Darjeeling, Barrackpore, and St. John's, Calcutta, he was able to give full scope to his manifold interests, and speedily attained to acknowledged authority. In particular the associations of Darjeeling inspired him to the study in which his life's work culminated—the language, literature, and natural history of Tibet. In the *Nineteenth Century* of 1889 appeared his first published work on Tibet, soon followed by other articles in various magazines. In 1888 his linguistic studies bore fruit in a *Manual of the Sikkim Bhutia Language*, of which a second edition appeared in 1895; and in 1894 he published a most useful *Handbook of Colloquial Tibetan*. An *Itinerary of the Route from Sikkim to Lhasa* appeared in 1901. At that time he began his heaviest task, supervising the publication of Sarat Chandra Das's Tibetan Dictionary; but even this labour could not exhaust his energies, for in 1904 appeared his *Exploration of Tibet*, and he was busied with the preparation of the present work.

But now his health, always delicate, gave way entirely. In June 1904 he was seized with tubercular laryngitis, and in March of this year, after sore suffering, the strenuous and noble life came to an end. *Manibus date lilia plenis.*

L. D. BARNETT.

LONDON :
August, 1905.

TABLE OF CONTENTS.

CHAPTER VII.

Monasteries and Nunneries.

CHAPTER VIII.

Inmates of Monasteries: their Grades, Discipline, and Occupation.

CHAPTER IX.

The Inhabitants in General.

CHAPTER X.

Lhasa: the Capital of Tibet.

CHAPTER XI.

The Mythology of Tibetan Buddhism.

CHAPTER I.

AT THE THRESHOLD.

Nature by her own arrangements seems to have decreed that Tibet should be the last country to be brought under the domain of modern civilization, therein completely siding with the opinion of those who actually hold the land. Intruders have not only to reckon with the policy of the Tibetan authorities which prohibits entrance to all strangers; but they have also to get the better of the physical defences which beset the portals of the forbidden regions on every quarter. Monstrous walls of mountain, stupendous glaciers and snow-fields, unbridged rivers, valleys of surpassing sterility, aid the inhospitable inhabitants in shutting out the traveller.

Mountainous as the country is within its own confines, it is enclosed on the borders by ranges as a rule much loftier and more bulky than those inside. Along the southern frontier, from long. 78° to long. 98°, stretch the massive ranges, chain within chain, of the Indian Himalayas. Turning up to the north we find on the western side the ganglion of mountains which, as a continuation of the Himalayas, spread themselves out in Kashmir, Ladak, and Nubra. Higher up and still forming the western boundary, there run in from the west the buttress-ends of the mighty Karakorams with K_2, Gusherbrum, Masherbrum, and the other giant summits which have been made in recent years so familiar to us by the graphic writing and vivid pictures of Sir W.M. Conway. Barriers equally gigantic in size (save in a few places where the lowness of the bounding range does not mean accessibility because of the terrible wilderness of sand and ice behind) are disposed along the northern limits. There, on the north, Tibet is shut in, as we pass from west to east, by the Kuen Lün, the Akka Tag, and Altan Tag ranges in succession. In the Tsaidam and Kökö Nor region is placed a north-eastern series of mountains which have proved less impregnable than the defences in other quarters. Through the easy defiles here and by way of the Hoang Ho, many adventurous spirits have penetrated. Nevertheless, the various parallel lines of the Nan Shan, the European names of which bestowed by Russian travellers read rather grotesquely, make a very substantial boundary in this direction. Crossing the Hoang Ho and turning due south, we have in the mysterious Amdo country the numerous minor mountain ranges which separate, very indefinitely, the various petty states which own allegiance according to fancy, some to Tibet, and some to China. While, further south, the eastern confines have, to guard them, not merely row behind row of rocky battlements, but also the mighty rivers running three and four abreast which pass from north to south and out into the world beyond.

Such are the boundaries of Tibet on cursory view. They shall be examined in detail later on.

As may be imagined, the tremendous portals of this mystic realm form, at every point, vestibules worthy of the marvels to be disclosed beyond. Mountains, individually of colossal proportions, stand in troops upon the threshold of the Forbidden Land, guarding as it were the Passes to be found at intervals all round, and which Passes offer the sole means of access within. Labyrinthine and dangerous are the pathways which lead to these strange entrances into the country. There is great similarity in the appearances about you on whichever side you approach; except perhaps coming from the north by Charlik over the Akka Tag, as did Bonvalot and the Littledales.

But take one of the more ordinary routes, by way of Sikkim, to some Pass into Tibet from the south. First, you surmount by zigzag path up, over, and down, the lower outer ridges of the Himalayas: then, through deep valleys strewn with enormous boulders, gradually ascending; then, darkly penetrating along the bottom of a profound gorge. So you go, ever striving to veer northwards; for northwards lies your goal. Next, up and up and up again, keeping perhaps to a string-course ledge which rounds the shoulders of the giant hills and creeps onwards along the sheer face of precipitous cliff and chasm rent asunder.

The mountains are everywhere about you. They tower above your head and clusters of peaks are revealed at the upper end of the valleys which open in so many directions; while the great brawny breasts of others lie far away with the mists rolling upon them. As you take your course along the back of some lower ridge, you notice that it is flanked with spurs which advance to meet similar projections from another ridge parallel to yours but loftier. They do not meet; but there and in between the protruding piers, in the depths below you, the trees are seen packed close together, an ocean of the darkest greens and russets. About you and above you are the great pines, *Abies Webbiana* and *Pinus excelsa;* but down there are the maples and rhododendrons and chestnuts and evergreen oaks peculiar to the Himalayas, with here and there a quaint tree-fern. The trees clothe completely the lower limbs of the mountains, and then ascend in seried flounces far up the skirts of the greater heights; each different species of pine visibly keeping to its own proper zone of altitude. And you know that in the remotest bottom—hidden by those weird throngs of trunk and leafy-crown – there winds a secret stream brought direct from snow-field and glacier; and, presently perhaps, an opening in the deep-down forest allows you a gleam and a flash from the tumbling waters.

As you near the frontier of Tibet, the ravines-ful of trees gradually disappear. The valleys soon become wider and very desolate, strewn with large stones and blocks of rock; whilst you procession of huge boulders marks the moraine of a glacier which some centuries ago travelled slowly downwards. The mountains, meanwhile, take a vaster scale, quite different from the view they presented at a distance, forbidding and fearful to look upon. Such shattered fantastic monsters they seem, holding themselves up to heaven in boundless defiance of harmony in size.

Then, in the fissures channelled on their great faces are perceived the swollen glaciers bulging forth. Spurs and protuberances of rock are connected by causeways of pure ice and the causeways bank up fields of lately-fallen snow. These ice-bridges, which often span deep gorges, allowing you to cross where otherwise it would be impassable, are styled by the Tibetan traveller *Lhá-i Sampa* "bridges of the gods."

In these regions, mists and storms sweep up very swiftly and suddenly. As the coming night lets fall its shadows about you the sleet and hail slant down in blinding showers and eye-sight is no longer of any guidance. Your only escape from utter bewilderment and the deathly cold is to creep to the southern lea of some rock which has been absorbing the sun's warmth through the day; and to wedge your form in there, embedded in blankets.

Darkness dyes the twilight black. The storm increases; and hark, those sounds of falling rocky masses! The mountains are speaking to one another. These uncouth giants have a hoarse and monstrous language of their own.

In this way and amidst such scenes, the traveller can approach to the confines of the Forbidden Land. Saddles of rock sunk between higher summits give access to the country beyond, and precarious paths lead up to all such depressions in the guarding ranges. These are the famous Passes which admit you into Tibet. At the head or culminating point of the Pass is invariably to be seen a cairn of stones artificially reared by native travellers. And there your Tibetan guides give vent to their feelings of relief at the ascent surmounted and of awe at the presence of the mystic spirits which guard the left-hand side of every Pass-top. Scattering two or three handfuls of their precious *tsampa* or parched barley-meal, they cry:

Lhá sollo, lhá sollo! Lhá gyallo, lhá gyallo!
Hail, hail, to the gods!
Victory, victory to the gods!

THE VIEW BEYOND THE BARRIERS.

But what is to be seen beyond those bounding ranges? The verge of the mysterious country gained, does anything new, do any of its reported marvels, as yet greet the sight? Naturally in a mountainous jumble such as that which fences in Tibet one would hardly expect much view from a Pass-summit, even though the summit lies cradled in the line along which the mountains reach their climax of height. Nevertheless the prospect from many of these gate-ways into the land beyond is something of a panorama—and from certain points a remarkably striking and extensive one, too.

Now, many European adventurers have actually travelled in the country itself; whereas formerly few could do more than wistfully gaze into regions whence they were irrevocably shut out from penetrating. However, whether he may be fortunate enough to go further or not, no man of the least degree of sentimental susceptibility can ever put away from his memory the recollection of his first glimpse into the Great Beyond. The features of the view are always, moreover, sufficiently distinctive to lie drawn upon the brain as an ineffaceable mental landscape.

Let us listen to a few of those explorers who have recorded their impressions of their first view into Tibet.

Sir Joseph Hooker, in 1849, having journeyed through Sikkim reached the summit of the Dongkhya La, "the frozen yak pass," the cairn on which stands at a height of 18,100 feet above the level of the sea; and he thus describes the view:—

The most remarkable features of this landscape were its enormous elevation and its colours and contrast to the black, rugged, and snowy Himalaya of Sikkim. All the mountains between Donkia Pass and the Arun river were of a yellowish-red colour, rising and falling in long undulations like dunes and perfectly bare of perpetual snow or glaciers. Rocks everywhere broke out on their flanks and often along their tops; but the general contour of the whole immense area was very open and undulating. Still further northwards, the mountains were rugged, often rising into peaks which from the angles I took cannot be below 24,000 feet and are probably higher. The most lofty mountains were on the range north of Nepal, not less than 120 miles distant ....

. . . . Cholamoo lake lay in a broad scantily-grassed sandy and stony valley; snow-beds, rocks and glaciers dipped abruptly towards its head, and on its west bank a lofty brick-red spur sloped upwards from it, conspicuously cut into terraces for several hundred feet above its waters . . . . The monarch of mountains (Kinchenjunga) looked quite small and low from this point, and it was difficult to believe it was more than 10,000 feet more lofty than my present position. I repeatedly looked from it to the high Tibetan mountains in the extreme N.-W. distance; and I was more than ever struck with the apparently immense distance and consequent altitude of the latter—I put, however, no reliance on such estimates. To the south the eye wandered down the valley of the Lachoong . . . . South-east the stupendous snowy amphitheatre of Donkia was a magnificent spectacle.

I had been given to understand that from Donkia Pass the whole country of Tibet sloped away in descending steppes to the Yaru river and was more or less of a plain; and, could I have trusted my eyes only, I should have confirmed this assertion so far as the slope was concerned, when, however, the levelled theodolite was directed to the distance, the reverse was the case. Unsnowed and thus, apparently, low mountains touched the horizon line of the telescope; which proves that, if only 37 miles off, they must, from the dip of the horizon, have been at least 1,000 feet higher than the observer's position.

General Macintyre, V.C., who was permitted to cross the Niti Pass from Garhwal into Tibet early in June, gives a striking description of the appearance of the country just over the border at that time of year before the new vegetation has begun to show. This part of Tibet is the southern portion of the Guge district of Ngari Khorsum, due north of the great glaciers in the Niti and Milam valleys of the Himalayas. He writes:—

A strange weird-looking land, to all appearance a desert, stretching far and wide before us towards distant ranges of barren undulating mountains, tinted with every shade of red, yellow, purple, and blue, rising tier beyond tier, and culminating in snow-clad ridges and peaks—all their features looking marvellously distinct through the clear rare atmosphere. Broad table-lands, averaging about 15,000 feet above the sea-level, bare, brown, and monotonous, sloping gradually down from the foot of the great snowy chain of the Himalayas behind us, and intersected by huge ravines growing deeper and wider as they all trend northwards towards the river Sutlej flowing hidden among their mighty labyrinths far away below us. The solemn waste diversified here and there by low arid hills of a brick-red hue. In the dark sapphire-blue firmament, a blazing sun shedding a cheerless dazzling glare on all around us. Not a sound but the wailing of the wind to break the dead depressing silence, save perhaps the croak of a big raven or the snorting of a troop of *kiang* (wild asses), as the startled animals stand for a few seconds to gaze at the intruders ere they wheel simultaneously about and gallop madly away over the rolling wind-swept slopes of shingle and sun-baked earth.

Here in small flocks, few and far between, roams the ponderous-horned *Ovis* ever watchful and wary. A wolf may be occasionally detected slinking stealthily off. Sometimes a shy hare starts from the cover of a scrubby tussock of the stunted herbage that is sparsely scattered over the stony soil; or a grey marmot may be seen sitting erect on some sandy knoll, disturbing nature's silent repose with its shrill chirping whistle ere it vanishes into its burrow hard by. Even the Tibetan hamlets, which very rarely occur in these dreary wilds, have a decayed and forlorn look that is quite in keeping with their desolate dream-like surroundings. Such were my general impressions of the country we were now in.

THE WAY INTO TIBET.

The country has been approached with a view to gain entrance from every point of the compass. In some regions access is comparatively speaking easy; at other points the natural difficulties are so enhanced by accumulations of snow and ice that the way is open only during a limited period of the year; but in no quarter of the extensive border-line of this great territory is communication from without an absolute impossibility. Although this secluded Tibetan world lies apparently so blockaded by physical barriers—so fast-bound by mountain and glacier and violent winds—it is, nevertheless, a fact that all round the frontier there is constant intercourse of some kind going on with the countries outside except perhaps in the depth of winter.

With China this intercourse is in many districts abundant and continuous. So, too, is the traffic between Tibet and Mongolia on the north-east. Communication from the north—from Yarkand, Dzungaria, and from Central Asia generally, although not considerable, is yet carried on regularly, at stated times, by caravans and small parties and does not appear to be restricted by either political or fiscal conditions.

The admission of traffic into Tibet from the west and south seems to be governed by regulations more or less complicated. Native traders coming into the country from Ladak and from the petty states in the Western and South-Western Himalayas are only allowed entrance during the period from April to October each year. A Tibetan official has to journey to most of the important Passes on the Ladak, Lahoul, and Kumaon frontier early in the spring to inspect each one and to declare whether or not it shall be regarded as open that season. Some years smallpox or other severe sickness prevails in certain of the valleys of the Western Himalayas, such as the Byans, the Milam, or the Mana valley; and then the particular Pass leading out of such valley into Tibet is said to be sealed or shut for that year by the official and no traffic allowed to come over.

Furthermore, even the native denizens of every state actually touching Tibet are not all allowed general access during the period when the Passes are free. The inhabitants of certain bordering districts are suffered to proceed to only one or two trading centres within the Forbidden Land. Thus the Lahulis and Kulu folk may carry merchandise to such centres in the west of Ngari Khorsum as Gart'ok and Totling but no further into the interior. The dwellers of most of the valleys of Garhwal and Kumaon are limited to Gya-nyima, Dongpo, and Tsa-parang. On the other hand the Bashahri and Kunuwari people, living adjacent to these last, have by prescription freedom to go anywhere in Tibet and to penetrate even to Lhása and Eastern Tibet.

So, likewise, in the case of the frontier states further east. The Assamese may not trade direct with the Tibetan provinces; but all traffic must be carried on through the natives of the Tawang Raj who receive merchandise either at Tawang itself or bring it up from Assam *viâ* Odalguri. The Bhutan people appear to have secured unrestricted intercourse between themselves and the north, but at the same time heavy customs duties and personal bribes are extorted by certain officials of Bhutan itself from every single packman or pilgrim of their own land who passes into Tibet. The many rival jurisdictions in Bhutan offer frequent opportunities for this kind of exaction. Between Nepal and Tibet there is considerable liberty of communication; but Kirong and Dingri are thought critical points for traders to get through unmolested or unmulcted by the semi-authorised levellers of black mail. Nepali subjects are not permitted openly to enter Tibet by Takla-khar on the Kumaon border.

The Indian Government has been at much trouble to secure a certain degree of mercantile traffic between India and Tibet by way of Sikkim. The natives of Sikkim have for many generations enjoyed the fullest rights of entry beyond the frontier; but Hindu and Bengali traders have usually fallen under the same ban which excludes Europeans. However, now, after considerable negotiation, a station named Yátung, situated within Tibetan territory in the Chhumbi valley, has been opened as a centre of traffic; and Hindus and even Englishmen may proceed there for trading purposes without let or hindrance, even though the place is technically in the sacred land itself. The customs officer placed there by the Chinese Government happens to be an Englishman, but even he may not pass the barrier wall Tibet-wards.

Many Tibetan pedlars undertake trips into India in the autumn and winter months. A certain number may be observed in the Calcutta bazars every Christmas-time. Some are from Bhutan only; but a few come even from Lhása.

But all which we have said, so far, concerns but little the actual pathways over the Tibetan border-line. Moreover, when we have detailed and pointed them out as we wish to do, that information will hardly have made easier the passage thither for us Europeans who are so rigidly prohibited from entrance.

Lonely the Pass may seem; beset by cascades of stones and beds of snow; of unbreathable altitude; far away on either side from village or outpost; nevertheless, when any English traveller has set his mind on making his way thither and quietly slipping over into some unfrequented corner of the territory, somehow by magic the news of his intentions is wafted over the mountains and sure enough a party of dirty-faced Tibetans will reach the Pass before him. Then will follow the usual result. First bluster and threats from the headman of the party; next entreaties and miserable appeals as to the fate awaiting them all if the traveller persists in pushing on into the country. Finally the latter becoming moved to magnanimity and contenting himself with a stroll on the northern face of the Pass just to say he has been in Tibet, retraces his steps hardly knowing why he has so readily yielded. Sometimes, when eager determination over-rides the remonstrances of the Tibetan official, and the young adventurer refuses to turn back, an *émeute* is raised among the nearest inhabitants and the traveller is seriously maltreated. That was the consequence when a young lieutenant, in 1896, made his way beyond Takla-khar in Purang, regardless of official protestations. Three hundred natives assembled and stoned him.

There are, however, several vulnerable bits in the cordon encircling these fascinating regions where peaceful entry into the land may be accomplished and where many days' march into the heart of the territory could be stolen before information of the intruder's presence became known. The entire length of the northern frontier-line of Tibet, we believe, remains practically unguarded. So distant from any settled district or even from any temporary pasturage of nomadic tribes are the Passes over the (so-called) Kuen Lün, Akka Tag, and Altan Tag ranges, that no watch is kept by the Tibetan Government anywhere near that region. Much the same might be said of the north-east boundary round about Kökö Nor. There, however, as a Chinese Amban is specially stationed at Sining in order to watch Chinese interests in the neighbourhood, there is some risk of interference. Nevertheless, as the stream of traders of all sorts and conditions is unceasing through Sining, Lanchou-fu, Tankar, and other adjacent towns, the likelihood of recognition or hindrance is small. Moreover, the Kökö Nor districts and Tsaidam, which lie beyond Sining, are admittedly open to foreigners and are every year visited by Russian and other European travellers. To pass further to the south-west, across the Burhan Bota range and into the Di Chhu region, without exciting suspicion, is therefore comparatively a simple matter. It was in this fashion and by this route that Huc and Gabet, Przhevalsky, Rockhill, and Kozlov gained an easy entrance into Tibet.

Of necessity the great factor in any successful incursion by these unwatched doorways is the possession of ample funds wherewith to procure supplies of food, baggage, animals, and servants. The way into Tibet by the passes over the Akka Tag and Kuen Lün ranges which involves previous lengthy journeys through Asiatic Russia and Chinese Turkistan is practically closed to all European explorers save the very rich. The parties of Mons. Bonvalot and of Mr. St. George Littledale who successfully tapped Tibet through these savage and unpeopled wilds were provided with unlimited means for purchasing resources of every kind. Thus Mr. Littledale was in a position to buy at Khoten and Cherchen, previous to attempting the passage of the Akka Tag, 120 mules, ponies, and asses, as well as to hire 130 more, besides carts, tents, and enormous consignments of food. He bought, he tells us, at these the last towns passed before entering the desert tracts along the northern frontier of Tibet, "25,000 lbs. of Indian corn for the animals and six months' provisions for ourselves and men."

By the Sining, Kökö Nor, and Di Chhu route, such resources and such an outlay are not certainly indispensable; and persons with slender means able to push their way and travel under the stress of hardships, might with circumspection and with good fortune find their way far into untraversed districts of East Tibet. Mr. Rockhill, without excessive expenditure, has indeed broken far into these tracts. If Chhamdo be evaded, however, something might be done by such undaunted spirits to unravel the mystery of the upper waters of the Salwin and the Mekhong rivers, the sources of which still continue absolutely unelucidated—in spite of the wild speculations and asseverations of Prince Henry of Orleans, and, later, of Messrs. Kozlov and Ladyghin.

Another pathway of access to the country left unprotected is the difficult detour by way of Leh, the Changchenmo valley, the southeast corner of Lingzhi T'ang, and over the Lanak La, into the districts along the 34th parallel of latitude. This was the track of ingress adopted by Captain Bowen with Dr. Thorold and Atma Ram, and, subsequently, successfully followed by Messrs. Wellby and Malcolm, and by Major Deasy. Admission further south *viâ* Tangtse and eastwards along the Pangkong Lake is generally out of the question, although the route this way into Central Tibet is physically the easiest of any save that through Sikkim. The Dokpa shepherds around the eastern end of the Pangkong Lake are ever on the alert to give information of approaching travellers; and a messenger despatched from Noh into Rudok at once arouses the Jongpön of that fortress and his retainers.

Finally, one of the most feasible entrances to the south-western districts is, after all, the old route from Almora by the valleys of the Alakananda and the Dauli and so into the peak country east of the Milam glacier region; whence one of the Purang Passes, preferably the Lipu Lek La or the Mangshang La, gives ready access into the tracts south of lakes Map'ang and Lang-gak. It is near here that the defensive station of Takla-Khar in Purang is located, however; and unless the out-look kept there is either eluded or beguiled, admission is not to be gained, the people of the place being hostile and turbulent to a degree greater than is common with Tibetan folk. Travellers of note have, in several instances, succeeded in entering the country by this way for the past 100 years. Moorcroft was the first to try it, on his journey to the lakes in 1812; Henry Strachey following in his tracks in 1846, Richard Strachey in 1848, and Dr. Thomson a few years later. This route was, furthermore, the path of access chosen by Mr. Ryall in 1877, and by Mr. H. Savage Landor in 1896.

CHAPTER II.

TIBET IN ITS GENERAL ASPECTS.

We must at once dispel from our minds the usual idea that Tibet itself is one vast table-land, remarkable only for lofty altitude throughout. Great undulating plains are a feature in certain parts, as we shall presently see; but even these desolate expanses are, at short intervals, crossed by long ranges of mountains, carrying peaks which often in height nearly equal the average of the summits of the Himalayas. Doubtless the immense elevation of the general level of the whole country detracts from the apparent height of Tibetan mountains; but, with an actual attitude of 24 to 26 thousand feet above the level of the sea, these ranges of peaks are thus frequently 10,000 feet and more above the level even of such elevated plains and valleys as exist in Tibet. Interlocking lines of lofty mountains; mighty rivers; extensive plains, sometimes undulating and fertile, sometimes rugged and of awe-striking sterility and desolation; together with many districts broken up into networks of ravine and gorge—all these features are comprised in the physical conformation of this uplifted land.

Unquestionably the leading characteristic is the great elevation of the entire territory. However, this elevation varies markedly. The average height of the surface varies with the latitude and not longitudinally. This seems to be a general rule governing the altitude throughout, but more uniformly so in that portion of Tibet lying westof longitude 92°. The rule is that there is substantially one level or superficial plane, independent of the traversing mountain ranges, running mostly in zones or belts which maintain an uniform altitude along the same latitude. The greatest height of the general superficies of Tibet is found in a broad band from west to east occupying the northern tracts, and again in a narrow belt from west to east running adjacent to the southern frontier. Between these elevated areas, and also following in the main this latitude, there occurs a long depression which is in fact the valley or basin of the Yeru Tsangpo—the great arterial water-way of Tibet. Along the latitude of the main course of this river—in parts not more than 90 miles north of the line of our Indian border—the plane of elevation sinks to an average of 11,150 feet above sea-level; and this depression of elevation continues along the same latitude (29° to 29° 30′), even where further east the river leaves this parallel for its northward bend.

The northern tracts of this territory, which, from the steppe-like character of the more western parts, are known as the Jang-t'ang ("Plains of the North"), or simply as the *Chang* or *Jhang,* attain the loftiest general altitude. That portion skirting the base of the Kuen Lün Mountains is uniformly lower than the desolate plains stretching from west to east, some 50 miles further south. Here, keeping to the parallel of latitude of 35° N., the Jang-t'ang reaches its highest level, one of over 17,000 feet above the sea. In the Lingzhi T'ang, in this latitude, near the Karakorums, the altitude is 17,300 feet; and 700 miles further east (longitude 89° E.) we find the plains and a lake in exactly the same latitude with a reported altitude of 17,400 feet, said to have been accurately measured. Again, take another test case. Captain Bower gives his altitude at "Camp 30" as 16,907 feet. We find his latitude then was 32° 45′ N. and his longitude *circa* 85° 15′ E. Now, after three months' time, he is again in that very same latitude but much further to the east, namely, 88° 40′, yet his altitude is practically the same, namely, at "Camp 71," 16,838 feet. Further south of this parallel, the average elevation of the Jang-t'ang decreases considerably; and the regions of Tibet lying between the 31st and 32° 30′ parallels must be placed at an approximate altitude of 15,000 feet. Further south again, as we have seen, the level is much lower.

East of the 92nd meridian, however, our rule of latitudinal zones of elevation fails so far as the more northern districts are concerned. In or about that meridian, a decided drop in height occurs, the average altitude of the general plane of the country to the east being 13,500 to 14,200 feet in all latitudes N. of 30° and S. of 36°. Further to the north-east the decrease in elevation is still more marked; so that in the Tsaidam plains, west of Kökö Nor, and beyond the Tibetan confines, 8,000 to 9,000 feet is the usual height. So again, in those parts of Tibet far to the south-east, there is likewise a fall, the descent being much greater and the valley-level between Zayul and Bat'ang being ordinarily under 8,000 feet. Indeed, the deep valleys in Zayul itself, bordering on the ranges which wall off Burmah, have mostly an altitude under 6,000 feet.

THE HIGHEST COUNTRY ON EARTH.

Taken generally, the claim of Tibet to be deemed the loftiest country in the world cannot fail to be admitted. The great northern tracts for hundreds of miles, as we have seen, average an elevation of from 15,000 to 17,300 feet. Its very valleys in the main territory scale 11,000 feet. Its people live and breathe and dance and sing and pray in towns and villages which rarely stand lower than 12,000 feet. The monasteries sheltering large communities of men or women are, by choice, erected on picturesque ledges at an elevation as high as the summit of Mont Blanc. Shigatse, second city in Tibet and a great commercial mart, has been built 12,250 feet above the sea; and Lhásá, the capital, is laid out on an alluvial plain 11,600 feet above the same level. Derge, the Tibetan Birmingham with a population of 6,000, stands at 12,700 feet; and Chhamdo, with 11,000 inhabitants, scales 11,500 feet. And all this only concerns the general superficies of the country; for, in the regions where it has been flung up into peaks and mountain ranges, 25,000 feet is reckoned in this land no extraordinary elevation; whilst the Passes daily surmounted by man and beast scale anything up to 19,800 feet. Yet, in contrast to these immensities, we have one town in the south-east corner of Tibet, Shikha, capital of the Zayul valley, pitched at only 4,650 feet.

FOUR CLASSES OF TERRITORY.

More or less, it is mountainous everywhere in Tibet; even the great plains, of which so much has been written, being traversed at intervals by mountain chains complex though not lofty. Nevertheless the territory is not of one character throughout. Both climate and configuration vary in the different zones included within these regions. Speaking generally, Tibetans classify their country as divisible into four sorts. They discriminate the *T'ang* districts, the *Dok* districts, the *Rong* districts, and the *Gang* districts; and this classification will be found a very convenient one.

T'ANG DISTRICTS.

The *T'ang* country is the region of the plateaus or steppes, those parts already alluded to under the specific name of Jangt'ang, and restricted almost exclusively to the north, and more especially characteristic of the western half of the northern tracts. Rising to the summit of a low ridge, you suddenly look athwart an immense plain which begins perhaps a few hundred feet below you and stretches without a break, generally a distance of 15 or 16 miles to a bounding range of hills, but sometimes uninterrupted to the horizon in a clear sweep of 30 or 40 miles. And this must be taken as the real feature of the country. We have not level desert plains as in Russia or Mongolia; Tibetan plains are more in the nature of *wide shallow valleys* running up on either side to bounding ridges. Moreover, the run at right angles to that which we have termed the sides is usually a slope up to some higher level where lies a *T'ang* of similar configuration but at a greater general elevation.

Many of these plateaus are bare and desolate to a degree hardly realisable. Undulating slightly, the whole surface seems strewn with flaky fragments of brown calcareous biscuit—mud-hardened and splintered by frost and by burning sun. In places the ground may be brown and white in alternate patches, according as the whitish clay, which in western regions is the foundation soil of the whole, is exposed or is overlaid with caked loam and stones. Where the *T'ang* has any decided slope, in the lower levels are generally found shallow lakes, usually intensely saline, and with sodas and salts lying, a dirty white frilling, along the margin. Certain plains, especially the great tracts extending from west to east to the north of latitude 33° and between longitude 82° E. and the mountainous country north of Lhásá, are distinctly salt deserts, holding huge reservoirs of saline waters where the drainage of the land has been massed into swamps and lakes. Large areas, moreover, dry and waterless, are perfectly snow-white, being completely covered with saltpetre. This is the case throughout vast tracts directly east of Rudok.[1] Much of this elevated region in the N.-W. comprises sheer arid flats nearly devoid of vegetation. A few scrubby bushes occur here and there, but very little pasture, and that only in the dips where water has been lying.

However, south of latitude 33° N. and east of the 82nd meridian, the *T'ang* country assumes a very different aspect. Although the broad open valleys continue, they are now covered everywhere with verdure, and though the average altitude may be taken as 15,000 feet, the coarse thick-growing grass affords sustenance to troops of wild asses and deer, as well as to the tame flocks of the Khampas and Changpas—the only denizens of the Jang-t'ang proper. This pasturage is most luxuriant in a broad belt, some 40 miles from north to south, which stretches to the east, running between latitude 32° and 33°. Here, also, dandelion, hawkweeds, and wild rhubarb, are met with.

North of the lake-district of those parallels, the lands seem dry and saline but yield much grass. In places the plains are covered with

[1] "During the last three marches to Dak-korkor no water of any kind was met with, and the party were forced to carry a supply in skins. In this arid part of the country the soil was of a dazzling white, a peculiarity which extended as far as the Pundit could see. The Pundit was informed that five days' march to the north there was a large district called Jung Phaiyu-Pooyu, and that throughout its whole extent the earth was of the same white kind as that they were crossing over, so white indeed as to cause people to suffer as if from snow-blindness."—*(Pundits' Reports for 1869.)*

congealed lava, and slabs of pure salt stand in piles; but, in certain districts much further to the north-east, extensive savannahs of herbage occur. Beyond the abundant grass up there, little else seems to grow; no crops will seed, and a few bushes of "camel's thorn," tamarisk, *Caragana* furze, and *Eurotia* are the only shrubs, and these are very rarely seen. Herds of wild animals of large graminivorous species, which feed here in the summer, supply manure for each season's growth as well as dung-fuel *(argols)* to nomads and travellers. East of the meridian of Namts'o Chhyidmo (*i.e.* Tengri Nor), the *T'ang* country narrows up to the north, lying as a belt of some 150 miles along the base of the Akka Tag mountains and reaching as far to the east as the 90th meridian. Here the grass-land is reported to be still more fertile, and the animal life even more profuse than in the west. Frequent mountain ranges (such as the Kököshili) and many river-feeders, however, bring these eastern regions, in most respects, out from the *T'ang* category into another class.[1]

DOK DISTRICTS.

The great upland pasture-grounds form the next feature in Tibetan cosmogony, and these are known as the *Dok* lands. These lie chiefly in Southern Tibet; but not exclusively so. In some respects they resemble the moors and heaths of Scotland and Yorkshire; but, perhaps, a closer analogy might be found in the *tundras* of Siberia. Bogs and swamps and gullies, with much broken country running up into shaggy ridges, also moss-covered knolls with a soft black peatty soil, are characteristic qualities. Low-growing barberry, *Myricaria,* and furze, are in places intermingled with wiry herbage. But all these lands lie lifted up on the backs of mighty mountains, or are entrenched amid huge cradling hills which protrude spurs and forking buttresses into each basin of moor or fen. Very wild and weird are these dark moors. But excellent pastures indeed are all the Dok tracts—less frequented by large game, save *Ovis Ammon* and wild asses, because given up to the herds of tame yak and sheep owned, patriarch-like, by the Dok-pa or semi-nomad inhabitants.

Doubtless, there is infinite variety under the general characteristics of regions of this and other kinds in Tibet. In this Dok country you may find yourself at one time hemmed in by peak-crowned slopes as at home in North Cornwall; whence, coming forth, you have the narrow val-

[1] The T'ang country in a measure re-appears in the South in a portion of territory known as Ding-tsam abutting on the north of Eastern Nepal and Sikkim. These tracts have a mean elevation of over 15,000 feet, are shrubless, but with plenty of coarse fescue grass, and are characterised by the same broad flat valleys separated by ridges of rounded hills which belong to the Jang-t'ang country of the north.

leys merged into absolute plains, descending gently down to the bed of some great river which has cut deep below the general level; the plains there, on either side, being broken up into narrow spurs separated by ravines. Here, again, is another glimpse of Dok scenery south of Yamdok lake, from the narrative of U.G. in the Survey Report:—

The pass was difficult and the ascent was rough and trying, passing along snow-covered slopes, flanked by deep gorges; but, after a descent on the southern slopes of the pass of about 2,000 feet, we reached a beautiful flat country which gently sloped up to the foot of mountains, carpeted with exquisite verdure and lovely flowers, with bushes of different shrubs. At the head of the lake is the monastery of Tong-tso Padma-ling, looking from which to the south-east the view embraced the crystal surface of the thrice holy lake flanked by a range of billowy mountains overtopped in the distance by the lofty snows of Kulha Kangri. The Kulha Kangri, with their snow clad peaks standing in most picturesque array, resemble (to compare great things with small) the Buddhist prayer offerings called *Torma*. To the north is the dome-like peak called Kulhai Cham, "the wife of Kulha;" on her sides stand exalted the sublime peaks of Chenresi, Chhiyagshi, Lonchhen Lhat'oi Gar ("the hoary headed premier Gar"), Namgyal and others. After visiting a celebrated cave, consecrated to Guru Pema, and surrounded on three sides by glaciers, we started to the south-east over this elevated plateau to find our way back into the Lhobrak Valley.

So pleasing an aspect of nature as this plain presented at an elevation of nearly 15,000 feet is no uncommon sight in Tibet The time of U.G.'s visit was early in September, when, in these realms of snow, vegetation has attained the climax of maturation.

It should not be supposed that the whole Dok country is peopled by nomads. Small towns of stone-houses are to be found in most parts, especially in the lower valleys where the altitude descends to 13,000 feet. Here, too, on the valley-cliffs junipers and small fir grow, with willows and poplars below near the river-side. In Dok-de (to the far N.E. of Lhásá, from 150 to 200 miles' distant) the country developes into really fine and pleasing scenery.[1] This part includes Tsog-de, through

1 After A. K's exploration, the whole of these tracts north-east of Lhásá were, by the unfounded theory of the gentleman who made the details public, included as parts of the Jang-t'ang. That Mr. Hennessey's view was erroneous is certain. The only ground for classing this portion of the country with the great salt plains to the west in the same latitude, seems to have been the supposition that the lofty elevation of the west in this parallel was continued here in the eastern regions. However, the many mountain ranges, which are of great intricacy, and the character of the pastures on the table-lands, as well as the lower altitude, sufficiently distinguish such districts from the *T'ang* country west and due north of Namts'o Chhyidmo. Moreover, the very names given in a native geographical work, "Dzambuling Gyalshes," of Dok-yul and Dok-de, identify the tracts as *Dok* (lit: *abrog*) or upland pastures; whilst in the account of A. K. himself the denizens are designated Dokpa or "herdsmen."

which runs the upper waters of the Gyama-ngül Chhu. Here are wide valleys in which cultivation is carried on, with villages nestling on the spurs and in nooks high up the steep slopes, and monasteries perched in places inaccessible apparently to anything wanting wings. Moreover, the rounded knolls of the *T'ang* mountains are replaced by bold crags and sharp snow-capped peaks. Fine rivers, feeders to the Sok Chhu, are seen at short intervals, all flowing southwards. This is the kind of country from Nag-chhu-kha, N.E. of Lhása, to Chhamdo with intervals of bare upland moors.[1]

WINTER ASPECT OF T'ANG AND DOK.

The prevailing tints of the loftier parts of Tibet, that is of the greater portion of the whole territory, are red, purple, yellow and brown. Where streams and swamps occur the bright emerald green growth of grass and herb produces a wondrous contrast. But only for four months is the natural colouring of the land seen.

In winter-time the appearance of both the *T'ang* and the *Dok* country is very different. The early falls of snow in October soon alter the face of the landscape to one of utter desolation. After frost has succeeded frost, and the bitter hurricanes have swept up the snow to be refrozen hard as rock in fantastic monuments, nothing save a few antelopes, hares, and foxes, which "flee like shadows," remain to witness to the moving life once there. But we had forgotten, these are not the sole survivors. Large numbers of yak and wild asses still roam about; and many may be seen perched on inaccessible crags rooting out herbage from deep beneath the snow. Still all is silent and death-like. The Dok herdsmen have retired to stone-huts in the sheltered valleys; the Golok robbers from the east, who scour the Jangt'ang, have retreated to the lower plains of Amdo and the small towns on the Chinese borders. One of the most distinctive accessories of the *T'ang* country in Western Tibet, north of lat. 33°, is the many great sheets of water, all saline, but some more intensely so than others. It is a noteworthy fact that in the depth of winter with the night temperature even 45° below zero, lakes holding more than saturated solutions of salts never freeze. These liquid pools and swamps upon the ice-bound plains are all the more startling to behold, when rivers of the strongest current lie hard-by con-

[1] As to the chief localities of the *Dok* lands, we should enumerate: (1) the region of Lake Map'ang and the greater portion of the Province of Dok-t'ol, bordering the north-east of Ngari Khorsum; (2) the country south and south-east of Lake Yam-dok, including the tracts round Tign Ts'o and P'o-mo Jhang-t'ang Ts'o; (3) the vast stretch of territory north-east of Lhásá and north of the Gyalmo Ngul Chhu, known as Dok-Yul and Dok-De. The last mentioned is by far the most extensive *Dok* region in Tibet, reaching as it does northwards to the Dungbura Range.

gealed and motionless, and even a goodly number of the geysers of hot water, so common near lakes in Tibet, have been frozen into tall white columns. As M. Bonvalot remarks, the power of ejection of these fountains of boiling water is not sufficient to cope with the frost. Upon the mosses and crags of the *Dok* territory, the snow in January lies in mighty sheets of many feet in thickness; while in the lava-strewn plains of the verge of the Jangt'ang, due north of Namts'o Chhyidmo, there seems to be less of snow. There flats and rocks and the recurrent mountain ranges belonging to the Tibetan steppes are not clothed in white, but are completely plated with pure ice, as though rolled up in glossy armour which had somehow been put on when liquid, and which thus holds them so tightly as to appear contorted and quilted.

RONG DISTRICTS.

Certain parts of the country are much cut up with deep ravines and rocky gorges, between the high cliffs of which rattle rapid affluents of the larger rivers. These narrow valleys mostly contain considerable raised beds of alluvial soil, especially where any conjunction of streams occurs. On the ledges of such ravines numerous hamlets and gompas are built everywhere; and the denizens industriously cultivate the strips of alluvial accumulation. Much artificial ground, derived from the river, is contrived, as well, on hollowed recesses in the cliff-sides. Indeed, these ravine or *Rong* districts are favourite spots for villages. One recommendation is the abundant water close at hand, another is the richness and softness of such soil as exists; and a third advantage seems to be the general low altitude of the districts where this conformation is found. One of the chief *Rong* districts, that one which lies between Shigatse and Lake Yamdok, is a perfect net-work of defiles, but literally swarms with villages and monastic establishments.

GANG DISTRICTS.

This conformation of country is peculiar to Khams the great province of Eastern Tibet. Khams holds both *Rong* and *Gang* districts, but the latter class is its speciality. In some respects this style tallies with the *Dok* lands further west, and indeed here it replaces them; only the morose and desolate aspects of the other are here absent, and moorland is replaced by downs. Moreover the whole elevation is much lower, and consequently vegetation richer and more varied. Still we are in the uplands, the Tibetan word *Gang* having that bearing. Captain Gill, who viewed Tibetan scenery from the east in September, just over the frontier of Szechuen, gives this glowing picture :—

On passing the crest of Chah-toh-shan, the great upland country is at once entered. Standing on the summit of the pass, stretched below was a fine valley, closed in on both sides by gently-sloping round-topped hills, all covered with splendid grass. The richness of the pasture was something astonishing; the gronnd was yellow with buttercups and the air laden with the perfume of wild-flowers of every description. Wild currents and gooseberries, barberries, a sort of yew, with many other shrubs, grew in profusion. By the side of a little tent some Tibetans were lying abont; their fierce dogs tied up to pegs in the ground, and great herds of sheep and cattle grazing round them. The sheep are taken in vast flocks once a year from Lit'ang to Ta-chien-lu, and thence to Chheng-tu for sale.

Near Chhamdo, in the north of Khams, the landscape is of the *Gang* character, this quality succeeding to the *Dok* features further N.-W. and West. It is of La-gang, a little west of Chhamdo, that Captain Bower is speaking when we read this entry in his diary :—

Through the most lovely country over which it has ever been my lot to travel. The path ran through a forest one or two hundred feet above the river, with here and there open grassy patches with trees scattered about. Each bend in the river disclosed to view a panorama of surpassing beauty. In no part of Kashmir does the beauty of the scenary excel that of this part of Tibet. Game is plentiful, but shooting is forbidden in all the country having any connection with the monastery of Riuchi.

Such scenery is not of the description one would expect to meet with at an elevation of 12,500 feet. But it is only so in Tibet.

South of Chhamdo, the country presently becomes rugged and sterile, and it is only in the main river valley that the smiling aspect of nature is maintained. It is so, too, in the important Derge kingdom of Khams, 150 miles north-east of Chhamdo. At this height all is forbidding and unproductive save in the great river-tracks. Mr. Rockhill thus pictures the change from the *Rong* country of the Gyekündo district to the *Gang* country further south, as Derge is entered by way of the Ḍengo valley. We preserve in our quotation the writer's orthography of names :—

The face of the country remained as we had seen it north of Jyékundo bare and bleak; in some rocky nooks a few stunted juniper trees, but no shrub or flower, no singing-bird or anything to relieve the awful stillness and dreariness of the scene.

After a miserable night during which sleet had fallen continually, we were off again by daylight; and entering the Dren-kou valley, which leads down to the Dré Ch'u, the scenery changed as if by magic. A brook flowed down the glen, its banks covered with soft green grass powdered over with little white and pink flowers. On the mountain sides grew juniper and pine trees, and by the roadside were wild plum, gooseberry, honey-suckle, and other shrubs, the fragrance of their blossoms filling the air. From cavities in the tufa rock pended creepers and ferns from which the water fell in crystal drops; and we heard the cuckoo's cry echoing across the valley. . . . . .

About two miles below Lori we came once more on the Dré Ch'u, and the scenery grew even finer as we wound along the steep mountains sides, some 500 feet above the blue river which went dashing by in eddying and seething masses in its narrow bed. The mountains rose several thousand feet on either hand, those on the left bank reaching to above the snow-line and stretching as far as the eye could reach along the river's sinuous course. Lamaseries and villages, around which were little patches of cultivation, were numerous on either side of the river; and great droves of yak were grazing around the white tents of parties of tea traders, whose goods were piled up under white cotton awnings to protect them from the frequent showers of rain.

Of course, in discriminating the characteristics of the different classes of country, it is impossible to do more than generalise as to the leading features. Indeed, in Tibet, as in every land, we often find the qualities of each class blended, so that it would be hard to distinguish to which class the district should be assigned. It is enough, however, to shew how various is the character of this territory, and yet how to some extent it admits of systematic apportionment. Moreover, as we have said, our classification is that of native Tibetan writers.

There are said to be six *Gang* districts in the topographical sense, namely; Mabja Zabmo, Ts'a-wa, Pömpo, Mar Khams, Minyag, and Yarmo. These are sometimes separated from the province of Khams, and the whole is designated Gang.

CHAPTER III.

CLIMATE AND METEOROLOGY.

One might reasonably look for eccentricities in the climatology of Tibet. An extensive territory with a plane of elevation so exceptionally lofty and yet so near to the tropics necessarily presents conditions unparalleled elsewhere on this globe. To put the matter more strikingly we have there in fact some 600,000 square miles of the earth's surface raised in general altitude from 13,500 to 17,500 feet above the level of the sea, traversed by numerous mountain-ranges varying from 19,000 to 26,000 feet, yet situated only from 5¼ to 14 degrees north of the Tropic of Cancer. Accordingly, the meteorology of such a country may well be unique. Moreover, the circumstances of the climate are still further complicated by the rim of lofty mountains enclosing the territory on three sides, those on the south cutting it off by their excessive height almost completely from the moist currents of the ocean. Probably, also, the great spinal column of plateau and dislocated mountain range, forming the main watershed of so many river basins, stretching from Aksai Chin to Zayul, produces further eccentricities.

Now, the altitude of this enormous country would lead us to expect terrific cold and its exclusion from the atmospherical effects of the ocean great dryness. And that is so in the larger half of the territory. We have in fact in those parts an Arctic climate, deprived to a considerable extent of that accessory in the shape of constant freshly-falling snow which in the Arctic regions does much to temper the severity of the cold. Deficiency of moisture causes the snow-fall in most parts to be exceedingly small. In the south-eastern districts adjoining Chinese territory, certainly, where the southern barrier is much lower than elsewhere, immense quantities of snow are deposited every year, much of it above the line of perpetual snow, much more below it, and which on melting adds materially to the volume of the three great rivers that quit Tibet in the S.-E. corner.

However, on the valleyed plateaus of the N.-W., S.-W. and North-

Central regions, heavy falls of either snow or rain, though indeed occasionally occurring, are rare. In those parts, extreme dryness is the leading feature. Only the round-topped ridges of very high mountain ranges, such as the Aling Gang-ri and T'ā-chhab Gang-ri, each scaling over 23,000 feet in altitude, receive any regular annual increment to their hoary load; and that is generally not a considerable dole. Moreover, the height of the snow-line in Tibet causes the small lodgments on the hill-sides and open valleys to vanish with the return of summer.

Nevertheless, the sweeping assertions often made concerning the utterly arid nature of the Tibetan climate need distinct qualification. Because at Leh in Ladak under 1½ inches is the annual rain-fall, it has been too hastily assumed, on the theory of similarity of hydrometric position, that the greater portion of Tibet receives no more. Now, though this may be the case in the extreme western tracts, there is actual proof that the deficiency in most other parts of Tibet is not in any way so great. The concurrent testimony of all traders who visit Darjeeling from Shigatse is that in that part of Tsang the rains of July and August are very heavy; while, in winter, at least 8 inches of snow fall five or six times every season. Again, even in the great salt-lake district, so far north as between the 32nd and 34th parallels of latitude, and so far west as between the 84th and 87th meridians, we have the strongest evidence of a considerable down-fall. Captain Bower and Dr. Thorold traversed this portion of their route (where the elevation averages 16,000 feet) from July 25th to September 4th, 1891; when, out of the 42 days therein comprised they record heavy storms with drenching rain on 19 days; and the implication from Captain Bower's narrative is that it was wet on other days also. It is interesting to note that these storms seemed to come mainly from the S. and S.-W. direction. Again, Captain Wellby, travelling in the districts due N. of Lhasa in 1896, noted in August only 11 fine days, rain or snow falling on 18 out of the 31 days with several severe storms. Even in the far N.-W of Tibet, supposed to be so arid, snow fell on 4 days in the first week of June. In July 1896 rain or snow fell on 10 days or nights in N.-W. Tibet. But we shall return to the subject later.

Furthermore, in connection with this question, we may mention the way in which native Tibetan authors constantly describe their country as "the White Land;" while their speech is styled by the poets *Gangs-chhen-kyi Skad* "the language of the great snows."

THE WATER-SUPPLY OF THE GREAT RIVERS.

How comes it—it might be asked—that Tibet is the grand home of so many mighty rivers? Their sources lie in the very heart of this land where the benison of the heavens is not lavishly showered down. Whence, therefore, do the fountains draw the great supplies necessary to feed the early reaches of all the water-thoroughfares of India and South-eastern Asia?

Well, it is possible to make reasonable elucidation of the apparent inconsistency. It is, after all, no great mystery. The truth seems to be that the climate of Tibet has not always in the past been the same as it is now; and that the results and productions of that different climate are by no means yet dissipated in that country, but survive as stupendous legacies—diminishing slowly it may be as time progresses, yet still effective in the present benefits they confer.

Let us extract a passage from Sir J. D. Hooker in one of the notes to his *Himalayan Journals:* "Were the snow-level in Dingcham as low as it is in Sikkim, the whole of Tibet from Donkia almost to the Yaru Tsanpu river would be everywhere intersected by glaciers and other impassable barriers of snow and ice, for a breadth of 50 miles; and the country would have no parallel for amount of snow beyond the Polar circles. It is impossible to conjecture what would have been the effects on the climate of Northern India and Central Asia under these conditions. When, however, we reflect upon the evidences of glacial phenomenon that abound in all the Himalayan valleys at and above 9,000 feet elevation, *it is difficult to avoid the conclusion that such a state of things once existed, and at a comparatively very recent period.*"

In addition, we find Captain (now Colonel) H. H. Godwin-Austen remarking in 1868 of the evident decrease in size of the Pangkong lake in Western Tibet: "The only deduction to make from such comparatively recent changes is, that the level of its waters has been alternating with moist and dry periods of time, the slow process of which may be even now going on almost imperceptible to man; the water of the Pangkong depending as it does mainly on the winter snow and the country passing through a period of diminishing falls—query: may not the snowfall in this part of the Himalayas be much less now than formerly?"

The explanation, then, takes this form. At the present day all the loftier mountain-ranges in Tibet are well stocked with enormous protrudent glaciers; and in concavities in elevated summits lie snow-fields, may be, several hundred feet thick. Moreover, the moraines in valleys and the signs of glacial action in the basal ravines assure us that, large as the glaciers still are, their bulk has been formerly exceedingly larger. The modern snow-fall and rain-fall at their current annual rate could in no wise bring about such accumulations. It is most probable, therefore, that the climate, so far as these discharges are concerned, has in later centuries undergone radical change, and the present fall of these is infinitely less in quantity than in by-gone times. However, so huge were these glaciers and other reservoirs of congealed water that, long as they have been furnishing the main demands of the great outflowing rivers, they are still large enough to maintain an adequate supply to them for an indefinite period to come. Nevertheless, the marked diminution in the size of numerous lakes in Tibet, as noticed by various travellers, which lakes depend to a large extent on glacial feeding, affords evidence that the drainage into them is not so copious as formerly. A certain falling-off in the supply is therefore betokened. Although a theory such as the foregoing is worthy of all credence, one point likewise must have due weight. We would re-assert our belief that, while the falls of rain and snow in the west and north are insignificant, yet in Central Tibet the amount of these has been greatly under-estimated. And it is *through the region where a fair quantity of both occur* that the Yeru Tsangpo and at least two other of the great out-flowing rivers pass in a great portion of their respective courses. Again, everywhere in Tibet, the annual renewal of *nevé* to counterbalance in some degree glacial waste on the higher mountains, is an appreciable factor even now-a-days. Some fresh snow—though only a moderate quantity—is still added yearly to snow-field and peak and does not melt. Comparatively scanty moisture reaches Tibet in modern times; and if this were only rain, we allow that the contribution might be hardly worth counting, as being nearly all lost by percolation into the thirsty soil. But, as on the lofty ranges, it comes in the form of snow and hail, on the contrary every atom is preserved and goes to increase those stores which replenish glaciers, and through glaciers—in due process—the resultant rivers.

In ways such as these we can readily account for the vast body of water brought from Tibet by the rivers which greet us in the plains of India and China; and yet not be surprised to learn that the amount of snow and rain falling in that hidden land is certainly, by itself, totally inadequate to produce such an out-flow.

THE SEASONS IN TIBET.

Let us follow the round of the seasons to gain some idea of the Tibetan climate in western and central districts.

SPRING CONDITIONS.

Starting with spring, we shall find that season slow to show itself, especially in northern and western regions. The end of April arrives before the snow fallen in the winter—little though it may be—

begins to melt; the outer crust is so hard and frozen. Even the great rivers, ice-bound to a considerable depth, are not unfettered before April has commenced; and every night there is a temperature below freezing point, in the moderately elevated tracts, right up to the end of June. Indeed, in the salt-lake district, on what is called the high plateau of Tibet, where the altitude ranges from 15,300 to 16,500 feet, the average minimum temperature in August is 28° Fahr., and in July 24°·5. So that we may say that in those regions the thermometer registers below freezing-point every night throughout summer, and therefore throughout the year.

Nevertheless the poor Tibetan, so hardly pressed by his inhospitable climate, endeavours in the earliest days of spring to turn over the iron soil and to sow his sixty-day barley. He cannot, as is the custom in the Tsaidam, begin his labours so early as March 1st. Even where no snow is lying on the ground, the frost holds it too tightly and the manure is too hard where it has been often laid ready through the winter on the surface.

At the end of March, however, the plough must be used and the soil prepared. Snow is still lying in many fields, and the contrivance to get rid of it is curious. During summer and autumn in general the people collect earth and store it in their houses in large quantities. In the spring, when they fancy no further snow is likely to fall, and when that already there has begun to melt and cake the sun's rays, they spread the soft earth over it, and that has the effect of melting the snow underneath. Sometimes snow falls again and again after this process, and occasionally even three and four layers of earth have to be used before the field is ready. In April all seed is sown; and early in May, so much care do they take, the green shoots are above-ground everywhere up to 14,000 feet.

VAST RANGE OF TEMPERATURE.

The air during April, May, and early June in Tsang, Ui, and all Central Tibet, is so wonderfully clear and pure—as a rule so free from the subtlest spiculæ of moisture—that during the day the heat of the direct rays of the sun is intense. When a traveller is protected by the north-thrown shadows of rocky heights he may feel, even at mid-day, chilled to the bones; but he rounds some corner and then, exposed to the unchecked glare, he is instantly in dread of sun-stroke. Captain Wellby, when in lat. 35° N., long. 82° E. in June, at an altitude of nearly 16,000 feet, speaks of the heat on a lake-side as insupportable, the thermometer in the open registering 105°. Even out of the direct rays of the sun, the temperature of the air, in the middle of the day, at great heights is often considerable. We observe it noted by Captain Wellby that on June 22nd at an altitude of 17,300 feet the thermometer inside his tent rose to 78°.

But the sun, which at 2 P.M. shone down with a force of 125° in the open, once sunk to the horizon, the bitterest cold can follow in the height of summer. On July 10th in North Central Tibet the reading at night was 6° Fahr.; on August 18th in lat. 35° 10′ long. 92° 12′ E., the minimum at night-time shewed 16° Fahr., the altitude being 15,700 feet above the sea. However, there are at night great variations of temperature. Travelling at an average elevation of 16,000 feet, Captain Wellby records 33° as the warmest night temperature in June and 40° as the maximum of the nights of August. In Lhása and even in Shigatse the evenings of summer up to 8 or 9 P.M., are generally most pleasantly warm. In travelling after sundown those pathways skirting heat-absorbing rocks often yield the balmiest of atmospheres far into the night.

Just at daybreak seems to be the time of greatest cold during the 24 hours. The difference between the *shade* temperature at 3 P.M., and that in a tent in the same place at 3 to 4 A.M., is often nearly if not quite 60° degrees in the early part of May at ordinary elevations. On July 10th 1896, in North Central Tibet, 54° was registered by day *in the shade*, but in the succeeding night the temperature sank to 6°. A quotation from Captain Wellby's diary must conclude our remarks upon this point. He and Mr. Malcolm were camping in June in the lake-district of N. N.-W. Tibet (lat. 35° 12′ N., long. 82° E.) at an altitude of some 16,000 feet: "Bathing in the lake itself, although the lake was partly frozen over with ice, the water was quite enjoyable, and we could remain splashing about in it for half-an-hour, and afterwards bask naked in the sun . . . . . A climate like this at such a height struck us as truly marvellous. After seventeen degrees of frost by night, we found ourselves basking in the open in a temperature of 106°, shewing a variation of ninety degrees in the 24 hours. At 7 P.M., again, the thermometer registered as much as 48° Fahr. . . . . . We were off before 5 o'clock, with a keen morning air in our faces, but after a couple of hours the heat became so unbearable that we would fain have halted." Again, on July 18th, the same latitude, but a good way further east: "At 7-30 P.M., at a height of over 16,000 feet, the temperature was 40° Fahr., and during the night there were nineteen degrees of frost."

THE SUMMER SEASON.

The temperature and hygrometric conditions are of great interest during the months of June, July, and August. As to the first, let a few readings of the Fahrenheit thermometer in shade be extracted from various sources for each month:

JUNE.

Average minimum temperature, N.-W. Tibet, at 14,000-16,000 feet	25°
Lowest minimum, N.-W. Tibet, at *circa* 16,000 feet (Captain Bower)	18
Lowest minimum, N. N-W. Tibet, as measured in 1896 by Captain Wellby	7°
Lowest minimum at Batang (at 8,150 feet) ...	27°
Average minimum at 12,000 feet in North Sikkim	33°·5
Average temperature at noon in Eastern Tibet, 12,000-13,000 feet	50°
Highest maximum temperature, N.-W. Tibet, at *circa* 16,000 feet (June 29th)	73°·5
Average maximum temperature at Lhása (11,600 feet)	72°
Highest maximum at Lhása during June ...	77° 4
Average maximum in Tsaidam plains (9,000 feet) ...	71°
Temperature in Tsaidam, June 4th 1880, at 6 A.M. ...	42°·9
Temperature in Lhása, June 8th 1879, at 6 A.M. ...	55°·4
Temperature in Tsaidam, June 4th 1880, at 3 P.M.	69°·7
Temperature in Lhása, June 5th 1879, at 3 P.M. ...	72°·4
Temperature at Mariam La, Purang, June 11th 1866, 8 P.M.	43°
Temperature at base Mt. Kailas, Manasarowar, June 17th, 6 A.M.	53°·5

JULY.

Average minimum, N.-W. Tibet, at *circa* 17,400 feet	24°·5
Average minimum, North Cental Tibet, in 1896 (alt. 16,500-17,000)	21°
Lowest minimum, N.-W. Tibet at 17,550 feet (July 4th)	17°
Lowest minimum, same district, registered by Captain Wellby	6°
Average minimum at 12,000 feet in North Sikkim	38°
Average maximum at Lhása (11,600 feet) ...	71°·3
Highest maximum at Lhása during July ...	77°·4
Temperature in Lhása, July 12th 1879, at 6 A.M. ...	51°·4
Temperature in Lhása, July 12th 1879, at 3 P.M. ...	74°·4
In Ngari Khorsum at 16,000 feet, July 30th, 1884, at noon:	57°·5

AUGUST.

Average minimum, North-Central Tibet, at *circa* 16,000 feet	28°
Average minimum, North-Central Tibet, in 1896 (Captain Wellby)	34°

Lowest minimum, North-Central Tibet, at 16,500 feet (August 18th)	19°
Lowest minimum, same district, in 1896 (same day of month)	18°
Highest minimum, ditto, at 16,000 feet (August 10th)	35°
Average maximum at Lhása (11,600 feet) ...	64°·4
Highest maximum at Lhása during August ...	70°
In shelter on Pass-top, near Gart'ok, West Tibet, 19,400 feet, in August at 9 A.M.	37°
In shelter on Pass-top, near Gart'ok, West Tibet, 19,220 feet at 9 A.M.	40°
In shelter on Pass-top, near Gart'ok, West Tibet, 17,650 feet at 9 P.M.	49°·25
In shelter on Pass-top, above Upper Indus, W. T., 18,750 feet at 3 P.M.	53°
At Töling Gompa, Upper Sutlej, 12,280 feet, August 5th, 4 P.M.	69°
On high plateau, West Tibet, 15,200 feet, August 11th, 5 P.M.	67°·5
T'ok Jálung gold-field, 16,330 feet, August 29th, 3 P.M.	55°
„ „ „ „ „ August 27th, 7 A.M.	41°

As to the falls of rain and snow in summer-time, it must be noted that the monsoon-season of India makes itself felt to a certain appreciable extent throughout Tibet. In Central districts rain-showers occur on very many days in July and August, the monsoon effects not reaching the North-western Central region until about July 20th. From the middle of June to the end of August, in the provinces of Tsang and Ui, including Yarlung, Yamdok and Lhobrak, nearly every day the sky is cloudy and frequently heavily overcast. In Western Tibet, rain falls in small quantities throughout July and August, but with a very moderate aggregate for the two months, probably 4 to 5 inches. Thus, Captain Godwin-Austen noted that, during the whole period of his wanderings in the Pang-kong Lake country, from July 22nd 1863 to the middle of August, with a few solitary fine days, "the weather was miserably cold—nothing but cloud, sleet, and rain." In the far north of West Tibet, as on Lingzhi T'ang, it seems, however, to be much dryer and clearer with only three or four days rain in August.

And now as to that phenomenon of Tibet, the not infrequent snowstorms in the height of summer. On the higher passes snow falls every year in July and August—no large amount, but often 4 or 5 inches in depth. It seldom lies longer than two or three days except in hollows and behind north-facing rocks, where, if the height be over 16,000 feet—though that is 4,000 feet below the perpetual line—it continues on to the winter. Occasionally, however, heavy snow comes down in Western Tibet in July, and remains for weeks upon regularly-used tracks. Thus on the road down on the Tibetan side of the Jhang La leading out of Ladak there is generally a considerable fall in the early days of July, and thus it lies two or three weeks in the full glare of the summer sun, a stretch of several miles' length. The Ts'omorang La between the valley of the upper waters of the Indus and the Tibetan gold-fields at T'ok Jalung is another locality for heavy falls in August which completely cover the Ts'omarang range from the ridge to the base, the latter part being under 16,000 feet, while the summits do not rise higher than 18,750 feet.

To us this seems so fascinating a subject—heavy snow falling in localities only ten or eleven degrees north of the tropics, in a latitude more southern than that of Greece or Sicily, in the months of July and August, that we would fain enlarge upon it. A few striking quotations from actual experience, however, will be more to the point. For instance, let a graphic word-picture from the hand of Godwin-Austen be introduced.

Here it is. He was camping early in August in the Chang Chhenmo valley on the bed of the Kyamgo Trag-kar stream; and he writes:—"It now began to snow hard, and we got under the lea of a low cliff and sat there until the coolies came up, when we pitched our tents with great difficulty, for the pegs would not hold in the gravelly bed of the stream; but by means of heavy boulder stones this was accomplished. It was a miserable evening, snow falling until sunset and lying on the top of the tents and in high dry spots. When the clouds broke at that hour, beautiful appeared the surrounding mountains with their white covering, and the fleecy clouds drifting up against their sides added greatly to their apparent height; the whole suffused with a lovely rose colour, and the sun shining upon the wet surface of the many-tinted rocks brought out their hues brighter than ever."

Captain Bower is not so descriptive in style; but he records tersely a similar incident at an altitude *circa* 16,500 feet in North-Central Tibet, dated August 16th: "Just as it became too dark to go on any further, a snow-squall struck us; we soon had the tents pitched and a kettle filled with snow was on the fire. Dr. Thorold, however, had gone after some goa just before the snow set in, and had not rejoined the caravan, so I fired several shots and, guided by these, he managed to reach the camp." Moreover, Atma Ram, one of the Bower party, mentions in his notes that from July 25th to August 3rd their route in N-W. Tibet was continually interrupted by repeated falls of snow.

AUTUMN AND WINTER.

All crops throughout the Central districts are got in before the middle of September; the early *grim* or naked barley having to be cut in July at least. By the middle of September the frosts at night, even as low down as 12,000 feet, are too keen for the stability of anything in the form of seed or flower yet remaining. Early in October the first of the winter falls of snow occur, and these October descents seem pretty general throughout Tibet.

In order to exhibit conclusively the generality and wide extension of the snow-fall in the early days of October, a few examples will prove useful. A.K., travelling in Yagra-töd, the valley just south of the Dang-la range, some 220 miles N. N.-E. of Lhása, at an altitude of 14,800 feet, notes heavy snow on October 7th and 8th, 1879; and, when he had crossed the range, we read: "during the night 3 feet of snow fell." Again on the 15th and 16th he was detained at one camp by continuous falls; and on the 17th he makes the entry: "Our day's march was almost entirely over snow." So, too, Captain Bower camping with his party on the shores of Chargyut Ts'o experienced similar weather from the middle of September to the 4th October 1891: "Snow off and on all day and night. What fell in the day-time melted at once, but that at night lay till the sun rose and then quickly disappeared." During October, in all localities that range above 13,000 feet, water outside becomes strongly frozen every night, melting in exposed situations during the day in the early part of the month; but by the end of the month the lake-shores begin to grow their permanent winter-fringe of ice, which in November generally extends all over the surface. Early in December the surface of Namts'o Chhi'mo or Tengri Nor, 1,200 square miles of water, has become one deeply-frozen solid block of ice. In this month, also, the larger rivers are set fast, being congealed several feet deep in the upper portion of their courses west of long. 96° E. East of that meridian and and south of lat. 32° N., the great southernly-flowing rivers, though often partially surface-frozen in January and blocked with ice, are rarely completely ice-bound. The Yarlung, Penam-nyang, and Kyi Chhu which are situated for the most part below an altitude of 12,500 feet, however, seem to be usually solidified for two or three weeks during the winter, though they have wide and strong currents.

Mons. Bonvalot and his friends must have experienced the severest effects of winter in the highest tracts of Tibet. They were travelling from December to March across the northernmost regions, from north to south, at an altitude generally over 16,000 and nearly always above 15,000 feet. Icicles 10 inches long clattering on their beards and frozen tears were regarded as sheer trivialities apparently by these sturdy travellers; and each day they record with the lightest of hearts readings of the thermometer anything from 12° to 40° *below zero!* And this state of cold they complacently endure 2 months at least at one stretch. We have the piquant Frenchman repeatedly making entries of this nature: "The thermometer marked a minimum of 35° below zero, and the morning was a lovely one." That entry is dated January 5th, 1890. The same evening Mons. Bonvalot goes a walk round a frozen lake: "The night is magnificent, and as I walk along the shores of this little lake, it sparkles almost as much as the moon, having, besides, a white halo of salt upon its banks . . . . . When I get back to the tent the thermometer marks 29° below zero. Prince Henry reminds Father Dedeken that they had come upon the traces of a wolf before turning in, and they suggest that, as I am up, I should go in search of it." Next morning, January 6th, he simply and cheerily records: "The thermometer marks 40° below zero, the point at which the mercury freezes, and there is still the west wind." Once more we read on January 30th: "Although we get a little lower down each day, the cold is still intense, the minimum of to-day being 31° below zero at an altitude of 14,200 feet."[1]

We can only admire the *verve* of these charming Frenchmen, always gay under circumstances so Arctic, while we envy their iron constitutions and presume the recording instruments they used were in good working order. The minimum temperatures observed on the Bower expedition were 15° below zero on October 31st 1891, in lat. 32° 43′ N. long. 89° 17′ E. at an altitude of 16,263 feet; and the same on the 2nd and 3rd November a little further east. However, as the cold is known to be more intense in January than at these dates, there is no improbability in the more startling records of Mons. Bonvalot.

We now proceed to give certain miscellaneous thermometric observations, derived as before from many sources and taken in various districts of Tibet. Let it be premised, merely, that the figures represent actual careful records and that the maximum and minimum temperatures were taken in the shade and out of the wind:

SEPTEMBER.

Lowest minimum in N.-E. Tibet (lat. *circa* 36° N.) 5 A.M., (alt. 16,000 ft.)	10°·9
Average minimum in North-Central Tibet (*circa* lat. 31° 25′ long. 89°)	27°

[1] Our quotations are from the translation of Bonvalot's narrative in which the Centigrade readings have been converted into Fahrenheit.

Lowest minimum during month, same locality (alt. 15,500 feet)	19°
Lowest minimum during month, at Mome Samdong, N. Sikkim (alt. 15,300)	31°
Lowest minimum during month in Tsaidam (alt. 14,000)	7°
Maximum for month in Ngasi Khorsum (alt. *circa* 14,500)	57°·6
Maximum at Lhása (September 4th, 1879) ...	66°·4

OCTOBER.

Average minimum in North-Central Tibet (*circa* lat. 32° 50′ N. long. 89°–90°)	9°
Lowest minimum during month, ditto, alt. 16,263 feet (October 31st)	15°
Highest minimum, ditto, ditto, alt. 15,560 feet (October 1st)	21°
Average minimum in Guge, Ngasi Khorsum (alt. *circa* 12,000 feet)	23°
Lowest minimum, same locality (October 9th) ...	12°
Temperature taken by Lt. H. Strachey near Mt. Kailas, October 4th, 1846, 6 A.M.	20°
Temperature taken by Lt. H. Strachey near Mt. Kailas, October 5th 1846, 3 P.M.	46°
Temperature at Janglatse, Tsang, alt. 13,800 feet, October 25th, 1866, 6 P.M.	54°

NOVEMBER.

Average minimum, North-Central Tibet (*circa* lat. 32° N., long. 90°–93° E.)	2°
Lowest minimum during month, ditto, alt. 16,113 feet (November 3rd)	15°
Highest minimum during month, ditto, alt. 14,925 feet (November 18th)	20°
Lowest minimum, at Shigatse (indoors) alt. 12,100 feet (November 18th)	21°
Highest minimum at Shigatse (indoors) ditto (November 14th)	30°·25
Average maximum at Shigatse (indoors) ditto ...	44°·5
Highest maximum during month, at Shigatse (November 14th)	50°·5
Average maximum at Golmo, N.-E. Tibet (lat. 8,760 feet)	44°

CLIMATE OF LHÁSA.

It was Father Everiste Huc who first noticed the general mildness of the climate in Lhása and its neighbourhood. Immediately he entered the Pempo or Pembu district just north of the capital, that which most forcibly impressed him was "the prodigious elevation of the temperature which we remarked in this cultivated plain. Although it was now the end of January, the river and its canals were merely edged with a thin coat of ice, and scarcely any of the people wore furs." The clemency of the weather remarked upon by the worthy priest does not, moreover, appear to have been an abnormal condition; as such has been generally confirmed as being the usual climate by our survey explorers, some of whom have resided during the winter in Lhása. Nain Singh, who dwelt there from the 10th December to 21st April, ought certainly to be a reliable authority, as he was specially deputed to report on the subject. He observed snow to fall only twice during that time in the city, to the amount of some 3 inches on each occasion, though on the low hills outside it seemed much heavier. However, the Kyi Chhu, the river on which Lhása borders, was quite frozen for 6 weeks; and water kept in the warmest parts of a house, freezing, burst the vessels holding it. But this is only as we often suffer in England; and Lhása is built between eleven and twelve thousand feet above the level of the sea.

We have a considerable series of temperatures taken at different seasons in Lhása; but their value so far as the minimum figures are concerned is insigificant from the fact of the thermometer having been kept in a room unexposed to the outer atmosphere. From these returns we ascertain that the mean maximum temperature during February at Lhása was 40°, and the mean minimum temperature indoors for the month was 31°; the highest register for February being 45° and the lowest 25°. The highest minimum during the month was about 36°. In March there was a decided rise all round; the mean maximum for that month being 48°·5 and the highest reading 51.° The mean minimum temperature during March, within the house but without a stove in the room, was 37°·3; and the lowest reading was 34°·5. After sunset in the city it is generally long before one feels any sensible decline in the afternoon temperature during these months; and in February the streets remain reasonably warm and tolerable up to 10 P.M.

THE SNOW-LINE IN TIBET.

One of the curiosities of the climate of Tibet is the height of the lowest limit of perpetual snow throughout the country.[1] Except in the eastern districts the snow-line may be drawn as lying at an eleva-

[1] Sir J. D. Hooker in his *Himalayan Journals* has dwelt fully on this fascinating subject. He was the first to make exact observations of the height of the Himalaya snow-line and the first to formulate the theory of it. All writers since on this theme necessarily tread over much the same ground as he did, owing largely to Sir Joseph in all their comments.

tion considerably higher than the summit of Mont Blanc. This extraordinary fact is doubtless to be chiefly ascribed to the extreme dryness of the atmosphere, cut off as it is throughout the major portion of the territory from the influence of the moist currents driven up from the Indian seas. The great wall of the Himalayas forms an impervious screen against the intrusion of more than the scantiest drifts of the monsoon vapours from the south. Such excessive dryness of the rarefied air causes the general evaporation to take effect with wondrous rapidity; and that serves to dissipate large quantities of snow without any process of ordinary melting. Another factor is certainly to be found in the violence of the winds which, except during the night, rage almost ceaselessly with immeasurable force across the plains and mountain-sides of Tibet. Other aids to the disappearance of newly-fallen snow are the clearness and attenuation of the atmosphere, almost free as it is from any rain-films, allowing, therefore, the sun's rays to penetrate unrefracted and unsoftened; also the great radiation from the sterile rocks unclothed with vegetation.

Thus we have the apparent anomaly that the southern and Indian sides of the Himalayas are loaded with perpetual snow down to a much lower limit than are the northern sides, exposed though they be to the intense cold of the Tibetan climate. Accordingly, in central districts of Sikkim and Bhutan, say along the axis of lat. 27° 15′ N., we find the snow-line ranging between 15,500 and 16,000 feet; and approaching the northern border of those countries we find it rise on the southern face of the mountains to 17,500 feet; but cross the frontier into Tibet, further north, and then, in the heights abutting on the Arun valley or in the range lying north of Chomolhari, the line of perpetual snow is nowhere under 19,300 feet.

Of course, it must be understood that when the lowest limit of perpetual snow is thus spoken of, the estimate concerns open mountain-sides and places offering a fair exposure to the sun and winds. In narrow gullies and in sheltered hollows facing north, the same deep beds of ice and frozen snow continue year after year even in Tibet at elevations of only 14,000 feet.

The tracts lying north of Eastern Nepal, which are among the bleakest, coldest, and most elevated in Tibet, are said to have a snow-line of 20,000 feet. This was also found to be the case west, where, for example, Dr. Thomson in lat. 35° 30′ estimated the snow-line as at the same height. At Lanak La, just a few miles N.-E. of the Changchenmo valley, Captain Basevi, we believe, reckoned the line below which all snow in properly exposed situations would melt, during every save a few abnormal summers, as averaging 19,800 feet.

Such estimates contrast strangely with the fixture of the same line in the European Alps which is only 8,500 feet.

East of the meridian of long. 92° E. the limit of perpetual snow drops lower; and the further east you pass the lower the line falls, especially in the southern regions, though in the tracts N. of lat. 31° N. the plane of this limit does not sink so rapidly. Thus, in the ranges about the sources of the Hoang Ho we find it adjusted by the Russian authorities at 16,000 feet. The estimate for Derge and Chhamdo is set at 15,800 feet. But much further south, as at Bat'ang (in lat. 30° 2′ N.) the level of perpetual snow is said to be under 15,000 feet; while in the ranges of the Dzáyul district we believe this line ought not to be set above 14,400 feet.

The cause of the comparatively low level of perpetual snow in South-East Tibet is not an obscure one. Several of the great rivers of Tibet make exit from the land just where the S.-E. provinces and the Chinese provinces of Szechuan and Yunnan meet. The country in these parts, which is exceedingly mountainous and broken up, there receives continuously voluminous supplies of humid air, which are brought up straight from the ocean along the courses of the mighty rivers. Such southernly-flowing water-ways as the Salwin and Mekhong, which quit Tibet at this corner, form permanent funnels of ingress for the moist currents which rush up their valleys from the southern seas. The result is not only an excessive snow-fall but also an atmosphere of exceeding humidity, and which during many months of the year is laden with rain-films and directly retards evaporation.

THE WIND.

One of the greatest embarrassments of travel on the Tibetan highlands is the wind. It is incessant all the year round. It starts up perhaps before 9 A.M., and at certain seasons earlier, and blows with great violence the whole day until after sundown. At the loftier altitudes in the winter months in exposed situations these winds are murderous and, unless shelter beneath hill-side or boulders is found, death or frost-bite is the result. It is the same in all parts of Tibet; a terrific wind which chiefly blows from the west or north-west seems ever present. Travellers in Ngari Khorsum in the S.-W., in the northern plains of West and Central Tibet, on the uplands and passes of Tsang, and amid the mighty parallel mountain-ranges of N.-E. Tibet, all speak of this wind with lamentable recollection. It is the same, although with certain seasons of intermission, in the more elevated tracts of Mongolia. South-East Tibet seems alone, of these central regions of Asia, to enjoy comparative immunity; for, there, the moister and less continuous currents from the south and south-east prevail, displacing the awful winds from the west.

The picture on the covers of Mons. Bonvalot's volumes of Tibetan adventure—a picture repeated more clearly in the text of the book—gives one a most impressive sense of the life of the nomads of the wind-swept plains. It represents a party of natives cowering round a tiny fire amid stones and trying to snatch a meal. A singular fact concerning the strength and velocity of the wind deserves special record. At an altitude of over 18,500 feet the currents of wind seem, curiously enough, to lose something of their force. On heights of 19,500 feet, and at loftier elevations on passes and ranges, there is a marked diminution of speed and strength. The currents of greatest power and violence are experienced in open tracts ranging between 15,000 and 18,000 feet. In fact, at such elevations the westernly winds blow furiously from about 8 A.M., acquiring the greatest speed, that of 35 to 38 miles per hour, at 2 P.M. or thereabouts. The temperature at that hour generally begins to fall, but the force of the wind does not abate for at least 2 hours further. As the sun lowers and the temperature falls, the velocity diminishes; but frequently the wind does not totally subside until long after dark, only to re-commence its vigour soon after sunrise the next morning. The wind rushing over most of the Tibetan and Himalayan passes in the day-time is usually little short of a hurricane. Strange to say, however, as already noted, in those passes which scale nearly 20,000 feet there is only a smooth and fairly brisk current.

The late Mr. E. C. Ryall, who did much work for the Survey of India on the Ngari Khorsum border, writes:—"Whirl-winds sometimes occur on the passes. I heard of a fatal accident on the Balchadhura pass. A Bhotia of Tola village in Johar, on arriving at the top of the pass, was lifted off the ground, carried away some 100 yards or so, and then dropping was dashed to pieces. I had always in Hundes to take my observations in a very respectable kind of storm. The only way to get on with the work was to shelter myself and my instruments as much as possible, by putting up a protecting *khanat* 6 feet high, to keep which in position I had to get 10 or 12 men to lean against it and frequently 5 or 6 more."

These powerful and continuous winds must, also, exercise considerable effect in transforming the physical surface of the country. Sven Hedin makes some pertinent observations as to the process: "In these high altitudes the abrasive power of the wind plays a very important part. The west wind, which is said to be the prevailing wind, sweeps away all the finer materials, leaving the gravel behind and exposed, until that in its turn becomes disintegrated and is swept away. The surface of the mountains was everywhere weathered and porous. It was evident there was an enormous difference between the temperature of the day and the temperature of the night; and this is the most destructive of all the disintegrating agencies. Next after it ranks the wind, which carries away all the fine particles of detritus."

CHAPTER IV.

THE SALT AND FRESH-WATER LAKES.

The great sheets of water held in the hollows of this uplifted land now claim notice. Although several of these are almost large enough to be styled inland seas, the supply to nearly all of them is kept up merely by the ordinary glacial drainage from the mountains in which each lies entrenched. Not one, as it appears, is fed by any considerable river. Two or three minor affluents meander into the larger lakes, but they are hardly more than mountain-streams draining not very distant uplands.

Tibetan lakes have several peculiarities. First, the great altitude at which they occur. Secondly, the excessively saline nature of their waters. With few exceptions they are emphatically salt lakes; potash, soda and borax being found in such extensive deposits encrusted round the margin, and in the waters themselves, that most of the lakes north of the central lateral chain are not denominated *ts'o* or "lake," but *ts'akha* or "salt-pit." Thirdly, few of the lakes seem to have any important outflowing river, and in this way, doubtless, their great size is maintained.[1] Fourthly, in the closest proximity to every Tibetan lake rises up an extensive system of hot springs. These geysers in Tibet, as they occur near lakes almost exclusively and not in other situations, suggest the theory of volcanic fires being near the surface and exercising by conduits, the gases of which are in spasmodic play through the heat, a syphonic action on the waters of the lake.

1 "As far as my experience goes, no lake in the Himalayas has two exits, nor do I think that it is common elsewhere, and indeed I know of but one case of the kind where a small pool has two exits. It is obvious that, if there is any great flow of water, one exit will probably be cut quicker than the other, and eventually become the sole channel"—(the late) *Colonel T. G. Montgomerie*, R.E. The earliest source of the Sutlej is undoubtedly Ts'o Lagran; but the outflow is intermittent, during some periods ceasing altogether, the main feeders of the river being streams from mountains to the north and south of its early course. The great Di Chhu of East Tibet is also affirmed to start from Chargyut Ts'o in North Central Tibet.

Stupendous reservoirs of water lie in every quarter of the country. From Kökö Nor on the Mongol border in the extreme N.-E. to Manasarowar or Ma-p'ang in the S.-W., and from the lakes noticed by Mons. Bonvalot along the base of the Kuen Lun range to the Kyema Ts'o on the Nepal frontier and Tigu Ts'o near Bhutan, such masses of liquid held in bond are constantly recurring. They do not stand in the course of the huge rivers of the land—if that were so they would probably have never existed—but always on the higher grounds apart. Sometimes in wide shallows on the flat desolate plains; sometimes engulfed amid amphitheatres of mountains; and again in lengthy series, the links of a mighty chain of many waters laid across ridges and moorland for several hundred miles together.

Imagine, if we can, the height at which the lakes of Tibet are resting! No such elevated sheets of water are found throughout the world. A few minor sheets are met with in the neighbouring Afghan and Pamir regions at altitudes equalling those of the lower waters of Tibet; but none even there at all approaching the elevation of the higher or the majority of the Tibetan lakes. In truth these last seem unapproachable, as to loftiness of situation, by any others in the world.

A short comparative table will at once exhibit the fact of the great superiority in altitude of Tibetan lakes to all others elsewhere :—

Name.	*Situation.*	*Circumference.*	*Altitude above sea.*
Horpa Ts'o	N.-W. Tibet	36 miles	17,930 feet.
Tsarol-ohhe Ts'o; otherwise Ige Námur Nor	N.-W. Tibet	84 miles	17,150 feet.
Yagmo Ts'o	North-Cent. Tibet		16,110 feet.
P'omo Jangt'ang Ts'o	South Tibet	54 miles	16,050 feet.
Tigu Ts'o	South Tibet	51 miles	15,550 feet.
Ts'agyud Ts'o (Chargut Ts'o)	North Tibet	112 miles	15,526 feet.
Manasarowar Lakes	S.-W. Tibet	96 miles (together)	14,960 feet.
Airán Kul; or Victoria Lake	Wakhán in Great Pamir	65 miles	13,950 feet.
Barkut Yasin	Little Pamirs	16 miles	13,300 feet.
Kara Kul	Kargoshi Pamir	46 miles	13,194 feet.
Guatapuri Lakes	Colombia, S. America	...	13,070 feet.
Yeshil Kul	Alichur Pamir	58 miles	12,460 feet.
Kökö Nor	Nan-Shan Range	168 miles	10,250 feet.
Tosun Nor	Tsaidam, N.-E. Tibet	42 miles	8,850 feet.
Issyk Kul	Semiryechinsk; Russ. Asia	247 miles	5,330 feet.
Lake Waterton	Rocky Mountains, N. America		4,200 feet.

Name.	*Situation.*	*Circumference.*	*Altitude above sea.*
Victoria Nyanza: (including Lake Bahringo)	East-Central Africa	860 miles	3,740 feet.
Lake Tanganyika	East Central Africa	780 miles	2,691 feet.
Ulungur Nor	Dzungaria	80 miles	1,550 feet.
Lake Baikal (Ozero Baikal)	Siberia	928 miles	1,540 feet.
Lac de Neufchatel	Switzerland	61 miles	1,437 feet.
Lac de Geneva	Switzerland	48 miles	1,152 feet.
Lake Chad	Bornu, West-Cent. Africa	1,060 miles	800 feet.
Lake Balkhash	Semiryechinsk; Russ. Asia	680 miles	910 feet.
Lake Superior	Canada	1,125 miles	609 feet.
Sea of Aral	Russia in Asia	705 miles	133 feet.
Caspian Sea	Caucasus	1,880 miles	84 ft. below sea.
Dead Sea	Palestine	...	1,308 ft. below sea.
Lakes Melghik, Kebir, and Hajila	Algerian Sahara	...	1,325 ft. below sea.

THE HIGHEST LAKE IN THE WORLD.

The lake in Tibet which may be accounted as the one situated at the highest altitude above the level of the sea is apparently that which Bower marks in his map as Horpa Cho, and which in elevation nearly approaches 18,000 feet. This is consequently the loftiest lake anywhere on the earth's surface. Bower describes it as of considerable length, running roughly N. and S. at a height of 17,930 feet above sea-level with several islets on it. Its area is about 118 square miles. One or two small pieces of water near and upon the Lingzhi T'ang or Lingzhi plains, hard by Horpa Cho, approach this altitude; whilst about 570 miles further east, but in exactly the same latitude, is the "Lac de Montcalm" which Mons. Bonvalot estimated as scaling 17,404 feet above the level of the sea.

SEX OF LAKES.

To peaks standing adjacent to lakes Tibetans assign masculine appellations, affixing the male particle *p'o,* or the honorific term for "father" *yab;* whilst to the lakes themselves, titles of female import are always given, or else to some other particular name a feminine affix is annexed. Thus we have the Dangra Yum lake in the Dokthol district, that is "the Mother Casket of Purity" lake; and beside it shoots up the Targot Yab mountain summit which is thought by intercourse with the lake to have bred many minor peaks. So, we have likewise the Ts'omo Tel-t'ung, near the Nepalese frontier, *i.e.,* "the female lake where the mules drink"; and Ts'omo Mabang is the vulgar designation of the eastern Manasarowar lake. Although *yum,* the honorific for "mother," is also an appendix to lake-names; nevertheless the frequent lacustrine appellation in books *yum-ts'o* comes from *gyu-mts'o*, "turquoise-lake," and refers to the blue-green hue which seems to be in an intense degree the characteristic colour of Tibetan waters.

THE SALT LAKE DISTRICT.

In the physical geography of Tibet there are surprises ever recurring; but among the more distinctive of these may be singled out the extraordinary natural deposits of soda, potash, and borax. Such deposits take the form of lakes and swamps. The salt-lakes of Tibet are unique and exist in remarkable numbers, whilst the size of many of them is equally notable. They are confined to the vast tracts which we have denominated the *Tang* districts; for the lakes of the *Dok* regions in the south, such as Manasarowar, Yamdok, Ts'o-mo T'el-t'ung, Palgo, and Tigu, are of fresh water, the adjacent soil there being black, peaty, and non-saline.

We have already indicated the salt-lake country. It occupies really a most extensive area—comprising, roughly, the whole of Tibetan territory north of latitude 31° in the stretch eastward from the 80th meridian to long. 91° 30′ E. The chief series of salt-lakes as yet discovered is that wonderful chain traversing a southernly-dipping belt from Pang-kong Ts'o to Nam Ts'o Chhyid-mo, the latter lake being only some 80 miles N.-W. of Lhása. They were first brought to our knowledge by the travelling-surveyor Nain Singh; and in their course from west to east drop gradually south from lat. 34° to lat. 30° 45′ N. The journey of Captain Bower and Dr. Thorold revealed another similar southernly-dipping series, running likewise from west to east, almost parallel to Nain Singh's chain and lying on the average about a degree further to the north. This new series makes a drooping chain from Lingzhi T'ang on the Ladak border to the immense sheet of water designated Naksung Satu in Bower's map and placed by him 75 miles N.-W. of Nam Ts'o. Doubtless other series of lakes take up a somewhat analogous course from west to east, both north of Bower's chain and south of Nain Singh's. Possibly Bonvalot's "Lac de Montcalm" is one of a northern series of the kind; whilst the lakes discovered by Captain Bower's party far to the north of Ts'a-gyut Ts'o, and thence further east to the longitude of Lhása, would also form part of this northern chain. But, indeed, after all, it is an arbitrary assumption on our part to group any of these as chains or series; because it may be proved by fuller investigation hereafter that the whole tract concerned is chequered everywhere with sets of large lakes without any systematic grouping of them in latitudinal zones. However, whether the theory of southernly-trending chains of lakes linked across country from W. to E. be true or not, on the whole it may be assumed that north of lat. 31° and west of long. 91° 30′ the whole of Tibet, even to the very base of the Kuen Lün Mountains, is thickly strewn with lakes.

The whole of this northern region seems also to be salt-country. In the unexplored tracts north and north-west of Namts'o Chhyidmo the vast natural store of saline matter is positively phenomenal. Native collectors of these salts relate curious accounts of their abundance or rather redundance. In some places pure chloride of sodium is found piled in stacks of apparently artificial formation. However, the piles are the work, not of man, but of nature. It must be supposed that floods from rivers, and the torrents of melted snow from the surrounding hills, draw great quantities of salt from the soil, which they subsequently deposit in thick beds. The succeeding terrible winds of these plains sweep the layers up into huge mounds, which the intense frost of the winter splits and separates into blocks and slabs resting one upon another. Strangely symmetrical seems to be the power of cleavage exercised in those bitter regions by cold upon the solid salt.

All the lakes hold the saline minerals in strong solution, and yet some of these sheets of water, in the more northern latitudes, are of large area; Ts'a-gyud Ts'o being reported to be 80 miles by 30 miles, and M. Bonvalot assigning to his "Lac da Montcalm," 180 miles further north, dimensions of 45 miles by 12. When the smaller lakes dry up, as seems commonly to happen, they leave pits and sheet-like deposits several feet in depth.[1] Indeed, it appears to be the general tendency of Tibetan lakes in modern times to dwindle. All show signs of having been once considerably larger than they are now. Captain Godwin-Austen when he surveyed the Pang-kong Lake 30 years ago found unmistakeable traces that its old level was much above its level then, and pointed out the probability of the two lakes of this name having once formed a continuous sheet of water together with the Nyok Ts'o. Captain Bower noted the same signs of rapid shrinkage in his series; and the thick far-reaching margins of saline crust encircling all these lakes is evidence of an evaporation which in the present day, for some un-

1 Most of the common salt found encrusted round lagoons abutting on Tibetan lakes contains some admixture of a salt of magnesia; but, though slightly bitter, it is consumed all over Ladak and Tibet. Dr. Frankland once made an analysis of the water of the Pang-kong Lake, and his examination shewed it to contain about 1·3 per cent. of salts. Nearly half of these was chloride of sodium; and the remainder comprised sulphate of magnesia, chloride of potassium, and sulphate of soda. Ordinary sea-water is about twice as salt as the Pang-kong waters, which at the western end are probably a good fair sample of the quality of most of the salt-lakes of Tibet.

explained reason, does not seem to be counterbalanced by any replenishing supply.

As we have stated, Tibetans discriminate the saltiest lakes as *ts'á-kha* (the *cháka* of the maps), the others as *ts'o*; while some even in the salt-country appear to be nearly free from saline matter, as are the great Dangra Yum and Captain Bower's sweet-water lake abutting on the southern shore of Náksung Satu. Near certain *ts'á-kha*, moreover, in the most nitrous plains, springs of beautifully fresh water are found gushing forth and flowing into these brine-pits. Writing of the Pang-kong Lake, Colonel Godwin-Austen speaks of springs bubbling up for some distance out in the lake rendering the water around quite fresh.

Explorers state how large is the trade in the salt products of these waters, which is carried on by the Dokpa tribes inhabiting the Dok regions south of the series. Here the salt (*ts'á*) soda (*bhül*) and borax (*ts'á-le*) are principally collected from the thick deposits fringing such lakes and, being filled into 20lb. bags, the bags are placed in couples on the backs of sheep. Flocks of seven hundred sheep thus loaded are to be encountered patiently bearing these products either west into Ladak, or south to the markets of Nepal. Borax seems to occur most profusely on the plains of Majin, a district N.-E. of Ngari Khorsum near the gold-fields. It lies there near the surface in vast tracts, and any amount may be had for the digging.[1] Some lakes yield likewise an impure nitrate of potash which, under the name of *shora*, fetches a fair price, being conveyed to Gyangtse and Lhása for use in the manufacture of gunpowder.

Hot springs, as we have said, abound near salt lakes as well as near fresh waters. Sometimes they also are strongly impregnated with salts, chiefly the chlorides and sulphates of potash and magnesia; some, too, contain iron. Often, however, they eject water quite pure and sweet, which, in winter on the desolate plains, is of ineffable value to travellers, who find even the ice not sufficiently freed by the freezing operation from its saline flavour. Tibetans attach considerable faith to the curative virtues of these geysers, the only bath of their lives being frequently a single week's course in the hot waters. In severe weather, nevertheless, natives have been known to take refuge from the cold by squatting in the rock-hewn basins whence the warm fountain issues.[2]

1 As to borax, the Tibetan Government exacts from the diggers a tax of only two khághang or 2½ annas per maund. Borax sufficient to supply the potteries of Dresden, Staffordshire and all Europe is here lying unused, if the yield from Tuscany should ever run short. In the Tibetan fields, however, great slackness of demand now prevails; nevertheless, in one borax field in the plains bordering on the easternmost sources of the Indus, one survey explorer noted 100 men at work.

2 See Sir J. D. Hooker's *Himalayan Journals*.

But in the rigorous regions of N. Tibet even the hot springs freeze. Says M. Bonvalot: "It is surprising to see in the midst of this plain of hot springs, cones of ice, twenty feet or more in diameter, about the height of a man, and speckled over on their surface—which is just like crystal—with grit and stones from the plain. These blocks, moreover, have split perpendicularly like certain kinds of over-ripe fruit. We have before us frozen geysers, which have become covered with this solid head-dress when their power of ejection grew insufficient to cope with the frost."

The fertility in places of the salt-tracts has also to be referred to, though it forms part of the general phenomenon of the comparative fertility of a table-land so lofty and ice-bound as Tibet. Not only do pasturage and such shrubs as Eurotia, tamarisk, Hippophae, and camel-thorn rarely fail in these regions, but on the margin of certain lakes, such as Dangra Yum at 14,800 feet, barley is extensively cultivated. Captain Bower found grass "particularly plentiful" in shallow nullahs near some of the loftiest lakes. He writes of large grassy plains at 17,600 feet, and notes, on the shores above his big "Aru Cho" at 17,276 feet, how he made his way "over a plain lying between the water and the mountains covered with grass and flowers." Mons. Bonvalot, who traversed the salt-country much further to the north, remarks only on its fearful desolation and barrenness; but his party journeyed in the winter, Captain Bower's in July. We now proceed to refer to particular lakes in some considerable detail under separate headings.

THE NORTH-WESTERN BOWER SERIES.

Probably the most remarkable chain of lakes is that which was brought to our knowledge by Messrs. Bower and Thorold as existing in the extreme N.-W. corner of the country. The most westernly of the chain was already entered in our maps; and one or two of the others appeared, though by no means in accurate position, under their Mongol names as transmitted from the maps of the Chinese Survey of the 18th century. But Captain Bower introduced us to a regular series.

The most notable characteristic of this lacustrine chain was the marvellous altitude at which it lay, between 17 and 18 thousand feet above the level of the sea; while the very large dimensions of certain members of the series rendered their occurrence at such an elevation still more extraordinary. Starting from the Lingzhi T'ang (the great saline plain abutting the easternmost roots of the Karakoram Himalayas), the series extends in almost regularly re-current links in an E. S.-E. direction through several degrees of longitude. The most westernly of these lakes are comparatively small in size; but as the travellers proceeded eastwards they found the sheets of water in this direction grow larger and larger the further to the east they lay. Some of the eastern-placed members of the chain were found—as we shall presently particularly indicate—to be even many miles in circumference. Another remarkable feature of the series was the unanticipated fertility of the lands surrounding the majority of the lakes, notwithstanding the tremendous general altitude. Not only grass of luxuriant growth occurred, but the grass was variegated with gay-looking assemblages of flowers—small-stalked it may be, yet brightly coloured.

Taking the chain *seriatim*, we find the most western members in the two fast-dwindling lakes of the Lingzhi Tang. These were not visited by Captain Bower's party; but they are of a certain degree of importance in that they form the reservoirs which receive the entire drainage—such as it is—of this extensive but sterile plain. No grass or flowers would have been met with, here at least, if these lakes had lain in the travellers' line of march. TSO-T'ANG TS'O, the westernmost of the pair of lakes, has been passed by most of the European explorers who have journeyed from Leh to Yarkand. It lies at an altitude of 17,250 feet, in lat. 34° 54′ N., long. 79° 26′ E. as to its central axes. The other lake, the southern end of which is barely 10 miles N. of Lanak La, is twice the size of the first-named, and is fed by a river from the Log-zhung range to the north. This sheet of water may be termed the SHUM-T'ANG TS'O.

Thirty-eight miles due east is the next considerable lake, one with saline waters, the MANGTSA TS'O. It lies in a district where for a space a temporary drop in the general elevation occurs, its altitude being only 16,500 feet. The circumference is about 24 miles. The bordering grounds are noted in the neighbourhood for their fertility, or such as is estimated fertility in regions so inhospitable: hence the name which signifies "Much-grass Lake." Captain Bower describes it as a fine sheet of water of a deep indigo-blue, and he notes the profusion of grass. Carey and Dalgleish visited the lake *en route* to the Kuen Lüns. It has been since visited and surveyed by Major Deasy and Mr. Pike. Two or three smaller lakes lie in the vicinity.

Passing some 25 miles further east, maintaining the same latitude, we find in long. 81° to 81° 6′ E. one of the most remarkable lakes of the series. The lofty plane of elevation has been not merely re-gained here, but is carried to a point positively higher, so far as general plane goes apart from intruding mountain ranges, than anywhere else in Tibet. Consequently this lake is veritably the highest-placed of all in the country; and not only that, but also the highest-lying lake in the whole world. The name of this sheet of water, thus to be regarded as unique from its situation, is set down by Captain Bower as the HORPA TS'O. On Major Deasy's map it has a different name—Gurmen Ts'o. It is located at the amazing altitude of 17,930 feet, and in its dimension seems to be a really magnificent lake. To this lake, however, we have already alluded on a previous page.

We now turn more decidedly to the S.-E.; and, dropping S. S.-E. from lat. 34° 30′ to 34° N., we come into the region of two large lakes which under other names and in positions far from accurate had been often set forth in the larger maps of Central Asia. These lakes appeared under the designations of BAKHA NAMUR NOR and IKE NAMUR NOR. It was strange that we should have had only the Mongol names of such extensive pieces of water, and that the Tibetan names should have been unknown. The Mongol appellations signify "Little Harvest Lake" and "Big Harvest Lake"; and doubtless the Jesuit mappists of the Chinese Survey denoted them by those names because their assistants who did the survey work in Tibet were Mongols of Peking. Their Tibetan titles we shall mention presently.

In the maps published previously to Captain Bower's journey, the location of these lakes was woefully out of place, both actually and relatively to each other. The Bakha Namur was marked half-a-degree further to the W. than it really is; while the Ike Namur was placed half-a-degree further to the E. than it ought to have been. Thus the distance between the two lakes was increased by a whole degree above that which is actually correct. The given latitudes, though not so far out, were by no means accurate.

Captain Bower furnished us with only an approximately-correct location as shown in the accompanying map. He was also able to exhibit in some measure their general size and shape with the run of their shore-line. From his observations we see that the two lakes are not more than 35 miles apart, and that they lie in substantially the same latitude. The size of them has not so great a disparity as was supposed; though the more western, the Bakha Namur, is the smaller of the two as its name indicates. We may venture to adjust approximately the circumference of the Bakha Namur at 80 miles and that of the Ike Namur at 108 miles. However, the most remarkable point of difference is that of the respective elevations at which they lie. Though so near to one another, one is full a thousand feet higher in situation than the other. The Bakha Namur has been formed in a very distinctive depression of large extent in the surrounding country, its altitude being only 16,180 feet. A lofty range runs betwixt the Horpa Ts'o and this lake, and on the southern slope a rapid descent in elevation occurs, the valley dipping 2,000 feet in 18 miles to the shores of the Bakha Namur. East of the lake the elevation again ascends and rapidly; for we find the Ike Namur, large though it is, perched on a mountain-flanked plateau 17,150 feet above sea-level.

Captain Bower gives the names of the district in which the lakes occur as Aru; and assigns the name Aru Cho to the larger, the Ike Namur Nor. Our own inquiries yield Tsarul or Tsarol as the correct designation, a name which the traveller could readily have interpreted as Aru, the final *l* in Tibetan being always nearly inaudible. Now *Tsarol* is in Tibetan the exact equivalent of the Mongol *Namur*; and thence we get at the most probable reading of the Tibetan appellations of the lakes, of which the Mongol terms are doubtless only synonyms; namely, TSAROL-CHHUNG TS'O, *i.e.*, "Little Harvest Lake" for the western water, and TSAROL-CHHE TS'O, *i.e.*, "Big Harvest Lake" for that to the east. It is noteworthy that many of the lakes in this region of Tibet have names bearing reference to the amount of verdure in their vicinity—a most natural style of nomenclature when one remembers the importance and scarcity of good pasturage in these windswept and lofty wastes.

The neighbourhoods of both sheets of water seem to abound in animal life. When in camp near Bakha Namur Nor or Tsarol-chhung Ts'o, Captain Bower wrote: "This is a great country for game; in the broken ground close to the river hares swarmed, antelopes were to be seen in every direction, and *Ovis Ammon* skulls lying about denoted that the living animals were to be found in the neighbouring hills." Again, he gives us this inviting picture of the Ike Namur Nor or Tsarol-chhe Ts'o:—" Over a pass 17,876 feet, and then down a long, narrow valley which suddenly debouches on Lake Aru Cho (17,150 feet), a fine sheet of water running north and south, salt like nearly all the Tibetan lakes, and of a deep blue colour. To the S.-W. and N.-W. some fine snowy mountains rise up into the blue sky; while on the east low undulating barren-looking hills are seen. In every direction antelope and yak in incredible numbers were seen—some grazing, some lying down. No trees, no signs of man, and this peaceful-looking lake, never before seen by a European eye, seemingly given over as a happy grazing ground to the wild animals. A sportsman's paradise."

We may add that it was in proximity to these lakes, notwithstanding the elevated altitude, that Dr. Thorold made some of his best botanical finds. Amongst these were *Adonis cœrulea* (at 17,200 feet), *Ranunculus pulchellus* (at 17,300 feet), *Erysimum funiculosum* (at 17,600 feet), *Draba canescens, Draba alpina, Christolea crassifolia, Astragalus Hendersoni, Microula Benthami*, and *Nepeta longebracteata.*

THE MANASAROWAR LAKES.[1]

(*Altitude above sea-level : 15,200 feet.*)

There is a fascination about the sheets of water comprised under the above name, not only because of the sanctity which so long has been attached to them, but also because of the fact that, notwithstanding their proximity to our Indian frontier, we are politically shut out from visiting or even seeing them.

In Tibet the name Manasarowar is quite unknown; the two lakes embraced in our maps under that title being popularly styled, the eastern one Ts'o-mo Má-pang, and the western one Ts'o Lang-gak. In Tibetan literature, however, where we find them occasionally introduced, the lakes seem to be known as མཚོ་མ་ཕཾ་ *Ts'o Ma-p'am* and མཚོ་ལྷ་འགྲན་ *Ts'o La-gran* respectively; while together they are designated མ་དྲོས་པ་ *Madrospa*, "that which does not grow warm." The name *Lágan* is also heard in common talk. As to the ordinary colloquial appellations they probably signify: *Má-pang*[2] "the Peacock's Breast," and *Lang-gak* "the Bull's Throat." In Sanskrit works the name *Manasarowara* seems to be applied to Ma-pang only, the Lang-gak lake being termed *Ráwana-hrad.* Finally, at the present day, the Hindus of the Himalayas call the latter lake Rakas T'al.[3]

These twin waters, which lie almost immediately on the northern face of the Kumaon Himalayas, a few miles N. from the base of the descent into Tibet, are well-known to have been of mythological importance in both the Brahman and the Buddhist pantheons of India. In sacred literature they were held to be the sources of the Ganges, the Indus, and other large rivers; although in reality the Sutlej alone has any connection with the lakes. A lion, a peacock, an elephant, a bull, and a gigantic horse-like creature vomited the sources of these rivers from their mouths laid open somewhere in these holy waters. Moreover, the lakes were reputed of enormous size, some 500 miles across—a sea where Sita and the gods bathed and sported; whereas the

1 Mentioned by Pliny and Ctesias, the latter stating that a liquid matter like oil found on the surface was valued and collected by the inhabitants. Marco Polo refers to one of the lakes but not by name, mentioning that pearls were to be found in it. Purang-gir notes a sugar-loaf hill named Khyem-lung as rising at the base of "Cantaish."

2 However, the Revd. A. W. Heyde, formerly Moravian missionary in Lahoul, informs me that the real name of the lake is Map'am not Mapang, and that the local tradition is that it was so called because Milaraspa contended with a Bon priest in miracle-working on its shores and was མ་ཕམ་ *ma-pham* "unconquered."

3 It is also popularly styled *Woma Ts'o* "milk lake."

greatest diameter of either in any part barely exceeds 20 miles. Tibetan writers of modern times endorse these legends; explaining, however, the disparity between such assertions and the present aspect of things by the dire decrease of moral merit in the land in recent years. "It is probably owing to the smallness of moral merit in us," writes Lama Tagtse Cho-wo, "that we do not see these sacred places in their original state as our ancestors beheld them. There is no other explanation, except this, why great things should now look small."

Another circumstance enhancing the religious dignity of the lakes is the fact that they lie at the feet of the ever-sacred peak of Kailas, the mountain whereon the 33 greater deities of Brahmanism and Buddhism are enthroned. This indeed is Mount Meru, where the four Dik Rajas protect the greater gods from intrusion, and down the sides of which are ranged the spheres of the lesser deities who are ever at war with one another.

A few words as to the geographical situation of the lakes. They may be placed as between the parallels of 30° 37′ and 30° 53′ 12″ of northern latitude, and between the longitudinal meridians of 81° 7′ E. (the westernmost reach of Ts'o Lang-gak) and 81° 38′ E. Both the lakes lie within these limits. The Pass out of British territory into Tibet which is located nearest to them is the Mang-shang La ("Many Nose Pass") giving exit from Garhwal, which Pass is distant as the crow flies about 30 miles from the southern margin of Ts'o Langgak.

No English professional observer has actually seen the lakes since Lieutenant Richard Strachey and Mr. Winterbottom visited them in September 1848. The former, now General Sir R. Strachey, is still living and published his narrative only in 1900. His brother, then Lieutenant Henry Strachey, of the 66th Regiment Bengal Native Infantry, had previously in 1846 made the same journey and reported on these lakes after his trip to their shores exactly 54 years ago. One or two military officers, nevertheless, are said to have succeeded in penetrating these forbidden wilds in quest of sport. The redoubtable Mr. Savage Landor also came here in 1897. Previous to Mr. H. Strachey's visit in October 1846, no European had reached here since Moorcroft who journeyed to the same shores in 1812. Nain Singh, A. K. (then known as "Pundit D."), and one or two others of our trained native explorers have, however, taken Manasarowar in the course of their peregrinations. In 1868-69 one of these agents made a careful traverse round both lakes; and this survey, coupled with the observations of Henry Strachey, who compiled a map of the region, gave sufficient material for the topographical delineation of this part included in Mr. Ryall's map of 1879.

The Himalayan hill-station nearest to the lakes, and from which with care and rapid movements they might prove accessible, is Almora. The route therefrom passes *viâ* Pitoragarh and the valley of the Kali river, which is followed up to Kangwa, just above Garbyang, by the right bank. Here the river separates into its two main feeders, the northern one of which is taken, and thence the Lipu-lek Pass into Tibet (altitude 16,800 feet) may be gained. It was by this route that Colonel H. B. Tanner went in 1885, when by quick marching he was able to get as far as Takla Khar on the Karnali river before the authorities were apprised of his movements. He reached, thus, within some 23 miles of the famous sheets of water. Strachey, however, does not recommend this way, as it lies through country comparatively well-peopled. He approves of the route *viâ* the Mang-shang La, which, though a Pass much higher then Lipu-lek and heavily-snowed, leads in Tibet through an uninhabited yet not difficult region, and is the shortest road to the lakes. Strachey himself took a Pass near the Mangshang but further north—the Lang-byang (or Lankpya) La, 18,150 feet in height; but that caused a considerable detour when Tibetan ground was reached. This, moreover, was the Pass by which Mr. Landor entered Tibet. The route to both these last-named Passes strikes off from the Kali 8 miles above Garbyang, turning N.-W. up the Kunti Yangti valley.

Let us now try and realise the scenery around the lakes themselves. It is worthy the fame of old attaching to the locality. Lang-gak Ts'o, it must be remembered, lies to the left or west, and the more sacred Ma-pang to the right or east. The two are separated from each other by a low rocky isthmus named Tung-kang which varies from 5 to 2 miles in breadth; and together they are encradled amidst massive mountains except to the S.-W.

The great Kailas, or Gang Tise as the Tibetans style it, stands directly to the north of Lang-gak. It rears itself up rather to the south of the main Gang-ri range from which it is partially detached, and its buttress-like spurs protrude to within two or three miles of the northern shore of the lake, the intervening valleys giving off considerable feeding streams. Mr. Ryall viewing it from a distance compared its blunt peak, which rises to a height of only 21,830 feet above sea-level, to a Hindu *math* or Pandu temple with the top of the steeple broken off.[1] Strachey, who beheld it close at hand from the very mar-

[1] The heretical Bonpo priest says to Milaraspa with some truth: "Snowy Tise and this Mapang Lake are like yourself. Only at a distance their fame is great; but near at hand they are nothing remarkable." In those pages, however, it it implied that the waters of Mapang were really extensive and hence the miraculons

gin of the Lang-gak lake lying there at its feet, gives a striking and enthusiastic description of its appearance there:

"The most remarkable object here was Kailas, now revealed in full proportion to its very base, and rising opposite (northward) straight out of the plain only two or three miles distant. The south-west front of Kailas is in a line with the adjacent range, but separated on either side by a deep ravine; the base of the mass thus isolated is two or three miles in width. The general height of this I estimate to be 4,250 feet above the plain; but from the west end the peak rises some 1,500 feet higher in a cone, or dome rather, of paraboloidal shape—the general figure not unlike Nanda Devi as seen from Almora. The peak and the upper part of the eastern ridge were well covered with snow, which contrasted beautifully with the deep purple colour of the mass of mountain below. The stratification of the rock is strongly marked in successive ridges that catch the snow falling from above, forming irregular bands of alternate white and purple; one of these bands more marked than the rest encircles the base of the peak, and this, according to Hindu tradition, is the mark of the cable with which the rakshasas attempted to drag the throne of Siva from its place."

To the south of the basin of the lakes, but more immediately to the south of Ma-pang and away to the S.-E. of Lang-gak, rises the huge mountain matrix known sometimes as Gurlha and sometimes as Nyimo Namgyal, the highest peak of which touches 25,360 feet, *i.e.*, 3,500 higher than Kailas.[1] Mighty glaciers fill the upper hollows of these summits which contribute to the maintenance of the waters of Ma-pang to the N. and the Karnali river to the S. The rocky isthmus separating the lakes is in part a long spur from Gur-lha. A long ridge from the same matrix running first east and then E. S.-E. forms eventually the boundary between Tibetan and Nepalese territory.

We must now take the lakes *seriatim* for detailed description;

nature of feats such as these. The heretic priest straddles across the lake, one foot on either shore. Then Milaraspa sits down upon the waters; and, though his body does not become larger and Lake Mapang does not grow smaller, he covers the whole surface of the lake. Again, Milaraspa holds Lake Mapang on the tip of his thumb, "and this he does without injuring the living creatures which dwelt in the waters." But see Milaraspa: Gurbum; folios 79 to 84. (Nart'ang block-print edition).

1 There is some doubt as to the real designation of this cluster of peaks. Probably the whole mass bears the name of Nyima (or Nyinmo) Namgyal; while Gur Lha Mandhata is applied to the main summit. Strachey styles the mountain Momonangli, which is possibly the denomination of a subordinate peak. Mr. E. J. Peyton, the talented delineator of the intricate mountain systems of Kumaon and Garhwal, was the first to ascertain a near version of the true name Nyima Namgyal. Colonel Tanner's Nimo Namling is another approximation.

and first Ts'o Lang-gak or La-gran which, though the less sacred, is the larger of the pair.

The greatest length of Lang-gak is from N.-W. to S.-E., and such diameter may be reckoned at 21 miles. From W. to E. where in places there is a tendency of the two opposite shores to approach one another the diameter is barely 8 miles. The whole outline of the lake except to the N. and N.-W. is complexedly indented, forming many creeks, inlets, and bays, which are fantastically termed *ts'o-lak* or the "lake's hands." We find especially the south-easternmost corner recessed into a deep bay; while the waters are drawn far inland into a fine point on the west side. Moreover, the coast-line is not only broken, but also in places extremely precipitous. Several islets are seen off the western and southern shores, and on one of these to the west is a small monastery. In contrast to the rugged margin of the south, the northern shore lies low and flat with large stretches of heavy sand. It is in this quarter, also, where the chief feeders enter the lake. A considerable number of streams descend from the gorges of Kailas: these form one small river known as the Sersho Chhu. But the two largest feeding streams come from the ravines separating the western and eastern flanks respectively of Kailas from the adjacent heights. These, the Khá-lap Chhu and Jom Chhu, are each some 150 feet broad where they enter the lake; and much wider when abnormally swelled by the melting of the snows in May and June.[1]

Another small river discharges into the Lang-gak about the middle of the western coast; while, according to the Strachey brothers, there is yet another affluent in a stream of large volume which flows from the N.-W. corner of Ma-pang and enters Lang-gak at the N.-E., thus connecting the two lakes. But this question of communication between the lakes must be taken later in the present article.

As to any out-flow from Ts'o Lang-gak, that point is of particular interest because in this lake the Sutlej is commonly believed to have its earliest place of origin. A reference to the map shows the lake narrowing to a horn in the extreme N.-W., and it is thence that any effluence into the bed of the Sutlej could only occur. Nain Singh, who crossed the valley in which this bed would lie some two or three miles from the north-western point of the horn, noted in his route-survey a stream there, proceeding from the direction of the lake. He designated it as the Sutlej. Does this famous river, then, make exit from the lake, and so there take the first start on its course? Henry Strachey examined, in passing, the reputed outlet. He found a swamp with large puddles of standing water, and the inference from his

[1] H. Strachey designates these rivers "La Chhu" and "Barka Chhu."

description is that the drainage from this morass presently masses into a stream which, when joined by other feeders, both from the south and from the western Kailas spurs, developes into the Sutlej. Probably, if Strachey had visited the spot 4 or 5 months earlier in the year, he would have observed the undoubted efflux in more river-like form. At any rate, here, in this lengthened-out point at the N.-W., the lake ends; and through a marshy channel in continuation, a drainage, which soon becomes a stream, exudes into the bed of the combined feeders, and together with these forms the river in question. Moreover, the natives of the locality designate this point as the *chhu-go* or "river-door"; while the Himalayan traders style it the *nikás* or outlet of the lake.

The intricate outline of Ts'o Lang-gak, with the abutting mountains, imparts a picturesque appearance to this lake, which is absent in the case of the more sacred waters of Ma-pang. We must, however, quote H. Strachey's description forthwith; as he is the only European who has referred to it :—

"The western shore of the lake was undulating ground over which we had been travelling this morning at the foot of steep and lofty hills there and here streaked with snow. The water was of the clearest brightest blue, reflecting with double intensity the colour of the sky above; while the northern horn of the water, overshadowed by the wall of mountain rising above it, was darkened into a deeper hue, partaking of the fine purple colour that distinguishes the rocks of Gang-ri . . . . . Bright sunshine spread a warm glow over the whole landscape, entirely divesting it of the cold barren aspect that might be supposed inseparable from these intemperate regions. . . . . . The lake was beautiful; quite a little sea. Long rolling waves broke upon the shore close under our feet, and as far as could be seen the whole face of the water was freshened into the ανηριθμον γελασμα of old ocean."

Turning to the eastern one of the pair of lakes, namely to Ts'o-mo Ma-pang, it is noticeable that the immediate shore all round (except perhaps along the southern banks) lies in flat sandy reaches. There are few cliffs and few indentations, which facts make the circumambulation of the lake a comparatively easy performance to the hundreds of pilgrims who journey hither for the purpose. The shape of Ma-pang is almost artificially regular to look at, the general configuration being obloid or an oblong with the corners rounded off, rendering it nearly elliptic, the major axis running east and west. Along the flattened litoral are the remains of many disused gold-workings. These are said to have been abandoned not because of the exhaustion of the precious metal, but on account of the remonstrances of certain prominent lamas who declared that the *shib-dag* or god of the soil was mortally offended by the extracting of so many large nuggets from his property. The more sensible persons affirm that the head-lama of the Gyang-t'ang Gompa, at Darchan, was animated by a dog-in-the-manger kind of feeling that the ground around the lake was being rendered somehow less valuable by the gold-digging operations—which we suppose in one sense was true—and by his influence the work was finally prohibited.

The task of making the circuit of Ma-pang on foot is denominated *parkor*, and including the requisite stoppages the journey is held to take 4, 5, or 6 days according to the length of such stoppages. To go round both Gang Tise (*i.e.*, Mt. Kailas) and the lake at one stretch is styled *p'i-kor chhempo,* "the great outer circle," and is reckoned as a week's business. To emphasize the sanctity of Ma-pang and the importance of the work of circumambulation, no fewer than eight *gompas* or monasteries have been erected at various points round the lake. These in the order in which they occur, passing as devotees do round the lake from W. to E. to S. to N., are :—

Jho-o Gompo	The Lord's monastery.
Jang-kyab G.	Northern refuge m.
Langpo-ná G.	Elephant's trunk m.
Band-dhe G.	Chinese monks m.
Serlung G.	Golden valley m.
Pang-go G.	Beggars' m.
T'o-kar G.	White head m.
Go-ts'ul G.	The Way-out-of-the-door m.

All these are establishments belonging to the Lho Dukpa sect of Buddhists and, curiously enough, are under the jurisdiction of the Dharma Raja of Bhutan, who also governs the monasteries standing round Mt. Kailas. The head-lama of each is always a man who has been at one time an inmate of Táshi-chhödzong, the chief lamassery of Bhutan; and such of the members who desire to take priestly degrees invariably proceed all the way to Bhutan for the purpose, a longer and more difficult journey than it is to Lhása. They are, however, all very small monasteries; and several are said to be now ruined and deserted.

Every pilgrim making the *parkor* of Ts'o-mo Ma-pang has to stop at, and present offerings at, each one of the eight gompas built round the lake. No one performs *parkor* round Ts'o Lang-gak, and only one monastery stands on the shores of that lake.

Although there is a belt of plain encircling the margin of Ma-pang, lofty mountains practically surround this lake also, except on the western shore where lies the isthmus separating the two sheets of water. There is a protuberant ridge from Gang-ri Gur-gyab which runs down from the N. N.-E. almost to within 3 miles of the northern bank and which carries peaks up to 19,500 feet. The main post-road between Gar-t'ok and Lhása passes over the flat space lying between the lake-shore and the foot of these peaks. But Gur Lha and its series of subsidiary peaks abutting the southern shore are the dominant mountains of the sacred lake. The two nearest summits are 22,850 and 22,670 feet respectively, the main peak rising up to the rear of these lesser heights.

Several river-like feeders supply Lake Ma-pang with its fluid contents. The two principal of these come from the Gang-ri Gur-gyab range which forms the eastern continuation of Kailas. The Some Chhu is the larger of the two and is fed by the Pempo-Kyi Chhu (River of Profit and Happiness) from the latter range, and by another branch stream from the heights surrounding the head-waters of the Yeru Tsangpo. Strachey believes that four affluents discharge into the lake. He, however, takes no account of the undoubted large supply of water which is emitted from the glaciers and spurs of Gur Lha. In fact four or five glaciers are said to lie on the northern or lake side of this mountain mass. The streams draining therefrom into Ma-pang are named fantastically *chin*, that is "urine"; and so we have Langpo-chhempo Chin "the mighty elephant's urine," Seng-ge Chin "the lion's urine," etc., as denominations of the various glacial feeders pouring into the sacred lake from the flanks of Gur Lha, or rather Nyin-mo Namgyal Ri "the mountain that completely vanquishes the sun." It should be added that no water comes to Ma-pang from Kailas.

With so large an affluence, it might be well-expected that there would exist some effluent streams from Lake Ma-pang. The lakes of Tibet do not as a rule seem to require much tapping in the shape of outflowing rivers to restrict them to a normal level. In fact, not any large lake in the land possesses a single considerable stream of exit from its waters, yet shrinkage is the usual present-day process observable in these lakes. The truth is that the loss through sub-soil filtration in most Tibetan lakes is phenomenal, sand and porous gravels being the basal setting of nearly all.

Moorcroft declared that there was no effluent river attached to Ma-pang. But Henry Strachey brings forward his own ocular testimony to the contrary. Moreover, his assertion is rendered of greater consequence when he states that the out-flowing river directly connects the waters of the two lakes. Despite Moorcroft (whose observations were not minute) we cannot refuse to credit Strachey when he saw with his own eyes "a large stream 100 feet wide and 3 deep running rapidly from E. to W. through a well-defined channel." He goes on to say:

"This was the outlet of Manasarowar. It leaves that lake from the northern quarter of its western shore, and winding through the isthmus of low undulating ground, for 4 miles perhaps, falls into Rakas Tal." The native surveyor who made the circuit of the lake in 1868-69 agrees rather with Moorcroft than Strachey; but as his attention was not called to the point before he made his traverse, but on his return home afterwards, his opinion is not of much weight as against the plain averment of Strachey. Indeed, the latter traveller gives a cogent reason why the outflow from Ma-pang might be easily overlooked by a superficial observer. The entrance of the effluent channel, which leaves Ma-pang lake just south of the Jho-o Gompa, has a large bar of sand and gravel continuous with either shore of the lake, the out-going water running in small streams which pierce the bar in many places. Pilgrims, making *parkor,* traverse this broad sandy bank, and the point where the streams combine to form a river is hidden behind a bluff upon which Jho-o Gompa stands. Mr. Savage Landor, it may be added, denies the existence of any connecting river; but his authority cannot be accepted because he did not reach the northern part of the isthmus between the lakes.

On the whole, admitting the definite evidence of the Strachey brothers, it may be said that a small river quits the eastern lake at its N.-W. angle, and after a 4 miles' course enters the eastern side of the western lake, but only intermittently; so uniting, though in scanty measure, the waters of Ma-pang and Lang-gak. As Ma-pang is so well supplied with feeding streams, such overflow has been probably rendered necessary notwithstanding the counter-operating processes of filtration and evaporation ever actively at work. That the two lakes at any previous period formed one, seems improbable in face of the height (averaging 250 feet) and constituent material of the dividing isthmus. However, the present connecting river runs through a valley which at one time may have been a channel of communication, not as a river but as a neck between the lakes.

Finally, it should be stated that the waters of both lakes are free from saline ingredients and perfectly drinkable. Certain deposits of soda at two or three parts of the litoral are probably, therefore, derived from the under-lying ground, not from the adjacent waters.

YAMDOK TS'O.

(*Elevation : 13,800 feet above the sea.*)

Perhaps the most remarkable sheet of water is that one which, for quite 160 years, was figured as a perfect ring of water surrounding a large island, the name given being Lake Palte. This name in the old maps is a misnomer, the real designation being Ts'o Yamdok; whilst the supposed island is an island-like peninsula connected in a very quaint fashion, on the western side, to the main shore by two narrow strips of land. The natives aptly compare it to a large scorpion on the waters, holding on to the land with its two nippers.[2] Between these two claws is enclosed another smaller lake, 500 feet higher in level than Yamdok itself, and bearing the warning name of Dü'mo T'so, the She-Devil Lake.[3] U. G.—with the single exception of A. K., the most able of all the survey explorers—has the credit of having been the first to investigate the physical features of the lake and its curious peninsula, and from the information brought by him from over the Himalayas the correct outline can be now delineated on our maps. Just at the point where one arm of the peninsula grasps the shore has been built the famous Samding Monastery—a joint community of monks and nuns both under the rule of a young woman of high family who is held to be the incarnation of Dorje P'agmo "the sow with the thunderbolt."[4] On the scorpion-shaped peninsula (named To-nang or Dora-nang) are lofty ranges of hills radiating from the centre, in the recesses of which are four other monasteries owning allegiance to the Great Mother Sow; and the mountains swarm with game which she strictly preserves. Colonel H. R. Thuillier, reporting U. G.'s narrative, writes: "Dumo Ts'o (the inner lake) impressed him greatly; its deep still waters, embosomed amongst mighty cliffs; the silence which hung over the stupendous crags which encircled it, broken only by the hoarse roar of falling masses of mountain—associated in his mind with traditions of demons and genii who inhabited the lake—struck his mind with unwonted awe. He declares that he experienced sensations hitherto strange to him." Yamdok Ts'o is 13,800 feet above sea-level, and has a circumference of 109 miles. Its deep blue waters are perfectly sweet and non-saline, and it lies softly and darkly amid

1 However, the Augustinian monk, A. A. Georgius, the historian of the Lhásá mission, writing so far back as 1762, gives the lake its proper designation, styling it *Yamdro* or *Yang-so*. He adds, moreover, that so large is its size that a man travelling 20 miles a day takes 18 days to go round it. So he estimates the circuit at 360 miles—as we now know a wild exaggeration there being no signs of the lake having dwindled in area.

2 The statement of Colonel H. B. Tanner (in Survey Report 1883-84, appendix, p. xlv.) that Yamdok Ts'o means "Scorpion lake" is quite an error. In Tibetan *dikpa* is a scorpion; and *Yamdok* signifies merely "upper pastures."

3 Sarat Chandra Das estimates the Dūmo lake as being 1,300 feet above the Yamdok Ts'o, which seems hardly probable.

4 The woman who was the incarnation of the goddess when the above was written has since died, and the present Dorje P'agmo and lady abbess is a girl of 5 or 6 years' old.

mountains which Tibetans poetically compare to the corolla of a lotos.

It is separated on the north from the deep broad bed of the Yeru river by a very narrow space of ground; but what this barrier lacks in breadth it makes up in height, ruggedness, and solidity. These northern ramparts which keep back the waters of the lake from draining off into the great Tsangpo form the lofty Khamba La range, which is the southern wall of the river-flats for many miles just here. The mountains of the range bank up the lake so high that, although in places the distance between it and the river is only 8 miles, yet the level of the waters of the lake is 2,000 feet above that of the waters of the river.

The southern shores of Yamdok are not mountainous, but low and flat with extensive grassy savannahs of the *Dok* or dark-soil character. These form luxurious grazing for the flocks of Dokpa nomads; and indeed the name Yamdok Ts'o or "lake of the upper pastures" is founded on these famous feeding grounds. Here also dwell numerous *dolpa* or fishermen, who make a livelihood out of the fresh-water fish which throng the shallows of the southern reaches.[1] To the east of the lake, also, but separated therefrom by mountains, is another broad plain utilised, as it seems, for pony-grazing, and denominated Yamdok Karmaling—"the Yamdok plain of stars."

Besides the semi-island of Tonang, a large mountainous island named Yambu occurs off the southern coasts. On this another branch house of the Samding monastery has been erected; and the island is noted, further, for a remarkable series of caverns. Not far from this quarter a long lake adjoins Yamdok, but is walled off from the main waters by a loop of rocky-cliffs most curiously disposed. It bears the quaint appellation of *Rombu-dza Ts'o* or "the Bottle of Corpse-worms Lake"—a name said to have been bestowed because of the numerous bodies of monks devoted as food to the fish of its waters. By this observance the Lu spirits inhabiting the lesser lake are propitiated, and restrain its waters from being overflowed into by those of Yamdok and so inundating valuable pastures. In truth the whole regions round

[1] Fish in Tibetan lakes are mostly of the genus *Shizopygopsis* differentiated by Steindachner as of the following species:—

S. Stoliczkae:	Pangkong and western lakes
S. Prshevalskii	Koko Nor
S. leptocephalus	"
S. gracilis	"

Other genera are *Aspiorrhynchus Ptychobarbus* and *Diptychus* (Steindachner). All four genera are peculiar to Tibet.

these shores are deemed by Tibetans enchanted ground, and the fantastic style of scenery attunes itself naturally to the eeriest superstitions. While the great snow-capped peaks near at hand stand there, as it were, to yield assent to the wildest play of the imagination.

One river, the Rong Nag Chhu, has its uppermost source in Yamdok Ts'o, departing from the N.-W. corner and reaching eventually the Yeru a few miles below Shigatse. However the outflow this way is inconsiderable and by no means constant.[1] Three small rivers enter the lake from the south and with the glacial drainage on the N.-E. maintain it at its level.

KÖKÖ NOR.

(Elevation above sea-level : 10,320 feet.)[2]

In the written Mongol language the spelling of the name of this extensive inland sea runs : *Küke Nagur,* meaning " Blue Lake," but the ordinary pronunciation is as above. Among the Chinese the appellation is *Tsing Hai* with the same signification as the Mongol. Tibetan traders, also, bestow a similar title, styling it སོག་པོ་མཚོ་སྔོན་ *Sokpo Ts'o Ngön* " the Mongol Blue Lake," or more tersely Ts'o Ngömbo.

These waters are rolled out in the lap of a long elliptic plain—sandy but verdant—formed in a wide open loop in the southern ranges of the Nan Shan and east of the deserts and hilly swamps of Tsaidam. The run of the plain is from N.-W. to S.-E.; and so extensive is it that

1 Colonel H. B. Tanner (in the Survey Report 1883-84) attaches credence to the statement of Lama U. G. that the Rong Nag Chhu sometimes flows into the Yeru Tsangpo and sometimes into the Yamdok lake, *according to which happens to have its waters the higher.* If Colonel Tanner had recollected that the mean level of the lake is at least 13,800 feet, while that of the Yeru Tsangpo below Shigatse is in every place always under 12,000 feet, he would hardly have expressed such an opinion. The Yeru would be a wonderful river indeed if its waters could ever rise 1,900, or 2,000 feet above their normal level!

2 The height above sea-level of Kökö Nor is hardly yet determined accurately, considering the remarkable differences in the estimates of various travellers who profess to have measured it. The chief assignments are :—

	feet.
G. E. Groom-Grzhimaylo	11,207
Count Szechenyi (1879)	10,934
W. W. Rockhill (1889)	10,900
N. Przhevalsky (1884)	10,700
G. N. Potanin (1886)	10,580
Captain Wellby (1896)	10,208
Dr. Sven Hedin (1897)	9,975

No doubt in different years the water stands not always at the same level, but such level can never vary so much as even 50 feet. Dr. Hedin's observation, taken in 1897, is unquestionably below the mark. The most probable altitude of these waters may be put at 10,250–10,400 feet above sea-level.

from the N.-W. apex to the point in the S.-E. where the embracing mountains again come together can hardly be estimated at less than 150 miles, whilst the greatest width (N.-E. to S.-W.) to which the valley opens is about 80 miles across. We do not mean to assert that the whole Kökö Nor valley displays one flat surface. Indeed a medial range of hills skirts the southern banks of the Pouhain Gol for some 40 miles, but the altitude being much lower than that of the bounding ranges of the Nan Shan the idea of a vast mountain-locked enclosure or plateau is hardly interfered with. The whole plain is by far the largest of the many great valleys which lie between the various lines of the Nan Shan; and numerous rivers all drain into the famous lake in the S.-E. portion of the plain.

The separated branches of the mountains circling the Kökö Nor valley and which run mainly parallel from N.-W. to S.-E. are usually distinguished as the Northern and the Southern Kökö Nór Ranges. As the Northern Range is less continuous than the Southern, and at certain points changes its direction, different names have been assigned to the different lengths which make up the former. Thus the westernmost portion of the Northern Range bears the Mongol name of Khorbana Ger "the dwelling-place of Khorbana." To the next stretch the Russian explorers have given the title Zussa Range; and round to the east, where a decided dip S. S.-E. occurs in order to meet the Southern Range, we have the Potanin portion. With the exception of the last-named portion (which is detached from and does not properly belong to the main Northern Range) the better name for the whole series is the Chinese one of Su-lei Nan-Shan. This Northern Range is considerably loftier than the Southern Kökö Nor Range throughout; while the latter averages 14,000 to 15,000 feet, the former in most parts reaches 20,000 and carries peaks up to 22,000 feet, as measured by Obroochev. Moreover, the Su-lei Nan Shan stands in perpetual snow wherever it exceeds the line of 16,000 feet. Such, then, are the mountainous surroundings of the Kökö Nor; a notable feature of the plain thus enclosed is its great elevation above the general level of the country just outside the encompassing mountains, especially above that to the E. and S.-E.

The lake itself lies towards the S.-E. termination of the plain; the bounding ranges approximating but not quite meeting some 20 miles or less S.-E. from the eastern head of the lake. In size this large sheet of water has been variously estimated to have a circumference of from 166 to 180 miles, the shores being in no part deeply or much indented. The general flow of the waters goes from N. N.-W. to S.-E., and the greatest length along this the major axis does not exceed 68 miles; while the width between the N.-E. and S.-W. shores varies from

40 miles towards the western end to 22 miles in the eastern section. As to the geographical position of the lake, recent investigations have placed both it and the adjcent localities further to the east than they are made to appear in the maps. In fact the meridional situation is now said to be 22′ further E. than was till lately supposed. Accordingly the actual position of the centre of the lake, or the point of intersection of the major and minor axes, may be adjusted at lat. 30° 56′ N., long. 100° 32′ E.

Mr. Rockhill thus describes the approach to the lake :—

"As we went on, the valley grew wider and the adjacent hills lower. The ground was well-covered with grass, and the water from numerous springs trickled down the hill-sides or formed bits of bog through which we picked our way. The few camps we saw were some of them Mongol, others Tibetan, but the former seemed to predominate. They are a very poor people, their flocks rarely exceeding 100 for each tent. They live in constant dread of their Tibetan neighbours who rob and bully them shamefully. On the third day from Tankar we reached the watershed between the Hsi-ho and the Köko-nor, and from the top of a low pass of 12,248 feet we got our first view of the great lake. It lay a glistering sheet of ice stretching to the west as far as the eye could reach and bounded to the south by a range of high black mountains with snow-tipped peaks."

Along the northern shores of the lake are immense stretches of undulating grassy savannahs affording luxuriant pasturage. In fact the greater portion of the Kökö Nor lands comprises a series of fine meadows passing over hillocks and hollows to the roots of the spurs of the distant mountains.[1] Sand forms a considerable constituent of the soil but with sufficient loam to produce a soft and nutrient herbage. The shore line is clayey slate interpenetrated with gravel.

On the southern margin of the lake the tracts of pasture are very narrow and the banks are steep and cliff-like. The mountain range there runs within a very few miles of the shore, giving off spurs with rounded glens between and hardly any rocky ravines. A scanty drain-

1 "The vast plains which adjoin the Blue Sea are of very great fertility and of a most agreeable aspect, though entirely destitute of trees. The grass is of prodigious height, and the numerous streams which fertilise the soil afford ample means to the herds of the desert for satiating their thirst. The Mongols accordingly are very fond of setting up their tents in these magnificent pastures."—Huc. II. p. 99. (Hazlitt's Edition).

Przhevalsky described the lake as "very beautiful." He writes of it, also, thus: "In the middle of March we reached the plateau of Kökö Nor—the absolute height of which is 10,800 feet. The forests of the Nan Shan had disappeared and had been replaced by meadow-like steppes, affording excellent pasture for domestic cattle, alongside of which roamed large herds of antelopes and wild asses. The ground was honeycombed with the innumerable burrows of marmots which both here and in Tibet often lay waste large tracts through devouring the roots of the grass."

age into the lake is contributed in the early summer months; but only one stream deserving the name of river enters the lake from the south; the Ara Gol in the extreme S.-E. corner having hardly any access to the lake. The southern shore is asserted to be the main stronghold of the shepherd brigands; but Gn. Obroochev is the only European who has traversed the southern margin, and he encountered none. It is noteworthy that, while the northern coast has been so well explored, the way along the south side has been always neglected.

The waters of the Kökö Nor are not very deep, and those parts adjoining the shore form shallows 4 or 5 feet in depth and in places even less. The water itself is described as salt and undrinkable, and is inhabited in some plenty by three species of fish belonging to one genus, that distinctively Tibetan genus *Shizopygopsis*, none of which exceed 9 inches in length. Obroochev, however, noted off the southern shore large numbers of fish of another genus and of much larger size, 1½ to 2 feet long. It must be these fish which are spoken of with commendation by the Chinese of Sining. The Amban of Sining is said, when on tour, to be in the habit of halting his party for several days on the verge of the lake for the fishing.

A beautiful deep blue colour which characterises the waters is stated to be the result of excessive saltness and to be so distinctive as to have suggested the name of the lake. Storms are common only in the southern reaches; but such a thing as a boat appears to be an unknown sight on the lake. There are a few islets along the southern coast where the water lies deeper than elsewhere. However there is one rather large island almost in the middle of the lake in the western quarter, some 20 miles S.-E. of the mouth of the Pouhain Gol and 14 miles from the south bank of the lake. This island is known as Ts'o Nying "the heart of the lake"; the Chinese designating it "dragon's colt island" in acceptance of a legend that certain mares placed on the rocks bred with a *lu* or serpent-god of the adjacent waters. On these lonely crags so far from the shore has been long established a small gompa harbouring about a dozen gelongs. The inmates have no communication with the distant coast except during the winter months when the intervening space is hard frozen.[1] It is then the custom for pilgrims from Kumbum to cross the ice to the islet and present offerings of butter and cloth to the holy anchorites. Tradition accounts for the island as having been originally a huge rock dropped into the rising

[1] When Dr. Sven Hedin visited the lake in the middle of November 1896, he reports "there was no ice on the surface, and, though the temperature of the air was 35°·4', the temperature of the water was 44° Fahr." According to Przhevalsky the ice breaks up in April.

flood by a *Khyung* bird to afford a refuge to fugitives from the waters then fast filling the plain. [1]

In the N.-E. corner of the lake a portion has been cut off from the main body by a bar of sand now of great width; and thus has been formed a small detached piece of water known to Mongols as *Norun Hübün* "son of the lake." Again, in the extreme S.-E. corner, are three lakelets in a chain which receive the waters of the Ara river and discharge them eventually by an outlet into Kökö Nor.

The rivers feeding the lake are commonly reckoned to be eight in number; the majority coming in along the northern coast. Some of these as they approach the lake display very broad beds abounding in boulders and sandy flats. Perhaps the widest-mouthed feeder is the Zikhe Ulang Hoshang Müren entering about the centre of the northern shore. But the most important and certainly the longest affluent is the one flowing in on the west, mentioned by Huc and called by him Pouhain Gol—really Bukha Gol or "Bull Yak River."

The Pouhain or Bukha river is so decided a feature of the Kökö Nor plain as to deserve some further remarks. It rises in two large-sized branches, one having its origin in the southern Kökö Nor range somewhere about 37° 18′ N., long. 98° 12′ E. and named Oring Gol. The other, the more important branch, the Pouhain Gol proper, rises either in the Khorbana Ger range or perhaps penetrates through a gap in the latter from the long valley which separates the Ritter and Humboldt ranges. No traveller—not even the Russian Obroochev—had followed its course down from the mountains to the point of entry into the Kökö Nor, until in 1893 Mr. and Mrs. St. George Littledale made their famous journey from Lob Nor to the latter lake. They seem to have first seen the river after crossing the Khaltan Kütül or Katin La, and passing down the valley of the river they noted no deep ravine but a broad bed bounded by low grassy hills. Its size is apparent from the fact that when 6 days' journey (some 120 miles) from the mouth in the lake, the river was too broad to ford. They also speak of a considerable stream from the north joining the Pouhain Gol not many miles below the Katin La. We find in the narrative no observations as to the direction from which the river was seen flowing when they first sighted it; and comparing Mr. Littledale's map with that of Obroochev there are radical discrepancies which weaken reliance on either. Thus, how

[1] "We still continued to travel due east at about a mile or a mile-and-a-half from the lake shore, which glittered a dazzling bright line on the south. All day we had the rocky island in view, rising above the surface of the water like a dromedary's back, and thrown up in dark relief against the scarce perceptible mountains on the south."—*Sven Hedin.*

far to the west the source of the Pouhain lies is hardly yet determinable. Its great size, which Huc had averred and which Przhevalsky had ridiculed, is confirmed by Messrs. Rockhill, Sven Hedin, and Littledale. Mr. Rockhill's observations shew a number of small affluents in the lower portion of the river and the names of which he ascertained. At the point of discharge into the lake the whole bed of the river which is traversed by several separated streams measures two miles across.[1]

Other incoming rivers are the Aling Gol and Balamat Gol entering from the north. Then the Tsaidza is a considerable affluent draining in from the S.-E. However, the only stream entering really direct from the south is the Ta-nyingma Chhu; unless we reckon the fitful inflow from the Ara Gol at the S.-E. corner which reaches the Kökö Nor by way of the lakelets already referred to. The Rhirmo-Jong of Mr. Rockhill's second journey does not, as we believe, ever arrive at the lake.

There exists no outlet from Kökö Nor at the present day; and, unlike the majority of Tibetan and Mongolian lakes, its size seems rather on the increase. The Russian explorer Obroochev who skirted the southern shores in 1893 detected below the present surface of the water two continuous terraces one beneath the other, which at different previous periods had evidently formed the margin of the lake. The upper terrace lay about 16 feet under the present level, and the lower terrace lay some 20 feet deeper still; while the run of both terraces was traceable for at least 12 miles. As already mentioned, the southern waters shew considerable depth. Possibly in earlier times there was an out-flow from the lake. If that was the case, the effluence took place in the south-eastern apex *viâ* the Ara Gol which even now makes no constant flow towards the lake. This idea is rendered all the more probable because at the extreme S.-E. point of the Kökö Nor valley, where the Potanin range from the N.-W. approaches close to the southern Kökö Nor range to form the termination of the valley, there is a wide passage between the two ranges. This passage gives an exit out from the Kökö Nor valley into the basin of the Hoang Ho which lies much lower than the basin of the Kökö Nor. Across this same passage is a low and very flat ridge, from the N.-W. side of which flows the Ara Gol towards the lake, and from the S.-E. side of which rises a feeder

1 Dr. Sven Hedin notes of this river: "The stream was 250 feet wide and had a volume of 600 cubic feet in the second. Beautifully clear and bright, and gliding along without a sound, like a river of oil; the current travelled at the rate of 3 feet in the second. Beyond the principal stream came six other arms, but they contained nothing except frozen pools and fragments of ice. Beyond was yet another arm with a volume of 140 cubic feet per second."

running into the Hoang Ho. At the present day the flat ridge is really the watershed between the basins of the Kökö Nor and the Hoang Ho; but probably in former days the rivers either side had not opposite courses but were connected and flowed as one stream down from the lake into the Hoang Ho. The alluvial nature of the present watershed demonstrates that it did not exist in times not very long gone by.

Sining-fu (or Ziling, as Tibetans term it), the centre of Chinese rule in these regions, though nominally the capital of the Kökö Nor district, lies distant 70 miles to the east of the lake and separated by the Potanin and another minor ridge from the plain. As shewing the remarkable elevation of the plain and lake above the adjoining tracts, it may be noted that Sining-fu (lat. 36° 33′ 32″ N., long. 102° 24′ E., according to Mr. Easton) stands 3,000 feet lower than Kökö Nor. A Chinese Amban resides there and the town has a considerable population. Tankar (or Dung-kor "shell-whorl," as the Tibetans name it) is another commercial place, in altitude 8,760 feet, some 25 miles nearer the lake than Sining; and from thence the road to Kökö Nor branches into two, one leading to the southern pastures of the lake, the other carrying over a pass of 12,000 feet and on to the north shore. Other towns are Hanchu to the N. of the lake, Mu-peshing-ta or "Mobaishen" (Chinese name Seng-Kwan) 10 miles N.N.-E. of Tankar, and Dá-tung.

Some flourishing monasteries are in the neighbourhood. The great Kumbum, 18 miles S.S.-W. of Sining, is the principal establishment, with 3,500 inmates. It stands in Tsong Kha valley and was built in honour of Tsong-khapa 450 years ago.

The abundance of pastures in the vicinity has caused the plains round Kökö Nor to become a general *rendezvous* where various caravans assemble with the view of proceeding together for mutual protection the remaining 900 miles to Lhása. Both the local Panakha robbers and the Golok marauders from the east and south-east make constant raids on the weak and unguarded parties.

NAM TS'O CHHYIDMO.

(*Elevation above sea-level : 15,190 feet.*)

The full name of this famous sheet of water is བྱང་གནམ་མཚོ་ཁྱིད་མོ། or "The Frozen Lake of the Sky in the North." However, it is commonly termed Nam Ts'o by Tibetans and Tengri Nor by Mongols, each name meaning simply "Sky Lake"; while the Chinese apply, in their T'ien Hai, a kindred designation.

Although, in truth, merely one in the great medial chain of lakes brought to our knowledge by Nain Singh, it has long had a distinctive interest to geographers from its large size and from its proximity to Lhása, which city lies only some 80 miles distant to the S.S.-E. Moreover, its whereabouts was substantially known previous to the discovery by Nain Singh of the chain of which it forms the easternmost link. It is marked in d'Anville's map which was compiled by the "lama mathematicians" in 1717.

Most of the particulars ascertained concerning the lake and its surroundings have been derived from the explorations of Pundit D. (afterwards known as A. K.) and Nain Singh. The surveys of these two were made in 1872 and 1874 respectively. However, since their time, the lake has been reached by three sets of European travellers. In 1890 Mons. Bonvalot and his party traversed the N.-E. litoral of these waters. Notwithstanding their good fortune, this is all the description the sight called forth :—

"Although we are the first Europeans actually to behold it, it is marked on the maps, thanks to the researches of the Pundit Nain Singh. . . . As we go southwards, the lake seems to open out in a S.-W. direction; and so long as the mist prevents us from seeing the end of it, we might take it to be a boundless sea. The evening sun, striking the ice, makes it sparkle like jewels; and we can well appreciate the origin of its name "the lake of the heavens."

With such poor platitudes do these travellers allude to the famous Tengri Nor, notable since the days of Marco Polo—they "the first Europeans actually to behold it." In August, 1895, the region of the lake was reached by Mr. and Mrs. Littledale and Mr. W. A. L. Fletcher. Although this party had an excellent view of the lake from the surrounding heights, none of them descended to its shore: consequently the diligent and accurate observations of Mr. Littledale only indirectly touch the lake itself and reveal little previously unknown.[1]

Accordingly, taking our details from Pandit D., whose notes were much fuller than Nain Singh's, we learn that Nam-ts'o Chhyidmo has an area of about 1,500 square miles, and is hemmed in on the northern and the southern sides by lofty mountain ranges. The southern-bounding range, however, which runs parallel to the shore-line in an E.N.-E. direction, is much the loftier and more striking. It is said to display as many as 360 peaks, supposed to represent Chhakna Dorje, the king of the mountain gods and his retinue. Both Pandit D. and Mr. Littledale name the range Ninchen T'angla, which we suspect ought to read Noi-jin T'angla—the "Noi-jin" being the Tibetan mountain deities.

[1] Messrs. Dutreuil de Rhins and Grenard in 1894 also reached the lake but have little to say of its appearance.

The general height of these mountains over-passes 20,000 feet and the peaks run up to 24,000 feet. The range along the northern litoral must also be of considerable altitude, the Pass across it being 17,400 feet.

The waters of Nam Ts'o are intensely salt, but plentifully supplied with fish, and from November to May they are thickly frozen over. A number of small islands lie close to the shore in different parts, and on all of these monasteries seem to have been established, one of which, as at Yamdok, is a joint community of *gelong* and *ani* sacred to Dorje P'agmo. As there are no boats on the lake, these lamaseries are only accessible during the ice season. It seems a singular fact that all the shrines and gompas set up on the lake-shore and the island, should have been endowed with names of which the word *do* "a stone" forms part. Even the various islets are denominated *do-bong* or "round cairn." Some extraordinary cones of hardened mud, of great height, each alleged to be 500 feet in circumference, are situated near the Chhyak-doṙ Gompa on the northern shore. There are numerous hot-springs in the neighbourhood of the lake, and from some of these the hot water is spouted up with force to a height of 35 feet. Sulphur is present in the springs, and the heat of several of them touches boiling point, which at that altitude is reached at about 183°.

Glacial drainage must furnish the bulk of the water-supply of this lake; for all travellers concur in noting the size and number of glaciers along the northern slopes of the Noijin T'angla. However, several affluent rivers have been observed. The Gya-kha or Chhoi-kha Chhu is received from the S.-W.; and both this and the Ngag Lobzang Chhu, which runs in on the eastern coast, are large rivers. One stream is reported to issue forth from the N.-W. corner of the lake—the Nag Chhu. It probably communicates with the series of small lakes lying W.N.-W. of Nam Ts'o.

On the western and eastern sides the shores are rather flatter than elsewhere; and on the east we have low-lying plains between the lake and the mountains. The western hills, as observed by Mr. Littledale, do not seem to rise more than 600 feet above the lake-level. Of course the scenery varies much; not, however, being so grandly mysterious and gloomy in character as others of the large Tibetan lakes. From the northern and western sides, the panorama of the great southern range is said to exhibit a magnificent spectacle.

CHAPTER V.

HOT SPRINGS OF TIBET.

Among the natural phenomena characteristic of Tibet the springs of hot water, so numerous and so remarkable, must certainly be included. Curiously enough those portions of the territory which have their general plane at the greatest altitude above the sea, and which are subjected to the intensest forms of cold, are possessed of the most and the hottest springs. Thus in the regions east of longitude 92° E., where the elevation of plains and valleys is commonly under 14,000 feet, these heated waters are known to occur in only two or three localities and the temperature of them seems to be rather low. On the other hand, in the uplifted tracts stretching *west* of that same longitude and the lofty altitude of which is carried as far to the west as the Lingzhi T'ang and the Karakorums, such springs are found at frequent intervals. Now the general level of those regions ranges from 15,000 to 17,400 feet; excepting in the S.-W., and there no hot springs are met with, *i.e.*, in Ngari Khorsum.

Furthermore, there appears to be a northern limit of occurrence also. This may be adjusted as just beyond the 34th parallel of latitude, north of which these springs have not been observed, although there is only a slight decrease in the average elevation. Accordingly, we may fix the boundaries of the region wherein waters of abnormally-raised temperature occur as edged by long. 78° 30′ and 92° E., and by the Himalayan southern range and lat. 34° 30′ N.; a hiatus existing within these limits, however (as we have said), in the S.-W. quarter.

Nevertheless, having given the bounds just laid down, it must now be pointed out that there is a certain portion of Tibetan territory which deserves to be specially demarcated as pre-eminently the Hot Spring Region. It lies immediately to the W. of long. 92° E. and to the N. of the Yeru Tsangpo. The northern limit seems to be still lat. 34° and the western limit is probably long. 88° E. Within these lines the number of boiling springs is truly extraordinary; while the high temperature and the force with which the water is expelled into the air are equally notable. We shall enter into particulars presently; but we must first call attention to the fact that the part of the Tibetan plateau which we have thus selected is that district where the majority of the large salt-lakes are congregated. So the Salt Lake district is substantially one with the Region of Hot Springs; and that in itself is a circumstance which leads to the point to be noticed.

The point in question is that in Tibet hot springs are found only in the closest proximity to lakes or, though less commonly, near to some large river. Nearly every important lake has more than one series of *jets d'eau chaude* bordering its banks. Many of the smaller lakes, only a few acres in superficies, have attendant geysers as well; and, within the limits of the region indicated above the adjacent hot springs are almost always present. In that district, also, several of the rivers are similarly furnished; and in these cases it frequently happens that the heated waters are thrown up not from openings on the banks but through valves situated in the midst of the river. In such instances the power of ejection is so strong as to cause a continuous column to rise above the surface of the river. Thus the phenomenon resembles the play of a hot water fountain in the midst of the stream, or perhaps the spouting forth of some amphibious monster.

Within the region of thermal springs above-mentioned, there seems to be an area where they are more specially concentrated; and that part lies to the S.-W. of the Namts'o Chhyidmo or Tengri Nor, between the lake and the P'unts'o-ling district of the Yeru Tsangpo. Here some of the hottest and most important examples occur.

Many of the springs simply bubble up quietly into basins naturally worn in the rock or soil. Others, however, are expelled into the air with considerable force; and in these cases they have generally the intermittent character of the Icelandic geysers. The height to which the waters are ejected, in the instances as yet reported upon, does not appear to equal that of the greatest of the geysers of Iceland which is said to ascend to a height of 146 feet from the ground. Between 50 and 60 feet seems to be the extreme altitude to which these natural fountains in Tibet spurt up their contents into the air. At Peting Chhuts'en on the banks of the Lahu Chhu (an affluent of the Shang Chhu of Tsang province) within a space under 80 yards in length eleven columns of hot water are cast up. These all rise to a height of between 40 and 50 feet, and produce so much steam that the sky is generally quite darkened with it, the noise being so deafening, moreover, as to prevent anyone speaking when near them. Hard by, in the middle of the Lahu river, are many similar jets which are shot up to the same height of 40 or 50 feet, as conjectured by the native explorer who observed them.

With regard to the temperature of the water, it has been proved to approach boiling point on issuing from the ground, in the case of several in the central region where experiments have been made. At certain springs on the Lahu river, where from the extreme elevation the boiling point of water stands at 183°·75 Fahr., the heat of the ejected stream was found to be 183°. At Chhu-t'ang Ts'áka, about 50 miles N. of Shigatse, on the river Shang, there occur 15 hot springs, and the average temperature of these was ascertained to be 166°, the boiling temperature of water there being 186°. At Peting Chhu-ts'en, referred to just now, the temperature reaches 176°. All these examples are only apparently much lower than the recorded heat of the Great Geyser of Iceland, which is given at 247°, the enormous altitude above sea-level of the Tibetan springs reducing the reading of the thermometer, while the elevation of the springs in Iceland being little, boiling point shews nearly 60° higher than is the case in the Hot Spring Region of Tibet.

However, in other districts of the country, we find that the waters are of considerably lower temperature than they are in the central region. A few instances will shew this. At the Kyam thermal springs in the Changchenmo valley, Godwin-Austen took the temperature of three of them and found them 98°, 102°, and 103°·5 respectively. In Sikkim on the Tibetan border are many springs: that of the Yumt'ang Chhuts'en is 112°·6 (at 12,000 feet), that of the spring at the base of the Jhangokang glacier 116° (at 15,850 feet). However, the explorer R.N. who visited the famous hot waters of Lhagpa Ts'á-chhu in South Tibet near the Bhutan frontier, and which are found at an altitude of 15,200 feet, mentions 50 hot springs at that spot, stating their temperature to range from tepid to boiling heat.

One remarkable characteristic of Tibetan geysers has yet to be referred to. As we have seen, the majority occur at an extremely lofty elevation where frost and ice reign supreme for nearly 8 months of each year. In the coldest months at altitudes over 16,000 feet above sea-level the atmospheric temperature sinks frequently 30° below zero, sometimes even touching 40° below zero. On many of these frozen plains at the lake-side at these stupendous altitudes do the geysers throw up their heated fountains. Nevertheless, although the waters on issuing forth are boiling, in the course of their lofty summersault through the air, so terrible is the cold that the falling stream congeals into ice before returning to the ground. This rapid reduction of temperature in boiling water in the space of half-a-minute is wonderful enough; but still more astounding is the practical effect. The freezing of the geyser in the act of falling produces, it seems, an enormous cylindrical column of ice enclosing as in a funnel the spouting hot fountain. On the banks of a river to the north of the Shang district are the famous Naisum Chhu-ts'á, two remarkable springs which throw up jets of boiling water over 60 feet in height. In the three coldest months the water in dropping down again freezes and forms pillars of ice which are nearly up to the full height of the jets. These twin pillars gradually grow from 30 to 40 feet in circumference each, and are pierced in a peculiar manner with holes like loop-holes, so that the general appearance is that of a couple of artificial ice towers. Inside the towers the water is thrown up with great violence and noise and the temperature touches the boiling point at that elevation. Mons. Bonvalot noticed similar results near his "Armand David Lake" in the region just north of Ts'á-gyud Ts'o (Chargut Ts'o). He writes:—

"It is surprising to see, in the midst of this plain of hot springs, cones of ice, 20 feet or more in diameter, about the height of a man, and speckled over on their surface—which is just like crystals—with grit and stones from the plain; these blocks have split perpendicularly like certain kinds of over-ripe fruit. We have before us frozen geysers which have become covered with this solid head-dress when their power of ejection was not sufficient to cope with the frost."

Again, further south, about 60 miles N.-W. of Namts'o Chhyidmo, he records "a frozen geyser about 33 feet in diameter."

In these cases, where the ejecting spring becomes gradually capped with a heavier and heavier cowl of ice, mud, and stones, it is possible that, in time and especially when it may chance that the summer season is prolonged sufficiently to melt the covering, the accumulation may eventually block up the spring permanently. Should that be the result, the geyser probably is diverted and breaks forth in some new place not always close at hand. A curious formation reported from the shores of the great Sky Lake (Namts'o Chhyidmo) suggests this idea. Near the Jádor gompa there occur three lofty cones of apparently sun-dried mud each (so it is asserted) about 500 feet in circumference. The mounds are partially hollow and one of them has an opening like a glass furnace through the apex above. Probably these strange and gigantic cones of solidified mire represent nothing more or less than extinct geysers; especially as they occur in such a realm of hot springs.

A marked constituent of these waters seems to be sulphur; and where the heat is excessive large quantities of sulphuretted hydrogen are evolved. There is likewise a considerable admixture of salts of sodium and potassium and certain lithates.

Averse though Tibetans as a nation are to bathing, there prevails throughout the country a general belief in the medicinal virtues of the outward application of these waters. Where any extensive series of thermal springs exists in the more populated districts, baths are usually constructed in connection threwith. Thus at Dam Chhuts'en, about 60 miles N. of Lhása, a large bathing establishment is attached to the springs; and most of the inhabitants of the neighbourhood are said to repair twice a year to the place for a bath. There are three tanks 21 feet square, lined with sun-dried bricks and cemented, which are always kept full of the sulphuretted waters. In these the bathers continue sometimes the whole day immersed to the neck. One of the main purposes of the bath is said to be the efficacy of the sulphur in the destruction of vermin with which all Tibetans are grievously affected; and in this way a clearance can be accomplished without any overt act of slaughter.

CHAPTER VI.

THE GREAT RIVER OF TIBET.

The great waterway of Tibet, which for nearly 1,300 miles makes strange progress through that land, is, we may say, at length universally admitted to be the parent stream of the mighty Brahmaputra of the Indian plains. Bit by bit, during some 38 years, have portions of its secret course been elucidated by the trained native agents despatched from India into Tibet. But the information ascertained in this and other ways exists for the most part in piece-meal form only. What we desire here to do is to collect and amalgamate the scattered facts and to present them as a connected whole. This question of the Tibetan river, and whether it eventually developed into the Brahmaputra or the Irawadi, has proved one of the most romantic as well as one of the most important problems of modern geography. As will be shewn later, the matter is now regarded as practically settled. But the details of the course of this wonderful river are in themselves worth setting forth; and we can here give not only a full summary of all that has been so far brought to light on the subject, but have also many new facts to add from native Tibetan sources.

Nearly the whole expanse, from west to east, of southern Tibet is traversed by a remarkable valley, rarely deep, but chiefly progressing as a broad depression in the lofty table-land at the back of the Himalayas. This valley forms the bed of a leviathan watercourse, running eastwards for several hundred miles, and draining large tracts of mountainous country to the north and south of its margin. It is, indeed, the gigantic gutter of the southern half of Tibetan territory; for, into its vortex, all the lesser rivers find their way at length.

The important fluvial artery, to which we are referring, is that so long known to geographers as the "Sanpo;" and the discussion concerning its ultimate development to which we have already alluded, has added considerably to its notoriety. Strange, however, it seems that Englishmen should have been dwelling for several generations within

100 miles of points a personal inspection of which could at once have ended controversy; yet they were and are physically shnt out from such visits. Indeed, the question as to which southern river receives the "Sanpo," has to this day been determined rather by accumulative inference than by actual observation. Still (1904) do a few savage tribes keep back Europeans from settling the problem with their own eyes. And yet now a railway station actually stands only fifteen miles from where the Tibetan river meets the Eastern Brahmaputra!

Quite apart from this discussion, the great river deserved special investigation. It is unique, as we shall see, in so many ways. To mention, in passing, but one such singularity: When flowing at the height of 13,700 feet above the level of the sea, it is a river habitually navigated by boats and made use of for the transit of merchandize. This can be alleged of no other water at such an altitude in the world.[1]

THE RIVER'S NAME.

First, as to the correct designation. This, of course, is not "Sanpo." That name came to be used only because the word *tsangpo* is the general Tibetan term for any large river; *chhu*, another word in common use, meaning merely "water," and being generally applied to smaller rivers, though loosely also to the larger. In the different districts through which this the Tsangpo *par excellence* passes, it bears different appellations. During the first 200 miles it still carries its ancient title, *Támchhok Khábab, i.e.*, "the downflowing mouth of the best horse"—the *Támchhok* being a fabulous steed petrified in Lake Má-pang from the rocky mouth of which creature the river is supposed to gush forth. Lower down in its course we hear the name Ngári Tsangpo. Below Shigatse it acquires the style most commonly employed in the civilised districts, that of Yeru Tsangpo (really *Gyas-ru Gtsang-po*) "the river of the right-hand banner;" and that denomination seems to be maintained throughout Central and East Tibet and until, in the Miri and Abor hills, it is yet again changed into that of Dihang or Dihong.

SOURCE OF THE TSANGPO.[2]

Despite the legend which has suggested the name for the early course of the river, it certainly does not rise, as alleged, in Lake Má-

1 A small-steam launch is stated to ply on the waters of Lake Titicaca, on the dividing line between Bolivia and Peru, high up in the Cordilleras. But the altitude of this lake is 12,750 feet above sea level, a thousand feet lower than the Tsangpo in Ngari Khorsum and Dokt'ol where there is a boat service for a length of 80 miles.

2 For convenience this term can be employed, and in Tibet it is often loosely so

pang. The real place of origin is situated some 20 miles S. E. of that lake—approximately in longitude 82° 10′ E. In fact the Yeru Tsangpo has its sources in a long narrow valley cradled in a remarkable manner between three separate ranges of mountains, each of which is literally loaded with glaciers.

Into this womb of the Ice Mothers which, conjointly, breed the mighty Brahmaputra, even Tibetans themselves have scarcely ventured. The only entrance seems to be at the S. E. extremity of this mountain-locked valley, at the end where the river issues forth. No tracks pass up the valley; for the mountains at the head of it, which separate the valley from the lakes at the base of Mount Tisé Kailas, have no way over them, and the whole terminates in a stupendous *cul-de-sac*. The actual place where the river first forms is said to be a large gravelly marsh, fed from the adjacent glaciers, and styled *Chema Yungdrung* "The Sands of the Mystic Wheel." This lies at an altitude of about 14,700 feet above the level of those plains of India whither the waters are destined eventually to descend.

Lonely, impenetrable, unknown, it seems meet that the weird and famous stream should thus be born in utter secrecy in this remote valley so far to the west.

But the solitude must be one not of barrenness, but of grandeur. On three sides, let us remember—N.-W., N.-E., S.-W.—the birthplace is girt about by monster sentinels crowned with helmets of never-melting snow and standing shoulder to shoulder with glaciers for each epaulette.

SECTION: NO. 1.

(FROM THE SOURCE TO CONJUNCTION WITH THE CHHORTA TSANGPO.)

"The Sands of the Mystic Wheel," whence the river takes rise, are closely hemmed in by parallel ranges trending south-eastwardly. The northern range, Gang-ri Gur-gyab, shuts off the sources of the Indus. The southern wall is a massive ridge developed from Gur Lha, itself a stupendous mountain-matrix flung up to the south of Ts'o Mápang (*i.e.*, "the Lake of the Peacock's Breast"). This ridge, bearing the name of Nyimo Namgyal, "that which completely vanquishes the sun," eventually makes to the S. S. E. to form the watershed lower down between the Tsangpo and the rivers of Nepal. The parallel ranges accompany the river for 25 miles, throwing up peaks from 18 to 22 thousand feet altitude and supplying it assiduously with glacial drainage. About 18 miles from the start, the valley opens out into a

designated. The Capuchin Missionaries, who were resident 150 years ago at Lhása, writing *circa* 1740, styled it, variously, *Tzhangpo*, *Tsang-ciu*, and *Tsanga*.

broad vale some 8 miles across; and there the river is found, with a swift current and deep waters, flowing in a rock-bound channel east by south. At this point it is said to be 70 feet in breadth. The southern bounding range here falls away south, though the glaciers and snowy peaks upon it continue and have still to contribute two or three feeding streams. And now, when the cradling valley expands and the northern mountains drop lower, we find the first fixed geographical point. For, into the river basin, from within an elevated ravine, there creeps down along this northern wall a well-beaten pathway from the much-used Mariam, or Már Yum La. This, the "Mother of the Lowlands Pass," has two main approaches or ascents from outer regions which converge at its climax, or *laptse*, into this the descent on the eastern side into the Támchhok valley. One approach is from the west, the direct official route from Gardok (Gart'ok) to Lhása; the other road is from the north and north-west, and ascends from the valley of the Indus. The latter is the route from Leh *viâ* Rudok, and is a well-used line of transit from Ladak both to Nepal and to Lhása. It is stated that merchandise can be brought up by the Indus to within ten miles of the foot of the northern ascending road to Mariam La. Thence the goods are transported over the Pass into the Tsangpo valley; and, it is said, are often again launched in hide boats some fifty miles lower down the stream, and so conveyed to Shigatse, which stands near the Tsangpo over 500 miles from Mariam La.

The descent we are now traversing from the Mariam La does not yet touch the great water-way. The combined route (comprising the two highways from Ladak to Lhása) at first keeps laterally along the northern side of the valley and is accompanied by a small river formed by streams from the heights abutting the Mariam Pass. This path has to be traversed some thirty miles further before the merchants, packmen, and pilgrims come in sight of the mighty Támchhok (or Támchhen) Khabab travelling grandly eastwards. However, the banks are not actually gained until the post-stage named Támchhen Tázam has been reached; and there, too, the branch-stream just mentioned falls into the main river, which by this has travelled some fifty miles from its source.

A word may here be interposed concerning these halting stages on the post-track which forms such a feature along a great part of the course of the Tsangpo. They are termed *tázam* or "horse-bridges," not because any bridge exists at them, but because the post-carriers to Lhása there change their horses, and so the long and difficult route to that city is thus metaphorically "bridged" from Tázam to Tázam. At each of these stages is a large rest-house, where coolies and beasts of burden are always held in readiness, but only for official use.[1]

From Támchhen Tázam down to the junction with the Chhorta river, a distance of 180 miles, the post-track follows the course of the Tsangpo; and thus it was that the native surveyor, Nain Singh, was able to report fully on this portion. At first during that part the great river has the southern snowy range only from twelve to twenty miles distant, and it runs along the base of some low-lying hills which form the northern bank. Beginning with dark shaly-slate, these hills soon pass into brown argillaceous clay, and eventually into actual red sandstone; they give off several small feeders into the main river. The first large tributary falls in forty miles S. E. of Támchhen; it comes in from the north, being styled the Chhu Nág-ku.

All this district is known as Purang; and the Tsangpo flows near the chief town Yá-tse Dzong, with its great gompa of Shingp'el Ling. After the influx of the Chhu Nág-ku, the river continues S. E. until where, about fifty miles further on, it is augmented by another tributary, much larger than the first, arriving also from the north. This affluent, the Ts'á-chhu Tsangpo, seems to be almost as large as the Támchhen Khábáb itself, being 500 feet wide, and only to be crossed by means of ferry-boats.

On the transit being made, you approach the Tádum rest-houses, the largest set in that part of the country.[2]

Tádum is a considerable vortex for trade, a fact to which the eight or nine post-houses surrounding the gompa bear witness; routes to the Panjab and Nepal being brought in here. And now the river deploys a peculiar loop, first due south, then curving north a little, but eventually making off once again direct to the S. E. Having absorbed another small tributary, the Mingchu Tsangpo, or "River of Ten

1 Between Gart'ok (near the Ládak border) and Lhása, a distance of 790 miles, there are 22 *tázam*, and the special messengers of the Tibetan Government are expected to traverse the whole space in 22 days. Although the horses are changed at each stage, the messenger is not: he goes the entire distance, travelling night and day. These men are said to have their clothes stamped at the fastenings with official seals to ensure their not undressing while *en route*. When their garments are first taken off, after the 800 miles' ride, the rider is always in a terrible state of exhaustion. There are similar despatch services between Lhása and Ba-tang, Lhása and Peking and Lhása and Phari Jong (near the Sikkim border).

2 Ordinary travellers use the stage-houses at a *tázam* on payment, but cannot claim ponies and yaks. Government officials travelling are provided with free transit of themselves and their effects, and invariably engage in extensive mercantile operations which have also to be given conveyance. Such conveyance becomes a heavy charge on the inhabitants of each district, who have to keep the *tázam* gratuitously supplied with beasts of burden.

Names," it takes a great bend some thirty-three miles below Tádum, flowing southwards for nearly twenty-seven miles, and afterwards turning up N. E. At the southernmost elbow there comes in the first important affluent received from the south. This is quaintly styled Shurtá Tsangpo, "the River of the Horse that Sits Still," while again, after a twenty-five miles run N. E., there joins the now majestic stream a duplex tributary from the north, said to be the largest received during the whole course of the Brahmaputra through Tibet. In opposition to the former contribution, this branch is known as the Chhortá Tsangpo, or "the River of the Horse that Runs Away"; and in size it fully equals the main water-way.

So ends what we shall term the first section of the big river's course; and it will be convenient to realise the position reached. By this time the number of miles traversed from the source may be reckoned with fair precision at 250. The progress throughout, with the exception of the loop just taken, has been S. E., and the longitudinal meridian arrived at is approximately 85° E.; but the latitude has dropped from 30° 40′ (at the source) to 29° 26′ E. Although so many affluents have been absorbed, the apparent size is hardly commensurate to the quantity of water brought in by these. As in the parallel case of the Indus, it is depth and rolling force which have been gained; and below Támchhen Tázam the river is never fordable, even where it spreads most widely. Not counting the early feeders from the glaciers of the southern range, important as they are to the primeval formation, all the tributary streams save one have come in from the North. The Shurtá, just received, is of course noteworthy as being the first considerable southern tributary. It rises in a wonderful realm of glaciers on the Nepalese frontier at the roots of the Ngo La or "Blue Pass," which leads over the southern bounding range so often alluded to. On the other side of the Pass we are amid the early fountains of one of the Gandak rivers of Nepal.

This southern bounding range (the Nyinmo Namgyal) is really of great consequence. Lying far to the back of the main line of monster Himalayan peaks, which line we have learnt long ago is not the actual watershed of Indo-Himalayan streams, it forms the true water-parting between the Indian and Tibetan river-basins. And the fact, that, during a course of 190 miles or so—from where its drainage supplies the nucleus of the Támchhok Khabab down to the Ngo La where the Shurtá rises—no Tibetan river is given off from a range well-stocked as this is known to be with snow-peak and glacier, is of great interest. It shows how considerable must be the supply to the Indian rivers of the North-West, especially the Kosi and Gandaks; for, after the Támchhok Khabab has left its flanks, the down-flow from the Tibeto-Indian watershed is almost exclusively Indian.

SECTION: NO. 2.

(FROM THE CHHORTA TSANGPO TO SHIGATSE.)

The rivers which debouch into the Támchhok from the north are all of such considerable volume that they must have had a lengthy run before reaching the point of junction. Accordingly we ought to set back the northern watershed of the Támchhok many miles further north than the actual valley line wherein the channel runs. The in-coming northern rivers cut through the low lines of hills bounding this valley on the northern banks: whence, then, do they hail? One would imagine that, in all probability, the massive mountain range, practically a continuation of Mount Kailas, known to geographers as the Gang-dis-ri range (really Gang Tise Ri) stretching east across Tibet, gave birth to these feeders. This range passes eastward from forty to seventy miles north of the general line of our river, and in the main forms the southern watershed of the great lake plateau. However, recent exploration shows that, in the case of several of the great northern feeders of the Támchhok, in the first and second sections, they rise further north still than the Gang-dis-ri range, and even on the lake-plateau itself. They pass through gorges between lofty peaks in this range, much as do the Indian rivers in their course through the Southern Himalayas. We interpolate these remarks here, because the Chhorta Tsangpo, which bounds our Second Section, is one of the great feeders, whose early course has been traced back north beyond the Gangdis-ri range; its primary sources being found in certain lakes to the S. W. and S. of Dangra Yum Ts'o.

East of the Chhorta tributary, the exact course of the Yeru Tsangpo (or Támchhok) has been traced for about thirty miles. Then for a length of, say, 150 miles, its line of progress is only conjectural. At that point the explorer, Nain Singh, left the river side, proceeding E. by N., while the river itself, as he observed, proceeded E. by S. Its course evidently takes the form of a shallow bow-like dip, first E. by S., then slowly slanting up again E. by N.; for it was near the important town of Jang Lhátse, 2½ degrees further east from where he had left it, and almost in the same latitude as at the point of his leaving it, that Nain Singh again encountered the wonderful water-way. Of this unknown portion of the river, we have personally ascertained that it first passes over an extensive plain named La-wa Mon-t'ang. Here the channel cuts deep down, evidently through soft alluvial soil. It then enters the mountainous district of Jong-nga, where glacier-charged streams again feed it, as in its very early flow. During the whole of this course, the river seems to bear the name of Me'-tsang Chhu, or "Lower Tsang waters" by which name it is still known at Jang Lhá-tse.

The exact point at which Nain Singh beheld the river next again was at Nupsi, fifteen miles above Jang Lhá-tse. This is classical ground to Tibetan Buddhists. Here, north of the river, are numerous large monasteries, notably Ngam-ring, a famous place of pilgrimage. Just before Jang Lhá-tse is reached, the river makes a sharp bend up northwards and then keeps N. N. E. for twenty-five miles. Jang Lhá-tse is an ancient place with a number of monasteries within and around its walls. Here, too, is one of the great iron-chain bridges erected across the Brahmaputra by T'ang-tong Gyalpo, 230 years ago. Just where the Ráka or Rákpa Tsangpo, a mighty tributary from due west, coalesces with it the river resumes its old S. E. direction. In this neighbourhood stands the lofty chhorten built by the engineer-saint T'ang-tong, or T'anang; and just below the apex of the river bend is the town of P'ünts'o-ling, with its fort and the large monastery of the heretical Jonangpa School built by the founder of the sect in the days of Kublai Khan. Here, and again a little lower down, are other iron-chain bridges. Four massive chains, with links a foot in diameter, run from pier to pier of masonry, thus spanning the wide deep bed of the river. A precarious footway of wood and rope is supported between the chains; but all these bridges are now very little used.

From P'ünts'o-ling Jong, and, indeed, from Jang Lhá-tse, there is a regular system of boat-traffic down to Shigatse, utilised for passengers as well as for goods and live-stock. Hide boats are the chief navigable craft. Midway between P'ünts'o-ling and Shigatse, the second great tributary from the south—the Re or Shre Chhu—flows in. It is a considerable river. The port of call for Shigatse and Tashi-lhümpo is Tungsum, about three miles from the former place which lies away from the main river. Two miles or so below Tung-sum is the mouth of the well-known Penam-nyang Chhu on the southern bank. This is the river upon which Shigatse actually stands; and its size may be estimated by the fact that at Shigatse it is spanned by a bridge said to be 380 feet in length. The Penam-nyang river drains the whole of these parts of the southern Tibet that border on Sikkim and West Bhutan, and its own tributaries ramify through much of the mountainous district south of Lake Yamdok. But the Penam-nyang is itself only a tributary of the Yeru Tsangpo, which therefore embraces within its southern scope the whole of those border regions. Taking the territory abutting Nepal drained by the Re Chhu, we may estimate within the basins of only two southern tributaries of the Tsangpo an area of some 6,500 square miles.

SECTION: NO. 3.

FROM SHIGATSE TO TSET'ANG.

Down to the point where the Penam-nyang Chhu joins the Yeru Tsangpo, we may compute the distance traversed by the latter at 545 miles. At length it has assumed the form of the larger Indian rivers. It runs in several channels separated by long bars of sand, and often spreads out into broad shallow reaches at least two miles across. At the mouth of the tributary flowing past Shigatse, the river widens in this fashion. It was exactly there that the Englishman, Samuel Turner, gazed upon those unknown waters from a rock above Tashi-lhümpo, in 1783. He notes that he beheld "the Brahmaputra flowing in a wide extended bed; and, as though the soil gave it an unwilling passage, it has forced itself through many channels and formed a multitude of islands in its way. But though its bed appears so wide extended from hence, I was told that its principal channel is narrow, deep, and never fordable."

Leaving the mouth of the Penam-nyang, the river is bordered on the right bank by the Rong country, a district noted for its rocky defiles and gorges; on the left lies the district of Shang. Although bounding a district of ravines, so much of the right shore as lies adjacent to the river is an undulating fertile expanse most carefully cultivated. Numerous valleys from the interior open out along this side, and these are neither wild nor rocky but are noted for their crops and general fruitfulness. Many villages lie along the track, which is never far from the river-side. At places the bank is so low that floods penetrate inland. On the left or northern bank runs a plain from three to five miles in width covered with much sand blown in from the bed of the river. Rounded hills, about 1,000 feet higher than the surrounding country, bound these plains to the north. About fifty miles from Shigatse this range falls into the left bank of the river. Opposite this promontory, on the right bank, is the point to which the stream is navigable from Shigatse. The landing-place is styled *Tag-sa dru-kha.* Past this the river narrows and becomes too rough and shoaly for hide-boats. Also it here bends south, and, after a four miles run, a lofty offshoot from a mountain range to the south bears down to the river-side and stops from this point the land-passage along the right bank. Along the base of the range, also, there comes in from the south-east a rapid river, the Rong Nag Chhu; wherefore up the left bank of this tributary the road leaves the Brahmaputra and makes for the shores of Yamdok Ts'o wherein the Rong Nag Chhu rises.

Beyond the junction of the tributary from the south-east, the main river for the space of eighty miles, as far as the famous Chaksam Chhuwori (the bridge near the mouth of the Lhása river), is at present unreported upon. It enters a hilly country, and, it is said, falls over many rapids. But where it has next been touched by our explorers is one of the best known spots in its whole course. For there the great route from the west, *viâ* Shigatse, Gyangtse and Palte Jong, climbs up from Lake Yamdok over the Khamba La range, and descends from the south into the Yeru Tsangpo valley, the name under which the Brahmaputra now travels. This route is the main one to Lhása; it passes over the Chaksam Chhuwori ferry (as the great iron-bridge is now unusable), and up the valley of the Kyi Chhu to the sacred city.

Sarat Chandra Dás, in his exploration report, thus describes the scene which breaks upon you as you descend from the Khambala Pass into this part of the Yeru valley:—

> The height we had reached was about a thousand feet above the level of the lake, though much higher than that above the level of the great river about to be seen. Passing the summit which faces the lake, we proceeded towards the *laptse*, the culminating point of the Pass. Here two large cairns stood on either side of the road, where my companions, taking off their hats, uttered mantras to invoke the mountain deities. . . . . . Advancing a few paces beyond the sacred cairns, I came to a point whence I saw one of the grandest views in Tibet. It was that of the valley of the far-famed Tsangpo whose sublime scenery, the like of which I had never beheld before, quite ravished my heart. My enchanted mind was made full with impressions of the scenery, and I liked to enjoy it to satiety. The great Tsangpo flowed at the base of a gigantic yawning chasm, which extended for miles between two ranges of lofty dark mountains, whose flanks, overhanging the river from the north, were covered with dark forests of fir-like trees. At the foot of these lofty mountains, but still in uplands above the river-brink, there were pretty-looking villages with castle-like white-washed houses, most of the larger houses being surrounded with tall trees. A village on the other side of the Tsangpo was conspicuous for the amazing depth in the valley at which it was seen from the *laptse* of Khamba La, being surrounded by rugged and sombre mountains.

The road to Lhása from the Khamba La strikes the river some seven miles north-west of the foot of the Pass, the point of contact being a little to the west of the mouth of the Kyi Chhu, and this is where the chain-bridge and ferry already alluded to are located. Great reaches of sand lie there, but the waters are so broad that the violent wind, very prevalent in the Tsangpo valley, raises frequent storms which make the passage across dangerous. Across the river, on the western jaw of the open-mouthed Kyi, is the port of Chhu-shul, with a gompa and 108 chhortens on a hill hard by, all said to have been erected by the same engineer-saint who constructed the various chain-bridges spanning the Yeru Tsangpo. From Chhu-shul there is a systematic service of large hide-boats down the main river towards Tse-t'ang, the first stage or half-way port being the notable wool and cloth mart of Kyi-desho Jong, some forty miles below Chhu-shul. In this course of the river the current is very sluggish, the bed in places very wide, great expanses of sand intersecting the waters. The plain bordering the north bank in these parts is from two to five miles in width, full of villages and small convents, and bounded on the north by a range of low hills which eventually culminate in a fine peak 3,000 feet above the river-surface. This peak is nearly opposite Kyi-desho, and on its crags, an imposing spectacle, has been placed the great and ancient monastery of Dorje-t'ag—an establishment still belonging to the old Nyingma school of Buddhism with a staff expert in Tantrik jugglery. At this point the river is described as flowing in one stream 800 yards broad, excessively deep from the contracted passage, and as teeming with fish. East of the T'ib Chhu, the southern affluent on which the cloth mart and port is built, the Yeru flows directly E. Here the enclosing valley is said to be grand and enchanting. In places it narrows into wild rock-walled gorges; elsewhere, and most frequently, it flattens out into great sandy reaches. Where wide and open, the lower spurs thrust out from the bounding hills are covered with verdure and scaling trees; grain crops and even fruit-trees, such as apricot, pear, and walnut, are made to flourish in every available spot. Large white-washed monasteries shine gleamingly in fantastic situations on the heights of the inner spurs; whilst many important hamlets and market-centres lie within easy access from this useful water highway. Twenty-four miles east of Kyi-desho, where the northern bank has flattened out into an extensive sandy plain sloping up inland, the mighty monastery of Samye is reached. Its temples, with golden and copper canopies within a great walled enclosure, are prominent objects from the river.

Tse-t'ang, otherwise Che-t'ang, lies forty-two miles further east, and here the Yarlung river disembogues its waters drawn from the southren glaciers into the main stream. And thus terminates our third division of the great Tsangpo's course, after a stretch of 240 miles from Shigatse.

SECTION: NO. 4.

(From Tse-t'ang to Gyalla Seng-dong.)

The large town of Tse-t'ang stands in long. 91° 43′ 25″ E., and from thence the river is seen trending away to the horizon in a wide valley in a direction about E. N. E. A great snow-capped range coming up from the south seems to meet the river in the far distance, and cut off further view. At Tse-t'ang low hills come close down both to the southern and the northern banks, and across the former the road continues along the right side of the river; but any passage that way is said to become presently very dangerous, being beset by thieves, and later on by the wild truculent tribes of the Tsari district. The best method of advance appears to be to cross by a ferry named Nya-ko-drukha, three miles below the town, and proceed along the northern bank, through what is described as a "wealthy district," full of opulent monasteries and richly-cultivated slopes, with woods, gardens and good roads. The chief monasteries on this side, within a few miles of Tse-t'ang, are Ngari Tatsang, Sang-ri Khángmar and Dansa T'il. Thence the river, after its slight northern inclination, flows nearly due east; but, just before the 93rd meridian is crossed, it drops somewhat to the south. Between Tse-t'ang and this meridian, it receives several fine branch-rivers from the north, the chief being the Mik Chhu, or Zingchi Chhu. The districts on the left bank are Wo-kha, Nang-po, and eventually Kong-po, which latter district occupies both sides of the river.

In Kong-po, in long. 93° 12′ or thereabouts, the Yeru Tsangpo makes a sudden and extraordinary bend to the N. N. E., the direction being about 23° east of N. The bend occurs just where the Khyimdong Chhu from the south flows in. This run continues about seventy miles, when it becomes rather more easternly, pursuing a N.-E. course for some fifty miles further, until, in lat. 29° 56′ N. and long. 94° 4′ E., its northernmost apex is gained.

This point in the river's course is the chief landmark in the whole run through Tibet; for now it starts on that great and sudden dive to the south, which is destined to carry it out of the country. At the northernmost point, therefore, we have the Yeru bending sharply on itself, with an inner angle of 80°, and proceeding first S. E. by S. then S. S. E. A lofty mountain range from the S. runs up to the apex within the bend, and, aided by another range above, or to the north of, the bend, running N. N. W. to S. S. E., seems to be the mechanical cause of this sudden southernly deflection. Passing now down the stream, we soon reach Gyalla Seng-dong, with the fort on one side and the monastery on the other side of the river, at a distance of sixteen miles from the northern climax above mentioned. From Tse-'tang to this stage, it is difficult to estimate closely the length, including winds and loops, but 295 miles may be considered a fair approximation to the truth.

This section, from a few miles east of Tse-t'ang to Gyalla Seng-dong, has not been subjected to very careful exploration. It has been traversed by two native agents of the Survey of India, namely, by G. M. N. in 1878 and by K. P. in 1886-87; but their surveying capabilities were only rudimentary. In our map we have placed several localities derived from other native sources, and have corrected the spelling of names given by G. M. N. and K. P.

From Tse-t'ang eastwards, the Yeru is bordered on the south by a country viewed with mixed horror and veneration by Tibetans of the Central Provinces. Here, between the 92nd and 93rd meridians to the south, lie the districts known as A-yul and Jya-yul, and then the mystic Tákpo country (spelt *Dvag-po*) is entered.[1] In Tákpo is the famous place of pilgrimage named Tsári T'ugka, and nearly forty miles S.-E. of this Tsári is the great snowy peak of Pal Tsári, which is the *ultima Thule* of Tibetan pilgrimage, involving a fortnight of hard travel from the banks of the Yeru Tsangpo. Tsári peak is said to be covered with thick pine forests at its base. The chief risk of journeys in Takpo and Tsári arises from the savage tribes dwelling across the ranges to the south of these districts, who appear occasionally to make raids on pilgrim bands. It is significant that the rest-houses, provided by the Tibetan Government in the country just here as well as in those tracts within the northern loop of the great river, are designated *Jik-kyop* or "fear-escapes."

Long ranges of hills radiate from the peak of Pal Tsári; those branching S. E. forming the water-partings between the head-streams of the Kamla and the Subansiri, which eventually combine to make the river known in Assam by the latter name. A lofty branch from Tsári, however, runs up N. E. within the loop of the Yeru Tsangpo, and that range makes the southern watershed of the river, effectually shutting its waters out from any conjunction with the feeders of ths Subansiri. Another range running N. N. W. from the S. E. forms with the Tsári range an inverted V-shaped angle right up within the northern apex of the Yeru, and again keeps the waters from joining the Subansiri stream during their great southern flight to the Abor country.

When, however, the river has turned the sharp northern angle, just before Gyalla Seng-dong is reached, one unaccountable characteristic concerning it seems to be this—the comparative want of breadth of the waters as reported by the two surveyors. In places, indeed, from so far back as the Tákpo (Dvag-po) district—before the northern bend begins—the river is spoken of as being very narrow. At Gyalla Seng-

[1] It was at a place named Drong-nge in Takpo that the Capuchin friars once had a branch hospice.

dong, where the level above the sea has sunk to 8,000 feet, it is stated to be only 150 paces or about 110 yards in width.

SECTION: NO. 5.

(FROM GYALLA SENG-DONG TO SADIYA IN ASSAM.)

At Gyalla Seng-dong the river seems to prepare for its drop into much lower regions than the Tibetan table-land. It here runs in deep gorges, probably more than one abreast—the explorer refers to two other streams besides "the Tsangpo"—and a cascade of 100 feet in depth occurs at this point. Politically and commercially the place is an important centre. Trade routes from the Lhása-China high-road through Kongpo, from Tsári, Tawang, Bhutan and the S.-W., from the P'oba country and Yunnan, and from Assam, appear to culminate here. Moreover, the barbarous border tribes to the south are not allowed to advance further than this in the traffic they carry on as middlemen in the commercial relations between Tibet and Assam. The numerous Jongs or forts presided over by representatives of the Central Government, which closely dot the country round, attest that vigilant supervision is deemed essential in these parts. From Gyalla Seng-dong southwards, however, there is only one Jong in the space to the frontier line 100 miles distant, the territory being of debateable ownership and being practically under the domination of Lho-pa tribes, who are probably identical with those known in Assam as Miri, Migi, and Abar or Abor.

The river from lat. 29° 35′ seems substantially to take a southern direction, making every now and then a slight advance to the east; but it does not assume a really eastern course until another degree to the south has been traversed. Indeed, the longitude at Puging in lat. 28° 35′ is apparently almost identical with that of Gyalla Seng-dong. The general level of the stream still continues to drop; and waterfalls are frequent. Some thirty miles beyond the last-named place, it passes over a cliff said to be 150 feet in height. Villages line the banks closely, and the further south one proceeds the larger and more populous are these communities. As we progress further south, the characteristics and customs of the inhabitants undergo a radical change. No monasteries are met with below lat. 29°, and the Tibetan language is no longer the vernacular. At Shobang, in lat. 28° 37′, that domestic system so distinctive of the aboriginal tribes of India—the provision in each village of a detached common sleeping place for the elder boys and of another for the unmarried girls—is first found. In the places lower down on the Tsangpo, this usage everywhere prevails.

At Shimong, in lat. 28° 26′, the great river commences a determined course to the east by south, and after the confluence of the Nyágrong Chhu from Dza-yul in long. 94° 34′ the course becomes almost due east. Below the latter point of junction, no agent of our Survey Department has penetrated. K. P., who reached this point from the north, mentions the name of the next place, about four miles lower down, as Miri Padam, and thence to the mountain gorges whence the Dihang embrochure opens is all *terra incognita*.[1] But at the outside the distance from Miri Padam to the highest point reached on the Dihang from the south cannot exceed sixty-five miles. However, the main run in that hiatus is evidently easternly, because, while the conjunction with the Nyágrong occurs in long. 94° 34′, the Dihang is first seen issuing from the lower broken ranges in long. 95° 25′. From the observed run of the valley and the "lie" of the mist-clouds above the conjectured bed of the river, doubtless the turn of the river's course from east to south, in order to cut through the last ranges of the Himalayas, is very abrupt. Moreover, at Miri Padam it has already reached too far south to allow room for any gradual bend. In a direct line due south, Miri Padam (as may be seen from the map) is barely twenty-five miles from our own territory. The river there, however, curves due east, and traverses a distance of some seventy miles to reach the known point where, turning abruptly S.S.E., it issues forth as the Dihang.

THE DIHANG AND EASTERN BRAHMAPUTRA.

But let our river now be considered in relation to the point where, as the Dihang, or Dihong, it joins the main stream of the Brahmaputra, which it meets sweeping in a broad channel from east to west. Now let it be borne in mind that the Brahmaputra is already fairly in existence as a distinct river long before the Yeru Tsangpo (as the Dihang) joins it; and therefore it is inexact to speak of it—as is the custom—as being a continuation of the Tibetan river. Indeed, prior to the conjunction, it has already been flowing in a noble expanse from the Brahmakund pool, the place where it freed itself, a turbulent mountain river, from the Mishmi hills. Further up in those hills, moreover, it has had a lengthy progress. The primary sources of the Eastern Brahmaputra are in fact in Tibet itself, although much further east than the upper waters of the Dihang. Those sources are the two rivers known as the Dzáyul Chhu and the Rong T'od Chhu, which drain and flow from N.

1 Mr. Needham expresses his doubts as to whether K. P. ever reached so far S. as he claimed; and says Miri Padam is a fictitious name. Still, as it is the name of a tribe, it might be so applied.

to S. through the twin valleys of Dzáyul-med in S.E. Tibet. Coalescing before escaping from that mountain-locked district, the united rivers cut through the southern range separating Dzáyul-med from the Mishmi country and thence, as the turbulent mountain river above mentioned, pass across the latter tract W.S.W. into Assam. Below Brahmakund, the waters, having developed into a considerable river, proceed from long. 96° 23′ due west. Thence, during a course of 80 miles, to the first union with the Dihang, the Brahmaputra—here sometimes styled the Taluka and sometimes the Lohit—receives no fewer than ten affluents of large draught, the chief being the Digaru, the Prenga, the Dhuli, the Dip'u, the Khundil, the Tenga-pani, the Noa Dihing and the Dikrang. Near Sadiya—fifteen miles above the first influx of the Dihang—the river has grown so broad as to include several large islands. Then the Dihang and the Dibang (which has just been augmented by the Sesiri) coalesce to meet the Brahmaputra in one combined stream, coming from the north at right angles to the Indian river. The Dibang-cum-Sesiri from the east unites with the Dihang about two miles previous to their general union with the Brahmaputra. This forms the principal mouth of the Dihang.

Another and smaller branch of the great Tibetan river makes entry about five miles lower down the Brahmaputra, the space between the two mouths of the Dihang being really the base line of a tall delta, the top angle of which lies far up the latter river. Its formation evidently has been brought about by the vast volume of water and the velocity with which that volume descends the steep gradients from the hills. An enormous mass of silt in solution, borne down thus violently, is suddenly checked, first by the Dibang stream meeting it with its output of 27,200 cubic feet of water per second, and next, still more determinedly, by the 33,800 cubic feet per second of the Upper or Eastern Brahmaputra, cutting it at right angles. The silt so checked has been deposited and in the lapse of centuries built up the pear-shaped delta. This second branch of the Dihang is much narrower than the main or first branch, the discharge being usually under 5,000 cubic feet. The bifurcation forming the delta occurs some fourteen miles up the stream; and, while the main limb retains the name of Dihang, the smaller is known as the Lali-pani. Above the point of bifurcation, the measure of the discharge of the undivided river must be estimated at about 60,000 cubic feet per second; for we do not think the late Captain Harman included the Lali discharge in his measurement of 55,500 cubic-feet made in 1878 for the Dihang near its junction with the Dibang.[2]

[2] Admeasurement of the respective discharge of these rivers has been carefully

Ascending the main stream of the Dihang, its appearance is majestic. Even where the waters exceed a mile in breadth they sweep on in a deep swift flow. Some ten miles up, where in places they narrow to 500 yards, the enormous discharge being thus compressed, the current developes into mighty rapids. Upward navigation consequently becomes a laborious task. Two or three Miri villages occur on the west or delta-side of the river, which produces larger than mere jungle timber. The left-hand, or eastern, bank is occupied by the Abors, whose villages, however, lie inland, the chief stronghold being Membu, some twenty miles from the Dihang. Large numbers of deer frequent the banks where the ground is low, and, notwithstanding the strong current, even swim across stream. During the high summer rise in the waters, which does not reach its climax until June, the breadth of the Dihang, even above the point where the river parts in two, again approaches one mile, and occasionally exceeds that width. Then, again, a mile or so higher up, navigation, though it is still resorted to by the villagers on the banks for short trips, is almost impracticable. Eight miles above the delta-angle, the low broken hills of the outermost range of the Himalayas begin to start up. Here and higher up the mighty waters are in places parted into two or three deep channels separated by vast reefs of rock, each channel with violent current chequered by several falls twenty to forty feet high over which the streams drop with thunderous roar and clouds of vaporous spray.

The route up-country, as followed by the Abor tribes who occupy the banks of the Dihang above the delta, keeps mostly near the riverside (though the large villages lie off the river), for the banks along the hills, though besetting and precipitous, are not at all lofty. Colonel R. G. Woodthorpe estimated the average altitude of the hills besetting this portion of the river at only 4,730 feet, and passes from the western valleys into the valley of the Dihang at 3,500 feet or under. Even much higher up, and as far as the valley can be traced with the telescope, it has been observed that the contour of the country round the river is low and undulating. Only a few isolated summits away to the north rise to five and six thousand feet, and the river, which bends abruptly in from the west, does not pass very near these northern peaks.

The river-banks, 25 miles up from the Brahmaputra, are all very

made more than once; first by Wilcox in 1825-26 and again in 1878 by the late Captain J. E. Harman. The calculations taken in December 1825 were not repeated in a winter month by Harman; so these stand alone as the record of the discharge of the rivers at that season. But measurements in spring were made both in 1826 and in 1878; and it is surprising how closely those estimates agree together, although taken fifty years apart. We have given above the spring record.

steep; but water is plentiful among lateral gorges above the banks on each side. Looking across the valley to the slopes on the other side, you descry waterfalls rushing down in every little ravine; and if you travel along the circuitous path-way which, at varying height, leads round each spur, torrents must be crossed at frequent intervals. The route to be traversed commonly follows upward the course of some stream, and that without evading the boisterous cascades, through the spray of which the traveller ascends with only such footing as is afforded by the wet moss-coated rocks, where the slightest slip would ensure immersion in the water.

No traveller of European birth (save, perhaps, Wilcox) had before the year 1885 ascended the Dihang river-side higher than within the first lower ridge of hills. The Abors, with their poisoned arrows and their murderous propensities, are the wholesome deterrent to all such enterprise. Such emissaries of the Abors as visited Sadiya to receive the annual payment bestowed on the tribes as a bribe to refrain from looting the cowardly Assamese spoke in big terms of their own prowess and their numbers. Nevertheless, Colonel Woodthorpe, who had good views from neighbouring heights of their principal villages, thinks that the size of the villages, and therefore their numerical strength, have been greatly over-estimated.[1]

Probably the furthest penetration in modern times into the Abor country has been made by Mr. J. F. Needham, political officer at Sadiya. He went first with some friends in 1885. They ascended the Dihang quite 24 miles, their craft being drawn by ropes up several rapids, and then landed on the eastern bank. Thence they pushed their way N.-E. through difficult country, and by dint of pluck succeeded in reaching the Abor village of Membu, or Mebor, quite within the mountains. Since then Mr. Needham ascended still further; and in 1902 he despatched two Gurkha sepoys who had received special training. The latter men met with much hostility and could not penetrate far; but reported seeing the Tsang-po flowing from the west due E. and as being one with the Dihang.

THE BRAHMAPUTRA IRAWADI CONTROVERSY.

The Dihang, by reason of its noble size, is worthy to be the continuation of the great river of Tibet; and that it is, in fact, one and

1 However, Colonel Woodthorpe's deductions cannot be accepted conclusively. For example, one of the places he viewed was Mebor, which was subsequently, in 1885, visited by Mr. Needham's party, who brought word that it contained about 300 dwellings, with a population which they estimated at 3,000, each dwelling harbouring a family of two or three generations.

the same is now deemed a certainty. This was Wilcox's theory even 80 years' ago. An emissary of the Survey of India has traced the Tibetan river almost down to the southern line of demarcation betwixt Tibet and Assam—roughly, it is true, but his narrative is circumstantial enough to enable our experts to assign the point he reached with tolerable exactitude. From the south, moreover, the valley of the Dihang has been followed up to the low hill ranges to a point 65 miles E. S.-E. of the other point laid down on the Tibetan river. The question was—does the great river connect these two points thus brought so close together? The Gurkhas of Mr. Needham report—Yes.

Captain Harman reasonably thought that the most conclusive way to prove the identity of the rivers without actual survey would be to throw in the water a certain number of marked logs at any place low down on the Yeru Tsangpo accessible to some one of the survey exploring agents. If, then, these logs emerged below in the Dihang, the problem was solved. In fulfilment of this idea, the emissary mentioned above, K. P., was sent into Tibet in 1880, with the injunction to make his way to Gyalla Seng-dong, and there cast 500 logs of a defined shape into the river. At the same time Captain Harman had arranged that watchers should be stationed at the junction of the Dihang and Brahmaputra to ascertain if any of the logs passed that way. Owing to the bad faith of a Chinese lama accompanying K. P., who when in Tibet sold him into slavery, the project for the time was not put into execution. Eventually, however, K. P. escaped, and after many vicissitudes, he, with commendable trustiness, succeeded in performing his portion of the scheme. He secretly cut his wooden floats and launched the whole 500 in a better place than that pre-arranged, namely at Bepung, about 35 miles lower down the stream, and nearer the frontier than Gyalla Seng-dong. However, this was done in 1883, three years after the time settled by Captain Harman, and when the watchers on the Dihang had ceased to expect the logs. Thus, whether the logs came down or not, the plan failed; but, even if the watchers had been on the alert, it must be remembered that the stretch of the river, with its currents and rapids, which the wooden messengers had to traverse from Bepung, was over 160 miles in length.

The attempt at ocular demonstration having miscarried, we may now state the inferential proofs :—

1. The first position is this. If the Yeru Tsangpo, brought down to a point 65 miles distant from that part of the Dihang daily visible in British territory, does not connect with that river, whither then does it flow? The southernmost place to which it has been fairly traced lies approximately in lat.

28° 18′ N., long. 94° 36′ E. Does it then suddenly turn S.-W. and flow into the Subansiri? But three great feeding branches of the Subansiri, each draining vast mountain-locked valleys to the west, have been already scientifically observed. If to their sources were superadded the waters of the mighty Tibetan river, could the discharge of the Subansiri in Assam by any possibility dwindle to 16,900 cubic feet per second, as measured by Captain Harman? No, indeed, avers the French School, the Yeru Tsangpo cannot flow S.-W. into the Subansiri; no, on the contrary, it turns and flows due east for some 100 miles or so, and then, when the northern verge of the Mishmi country has been reached just beyond the 96th meridian, it is diverted in a S.-E. direction to skirt the southern side of the mountains walling in the Upper Zayul valley to the north, whence it enters the recognised basin of the Irawadi about lat 27° 40′ N. and long. 97° 25′ E. However, a few glances at the revised map of these districts will demolish any such theory as the foregoing one. The Yeru Tsangpo has been followed south to lat. 28° 18′ N., and if we then carry it, as proposed, due east from there, where are we to work in the head-waters of the Dihang—the Dihang with its lowest summer discharge of 66,000 cubic feet per second? The course of this river, presumably from the west, would have to be pressed down, some miles at least, south of the parallel 28° 18′ N., that it might not coalesce with the course of the Yeru. Next, when we had traced it back west, it must somehow find its enormous water-supply amidst the feeders of the Subansiri.

It was lately argued that the northernmost of the valleys formed by the ranges radiating from Tsari—that valley high up within the loop of the Yeru Tsangpo in the Gipmochen tract, might prove the feeding-ground of the Dihang; *i.e.*, one small valley to make the mighty Dihang, while three of the same pattern further south are required for the Subansiri, which discharges one quarter the water of the Dihang!

2. Worse difficulties would occur from the east. The conjectured course of the Yeru into the Irawadi valleys must be manœuvred so as to avoid contact with the early course of the Dibang and Sesiri rivers, which rise at least as far north as lat. 28° 35′ N., so the Yeru ought to sweep up further north than that latitude before turning again South-East.

It would for this purpose have to mount to a district of *much higher general level than that from which it had flowed,* most probably ascending from 5,000 to reach 8,000 feet, the estimated level of the country north of the Dibang sources![1] Moreover, as it turned S.-E. and passed within the Mishmi country S.-W. of Lower Dzayul, the flow upward would be still steeper. An equally arduous task would have yet to be attempted before the Irawadi was gained. The mother stream of the Eastern branch of the Brahmaputra would be encountered in the Mishmi country running from N.-E. to S.-W. to enter N.-E. Assam. Unless, then, one large river can neatly cross the course of another, the Dzáyul Chhu (as the Upper Brahmaputra is here styled) would effectually bar back the Yeru in further progress to the Irawadi. Our map will show this clearly.

3. The exploration of A. K. proved that no great river from the west entered Dzáyul-med (Lower Dzáyul) through its lofty western barrier-mountains, to wit, the Ata Gang La range. Thus the possibility of any round-about route further to the north and thence into the Irawadi is put away.

4. By the later investigations of Colonel Woodthorpe and Major Hobday, confirmed by the journey of Prince Henri d'Orléans, the whole argument is practically disposed of; because the actual sources of the Irawadi have been almost exactly located. The three primary feeders have been traced nearly up to the base of the great Kha Karpo range, which, to the north, walls them off inexorably from Lower Dzáyul; while, to the East and North-East, another range clearly shuts off communication from any Tibetan river proceeding to the south *viá* the gorges of Western Yunnan. But, again, let the reader consult our map.

The conclusion, therefore, is irresistible. It is the Yeru of Tibet which passes south through the Assam-Himalayas, and which shows itself, in about long. 95° 20′ E., as the river known in Assam as the Dihang and ultimately as the Brahmaputra. Thus is the old conclusion of Rennell and, later, of Wilcox, confirmed.

1 That the general level of the tracts lying east of the traced southernly course of the Yeru (from Gyalla Seng-dong to Miri Padam) slopes upward as you pass eastward to the bounding ranges of Dzayul, is evident from the fact that all the observed rivers east of long. 95° flow determinedly westwards. Thus the great river which A. K. reported as leaving the Ata Gangla range in lat. 29° 25′ E., namely the Nyagrong Chhu, proceeds unfalteringly westward across the very district through which the Yeru, to join the Irawadi, would be flowing eastward!

CONCLUDING REMARKS.

As to length, our river may have assigned to it an extent of 1,308 miles up to its union with the Eastern, or Upper, Brahmaputra. Then, adding the course onwards to the mouth of the Megna, in the Bay of Bengal, we may put the full lineal measurement at 1,920 English miles from source to sea.

Again, the catchment-area of the river should be estimated. It rises, as we have seen in the morass, fed by glaciers, of the Nyimo Namgyal range, hard-by the Manasarowar lakes; and it drains the whole of Southern Tibet substantially from long. 82° E. to long. 93° 30′ E., its northern influence so far being limited to the south of lat. 31° N. However, further east its basin becomes more restricted, not extending so far to the south as is the case in the western parts. Having next abruptly curved up to the north as far as the 30th parallel of latitude, it there receives a drainage from about a degree of territory further north than that parallel. Then, as suddenly running down S. S.-E. for about 170 miles, near but beyond the 94th meridian, the river absorbs the waters from the country lying to the east of this southern course, even as far as to the 96th meridian. Thus, before the Yeru Tsangpo enters Assam, its basin has extended through 14 degrees from west to east with an average breadth, north and south, of 2½ degrees throughout; with a drainage covering some 112,000 square miles. Such is a rough estimate of the dimensions of the stupendous superficial area over which the great water-artery of Tibet causes its absorbent effects to be felt.

When the river rises in the Chyema Yungdrung springs, its bed lies 14,700 feet above the level of the sea. After a course of 540 miles to the neighbourhood of Shigatse, its elevation has fallen only 2,400 feet, giving a gradient of descent of nearly 4½ feet to the mile, or 1 in 1187. East to Tse-t'ang the rate of descent continues almost precisely the same, the fall being 1,000 feet in 242 miles. In the next 250 miles of the river's course, however, the downward gradient increases amazingly; the descent in that space being 3,300 feet or 13 feet per mile. South of Gyalla Seng-dong, where the altitude is 8,000 feet, we have no certain record; but the drop is believed to be very rapid, as the general level north of the Assam Himalayas, taking the height of the abutting peaks, can hardly exceed 3,500 feet. Then, when, as the Dihang, it has fairly cleared these mountains, the wonderful river, once a water-way 14,700 feet above sea-level, is found flowing at an elevation of less than 800 feet. Finally, at the tri-junction with the Dihang and Brahmaputra, the level is 420 feet.

CHAPTER VII.

MONASTERIES AND NUNNERIES.

One of the strangest features of this fascinating country is the religion of the inhabitants, and one of the curious circumstances of that religion is the apparatus it possesses of religious communities greatly akin to the monastic institutions of Europe. Indeed the conventual idea is carried out to an extreme in Tibet. Everywhere throughout the length and breadth of the land are to be found establishments harbouring small bodies of men or women living under religious rules more or less rigorous. As the Buddhist institution is in many respects not dissimilar to the Christian monastery, we may for convenience apply the name to these establishments, and say that we meet with Buddhist monasteries and nunneries in Tibet in every conceivable situation and in extraordinary numbers. We find them in the city and in the desert; we espy them perched on each available ledge among the stupendous mountains and seated on the shores of the ice-bound lakes. There is no confluence of rivers without its guardian monastic fortress placed at the junction; no fertile valley without its six or eight such communities; no rocky islet on the large inland seas uncrowned by a hermitage holding a dozen inmates; no village void of its *Shigön* or small temple flanked with huts for three or four religious. Generally, lofty and picturesque situations are chosen; and the buildings, sometimes massive and castellated, sometimes square houses purely lime-washed and striped with broad bands of red and blue or quaintly picked out with amber-coloured borders, and having protruding balconies painted bright chocolate, form a striking feature in Tibetan scenery. The rocky gorge; the open valley with its silvery river parting the meadows along the dividing line in the deep bottom; the dark mountains, red or yellow or grey-black in body and outstretched limbs, but stainless dazzling white upon head and shoulders—are all frequently relieved of the aspect of desolation by the range of huts, the central temple, the inevitable appendants of *chhörtens*, poles, and flags.

But when were these little social parties of religious folk living each in their own isolation established in Tibet? We do not ask when were they introduced into Buddhist countries generally; because monasteries in the ordinary sense of the term are not found everywhere as an intrinsic concomitant of Buddhism.

Monasteries as they exist and have long existed in Tibet, Mongolia, and the Chinese border-land, are really unique in constitution and character so far as the East is concerned. In Burmah, Ceylon, Siam, Kambodia, and Japan—the other countries where Buddhism prevails—establishments of this peculiar character are never found. Attached to the larger temples in the last-named countries are indeed communities of priests and mendicants who perform the services and live on the offerings of the devotees. But nothing analogous to the monastic system as found in Europe and West Asia is found there. In Tibet bodies of men or women—large and small—are housed in isolated societies often far apart from their fellow-creatures, much as in Christian convents. They dwell and work and worship together, and often form a community of 500, 1,000, or even in a few cases of 4,000 and 5,000 persons. There is in general outline a strong similitude between the Christian religious houses of primitive and mediæval times and these Tibetan lamaseries. And from eastern Christian countries (such as Armenia) do we venture to suspect was the institution in its Tibetan form imported into Central Asia.

Orientalists are in the habit of speaking of the old Sanskrit Vihara of the days of Indian Buddhism as something like unto the mediæval monastery. General Cunningham in his elaborate re-construction of the ruins at Budh Gaya expands the famous shrine into a mighty monastic establishment. But, so far as the actual evidence of the remains and foundations go, this was not so. What was Budh Gaya and what was the Buddhist Vihara of India? It was a school or college with a few cells for professors and ascetics and with verandahs or corridors where pupils were instructed. The general herd of Buddhist "hearers," such as they are made to appear in the Lalita Vistara, the Abhinishkramana and other later Buddhist compilations, were not housed together but lived more as the denizens of a modern Indian village. Moreover, with regard to the number of those who submitted to live by rules and attended the monthly "confessions," there is much to cause one to believe that these are instanced by the authors *quâ exempla* as to *what might be*, supposing their religious theories to be properly carried into effect. Those acquainted with the fantasies of Indian authorship know well with what an air of verisimilitude, as if they were relating actual facts, such writers can record their speculations. The vast scheme of disciplinary machinery of the books was, we are every day more and more inclined to believe, rather a well-built temple of fancy placed by enthusiasts on paper than a system ever on any full scale put into practical use.

As to the Tibetan form of monasticism—radically different even to the shape which certain writers are accustomed to assign to the Buddhist communes of India—there is strong evidence as to whence it was introduced. From the 6th to the 11th century A.D. was a period of remarkable activity on the part of the Nestorian Church in Asia. Christian missionaries were despatched under powerful organisation into the remotest wilds of Mongolia. The borders of China were touched and churches and conventual buildings erected. By the time of Jenghis Khan, so learned and reputable were the Nestorian priests accounted, that their Syriac alphabet was adopted in a modified form as the written character of the Mongol-Tartar language in which it is thus used to the present day. Now it was about the 9th and 10th centuries that lamaism and the general system of the northern Buddhist cult began to run in the channels which afterwards attained such distinctive development. We do not propose to set forth any elaborate argument here; but the influence of Nestorianism at that period taken in conjunction with the extraordinary parallism observable between Tibetan Buddhist ceremonial and the mediæval practices of the Eastern Christian Churches raises a strong inference which would be applicable likewise to the similarity in their monastic systems.

Not accepting the statements of the books unless supported by accessory evidence, it may be allowed that a large number of the monasteries in Tibet are of ancient foundation. The oldest establishments still existing may be set down as Samye on the Yeru (*circa* 830 A.D.), Meru Tá Chhoide in Lhása, T'o-ling or T'o-ding on the Sutlej in Ngari Khorsum, Rading to the N.-E. of Lhása, and Minḍol Ling. All these date from times prior to 1050 A.D., while Sakya, Daipung, and many others still flourishing were founded only a little later. The great monasteries on the Chinese border arose between 1400 and 1650 A.D. It is not chiefly in the more civilised and metropolitan districts of Tibet such as the Lhása region that the greatest number or the largest monasteries have been set up. In the border provinces of Amdo and Khams in the N.-E. and E., as well as in Ladak in the extreme west, these establishments are equally numerous and important. The Amdoan foundations are particularly wealthy and popular, and although they are located in the heart of a land of notorious brigands, such devout Buddhists are these dreaded marauders that the monasteries enjoy perfect immunity from their depredations. Such famous establishments as Jambabum Ling,

13

Serkhang Gompa, Labrang Táshi-kyil, Gonlung Gompa, Tsoni Parkhang, and the great Kumbum monastery 18 miles S.-W. of Sining, exist in the remoter wilds of Amdo. Moreover, in later times, the more noted Buddhist authors have hailed from those parts, as well as a recent Dalai Lama of Lhása.

With regard to the number of lamaseries in Khams in the districts adjoining the Chinese border, the statement of Mr. Rockhill may be mentioned, that in travelling from Gye-kündo to Darchendo, a distance of 600 miles, he passed forty, in the smallest of which there were 100 monks and in five of them from 2,000 to 4,000. So also in Rudok and Ngari Khorsum in Western Tibet, desolate regions though they are, and occupied almost exclusively by a semi-nomadic laity, there are said to be 104 of these establishments, large and small. In Spiti, now under British rule, with a population of only 2,862 inclusive of monks, there are 11 gompas, five of which are on a big scale. As a contrast, in the city of Lhása iteslf there are only 10 monasteries, with four others within a radius of four miles; but the inmates of the 14 reach a gross total of 18,500.

As to the power and influence of these mighty establishments all over the country, such can hardly be exaggerated. Moreover, the fact that the clerical fraternity draws recruits from all ranks and that every family in the land contributes its quota, cements the union of monasteries and people. So it is natural to find the central government at Lhása mainly in the hands of ecclesiastics. In Tsang, the southern province, the head of Tashi-lhümpo is *de facto* the temporal sovereign. In the eastern province, Khams, although the ostensible rule rests in the hands of hereditary chieftains, the presiding lamas of all the great monasteries, suchas Chhamdo, Riwochhe, and, Derge, are to a man either appointed from Lhása or, being born locally as "incarnate lamas," have been educated at the capital. These, then, exercise authority not only over the inmates but also over the householders dwelling on the extensive landed estates attached to each one of them. In fact, in most districts of Khams the head lama of the principal monastery is the real ruler of the district.

ARCHITECTURE AND INTERNAL ARRANGEMENT.

As might be expected the architecture of the Tibetan monastery varies with the different districts. In Ladak we find fortress-like buildings with massive walls and protruding bastions, portions being erected on different levels and seeming to climb one above the other; on one side the foundations may rise up from the edge of a sheer precipice of two or three thousand feet, of which the very walls of the monastery seem to be a part. In these the interiors are a curious labyrinth of passages, steps, cells, and halls, practically under one roof. Further east in Tibet Proper, where the sites though mountainous can generally command some portion of level ground, the buildings are not so crowded and heaped up. In such cases the plan of the smaller colleges at Cambridge would give the reader some idea of the Tibetan establishment. There is an open courtyard surrounded by blocks of houses two or three storeys in height and often with arcaded passages or cloisters running in front under the second storey. There are several ascents from beneath the arcades; sometimes stone-steps, very often inclined planes of wood, or only ladders. Upstairs are many small rooms opening on to another passage or frequently on to a gallery. Each cell belongs to a *ge-long* or fully fledged monk who has generally a *tápa* or boy-learner as attendant on him and occupying the same chamber.[1] In these cells are to be seen little furniture: a long padded cushion covered with dirty red material for sleeping and sitting on (*sim-ten* or *bölten*), a mat for visitors (*shúten*), a large wallet (*khom*) and a box (*dom*) as receptacles for utensils and other property, and a shelf (*pangkha*) for a long book or writing materials.

In the centre of the courtyard the temple (*lhá-khang* = "god-house") is usually placed; and adjoining it, as an ante-room or side-chamber, is the congregational hall or assembly-place where the reading of the sacred books in general concert by the gelongs is daily conducted. This hall is called the *du-khang*; it varies in size; and in the largest monasteries is a separate building apart from the temple. In certain other places, the assembly-hall is below the temple where the images are. At the larger gompa there are often more *lhá-khang* than one. Above the chief temple and *du-khang* are second floors where other shrines may be and where, if there be enough to form a real library, the books are kept; and leading out of the library is frequently the suite of little rooms (not more than two or three) occupied by the head lama of the monastery. Another erection in the courtyard is a long shed with pent-roof where a row of big prayer-cylinders is ranged.

There is, moreover, always a long barn-like edifice usually built of sun-dried bricks. This is the public kitchen, with the store rooms attached; but it seems to be only brought into use on festival days, on ordinary occasions all the denizens doing their own cooking in their respective rooms. While festivals are being celebrated and also during the harvest season when the inmates have, most of them, to work in the fields, the general kitchen is set going. All the monks mess together, eating their full of meat, tsampa, butter, curds, and tea; not to men-

[1] *Trápa* or *tápa* in also used as a general term for the all inmates of monasteries.

tion a plentiful supply of *chhang* which is drunk warm, causing great hilarity. These "*mang-ja*" or general teas take place in the *du-khang*.

SOURCES OF REVENUE.

The wealth of the greater number of regular establishments, as distinguished from the many small out-lying gompas, is derived mainly from landed property. Upon these estates are usually numerous small farmers and householders (*mi-ser*) who cultivate the land as hereditary tenants. The occupiers pay no direct rent for their farms but are bound to yield up a third of the produce or one-third of its value every year to the over-lord which in these cases is the monastery. Such proportion is collected annually; sometimes by an agent who travels for the purpose; sometimes, where the monastery is the sole proprietor of the district and appoints the governor or fort-master of the Jong, by the Jong-pön (fort-master) himself. These amounts are paid in butter, wool, or money; and the collector must be supported lavishly during his visits. Moreover, as a rule, a certain number of bricks of tea and other commodities which he brings round must be purchased by tenants, the profits on which are shared between the agent personally and the monastery or other owner. If the agent is the Jong-pön he has unlimited facilities and powers for enforcing compulsory purchases.

Again, the occupants of monastic lands must provide without charge sheep, cattle, and ponies to carry borax, salt, or wool, through their territory, if the monastery authorities trade as they often do in such merchandize.

Individual gelongs are frequently money-lenders to both householders and their brother monks, charging large interest.

As to the general revenue of a gompa, it is not doled round to the inmates. Some of the higher officials secure their pickings and perquisites therefrom; but it is legally supposed to be devoted to three objects: (1) Repairing and embellishing the fabric and purchasing new implements for the temple use; (2) Supplying butter for the sacrificial lights before images; (3) Providing meat, tea, and beer consumed by the inmates on festival days, which days are numerous.

Let it then be understood that in general the dwellers in a monastery are not clothed and fed from monastic funds but have to support themselves by their own earnings or from any other private source. The principal means of his being able to subsist, if the man be an ordinary member of the fraternity, is the produce which his family at home transmit him from a field which they set apart and call *lama-i-zhing* "the lama's field." Again, if he be a full gelong who has been ordained at Táshilhümpo or Lhása, he can earn considerable sums by attending at persons' houses for marriages or in cases of sickness, and for the casting of horoscopes at birth and on other occasions. He may also at certain seasons hire himself out for field work.

There are, however, certain forms of income which the denizens of a religious house receive in their corporate capacity which yet benefit the individual members. These are the *bu-la* or funeral fees, and the alms contributed at harvest-time. The first are derived from attending at the house of the deceased where a large body of monks go to read the sacred books in the presence of the dead, and from similar readings in the *lhá-khang* when the nearest relative comes to take part in the *kang-sha* rites. Harvest alms are got in by parties of monks just after the crops have been reaped. These go about the country on begging expeditions in gangs of five or six dressed in their best robes and *chhoi-shá* or religious hats. Passing from house to house they chant various rhymes and collect grain at every door; for the response is never-failing. Each inmate of the gompa claims a share in all such sources of income, receiving in proportion to his grade and position. In eastern districts certain monasteries obtain subsidies from the Chinese Government, a part of which is distributed in food to the residents.

In Tibet Proper all monastic institutions are exempted from taxation on land or other property belonging to them. Neither are they liable to *be-gar* or forced-labour dues, nor to the supply of cattle to high government officials for draught purposes or of horses for the postal service. Such burdens, therefore, fall the more heavily on the laity.

GRADES OF RELIGIOUS HOUSES.

Monastic establishments are, of course, not all upon one level There are different degrees of standing, and the rank depends on certain recognized conditions. If the place is the dwelling of an incarnate lama of much sanctity, that is of count. But the grade of the bulk of houses is really of more technical sort, resting on antiquity and ancient prestige quite as much as upon the number of inmates and landed possessions; though in many cases those qualities exist together. Indeed the oldest institutions are often the richest.

A monastery of the highest rank is termed a LING; and is generally governed by a gelong of learning and note styled a *Khempo* in Gelukpa establishments and a *Lo-pön* (in Ladak *hlobon*) in Red-cap institutions. The word "ling" originally meant "an island" and thence came to be applied to spots separated by their sanctity from their surroundings; testifying, moreover, to the distinction and isolated grandeur of the edifices erected at such places. Only the older establishments seem to be called Lings, and in those early days they were indeed as islands in the desert-ocean of Tibet. Among the chief monasteries of this class are the four Lings at Lhásа; also Sákya Ling, the heads of which formerly governed the whole of Tibet; Sera Ling, with 3,000 inmates, near Lhása; P'un-ts'o Ling on the Yeru Tsang-po where the great Jonang-pa school of Buddhism originated; and Mindol Ling, the ruling abbey of the Nyingma section. Many Lings, like our abbeys with their appendant priories, have smaller monasteries attached to them and which pay to them a proportion of revenue. These branch houses may be either in the same district or in some distant locality. Thus T'ö-ling on the River Sutlej, the oldest establishment in Ngari Khorsum, has 25 minor appendencies.

The next grade is the CHHOIDE (ཆོས་སྡེ) supposed to be an institution where special provision is made for study of doctrinal works and Tantrik subtilties. These are in fact the theological colleges of Tibetan Buddhism and have the privilege of granting various degrees and diplomas which qualify the holders for offices of position in other monasteries. In strictness no one can become a full gelong unless he has resided a certain period at a Chhoide and passed there the requisite examinations. Two or three of these establishments have acquired special fame and dignity. The principal of all is Táshi-lhümpo in Tsang which might perhaps be designated an University, granting as it does its own peculiar degrees for special studies, and conferring also, it is said, certain similar distinctions on lay-students of good family. Other Chhoide of prestige are Tsi Nam-gyal on Potala Hill at Lhása where the Grand Lama is the resident head; Daipung with 7,000 inmates, an establishment particularly affected by Mongol and Kalmuk students who come there even from Urga in Siberia to take their diplomas as gelong; Sera Ling; the P'alkhor Chhoide of Gyangtse; Táshi Gomang in Amdo; and Ngam-ring on the Yeru Tsangpo west of Jang-lhátse. Certain others such as Dongtse Chhoide near Gyangtse and Shel-kar Chhoide have no reputation and are barely recognised as capable of granting lamaic rights.

A few of the larger Lings and all Chhoide have within their confines guilds or subordinate colleges known as TÁ-TS'ANG (གྲྭ་ཚང་) where fully-qualified lamas enter as students in order to devote exclusive attention to particular branches of doctrinal philosophy such as Tsan-nyid, Dü-kyi Khorlo, Madhyamika, and Tantrik lore. There are special edifices belonging to the college and the members dwell together in rooms apart from the other monastic residents. Endowed chairs with professors, or learned experts, are attached to each *Ṭá-ts'ang*, much in the manner of our own University professorships. However, the professor is usually of the Khempo rank, sometimes even an incarnation of some by-gone saint, and he manages his community in semi-independence of the main monastery. Thus in Sera Ling we find three of these establishments; Daipung has four, one of them Gomang Ta-ts'ang being the Mongol college; while at Ṭáshi-lhümpo there are four of great note, which seem to have the same relationship to the mother monastery that our individual colleges bear to the University. Chhamdo Chhoide in Eastern Tibet and Radeng possess well-known guilds for Tsan-nyid philosophy; while at Tse-chen Chhoide in Tsang are several schools for the study of Prasanga and Dükyi Khorlo mysticism. But at Gyangtse exists the largest number of Tá-ts'ang; for there we find no fewer than eighteen, each of which respectively is supposed to teach a separate doctrinal syllabus, namely, one of those peculiar to the eighteen ancient schools of Buddhism. Occasionally the fraternity is apart from any monastery, as the Waidurya Tá-ts'ang at Lhása.

The members of a Ta-ts'ang generally bear the name of *Ká-ram;* because, prior to admission, each must have taken a sort of doctrinal degree at a Chhoide, either that of *Ká-chan* ("possessed of the precepts") or that of *Dhung-rampa*. In summer the *Ká-ram* often go for out-door camp-meetings where under their Khempo they practise disputations and magical ceremonial exercises, reciting many folios of mystic syllables.

Fourthly must be enumerated the general mass of monastic establishments known as Gompa (དགོན་པ་ "a desolate or unfrequented place.") These seem to be upon every conceivable scale, from the edifice harbouring 8 or 10 up to the community of 2,000 or 3,000. Many of the large settlements in N.-E. Tibet, and over the Chinese frontier, with terrace above terrace of residences and often more than 2,000 regular denizens are known merely as Gompas. The term is likewise employed loosely to designate monasteries of any rank; so that we hear of Daipung Gompa, Tö-ling Gompa, Ṭáshi-lhümpo Gompa, etc. As to the small temples to be seen in villages with a few huts adjacent for the three or four ecclesiastics in charge, perhaps a single gelong with two or three ge-ts'ul, these also may be styled Gompa, though Shigön (གཞི་དགོན) is the correct and more usual appellation. Most of the big establishments bearing the general designation are of recent origin, comparatively.

In Tibet are to be found, furthermore, communities of women, vowed to religion and celibacy, and living in association. Such are commonly known as ANI GOMPA or as TSUNPO, but in Ladak and Western Tibet JOMO-LING is the proper term. However, the dwelling-place for nuns can hardly be dignified with the name of convent or nunnery. It is rather a small collection of huts forming a kind of settlement without any temple. Where the community belongs to the Gelukpa order, it is pitched more or less in isolation from all other dwellings or monasteries. Such is the Dzá-lung Nyá-gön, some few miles from Khamba Jong, where is a settlement of 15 huts; and only one Ani Gompa is permitted within great towns like Lhása on Shigatse.[1] In these lonely establishments the nuns or *tsunmo*, as they are styled, usually own many sheep and goats which they pasture themselves and keep in pens built on to each dwelling. But with other sects, there are nuns' quarters placed just outside the monastery of males, and they often have a room within the latter place where they may sit if they desire. They are in such cases mostly the concubines, more or less openly, of the monks. A nun's hut is called *tá-shak;* and sometimes two or three occupy one hut.[2]

Lastly, must be mentioned the P'UK or caverns tenanted by hermits or contemplative lamas. Sometimes the *P'uk* is a single cave with one ascetic living far apart from his fellow-creatures in a situation almost inaccessible to intruders. An excavation high up on a ledge in the mountains is a favourite site. Commonly, however, the term indicates a whole colony of such anchorites, who live in extensive ranges of caverns such as are frequent in the mountain formations of Tibet. These dwellers in caves are then styled *Ri-t'oi-pa* and, while supposed to pass lives of sanctity and deep meditation, they are not forbidden considerable intercommunion with one another. However the solitary *Ri-t'oi-pa* or *Ri-p'ukpa* are most highly venerated. Some have lived many years without any intercourse with their fellow-creatures, and are really absorbed in that concentrated meditation which Buddhism enjoins. At Shalu near Painam Jong in Tsang, a hermit lives in an underground cave and shuts himself out from communication with the upper world

1 In Lhása the one *ani gompa* is situated in the extreme S.-E. quarter of the city near the cemetery and the Kashmiri mosque. It is named the Tshang-kung Gompa.

2 It is related in the Tibetan Dulwa that Shakya-t'ubpa at first declined to allow women to be admitted to membership of the religious orders. His aunt and 500 other women, however, persisted in following the Buddha about beseeching him to receive them; so at length, at the request of his disciple Kungáwo, he permitted them to take the religious vows as Gelongma. Tibetan nuns at the present day never bear that name, but are styled variously *tsunmo, ani*, or *jomo*. Women are believed to be eligible to become both Bodhisattwas and Buddhas, and some are said to have become so already.

for spaces of 12 years; food being passed to him through a hole in the ground. Such men profess to acquire miraculous powers by dint of lonely contemplation with breath held in.

MODERN SECTS IN TIBET.

When we speak of Buddhism as representing the general religion of the country, we must remember that here this Faith has no one model form universally observed. There is not a really unified set of beliefs; for Buddhism is full of schismatic schools and dissents. In fact, there are eighteen different sects or "schools" existing; and some of these are bitterly opposed the one to the other.[1] But one of the eighteen is singled out as the State Church of Buddhism in Tibet.

Primarily the sects are divided into two main classes—the SAR-MA, *i.e.*, the Reformed, and the NYING-MA, the Old or Unreformed, classes. There are only three sects or branches of the Sarma division, and one of these Reformed branches is considered the national and established form of religion.

This orthodox branch of the Faith is that which was framed and embodied into a distinctive school of thought by the Reformer, Tsong-khapa, towards the close of the 14th century. The voluminous writings of this hero have yet to be examined by the learned.[2] However, the school he set up is known to be founded on the Madhyamika system, an offshoot of the *T'eg-pa Chhenpo* or "Greater Vehicle." It is not improbable that much of the new ritual introduced by him into the temples was an adaptation of that of the Nestorian Christians, who previously, as well as in the age of Tsongkhapa, sent, as we have mentioned, agents of the Higher Faith as far into Central Asia as the borders of China, and even gave to the Mongol Tartars the variety of the Syriac alphabet used by the latter in Buddhist writings to the present day. So powerful and popular a teacher was the worthy Tsongkhapa that he ranks as a deity now; whilst his followers are not only the strongest numerically, but also bear rank in Tibet as the only orthodox sect. The designation they take is that of the GE-LUK-PA or Gedenpa school; and they are distinguished everywhere by their general propriety of conduct, as well as by the peculiarity of their robes which ought to be mustard yellow in colour but which are usually red, the church hat alone being yellow.

1 These 18 do not in any way correspond with the 18 schools of traditional Buddhism. Probably the assertion of modern Tibetan writers that there are 18 sects in Tibet is only made in order to pretend a correspondence of this sort. We believe, however, nearly 18 sects can be enumerated in Tibet.

2 The *Lam-rim Chhenmo* of Tsong-khapon has, it seems, been examined by Sarat Chandra Das, who gives many references to it in his recently-issued Dictionary.

14

All the other sects, and even the followers of the Bon cult (who profess direct antagonism to Buddhism), are tolerated more or less; the chief practical restriction upon them being the prohibition against settling in Lhása. In other parts of the country they possess both large convents and well-fitted temples. The NYING-MA sects have innumerable supporters; and their establishments may frequently be recognised by the broad blue and red stripes with which the outside walls of the buildings are painted. The Government thus enjoins executive officers on this subject:—" In doctrine and principles, the Gelukpa school being the purest, you should follow it. But although the Nyingma school has some alloy in it, yet, as it is useful in religious services for removing certain diseases and injuries, its followers should not be treated with harshness. So also with the Sakya-pa school which is of the same source with the Gelukpa. People should be freely allowed to observe their funeral obsequies, and their services for the protection of the living, according to old custom. But although it is unfair to treat unfavourably the adherents of differing sects, yet the Karmapa and Duk-pa schools having opposed with violence the orthodox faith, and being heretical and making many converts, it will be your duty to put them down whenever you have the power."

The religious orders of Sikkim belong to the Dzokchen school of the Nyingma division; while those of Bhutan are of the Duk-pa persuasion; and the famous monastery of Samding, on the peninsula in Lake Yamdok, is a Karmapa establishment. The Sakya-pa school has many ancient monasteries, the great Sakya Ling, 50 miles due north of Mount Everest, being the leading establishment; others of that school being the Gong-kar, Nalendra, Já-yai, and Kyisho Rawana monasteries. Mindolling is the chief Nyingma institution and the home of the more intricate and mystic ceremonies belonging to Buddhist sorcery.

Reserving a description of the inmates of monasteries, their various grades and occupations, until the next chapter, we proceed to a lengthy appendix. In effect, we mean now to select a few of the leading lamaic establishments in Tibet; and to set forth all details concerning each that we have been able to collect. From the archæological and geographical point of view such particulars will have a value of their own. Moreover, these great convents, being centres of the political as well as of the religious life of the country, will assuredly assume an important part in any internal operations which may take our forces in the near future into Tibet. The value of such information is consequently proportioned to its exactness. The first three of the following are so pre-eminent that in public documents they are generally mentioned in abbreviated form thus: དགའ་འབྲས་གསེར་ " *Gá-Dai-Ser.*"

GALDEN OR GANDEN LING.

(དགའ་ལྡན་རྣམ་པར་རྒྱལ་བའི་གླིང་ "The Ling of Completely Victorious Joyfulness.") (Lat. 29° 38′ N. long. 91° 30′ E. *circa.*)

This famous monastery which is the headquarters of the Gelukpa sect—the established church of Buddhists in Tibet—stands enthroned upon the Wang-khor hill, about 25 miles E.N.-E. of Lhása, from which city it can be reached by proceeding along the banks of the eastern feeder of the Kyi Chhu or Lhása river.

It was founded, about 475 years ago, by the reformer Tsong-khapa, who raised the place to a high pitch of fame and filled the shrines with costly images. The chief object of veneration is the grand tomb of Tsong-khapa, which has been set up in the *tsuk-lá-khang* or principal worship-hall. It assumes the form of a lofty canopied mausoleum constructed of marble and malachite with a gilded roof. Inside this outer structure is to be observed a beautiful chhörten consisting of cube, hemisphere, and surmounting cone, all stated to be of the purest gold, though 5 feet in height. Within that golden casket, wrapped in embroidered clothing inscribed with sacred *dharani* syllables, are the embalmed remains of the great reformer himself, disposed in sitting attitude. No one is permitted ocularly to view the actual mummy of Tsong-khapa's body, save the reigning Panchhen Lama of Ṭashi-lhümpo who is believed to hold in his spirit the psychic essence of the saint and who must proceed once during lifetime to Galden for this purpose.

Other notable objects here are a magnificent representation of Jhampa, the Buddha to come, seated in European pose on a throne. Beside him stands erect a life-sized effigy of Tsong-khapa in the character of Jampal Nying-po, which is supposed to be his name in the Galden heavens. A rock-hewn cell is also shewn as Tsong-khapa's, containing a self-sprung image of the saint with impressions of hands and feet on the ground averred to be his. A very old statue of Shinje, the lord of death, with a circle of attendants, is greatly reverenced, as it is said to have been designed by the same hero. The floor of the large central nave of the worship-hall has been paved with brilliant enamelled tiles; whilst a side chapel holds yet another great image of the ubiquitous Tsong-khapa with other figures representing his chief disciples, Khá-ḍub Chhoi-je, Sherab Seng-ge, &c. In the library are to be seen the Lam-rim Chhenpo and other works of the founder of Galden in their original MS. form as written by the author, also his rosary, dorje, and other relics.

The Khempo of this monastery is an important personage in Tibet ranking third highest in the kingdom and above the Gye-ts'ab or Regent of Lhása. He differs from other heads of the larger Lings in that he is not a *ṭulku* or incarnate lama, being chosen by a conclave from among the most scholarly of the monks of Sera and Daipung, generally under Chinese auspices. So he is never a mere child as elsewhere is the case. The late Khempo of Galden, Khuro Gyalgo, held the office of Regent in addition.

The number of inmates here is reckoned at 3,300. There are two *Tats'ang* or schools of philosophy, the Shar-tse and Jang-tse.

SERA LING.

(གསེར་ར་ཐུགས་ཆེ་གླིང་ "The Ling of the Mighty Heart enclosed in Gold.") (Lat. 29° 40′ 50″ N. long. 91° 5′ 30″ E. Alt. 11,800 feet.)

One of the three largest Gelukpa foundations in the province of Ui and established in 1417 by Jam-chhen Chhoi-je. It is placed 2 miles due north of Lhása and is backed by some black barren hills, the nearest of which is Do-de-p'u, famous for its extensive deposits of silver; and indeed the monastery buildings run up the skirts of this hill.

Only two of the Survey agents seem to have penetrated the precincts of Sera.[1] One was "K. P." who went there in 1866. This was Nain Singh, whose report merely refers to the idols in the temples and comprises one terse sentence: "The images here differ in size and hideousness, some having horns; but the lower parts of the figures are generally those of men."

Father Huc gives a fuller description :—" The temples and houses of Sera stand on a slope of the mountain-spur, planted with hollies and cypresses. At a distance these buildings, ranged in the form of an amphitheatre, one above the other, and standing out upon the green base of the hill, present an attractive and picturesque sight. Here and there, in the breaks of the mountain above this religious city, you see a great number of cells inhabited by contemplative lamas, which you can reach only with difficulty. The monastery of Sera is remarkable for three large temples of several storeys in height, all the rooms of which are gilded throughout. Hence the name; from *ser*, the Thibetan for "gold." In the chief of these three temples is preserved the famous *tortché* which, having flown through the air from India, is the model from which all others, large or portable, are copied. The *tortché* of Sera

[1] The London *Morning Post* lately (September 15th, 1903) published a highly romantic description by a Japanese priest of a journey to Lhása and his residence at "The University of Sera," which he erroneously places "5 miles S.W. of Lhása."

is the object of great veneration; and is sometimes carried in procession in Lhása to receive the adoration of the people."

Besides the standard and original *dorje* of gold here mentioned by Huc, Sera holds likewise the model *p'urbu* or three-edged dagger of exorcists, which was procured by one Dub-t'op Dá-chha from the floor of his cave of meditation. In the Ts'okchhen hall is a huge image of the Blessed Chenraisi with eleven heads piled on the neck in curious fashion.

The gelongs and other inmates of Sera form an important community; but Huc's estimate of their number at 15,000 is an exaggeration. Our latest informants with one consent put the number in the monastery at from 5,000 to 5,500. However, this is a multitude large enough to render the monks of Sera a formidable body as a faction. A notorious Regent during the Dalai Lama's minority in 1843 raised with their assistance an insurrection against the ancient constitution of Tibet, having granted them certain privileges to induce them to join him. Again in 1899-1890 the Tengyai-ling lama got their aid in his plot to dethrone the present Dalai Lama. The ringleader was only imprisoned but eventually died January 1901.

There are three Tá-ts'ang for Tantrik studies, namely, the Má, the Ngakpa, and the Je-pa, Tá-ts'ang; and in the worship-hall of the latter college is a large image of one Pema Sang-takpo which is reported to have the power of performing miracles. The *Ser-kyem* sorcerers attached to Ramochhe Temple at Lhása are trained in this Ta-ts'ang.

DAIPUNG CHHOIDE.

(དཔལ་ལྡན་འབྲས་སྤུངས་ "The Glorious Heap of Rice.") (Lat. 29° 40′ N., long. 91° 0′ 30″ E. Altitude 12,050 feet.)

This is the largest-sized monastery in Tibet as well as the most populous in the number of its denizens which sometimes exceed 7,000.[1] It is situated high up on a hill-side about one mile to the north of the main western roadway into Lhása from which city it is distant 3 to 4 miles.

At the foot of the monastic buildings there stretches southwards and eastwards down to the Lhása roadway a sort of park well-planted with small trees—walnuts, maple, and willows, some of great age. This is known as the *damra* or "grove" of Daipung; and in a

1 The Capuchin missionary at Lhása, Cassiano Beligatti, in his Journal lately printed in the *Rivista Geografica Italiana* of Florence mentions the number of inmates in his time (1741) as being only 1400. He adds that the monastery is under 4 lama-heads and 10 assistant lamas or "vicars" as he characteristically terms them.

paddock of it near the main road is always kept a fine specimen of the Tibetan *Shau-ru-chu* stag (Cervus Thoroldi), which species is believed to have a propitiatory influence over the *Shibdag* or god of the soil. On the eastern flank of the grove are the temple and premises belonging to the Naichhung Chhoikyong, the chief oracle of Lhása; on the western flank and just beneath the western buildings of Daipung is seated the populous village of Daru, the *de-shol* or "sadder bazaar" of the monastery.

The whole range of edifices presents a striking appearance from a little distance, the mass of them lying together on a terrace but with out-lying portions lodged on various ledges of the hill and in some places overhung by higher porches of rock. In the main part of the buildings rises up a sort of citadel known as the Galdan P'odang crowned with a fantastic *gye-pi* or square concave-sided dome. This head-piece is seen to be decorated on the sides with vividly-painted deities and *lu*.

Inside the walls in the great central worship hall are ranged an unusually larger collection of images, the chief being a monster figure of Jhampa, the Buddha to come, and one of Chenraisi. There were formerly seven *ta-ts'ang* or colleges in Daipung, but these have been reduced to four, styled respectively Gomang, De-yang, Loksal, and Ngakpa, the last-named being devoted to the study of Tsan-nyid philosophy, *i.e.*, Tantrik ceremonial and miracles. The heads of these are each styled Khempo. Although Urgyen Gyá-ts'o and others of our native explorers have inspected the interior of this vast establishment they allude to few details. One explorer, G-m-n., seems to have been chiefly impressed with the enormous copper cauldrons in which on festival days the buttered tea, soup, and *chhang* are prepared for the monks. These cauldrons measure 20 feet across and are 6 feet in depth, being built up with massive masonry and having long planks laid over them for the cooks to walk on, the more readily to stir up the contents and ladle them out.

Mongol students resort in large numbers to Prai-bung, as they call it, with a view to qualifying there for full ordination; and indeed this huge and powerful monastery is held in high repute throughout Central and Northern Asia. However, the gelong of Daipung are in ill-odour in and around Lhása, where they are continually engaging in uproars and, outside the city, indulging in amateur highway robbery.

Daipung was so called after a famous vihara of Indian fable which bore the name of Sri Dhanya Kataka, the Sanskrit rendering of "Glorious Heap of Rice." It was founded in 1414 A.D. by Jam-yang Chhoi-je; but did not attain to any status until 1530 when Gedun Gyá-ts'o was transferred hither from Tashi-lhümpo where he had been

Panchhen Lama. He it was that erected the central palace of Galdan P'odang wherein the Grand Lamas always dwelt up to the period when the fifth of the dynasty having built Potala removed there in 1645. Huc avers that the Dalai Lama still repairs to Daipung once a year in order to expound to the inmates certain portions of the sacred writings, residing when there in the old palace of the place.

It may be of interest to mention that the Mongol lama so prominent in the secret negotiations with the Russian Government in the years 1900-01, and whose name was given as *Dorjieff*, is the Tsan-nyid or Ngag-pa professor here. His real name is Ngag-wang Dorje Rampa.

THE FOUR LINGS OF LHASA.

This quartette of monastic establishments belonging to the metropolis have a special standing in that the head of each is considered to have a claim in the ordinary course to be elected to the office of Gyalts'ab or Gyalpo, that is to act as Regent of the kingdom during the minority of the Dalai Lama and in any case to rank next to that sacred personage. However, the choice once or twice in recent times seems to have fallen outside the chief lamas of the four Lhasa Lings, the last Gyalpo having been the head of Radeng monastery; while at present the office is said to be in abeyance owing to the unusual activity of the now reigning Dalai Lama who will not brook a so-called "king" in his own sovereignty.

Of the four monasteries in question, two, namely, Tengyai Ling (བསྟན་རྒྱས་གླིང་) and Ts'omo Ling (vulgarly Chhomo Ling), are situated in the town itself; the other two, Kundu Ling and Ts'e-chhog Ling, stand outside the bounds, the former near the western entrance, the latter across the Kyi Chhu to the south of the river. All are antique in appearance and have not accommodation for more than 250 inmates apiece. Nevertheless they are handsomely endowed with lands and feudal tenants in different parts of Tibet, the major portion by far of each endowment belonging to the Incarnate Lama at the head of each establishment. The head of Tengyai Ling is the richest, having considerable estates in Kongpo district: it was the just-lately deceased holder of this office who for many years got up villanous conspiracies against the present Dalai Lama. He was eventually detected and for punishment imprisoned for a period in a small brick hut with only an opening in the roof. This incarceration is said to have induced his death which took place in January 1901. The head of Tengyai Ling is supposed to be always a re-incarnation of Sron-tsan Gampo's famous minister Gar

(སྨྲིན་པོ་མཁར) ; the head of Ts'omo Ling personates Ts'atur Nomankhan, a Mongol saint; and he of Kundu Ling the "Tats'ag Lama."

TASHILHUMPO MONASTERY.

(བཀྲ་ཤིས་ལྷུན་པོ "the Mound of Good Fortune.") (Lat. 29° 15′ 40″ N., long. 88° 54′ 40″ E. Alt. averaging 11,850 feet.)

This celebrated establishment, long known to European geographers as "Teeshoo Loumbo," is the best-conducted monastery in Tibet, and is also the seat of Government of the semi-autonomous Province of Tsang. It has been built partly at the foot, and partly on the lower declivities of a rocky hill named Dolma-i Ri—the hill of the goddess Dolma. The walls surrounding the extensive series of buildings are continued from the sloping ground at the base up to the southern face of the hill, meeting in apsidal form about one-third of the way up. From the base the land shelves easily down eastwards to the left bank of the River Nyange at a point about four miles from the confluence of that stream with the Yeru Tsang-po. On the opposite bank of the Nyang rise lofty cliffs, so closely adjacent as to seem to overshadow the monastery, though the river flows between, and is here 120 feet in width. Across the river has been thrown a substantial timber bridge on four stone piers. Tashilhümpo may therefore be described as situated at the southern base of a hill which protects it from the bitter north winds, and as shut in to the east and north-east by the lofty cliffs towering up across the river, which serve to shield it from the east winds also. On the top of Dolmai-Ki is a *lhá-khá*, or stone cairn, where banners are always fluttering, and where, on high festivals, huge bonfires are set ablaze. The lay capital of the province, Shigatse, lies on the upper ridges to the N.-E. of this hill, hardly a mile from this, the ecclesiastical capital. Shigatse, large town though it is, is deemed but an appurtenance to the great monastery, and is technically the *de-shol* or sudder bazaar of Tashilhümpo.

The lofty circuit walls, enclosing the town-like collection of buildings composing the monastery, are pierced by five gateways. Over the eastern gate has been placed, in large carved letters, a prohibition against smoking within the monastic precincts. The western gateway seems to be regarded as the main entrance. So, entering the monastic premises there, you find yourself in a sort of town with lanes lined by lofty houses, open squares and temples. In the centre of the place is the grand court-yard of the Tsug-lag-khang of Tashi-lhümpo. This open space, which is used by the monks for religious dances and other out-door ceremonies, is oblong in form and 900 feet long by 150 broad. Round this space are reared the halls of the Tsug-lag-khang, four storeys in height, provided with upper-floor balconies. North of these buildings are set up in a line the huge tombs of deceased Panchhen Lamas. The body of each is embalmed and placed within a gold-plated pyramid raised on a tall marble table; and this structure stands within a stone mausoleum, high and decorated with gilt ganjira and small cylinder-shaped finials made of black felt. One of these tombs is much bigger than the rest. It is that of the Panchhen Erteni who died in 1779.

There are four conventual colleges attached to Tashi-lhümpo, all of which receive students from every part of Tibet, who are instructed in Tantrik ritual and learn large portions of the Gyut division of the Kangyur and Tengyur. The names of these colleges are Shar-tse Tá-ts'ang, Ngag-pa Ta-ts'ang, T'oi-sam Ling and Kyil-khang Ta-ts'ang. Each of these institutions has an abbot or Khempo, who is the *tul-wa* or avatár of some by-gone saint; and the four abbots have much to do with the discovery of the infant successor to a deceased Panchhen or head of the monastery From these abbots also, one is selected to act as the prime minister or chief ecclesiastical adviser in the Government of Tsang. The most imposing building of the monastery is the temple and hall of the Ngag-pa Ta-ts'ang, known as the "Ngag-khang," which is decidedly the chief college, and, indeed, is the principal home of occult ritual and mystic learning in Tibet. Another college, the T'oi-sam Ling, stands at the extreme northern apex of the walls, some way up the slope of Dolmai Ri.

Hard-by the last-named premises is to be observed a lofty building of rubble-stone, reared to the amazing height of nine storeys. This edifice, which forms a very remarkable object on the hill-side, is styled Kiku Tamsa, and is used as a store-house for the shoals of dried carcases of sheep, goats, and yak, which are kept in stock for the feeding of the inmates of the monastery. A wide walled yard fronts the Kiku Tamsa, and this space is thronged by a motley crowd when (as is the custom in June and November) the gigantic pictures of Buddhist deities are brought out and hung high up on great sheets outside the walls of the tall building. Turner, who visited Tashi-lhümpo 100 years ago, noticed and made a drawing of Kiku Tamsa which, however, he styles "Kuga-pœa."

The number of *ge-long* and *ge-nyen* generally in residence at Tashi-lhümpo is said to be 3,800 Outside the walls have been erected certain club and lodging halls, where monks and pilgrims from different parts of the country reside during their stay here, each province having its own club-house, and the residents forming themselves into a guild or *khamts'an.* Thus, outside the eastern walls, are the Lhopa Kham-ts'an, the Dong-tse Kham-ts'an, &c.

The head of the whole monastic establishment is the PANCHHEN RIMPOCHHE, who is likewise titular King of the Province of Tsang. Formerly his rule was independent of all control from Lhása. During the last and the early part of the present century all British negotiations with Tibet were carried on with the ruler of Tsang. Now, though taxes are levied in, and pass-ports issued in, the name of the Panchhen Lama, yet in military and imperial affairs the authorities at Lhása are paramount. Lately, however, the inhabitants of Tsang have several times shown themselves impatient not merely of Tibetan, but also of Chinese domination; and any day, under an ambitious Panchhen, the ancient autonomy of Tsang may be re-asserted.

The present ruler of Tsang and head of Tashi-lhümpo during childhood resided with his parents and a retinue of 300 ge-longs at a monastery on the Bhutanese frontier. Towards the close of 1889 he was installed with considerable pomp at Tashi-lhümpo, and has already begun to hold his Court and Council at La-brang Gyalts'an T'onpo, the consistory-hall of the monastery. He resides now in his private monastic palace, styled Kün-khyab Ling, just without the eastern walls of Tashi-lhümpo. His parents are comfortably housed in a palace immersed in a plantation of trees, dignified with the name of "Grove," and called Kiki Naga, not half-a-mile distant from the domicile of their holy son from whom they are now parted. The Panchhen Lamas do not seem to have been subjected to the forced mortality which has beset their brothers of Lhása during the present century. In 1882 the late Panchhen, named Paldan Chhos-kyi Gragspa, died of small-pox, aged 28. He was the immediate successor of the little Lama whom Turner saw in 1789, an infant prodigy of 18 months, who proved an able governor. The present head of the monastery is named Geleg Namgyal and has now (1904) reached his 22nd year of age.

Each successive Panchhen Rimpochhe is held to be an incarnation of the fourth Dhyani Buddha Nang-wa T'á-Yai (Sansk. *Amitabha*) otherwise called Yo-pok-me; and includes therewith the psychic essence of Gedundub, the sage who, in 1446, founded Tashi-lhümpo. Each fresh incarnation is traced to some unknown infant, as in the case of the Dalai Lamas of Lhása; but the Panchhen is by no means so great a sanctity as is his brother of Lhása.

THO-LING GOMPA.

(མཐོ་ལྡིང་གསེར་གྱི་ལྷ་ཁང་ "The Golden Temple Soaring on High.")

(Lat. 31° 28′ 30″ N., long. 79° 52′ E. Altitude 12,200 feet above sea.)

This, which is one of the oldest and most celebrated of the monastic establishments of Tibet, is situated in Ngari Khorsum in the *khor* or circle of Gu-ge. It stands on a slight eminence on the left bank of the River Sutlej, about 88 miles above Shipkyi where that river enters British territory.

The buildings of T'o-ling—or Totling Math as it is styled by the hillmen who visit it on pilgrimage or trade from the Himalayas—are very ancient and very dilapidated and have been patched up from time to time in a manner very discreditable to the Tibetan Government, considering the historical fame of the place. The whole is enclosed by a wall about 300 yards in circumference which pilgrims have to make circuit of crawling on hands and knees.

At present this once popular institution is peopled by not more than 60 inmates; but it is still ruled by a Khempo who is also a Skushok or incarnate lama, being deemed a re-embodiment of one Rinchhen Zangpo a celebrated translator of Sanskrit treatises of the eleventh century, A.D. The Khempo of T'o-ling has jurisdiction over 25 subordinate gompas.

The monastery was founded 1025, A.D., by a King of Ngari known to Tibetan history as Lhá Lama Ye-shes-od. He was a great enthusiast in Buddhist literature, and it was on his invitation that the eminent Bengal pandit Atisha, or P'ul Jung as he is called, came on a mission to Tibet. Atisha, however, did not arrive until Lhá Lama was dead; but took up his residence with his successor Lhá-Tsunpa who seems to have had a palace at T'o-ling. It was here in T'o-ling Gompa that Atisha resided some years (*circa* 1045, A.D.) and composed there several of his best known writings, including the Bodhi Patha Pradipa. Subsequently numerous authors dwelt here; and many treatises in the Tengyur and Ká-gyur bear the superscription "at T'o-ling Lhakhang."

SAKYA LING (Sá-skya Gling). "The Yellow Earth Ling," (Lat. 28° 53′ N., long. 86° 54′ E.), a monastery of the semi-heretical Sa-kya school of Buddhists—their headquarters now and for the past eight centuries—and an establishment which has played an important part in the history of Tibet. Eight of the abbots, known as the Sa-kya hierarchs, were *de facto* kings of Tibet, their dynasty continuing from 1270 to 1340 A.D. Kungá Nyingpo, born 1090 A.D., and Sa-kya Pandita, born 1180, were famous lamas occupying the Sa-kya chair. The foundation of the monastery and its future fame are related to have been foretold by the Indian sage, Atisha, he, on his way into Tibet, having passed a rock, on the present site of the monastery, on which he saw the Buddhist symbol *Om* inscribed in *Rangjung* or "self-sprung" characters. Afterwards this establishment became the seat of much learning.

Sakya Monastery stands some 50 miles N.N.-E. of Mount Everest.

It contains a large temple and a spacious assembly-hall known as "the White Hall of Worship." It is still famous for its magnificent library, containing numerous unique treasures of Sanskrit and Tibetan literature unobtainable elsewhere. Some of these have enormous pages embossed throughout in letters of gold and silver. The monastery, though visited in 1872 by our exploring Pandit No. 9, and in 1882 by Babu Sarat Chandra Dás, remains undescribed at present. Its inmates do not dress in dull-red, but in bright deep-red robes. The Sakya Lama is still held to be an incarnation of the Dhyani Bodhisattwa Jamyang (Sansk: *Manjus'ri*), and to carry *las* or *karma* derivable from Sa-kya Pandita.

SAM-YE LING (Bsam-yas Mi-agyur Lhun-gyis Grub-pai Tsug-lag-khang: "The Academy where unchanging Wisdom from above forms itself into a mass.") (Lat. 29° 20′ N., long. 91° 26′ E.) (Alt. 11,430 feet). Notable as being the most ancient of all monasteries existing at the present day in Tibet, and as the first Vihara or academical school ever founded in this land. It was erected, as we read in native Tibetan accounts, by King T'i-srong Deu-tsan, *circa* 770 A.D., at the instigation of Padma Jungne and Santa Rakshita. These Indian sages drew up plans for Sam-ye, after the model of the Vihara of Uddandapuri at Magadha. Part of the original edifice remains in perfect preservation. The monastery is well situated on a gentle incline, 35 miles from Lhása, and some two miles from the north bank of the Yaru Tsangpo. The approaches to the place are deep in sand, which lies around in flats and hillocks, clothed with wiry herbage. A lofty circular wall, 1,700 yards in circumference, surrounds the place, with gates facing to the four cardinal points. Along the top of this wall there have been erected a large number of small chhortens and votive piles, built of burnt yellow bricks. The exploring pandit, Nain Singh, counted 1,030 of these; and they seem to be covered with ancient inscriptions in old Lan-ts'a characters, similar to those found near Gaya in India. In the centre of the enclosure stands the large *Tsuk-la-khang*, with radiating cloisters, leading to four chapels, facing, at equal distances, the four sides of the larger temple. The explorer found "the idols and images contained in these temples of pure gold, richly ornamented with valuable cloths and jewels. The candlesticks and vessels are nearly all made of gold and silver." Another survey agent mentions a famous image of Shakyamuni in copper and gold 10 feet high. Round the temple walls are Chinese and Lan-ts'a inscriptions in enormous characters.

Samyé is used by the Tibetan Government as a bank, where reserve treasure in bullion is stored. Considerable sums are said to be kept there.

SAM-DING MONASTERY (Bsam-lding Chhoide: "The Island of Thought College.") (Lat. 28° 57′ 15″ N., long. 90° 28′ E.) (Alt. 14,512 feet). An important establishment, noteworthy as a monastery of monks presided over by a female abbot. In adjacent buildings is a community of nuns, ruled by the same lady. This august woman is known throughout Tibet as Dorje P'akmo, or "the Diamond Sow;" the abbesses of Samding being held to be successive appearances in mortal form of the Tibetan goddess, Dorje P'akmo (*Rdo-rje P'ag-mo*). In 1889 the late incarnation of this goddess here was described as being 33 years' old; and as being a clever and capable woman, with some claim to good looks, and of noble birth.[1] She bore the name of Ngag Dbang Rin-chhen Kun-bzangmo Dbang-mo (pronounced Ngak Wang Rinchhen Künsangmo Wang mo, and signifying "The most Precious Power of Speech, the Female Energy of all good"). She was a member of the Phala family and sister-in law of one of the Privy Councillors or *kalons* of Lhása. Under this lady, the reputation which Samding has long enjoyed for the good morals of both monks and nuns was always well maintained, the worthy Diamond Sow enforcing a very rigorous discipline.[2] However, this incarnation seems to have died in the year 1898; and in 1899 a baby girl one year old was installed as lady abbess and incarnation of the goddess. The present Dorje P'akmo is now therefore only 6 years old. Among other rules, the inmates are forbidden to lend out money or other valuables on interest to the rural folk, usurious dealings being commonly resorted to by the monastic orders. Samding is a Karmapa establishment of the Namgyal school, and consequently unorthodox in doctrine; being much akin in its ritual and literature to the unreformed Buddhism of the Nyingma sect. The monastery was founded by one Je-tsun T'inle

1 When the party of Capuchin friars, whose journey to Lhása in 1740 is described by Cassiano Beligatti, reached Yamdok lake, they found the lady-abbess had gone on a visit to Lhása where they subsequently had an interview with her. From the description of her appearance it would seem that the incarnation of the goddess of that date was anything but prepossessing in appearance. Beligatti writes: "In the present Turchepamò nature herself seems to have been forced to produce a body equally strange as is the chimerical spirit of Changchub which has had to take shape in this way. This female lama, who had reached at the time of our arrival the age of about 30 years, is a woman less than 4 feet high, with a very huge head, a broad face, eyes and mouth disproportionately large. She has the neck sunk in her shoulders, her spine raised into a big hump, and the hands somewhat contracted—a monstrous mass of limbs in perfection!" (*Relazione inedita di un Viaggio al Tibet per Alberto Magnaghi*, pp. 64, 65.)

2 In Beligatti's time we fear the lady-abbess herself was only a poor example of morality; as he relates how that, a few years previous to his interview, she had given birth to an infant—"a little lamessina" as he quaintly puts it—thereby causing a scandal which her courtiers had in vain endeavoured to prevent.

Ts'omo, a follower of the philosophy of Po-dong P'yog Legs Nam-gyal, whose writings, to the amazing extent of 118 volumes, are treasured up in the monastic library.

Yamdok Lake is remarkable for the grotesque shaped semi-island anchored to the main shore by two necks of land. Samding is itself placed on the main shore at the juncture of the northern neck. Being built on a conical hill, it appears to be guarding the sacred island from intrusion. The monastery stands like a fortress on the summit of the barren hill, some 300 feet above the level of the surrounding country. Huge flags of stone are piled in ascending steps up this hill, and a long low wall mounts beside them like a balustrade. At the top of the steps, a narrow pathway conducts to the foot of the monastery, which is circled by a high wall. Samding Chhoide is finely placed. To the N.-E. it fronts the dark and precipitous mountain spurs which radiate from the lofty central peak of the islands. To the S.-E. it looks over the land towards the illimitable waters of the weird and mighty Yamdok herself. To the S. it frowns down on the Dumo Ts'o, the inner lake betwixt the connecting necks of land above-mentioned, into which are cast the bodies of the defunct nuns and monks as food for fishes.

On entering the gates of the monastery, you find yourself in an extensive courtyard, flanked on three sides by the conventual buildings. Part of the fourth side of the parallelogram is occupied by a kind of grand-stand supported on pilasters of wood. Ladders with broad steps, cased in brass, give admission to the first floor of the main building. Here, in a long room, are ranged the tombs of celebrities connected in past times with Samding, including that of the founder, T'inle Ts'omo. The latter tomb is a richly ornamented piece of workmanship, plated with gold and studded with jewels. At the base, on a stone slab is marked the reputed foot-print of the saint. In a private strongly-barred chamber, hard-by, to which no one may be admitted, are laid the dried mortal remains of all the former incarnations of Dorje P'akmo. Here, in this melancholy apartment, will be one day placed the body of the present lady-abbess, after undergoing some embalming process. To the grim charnel-house, it is considered the imperative duty of each incarnate abbess to repair once, while living, to gaze her fill on her predecessors, and to make formal obeisance to their mouldering forms. She *must* enter once, but only once, during her lifetime.

Another hall in this monastery is the *du-khang*, on the walls of which are frescoes illustrative of the career of the original Dorje P'akmo. There, also, have been put up inscriptions recording how the goddess miraculously defended Samding, when, in the year 1716, it was beset by a Mongol warrior, one Jung Gar. Sarat Chandra Das relates the circumstances somewhat thus: When the Mongol arrived in the vicinity of Yamdok, hearing that the lady abbess had a pig's head as an excrescence behind her ear, he mocked at her in public, sending word to her to come to him that he might see the pig's head for himself. Dorje P'akmo returned no angry reply, only beseeching him to abandon his designs on the monastery. Burning with wrath, the warrior invaded the place and destroyed the walls: but entering, he found the interior utterly deserted. He only observed eighty pigs and eighty sows grunting in the *du-khang* under the lead of a bigger sow. He was startled by this singular frustration of his project; for he could hardly plunder a place guarded only by hogs. When it was evident that the Mongol was bent no longer on rapine, the pigs and sows were suddenly transformed into venerable-looking monks and nuns, headed by the most reverend Dorje P'akmo! As a consequence, Jung Gar, instead of plundering, enriched the place with costly presents.

A certain amount of association is permitted between the male and female inmates of this convent, who together number less than 200. Dorje P'akmo retains one side of the monastic premises as her private residence. It is asserted by the inmates that the good woman never suffers herself to sleep in a reclining attitude. During the day she may doze in a chair; during the night she must sit, hour after hour, wrapt in profound meditation. Occasionally this lady makes a royal progress to Lhása, where she is received with the deepest veneration.[1] Up in Northern Tibet is another sanctuary dedicated to Dorje P'akmo. This convent also stands on an islet situated off the west shore of the great lake, 70 miles N.-W. of Lhása, the Nam Ts'o Chhyidmo, and is much akin to Samding, comprising a few monks and nuns under an abbess. At Markula, in Lahul, is a third shrine of the goddess.

With Samding our descriptions may be brought to a close. Many

[1] Georgi, writing in 1762, mentions this monastery and its lady-abbess thus:—"In Australi eorum latere Monasterium et Sedes est Magnæ Renatæ Lhamissæ *Turcepamò.* Eam Indi quoque Nekpallenses, tanquam ipsissimam Deam Bavani venerantur et colunt. Tibetani vero *Ciangciubium,* hoc est, Spiritum quendam sanctum atque divinum in hac deformi fæmina haud aliter quam in Supremo Lhama, renatum putant. Nec domo, nec lacu egreditur, neque vero iter facit unquam in Urbem Lhassa nisi pompa præeat; totaque via thuribula duo semper insensa atque fumantia præferentur. Tum venit Dea sub umbella advecta throno; illius lateri adhæret Asceta omnium senior tanquem spiritualis vitæ Rector et Institutor. Sequitur postremo ordo reliquus Religiosorum hominum ferme triginta, qui comitatum et aulam componunt. Ubi cohors Lhassam pervenerit, Divam adeunt veneraturi cum Trabæ ipsi, tum Laici præsertim, qui ter humi prostrati eam adorant, cumulantque muneribus. At illa nescio quod sigilli genus bonis adoratoribus osculandum præbet, eosque divinitatis suæ participes facit. Eadem porro Lhamissa est, quæ regit Cænobia omnia tum Virorum tum Fæminarum in ejus lacus insulis collocata." *Alphabetum Tibetanum:* p. 451.

other establishments might yet be referred to—KUMBUM, with its 4,000 inmates, near Sining on the Chinese border, and RADENG, to the N. E. of Lhása. Then, too, Gyang-tse Chhoide and Dong-tse Chhoide on the River Nyang; Sam-tanzing, in Upper Tsang; and Hemis and Hanlé in Western Tibet, where several of the old classical treatises were written 800 years ago, and still of fame in our own days. Again, in the far east, RIWOCHHE on the Ngul Chhu, governed by two incarnate abbots jointly; and the grim great CHHAB-DO or CHHAMDO GOMPA, a famous printing establishment, with 2,000 monks. All of these deserve more than mere mention. In conclusion, let us add that the total number of monasteries in Tibet is computed to exceed 3,100!

CHAPTER VIII.

INMATES OF MONASTERIES; THEIR GRADES, DISCIPLINE AND OCCUPATION.

The general appellation of all inmates of monasteries in Tibet is གྲྭ་པ་ or colloquially *trapa*. Various attempts have been made to estimate the proportion which the number of *trapa* or monastic personages in Tibet bear to the whole population of the country. As a fact such comparative reckoning would not hold good throughout the kingdom, as the tendency to adopt the calling as well as the hereditary custom of the district varies in different regions. In the agricultural parts where are many settled villages and farm-houses, every household may be said to contribute one member to the lamaic fraternity; but in pastoral tracts this custom is not so uniform. In the latter class of life, as a rule, those families only in which the parents have more than three sons follow the practice of devoting the number beyond the three to monasticism. However, most children left orphans, their parents dying before they have arrived at man's estate, are sent into the monastery, and nearly all illegitimate offspring.

In Khams and Amdo, the eastern and north-eastern provinces, the predilection for the religious life is often a passion. The monasteries there are huge, powerful, and popular; and every town is crowded with monks who wander about in idle vagabond groups. So, there, the proportion of full gelong and neophytes—the latter by far the larger body—is great as compared with other parts of Tibet. On the whole, it would not be wide of the truth to estimate one-fourth of the male population of Tibet as accreditable to the monkish section of the people. But in adjusting this proportion we would reckon in our estimate the considerable body of Nepalese and Chinese residing in the country, and of whom we may remark they rarely form any items of this one-fourth part that comprises ecclesiastics.

Now, let it be supposed that a *miser* or agricultural house-holder determines to make one of his three or four boys a *trapa* or Buddhist monk; and if he have four or even only three sons such is pretty sure to be his resolve. Moreover, we may remark that it is the eldest husband of the mother of the child, and not his younger brother or brothers who are co-husbands with him, who makes the decision in such matters. Well, suppose the determination come to; the lad is usually entered in some monastery at the age of nine to twelve. In many districts the house-holder will have some family connection with a particular establishment and probably the boy's uncle will be a member there. In that case he is sent to his uncle who takes him in hand as a sort of pupil, generally taking care to make use of him in a hundred ways in the domestic economies of his abode. Should there be no relative in any community of the neighbourhood, the lad is attached to some old monk who teaches him and employs him in his room or rooms. It is considered an advantage to despatch the little fellow to a distant, though not too distant, locality, in order that his training may not be frequently interrupted by visits from his parents and friends. In the jurisdiction of the Táshi-lhümpo monastery, indeed, such arrangement is compulsory; and no community of the Gelukpa order in the province of Tsang will receive a boy or adult novice whose native home is within forty miles. In Spiti, on the contrary, the lad often divides his time between the monastery and his parents' dwelling. There, in Spiti, every family appears to have its particular *ṭá-shak* or set of two apartments or more in the gompa to which it is by heredity attached; and in this all the monastic members of the family—uncles, nephews, and brothers—may be found living together.

On being informally entered on the establishment in this way, the youth undergoes a certain initiation. He is taken before the head lama, a *Khempo* if there be one, who receives from him a small offering and a scarf sent by his parents. The lama then seizes him by the hair and cuts off a small tuft which he hangs up in a certain place in the *du-khang*, and which is styled in Central Tibet *ṭra-p'ü* and in Khams *shtra-p'ut* or "hair first-fruits." He is now named indeed a *trapa*, but is not permitted to sit with the other inmates at services in the worship-hall. In fact he is generally either running messages for his tutor or else in the *chhö-ṭa* or school of the monastery learning to read, write, and recite.

And here it will be convenient to mention that in all establishments of any size there is an apartment reserved for the instruction of lads who are intending to become monks. Boys and girls sometimes attend here from the village if their parents have signified their intention to make them afterwards ecclesiastics male and female. But in Tibet these monastic schools are never, as in Burmah, open to general attendance. The teacher is styled *Gergan*.

In great monasteries such as Táshi-lhümpo, there are many *Gergan* of considerable attainments who can bring their charges on rapidly in their studies. But in the smaller provincial places, there is one man so entitled, and he hears the novices recite their pages of the sacred books which it is their main duty to get by heart. Nevertheless, nominally, it is also the chief business of the monk to whom he has been apprenticed to coach the novice in such mnemonic feats. But in most religious houses save the larger ones, the master is nearly as ignorant as his pupil, and either the *Khempo* or the *Gergan* must take the lad in hand—which they will do if he exhibits promise and comes of a well-to-do family, but not otherwise.

The next stage to be attained above *trapa potsa* or boy-monk is the rank of GE-NYEN(དགེ་བསྙེན). To be granted this step does not involve any degree of scholarship. In most monasteries, and at least in those of the Red-cap or Nyingma sects, an ordinary Khempo can confer the grade. Attended by a circle of the inmates he hears the students recite a few pages of the sacred text; and great accuracy is not indispensable provided fluency and the orthodox cadence characterise the recitation. The novice is then shaved completely as to his head save for one tuft in the centre of the crown; after which he kneels and makes offering of one *ser-sho*, a golden coin worth perhaps 15*s*., to the Khempo, his Gergan standing by as if presenting him. He next receives from the head lama a new name which is his *chhoi-ming* or doctrinal name and which he generally uses as his personal appellation.

To proceed so far as this grade is deemed in the provinces considerable advance. Many remain simple *trapa* all their lives; some attain a further step when 25 or 30 years' old, and a few before they are 20. But for such as begin their course in the great monasteries of the Central Provinces, they appear for this upper degree about 3 years after admission. At Táshi-lhümpo the previous textual recitation is quite the "little-go" of the curriculum. The number of pages to be said by heart is fixed at 125; and should he fail or the Ge-koi of the place in whose presence he must recite them is in any way dissatisfied, the lad may be turned out of the monastery. His tutor, moreover, at once receives ten strokes from the Ge-koi's staff and pays a fine of four *bo* of butter, *i.e.*, 30 lbs. But at Táshi-lhümpo, it must be remembered, the tutor is always well-paid for his services by the parents of the youth, or if the novice be an adult (as frequently is the case) he himself has been bound to heavy tutorial fees which are made heavier still if he successfully passes the ordeal.[1]

[1] Particulars of the usage at Táshi-lhümpo will be found in an interesting paper by Sarat Chandra Dás in *Journal of the Buddhist Text Society*, part iv of 1893.

Should any further advance be desired, the neophyte may now become a Ge-ts'ul (དགེ་ཚུལ་). This is usually a mere matter of form requiring no examination. It seems to be a *sine quâ non*, however, that the admission be performed by an incarnate lama. For at this stage the man takes upon himself the vows of a religious life and of celibacy and he obtains, as it were, deacons' orders (if we may use that as a comparative term), being thereafter allowed to read the sacred writings in chorus with the other monks.

At prescribed periods the Kusho Tulku or incarnate lama, of which order there is at least one in every district of Tibet, makes a tour of visitation to different monasteries round; he himself being the head of one establishment. Then may the candidate or candidates be presented to him for the ordination rite. Generally it takes place at one centre and the opportunity is seized to turn the occasion into a feast or fair for the surrounding district. Each candidate appears in a sort of doublet without sleeves or large waistcoat known as *tö-gak* which ought to be yellow but is nearly always red and is richly embroidered; also a many-pleated petticoat red in colour known as a *shamt'ap;* and, over his left arm and shoulders, a yellow or red cloak so folded round his body as to leave his right arm and shoulder bare. Kneeling before the Tulku, the latter functionary, calling him by his old ordinary personal name, puts a question asking if he is ready to be deprived of the one remaining tuft of hair on his head. To this the candidate answers in the affirmative. Whereupon the Tulku snips off closely the large button of hair; and, sprinkling his head with water out of a silver teapot-like vessel, he pronounces his new name or *chhoi-ming* which he henceforth finally assumes.

However, the individual thus far advanced is not really a fully-fledged lama yet. One further stage has to be passed; and, though considerable numbers in remote districts and in the petty states of the Himalayas proceed no higher, without this additional step the monk falls short of reaping the chief spiritual and temporal advantages of his profession. If he look for promotion or to be considered of consequence in his circle or to be sent for in the affairs of life by the laity—he must yet be ordained a Ge-long (དགེ་སློང་)—the equivalent of the Bhikshu or "beggar of virtue" of Indian Buddhism.

Nevertheless, this is not a rank which with propriety can be won in the monasteries of districts remote from the Central Provinces. To have any title to respect the Ge-ts'ul must in some way contrive to leave his own part of the country and proceed for further study and ordination either to one of the three great suburban lamaseries of Lhása—Sera, Daipung, or Galden, or else to that puissant establishment the

Táshi-lhümpo Chhoide in Tsang. In many parts of Tibet, especially in Khams, Ngari Khorsum, and the Tsaidam principalities, the last-named monastery is much preferred. In order to reach these centres many aspirants undergo great privations and usually make the journey on foot. Should the man have relatives or parents in passable circumstances he appeals to them for aid and to this request they invariably accede. In fact it is held to be the bounden duty of the eldest brother, who has inherited the father's property probably before the father's death, to make provision for his clerical brother proceeding to Lhása. The *khang chhempa*, as the holder of the family property is called, may possibly be the uncle—rarely the father, who retires from his farmstead on his eldest son's marriage—and he then must pay the lama-nephew's outgoings.

Young men arriving at the great seats of learning from the provinces, though endowed with the rank of Ge-tsul before coming, are yet not admitted to the priesthood unless they can first recite the necessary 125 pages of the Sher Chhyin text. Had the previous grades been passed at the metropolitan Chhoide, the recitation belongs to the earliest stage, but the laxity of provincial houses is known and thus the new arrival is not permitted to evade the test. It is there indeed that many fail, and a large number are stated to be obliged after two or three years' residence to go home, as they arrived, only half-rank or *tsun-chhung* monks, not fully fledged gelongs. Other courses include the acquirement of the pronunciation of Sanskrit syllables in Lants'ha characters, termed *gar*, and the orthodox fashion of a lama's gait, styled *t'ik;* also *yang*, the mode of chanting when reading sacred books.

When qualified to be ordained, the chief Incarnate Lama of the monastery performs the ceremony—at Daipung the Dalai Lama or a deputy, at Tashi-lhümpo the Panchhen Lama or the head of the Ngagpa Ta-ts'ang, and so forth. The candidate first humbly presents to the Lama a small collection of herbs of medicinal virtue in his gelong's bowl (*hlung-ze*) and then squats before the reverend personage in the manner of a suppliant. He protests thrice the Buddhist creed to the effect that he takes refuge in Sang-gye, in Chhoi, and in Gendun, *i.e.*, in Buddha, the sacred Doctrine, and the Priesthood. Whereupon the Lama puts to him certain formal questions, inquiring whether he has murdered his father or mother, whether his parents have ever acted as smiths or butchers, whether he has ever thrown poisonous drugs in a river or big stones down hillsides thereby endangering life. Among these interrogations is the important one, said to have been sanctioned by the Buddha Gautama on the request of his father (who never forgot his son's flight from his own roof), as to whether or not his parents consent to his entering the priesthood. But in the case of the illegitimate offspring of nuns or monks this question is not put. The candidate then takes the vows of celibacy and to keep the disciplinary rules as set forth in the "Sutra of Gradual Emancipation." Then a silk-scarf as *sung-dü'* or "knot of preservation" having been tied round his neck and his offering of ten silver *tangka* accepted, the admission rite is complete.

Above the rank of ge-long there is indeed a higher grade open to aspirants; it is that of GE-SHE དགེ་བ་ཤེས་ *dge-bshes.* It is reserved, however, to such as acquire a real knowledge of Buddhist literature and philosophy.

DISCIPLINE AND MORALITY.

According to the code alleged to have been promulgated by Shakya T'ub-pa, but in reality conceived and compiled at a considerably later date than his era, every gelong is bound to observe the 253 laws or *t'im* (ཁྲིམས་) laid down in the above-mentioned Sutra. This Sutra is styled in Tibetan "So-sor Tarpai Do" and is none other than the famous *Pratimoksha Sutra* of Pali Buddhism. It comprises in Tibetan books some 30 leaves containing 700 *slokas,* and may be found in the 5th volume of the Dulwa section of the Kangyur. The succeeding pages of this volume do not belong properly to the Sutra itself but—together with the three following volumes, comprising with them 1,733 leaves of two sides each—are occupied with a vast series of explanations of the rules, illustrated by innumerable stories of monks and nuns who ventured to disregard them.

Among the 253 laws thus made binding on every gelong, the primary ones are against marriage, immorality, destruction of animal life, stealing and murder. Then follow rules as to general behaviour, manner of walking, material of garments, mode of eating and drinking and kinds of food permitted. Washing of clothes by boiling, the water of which is afterwards to be deemed sacred, is enjoined; and the scratching of the body with tiles, bricks, or fish-scales is specially forbidden! Garlic may not be used with food, and umbrellas are not to have ornamented handles.

We understand from inquiries that, in reality, little provision is made for the rules being carefully attended to; and no examination on the subject or any public confession, as ordered in the books, is now practised in the monasteries. Many gelong observe the minor ceremonial rules but a less number are particular as to such primary prohibitions as those against concubinage and theft.

However in the larger Gelukpa establishment a considerable maintenance of discipline prevails. During prescribed seasons regular attendance in the *du-khang* at readings is exacted; early rising occasionally required; all outward violation of by-laws severely punished; and the sumptuary regulations of Buddhism enforced. In such monasteries immorality cannot be openly indulged in; and even in the smaller Gelukpa institutions a scandal of this sort—though naturally by no means rare—is always made the subject of some punishment. Sometimes the offender is scourged; and expulsion is, in the graver cases, meted out. Any inferior Gelukpa nun found with child would be most certainly discharged from her order; besides receiving 100 stripes on her back and having to pay a fine equal to 120 rupees. A nun thus expelled is styled a *jolok*. But in the village convents belonging to the Nyingma sects, such as those of Sikkim and East Tibet, even public concubinage is passed over.

In all the great gompas there seems to be a special officer named Ge-koi (དགེ་བསྐོས་) who exercises disciplinary functions. He is on the watch for offenders, suppresses turbulence, keeps order at public ceremonials, and administers castigations both casual and prescribed. When any great festival is in progress, and the head lama makes solemn procession, the Ge-koi, with his assistant beadles, marches first clearing the way with a huge bamboo to which thongs are attached; and no scruple is shewn in applying this formidable whip over the persons of spectators both lay and clerical.

Both monks and nuns keep their heads always closely shorn if of the orthodox sect. Nuns of the Nyingma and Dzokchen sects retain their hair. A Gelukpa nun on occasions of ceremony wears on her smooth-shaven head a large wig with rough curls of long brown sheep's wool. The party of nuns that visited the British Commission at Kamba Jong in September 1903 wore their brown woolly wigs.

LAMAS OF THE HIGHER RANKS.

The term which has crept into general use in Europe to designate all Tibetan ecclesiastics is that of *lama*. Travellers in the country and visitors to the villages of Ladak and Sikkim persist in styling every member of the religious orders and every doorkeeper and underling of the temples by that name. Now this practice is utterly incorrect. In Tibet the appellation is limited in its application, and indeed comparatively few can lay claim to the title. The general title for all is always *trapa*. In truth the word *lama* (བླ་མ་ *bla-ma*) signifies "the upper" or "the superior one"; and seldom are any monks in a monastery given the name excepting the head of the house and in some of the larger institutions those occupying specially honourable positions. Thus when we hear of "the T'up-gen Lama," "the Di-chhung Lama," "the Radeng Lama," those indicate the Superiors or rulers of the various establishments named. Monks of special learning often receive this honorific style; and in books the title occasionally occurs as a general term. However, it is an absurd mistake to denominate the ordinary gelong of monasteries, large or small, "lamas." In any case no one under the grade of gelong may bear the appellation.

We use the designation at the head of this section because we are about to describe those gelongs who succeed in advancing above the main multitude of their order.

Birth, particular abilities, and learning, each of these can be a special factor in such progress. Of course good fortune, earnest determination, unscrupulousness, and friends in power, have in Tibet as elsewhere, their share also in bringing about distinction and promotion. But in Tibet, it must be granted in common fairness, that learning of the peculiar style there cultivated and the principle of birth applied after a novel fashion, are the two leading paths to ecclesiastical position. By learning a monk may attain the grade of *Ge-she* already mentioned, or by magical studies a lucrative practice as a Ngagpa sorcerer; but the greatest elevation depends on the system about to be explained.

INCARNATE LAMAS.

The application of the birth principle in singling out individuals from among their fellows does not rest on any vulgar notion of physical or fleshly descent. That would ill assort with Buddhist idealism. It is the spiritual pedigree which is concerned and that is regulated by the lofty speculations of metempyschosis or rather metasomatosis. And this theory accounts for the veneration in which certain ecclesiastical personages are held in Tibet who have not acquired their position by zeal, learning or purchase, but who were born to it.

Thus it comes to pass that in visiting Tibetan monasteries one is every now and then confronted with individuals of transcendent pre-natal antecedents for whom is claimed extraordinary rank and sanctity. These beings are known as SKUSHOK in Ladak and Ngari Khorsum, as KARPA in Amdo, and as ṬUL-KU in the Central provinces. They are in fact INCARNATE LAMAS; or, in other words, a personage of this kind is believed to be the bodily form in which some great saint or hero of past history is continuing his earthly existence. Every Skushok or Ṭul-ku is the re-embodiment of the subtle pychic essence known as the *karma* of such by-gone person who persists in returning to earth, of his own good will to mankind, in a successive series of re-births. Thus the Being before you is great indeed—either he is the present shape of a saint or a warrior or else in a few instances he is the earthly counterpart of some Dhyani Buddha or Dhyani Bodhisattwa now existing contemporaneously in the Buddhist heavens. Moreover, it is the habit of each of these to unite his spirit continuously with the holder of some one particular office, so that whosoever may be born as the re-incarnation of the hero must be appointed to the office.

So it is always said that such-and-such a Dhyani Buddha or such-and-such an historical personage has taken this or that headship of a monastery or this or that great office of state under his special protection. Furthermore, he is not fickle, he rarely changes his patronage; once the choice of appointment is made, to that appointment will he cling at least during the current age of the world.

In this way we have it laid down that the occupant of the chair of the famous Sákya Monastery (50 miles due N. of Mount Everest) can only be the man in whom the Dhyani Bodhisattwa Jam-yang (*i.e.*, the Sanskrit *Mañju-ghosha*) is now incarnate.[1] So, too, the human being chosen to govern at Táshi-lhümpo may be nobody else save the existing embodiment of the Dhyani Buddha Wö'pakme' (Sansk. *Amitabha*); and he who presides over Radeng Chhoide must be a person animated and shaped by the *karma* of the reformer Bromston. Then, in like manner, the incarnate lama of Pyi-tak Gompa near Leh in Ladak is invariably the current bodily form of Wákula (or Sre-mong), one of the sixteen Naiten or "immovable saints" that aided Gautama in promulgating his religion 2,300 years ago; the present holder of office being the 17th re-embodiment. Again, near the lower end of the Kyi Chhu is a hermit's cavern known as Tag-ts'ang-rawa P'uk, and the ascetic dwelling there is the incarnation of Dawa Zanpo, the king of the fabulous city of Shambhala in Central Asia where the Dü-kyi Khorlo or Adi-Buddha theories were alleged to have been first proclaimed.

Feminine personages in Tibet can also be earthly manifestations of divine and other beings. Such are generally considered incarnations of some great goddess of Buddhism. The lady-abbess of Samding on Yamdok lake is an emanation of Dorje P'agmo, the sow-goddess. There is another incarnate abbess at Jang Tag-lung monastery 40 miles N. of Lhása; she is head of all of those belonging to the Tag-lung sect. Dolma, the mother of all the Tathgatas as she is termed, is at present dis-integrated into no fewer than 21 subordinate manifestations of her spiritual energy. She was divided at first into only two co-ordinate emanations—Dol-kar and Dol-jang, the White Dolma and the Green

[1] He is addressed as འཇམ་མགོན་ཆོས་རྒྱལ་པོ "the Lord Jam, king of the doctrine." *Vide* Yig-kur Nam-shag, by S. C. Das, C.I.E., page 11.

Dolma—and these took shape in the two wives of king Srong-tsan Gampo. Subsequently, this primary bifurcated psychic essence of the goddess was still further subdivided as above in order to enlarge her sphere of influence over mortals, but several of these branch emanations no longer manifest themselves in earthly guise. There is probably a scarcity of women of position as vehicles of such re-embodiments. This is made evident from the fact that the present incarnation of the Green Dolma is a *hubilgan* or male incarnate lama in Mongolia, and that the White Dolma who in the 18th century was proclaimed by the Buria lamas to be incarnate first in the Empress Elizabeth of Russia and afterwards in Catherine II, is currently believed (at least in Mongolia) to have gone on being embodied not in any woman but in the successive Tsars of Russia even to the present monarch.

One development of these quaint speculations deserves particular mention. In recent times they were brought to bear even upon Queen Victoria of England who, though of course no Buddhist, was as sole ruler of the vast empire of India regarded throughout Tibet with awe and admiration. Many years ago several prints representing her late Majesty as reviewing troops while seated on horseback found their way into the snowy land; and those pictures set afloat the theory that she must be an incarnation of the goddess Palden Lhamo. Palden Lhamo, otherwise Pánden Makjorma, is the most blood-thirsty and warlike female deity in the Buddhist pantheon; and one of her characteristic poses in Tantrik ceremonial is when represented riding on a chesnut mule which was the offspring of a red ass and a winged mare. Thus arose the idea current among Tibetans, which resulted in the installation of Queen Victoria as a potent incarnation outside their country.

Innumerable curious instances of the re-embodiment theory, as it touches great personages in Tibet, might be specified. And it is necessary that a few expansions of the system as engrafted into the original notion should be just mentioned. Occasionally the principle of physical descent has been coupled with the general rules affecting spiritual pedigree; and the incarnation in these cases is allowed to be controlled by fleshly generation. At the great Red Cap monastery of Mindol Ling on the Yeru Tsangpo there are always two incarnate lamas, one styled the Ṭ'i (or "throne") Lama, the other the Dongpa Lama. The latter ecclesiastic is bound to break the celibate rule and to marry in order to keep up the succession to the headship of the monastery which both lamas rule conjointly. If at least two sons are born to the Dongpa Lama, the elder succeeds to the celibate chair on the death of the uncle, while the younger becomes Dongpa Lama and marries to carry on the succession. However, should the married brother prove childless or have only one heir, then it is compulsory upon the celibate lama to marry some woman in order to raise up the requisite issue who shall be able to maintain the orthodox descent. Moreover the original *ṭulwa,* bearing the *las* or karma, invariably transmigrates in accordance with this arrangement. In one or two generations both lamas have died without children; and then the ṭwin incarnations have to be looked for from a new stock, but such an eventuality leads to widespread woes—war, famine, and general disaster. At the famous Riwochhe lamasery on the Gyama Ngul Chhu in Eastern Tibet a similar scheme prevails. There we find three *Ṭulku* with co-ordinate jurisdiction, two of them celibates and one a lay lama. The lay lama takes a wife; but if he have not sufficient issue, the others, one after the other, marry the widow; but the main object in this instance appears to be to keep up the succession of the lay incarnation, the two ecclesiastical lamas being always re-embodied in the ordinary way outside the family. So, too, the son of the Sikkim Raja, though a *ṭulku,* marries if necessary to keep up the royal succession. Again at Chhamdo Chhoide two incarnate ones preside jointly over the 2,800 inmates and are known as P'akpa Lha the father and Shi-wa Lha the son. They are not, however, connected by earthly relationship, the only condition being that the one shall ordain the other into the priesthood and thus constitute him his spiritual offspring. When the two visit Lhása in company, they seem to be highly honoured. At Derge in Kham are no fewer than 4 *ṭulku* lamas, one of whom must be by birth a Khampa.

All Ṭulku, let it be here noted, do not rank alike. There are said to be three grades, the highest of which is confined to those only who are incarnations of Dhyani Buddhas and Bodhisattwas. This class is named *Jang-chhub Kusho;* the lower ranks being termed *Alak-ts'an* and *Ser-kyi Jong pa* respectively.

From the Buddhist point of view the self-denial of the original saint in thus voluntarily undertaking these repeated appearances upon earth is of a sublime character. He was a being who might have gained Nirvana at once then; but, out of philanthropic motives, he put aside that boon when within his reach and offered to be re-born in order to help on the general welfare of the world and its inhabitants. And the self-sacrifice of such a decision is, we should fancy, enhanced by the possibility that some of the bodies in whom it may be his lot to be lodged may hereafter lapse from his own high standard, and causing a decline in the virtue of the transmitted *karma* disqualify it from the attainment of Nirvana for ages to come.

The responsibility of the successive incarnation of any saint or Buddha, one would accordingly imagine to be tremendous; and some consciousness of that ought to have considerable influence in causing him to lead a life of strict morality and sanctity. Many Buddhist authorities, however, contend that whenever an incarnate lama notoriously misbehaves, it is in some unexplained way the present individual's own evil disposition annihilating the spirit of the saint whose manifestation he is; and that the saintly *karma* does not deteriorate. The punishment of such misconduct is that in the next re-birth the *avatar* of the holy one is disintegrated from the spirit of the recent holder of the office which henceforth alone takes re-embodiment, assuming some degraded form suitable to his deserts; while the astral spirit separates itself for ever from the office on earth which it formerly patronised. As any such explanation stultifies the whole theory of Buddhist metempyschosis based on the inexorable rule that present actions must shape future *karma* for better or worse, it is evidently only a shuffling device to preserve intact the moral standing and memory of a departed saint or hero. More consistent rather are those who preserve his dignity by boldly asserting that it is our lack of moral merit at the present day which causes us to be unable to see the really grand motives which are underlying the apparent ignoble behaviour of the current representative of the astral spirit now in Dewachen.

For, it must be always borne in mind that such Bodhisattvas and saintly kings and holy lamas as consent to repeated incarnations upon earth have obtained by virtue of *sam-ten* or the highest form of meditation a dual existence. So it comes about that, in Galdan, Dewachen, or any other of the Buddhist paradises in heaven, the astral or ineffable spirit is ever continuing, whilst its copy or counterpart undergoes earthly re-birth in indefinite succession.

We must next explain the process whereby, on the death of an incarnate lama, discovery is made of the particular person in whom his psychic essence has or will presently take refuge. And first it must be understood that no true Buddhist ever speaks of the *death* of the holy man. He has migrated hence, they say—he has *zhing-la p'ep* "gone to the field"; while, of the ordinary man, they would affirm *shi song re'* "he has died."

After a period not less than 49 days, during which period the spirit (as the commonality aver) or spiritual essence (as the philosophic writers, whom our British authors quote from, prefer to put it) remains in the Bardo—the Buddhist region of disembodied ghosts—the saintly *karma* may take shape at any time and in any place. As he will then be absolutely *re-born*, he can only animate a human being at the moment of birth; and therefore the new incarnate lama must be some infant. Occasionally the *Ṭulku* himself, if conscious that death was approaching, will have forecast the exact locality where his successor was to be born, setting forth perhaps certain circumstances that would attend his birth and also the signs and prognostics which shall occur to those who go in search of the new incarnation when they are near the right spot. Frequently, however, the man has departed this life without any testament of this sort; and then resort is had to some recognised oracle or to one or more lamas learned in Tantrik auguries. We believe that in the majority of cases there is not any trickery or manœuvring to get the infant of particular parents indicated. Few persons seem to covet the appointment for their offspring; although when informed by those in quest of the new embodiment that a child of theirs answers the requirements of forecast or oracle the verdict is received with humble gratitude and complete resignation.

An infant thus singled out remains with his parents until he reaches four or five years of age. His identity must then be further confirmed in this manner. The gelongs of the monastery where the late lama died display before the child a number of religious apparatus and other chattels that belonged to the departed person, intermingling them with other articles of precisely the same kind in order to mislead if possible his little successor. If the latter manages to pick out, more or less correctly, those things which were the property of the late lama, he is hailed as undoubtedly the veritable *Ṭulku*. Any failure in this trial is said to occur very rarely, and probably only when those concerned find, subsequent to the first identification, that an unwise selection of parentage has been made. When approved, however, the child is at once despatched to the monastery over which in after years he will preside. Notwithstanding his tender years, there is no demur; off he goes in charge of his future subjects who bring him to their establishment with exceeding ceremonial and noise.

An incarnate lama, both when first brought in and afterwards in later life, never resides actually within the monastery. He possesses a small house of his own generally adjoining the main buildings, and there he dwells alone in a certain amount of state yet with a considerable display of austerity as well. He is not supposed to eat meat and never anything in the presence of others, passing many hours in study and systematic meditation. Whenever he attends functions in the temple, he always sits on an altar as if he were a deity. Ascetic rules are quite disregarded by some; but as a fact the majority are said to approximate closely to the orthodox conditions. This, of course, in adult life. So, at Lit'ang the lama dwells in a cavern as a Rit'oi-pa, seldom visiting his monastery. But so long as the *Ṭulku* continues a child, there is greater liberty from restraint and his parents make frequent visits, occasionally being accommodated hard by, though not suffered actually to dwell beneath the same roof as that which shelters the young prodigy. The parents of a Dalai Lama are housed in a palace and acquire large estates, however poor they may have been. Cassiano Beligatti mentions in his journal the high position of the man who in 1741 was father of the Dalai Lama.

At the age of 12 or 14 the boy is sent off either to Lhása or to Táshi-lhümpo for education, general training, and the all-important admission to the *gendun* or priesthood. His travelling expenses and sojourn in Lhása are no burden to his parents, everything being defrayed out of monastic funds. Usually the youth continues away from his domain for many years, up to the age of 23 or 24. He is retained by the authorities of the capital or of Táshi-lhümpo until he has become thoroughly imbued with a sense of the omnipotence of the central lamaic powers-that-be and has been quite weaned from provincial leanings or any admiration for his local home. Then, when at length he returns to his sphere of duty, he comes as a new man and another order of being; his old attendants and companions have forgotten the familiarities of past days; and his education and experience impart a bearing of superiority which is at once deferred to and even recognized as indicative of supernatural endowments. At Lhása he has been trained in worldly-wisdom and business attainments as well as in the mystic side of his spiritual character; and thus he frequently assumes the fullest control and disposal of the monastic revenues.

The Lhása Government surely exhibits great sagacity in enforcing the condition of so many years residence in the capital in the case of future rulers of the powerful establishments found in all corners of the kingdom. In the case of the mighty monasteries in Khams, Amdo, Palri, and along the Chinese border-line the State has in this way partisan agents, with all the prestige of supernatural rights and temporal experience, placed in positions of authority in localities the distance of which from the centre of Government would otherwise cause the inhabitants to grow disaffected or a prey to outside powers. Again in Ladak, which is no longer under the temporal rule of Tibet, the Lhása Executive has practically a considerable share in the ordering of affairs, because the heads of the four or five chief monasteries are incarnate lamas specially trained in the Tibetan metropolis. In furtherance probably of some such policy, it has been managed during the last 50 or 60 years that the *Ṭulku* of the principal foundation in Ladak, the wealthy and potent lamasery of Hemis, shall not even return to his native country after he has come to Lhása for training but continue in that city the rest of his days. Accordingly the general control of the great Hemis Monastery with its extensive property in Ladak is largely in the hands of the authorities at Lhása. There is indeed a resident *Lopon* or head at Hemis but, though endowed with much personal power, he is deemed subordinate to the genuine incarnate lama living in Lhása.

The great lamas of Lhása and Tashi-lhümpo are not of course sent away during their minority. They dwell in their own monastery, being provided with a special tutor who bears the title of Yong-dzin.[1]

Of course there are occasions when the *Ṭulku* exhibits independence of character and action; and it has been observed that when such individuality has proved obnoxious to the central power at Lhása, death through poisoning has been frequently the secret agent of his removal. In like manner where Chinese interests seem likely to suffer in Eastern Tibet or Mongolia, the Imperial Government appears always able to find, among the lamaic community surrounding a *Ṭulku*, unscrupulous tools ready to fulfil any underhand mission of this sort. In fact, so far as China is concerned, it is said she has found the incarnate system not so amenable to her will as is agreeable, the stupendous influence of these ghostly personages over a superstitious people being the strongest counteragent. It is believed to be due to Imperial dictation that at two such important political centres as Kumbum and Galdan monasteries the head lama is not a Kusho *Ṭulku*, but a mere Khempo,[2] placed there by the Government as a man of reliability and not chosen, as would be the case otherwise, in infancy.

It should be remarked that several sects nominally of the Red Cap or *Shámár* division of Buddhism have their head lamas, incarnate or non-incarnate, educated in institutions of the Yellow Cap order. Nevertheless that is not the practice of the sects more strongly opposed to this the State communion. So, the Urgyen sect, known as Dzokchhenpa, regard Mindol Ling as their head station for training and ordination, and have no dealings with the Gelukpa centres of Lhása; the Dukpa or Lhon-dukpa resort to Táshi-chhoi-dzong, the chief monastery of Bhutan where dwells the Dharma Gye'po; while the Nyingmapa establishments own allegiance to Dorje-ṭag Gompa on the Yero Tsangpo which is their seat of learning.[3]

[1] The tutor or Yong-dzin (ཡོངས་འཛིན) of the present Dalai Lama was the head of the Ts'e-chhog Ling monastery in Lhása. The full designation seems to be ཡབ་སྲས་ཀྱི་ཡོངས་འཛིན་

[2] This title Khempo or Khanpo is not necessarily indicative of rank; it is equivalent to our D.D.

The class distinguished as Tulku or Incarnate Lamas extends into Mongolia and China.[1] At Peking outside the walls, in the monastery attached to the Hwang Ssü or "Yellow Temple," there is a celebrated Hiro a Fo or "living Buddha" well-known as the Chang-kya Hutuktu, who is the incarnation of ལྕང་སྐྱ་རོལ་པའི་རྡོ་རྗེ་ So, likewise, within the walls of Peking are two others, one at the Chan-t'an Ssü ("Sandal-wood Temple"), the other at the Yungho-kung Ssü—"the Temple of Unending Peace." One of the most attractive of these mystics in China, however, is probably the hubilgan located at Wu-t'ai-shan in the Shansi province—the Dzasak Lama enthroned in P'u-sa-t'ing temple.[2]

In Mongolia from Kökö Nor to Lake Baikal in Siberia, both Mongols and Buriats venerate immensely a large band of this supernatural order to whom they give the general title of Khubilgan (sounds *Hubilgan*). As in Tibet there are three grades or classes recognized, the steps of rank from highest to lowest being Khutuktu, Shaberon, Gegen, and the Gegen are naturally the most plentiful. The principal individual of the kind, to whom, in some sort, all other Khubilgan dwelling north of Tsaidam are subordinate, is the incarnate lama of Urga the capital of North Mongolia on the river Tesla on the Siberian border. He bears rank as a Khutuktu and is held to be the current embodiment of Taranatha, the author of a Tibetan history of Indian Buddhism, who died in 1610 aged 70. In Urga he seems to be usually styled *Khüréni Bogda* "the Holy Chief of the Enclosure"; but in Tibet he is spoken of as Taranath Lama, or Je-tsun Tampa Taranatha or even merely "Ta Lama." The Taranath incarnations have not been seated at Urga for any length of time. They were indeed formerly attached to the Tábun Tura monastery at Khuei-hua-chheng in the Gobi desert. However, about 160 years ago, one of the incarnations was murdered by a Chinaman on the occasion of a visit of the great Emperor Khang-hi, when the Lama refused to rise in the imperial presence because he was more

[1] *Nyingma* is both a general appellation for all the unreformed sects of Tibetan Buddhism, and a particular designation for one of the unreformed bodies with its headquarters at Dorje-ṭag.

[2] In Peking sind vierzehn "lebende Buddhas" als feste Posten vorgesehen; davon weilt jetzt nur einer in der Stadt, denn die übrigen, welche alle in Tibet wiedergeboren werden müssen, erhalten zur Reise nach Peking wedel die Erlaubnis, noch das erforderliche Geld. Der wichtigste unter ihnen, der lChaṅ skya Khutukn, der einen etwa dem Grossal-mosenier entsprechenden Posten versehen soll, ist vor etwa zwölf Jahren zur weitern Ausbildung nach Tibet gesandt worden und dort gestorben—Grünwedel in his *Mythologie des Buddhismus in Tibet und der Mongolei*, pp. 92–3.

sacred than the Chinese monarch. Thereafter the Khutuktu was transferred to Urga as being more remote from Peking and destruction.[1]

The Khubilgan of Mongolia and China are mostly Tibetan by birth. Being "discovered" in the usual way in Tibet, they are sent for a few years to their seats in Mongolia or China; but at 10 or 12 are returned for training at Lhása, whence they are ultimately sent again to their respective monasteries.

1 The present Taranath Lama of Urga, now 27 years old, is said to be a dissipated character given to gambling and horse-racing and irresistibly fond of playing absurd practical jokes on his worshippers, a habit which in one case caused loss of life.

CHAPTER IX.

THE INHABITANTS IN GENERAL.

As one might expect to find, the whole territory under consideration is peopled by men of varying race and customs. In family, doubtless, there is a generic unity throughout; though certain Tibetan tribes exhibit a facial contour strikingly unrelated to that belonging to the great Mongolian stock under which the bulk of the inhabitants may be classified. Indeed the Grand Lama of Tibet at present reigning at Lhása is said to possess a distinctly Caucasian cast of countenance and Aryan features. Mons. Bonvalot, also, gives a picture of a Tibetan with the American Indian type of face. But if the stock of the Tibetan races be, as it undoubtedly is, of Mongol origin, the language, on the other hand, is singularly free from any Mongolian affinities. Spoken as it is throughout the entire territory in slightly-varying dialects, and even extending beyond the legitimate confines into parts of Western and North-Western China, neither in vocabulary nor in construction is the Tibetan language related to Chinese, Mongolian or Manchu Tartar.

In most of the provinces of Tibet are to be found two distinct classes of inhabitants, with instincts, domestic habits, and mode of livelihood as much apart as if they represented different nationalities. The denizens of the villages and towns, together with the inmates of the gompas or lamaseries, form apparently one race; while the pastoral tribes, occupying the Dok uplands, and leading lives either semi-nomadic or nomadic according to the region where they dwell, are quite as much a separate people.

RESIDENTS IN CENTRAL TIBET.

In the towns of the Central Provinces of Ui and Tsang, we find a quiet, orderly people, of domestic habits and warmly religious feelings. With the exception of such large places as Lhása, Shigatse, Tse-t'ang, Gyangtse, and Phari Jong, the towns are mostly communities gathered round some monastery, with the duties or interests of which all the residents are more or less connected. But there are hundreds of hamlets and villages all over the country occupied wholly by agriculturalists; and although a small gompa with a few lamas may be located hard by, still the majority of the residents would be laymen. But first a few words concerning the dwellers in towns. Tibetans themselves are not specially adepts at commerce, however much they may love its rewards. Accordingly, although in certain centres the smaller tradesmen are of Tibetan race, their transactions are paltry indeed compared with the enterprise of dealers and merchants who, belonging to other races, have entered the country to trade, and now monopolise all the more profitable departments. In Lhása and Tse-t'ang are large communities of Nepalese who carry on the goldsmith's and the jeweller's occupations, being also the chief metal-workers, chemists, and cloth-dyers. Kashmiri merchants are the cloth-dealers, woollen-yarn importers and money-changers; and other lower class Kashmiris engage largely in the business of butchers—for, Buddhist though Tibetans may be, they are diligent consumers of beef, mutton, and even pork. As to the Chinese who infest the country, they devote themselves to multifarious pursuits, a great number of course being professional soldiers. Most of the eating-houses and pastry-cook shops are in Chinese hands; and, as the custom of dining at restaurants is almost universal amongst pilgrims and merchants visiting the larger towns, the Celestial does a stupendous business. A. K. mentioned places in Lhása where 200 can dine together, men and women sitting down at the same tables. A man from Lhása, moreover, informed us of a huge restaurant near the Chokhang temple styled satirically the Ani Sakhang or "nuns' eating-house," full all day.

The present expedition of armed forces into Tibet has revealed to us many surprises concerning the character and capabilities of the Tibetan people. One of these revelations has been the skill in mechanical arts and metal work of the inhabitants of Lhása, as evidenced in the small arms which they have managed under pressure of circumstances to turn out. Having procured patterns from Russia (as it is to be supposed) of certain modern rifles, such as the Martini-Henry, they have succeeded in manufacturing them themselves in large quantities. Hitherto the Tibetans had been accustomed only to the old-fashioned muzzle-loading musket; but now some thousands of breech-loaders of the latest patterns have been produced by artificers in Lhása—probably under the supervision and direction of the Nepalese metal-workers. Such of these rifles as have fallen into our hands are described as being, though rough in finish, creditable imitations of the European article and put together skillfully enough to be of effective service in a fight.

Though the Tibetan is not by nature a shop-keeper, he does not despise traffic when he has donned the ecclesiastical garb, and many of the immates of the larger monasteries do a profitable business through being granted by the chief lama concessions for the supply of tobacco, butter and tea to their brothers in residence. By far the major portion of better class folk in Tibet belong to the religious orders dwelling in the numerous gompas which abound in town and desert. Certain laymen of the towns have private estates bringing in rents, and others are employed in the civil service as *Jongpön*, or governors of forts and district revenue collectors, and as *Dungkhor* or Government clerks in Lhása. A number of the latter class are said to reside in the villas built in the suburbs of the capital. The Jongpön in a provincial centre is a great personage with unlimited powers of extortion and oppression. On the whole taking the denizens of the towns in the bulk they belong to only two classes—ecclesiastics and tradesmen.

The inmates of the monasteries of Central Tibet hail from all parts of Mongolia and Tibet. Though of heavy build, they are athletic and healthy, most of them being not of sedentary habits but engaging in active exercise and sometimes in field labour. A leading characteristic is a love of broils and fighting; some to indulge this predilection making up small predatory parties in imitation of the more warlike bandits of the North and North-East. These men of the church are truly militant and they are often brave and patriotic to a degree when banded against a common outside enemy. In recent years moreover they have been regularly drilled.

It is asserted on the best authority that the majority of the most ardent fighters who have been engaged against the British in the present campaign in Tibet (1904) have belonged to the monkish classes; and in general the captains and leaders of assaulting and defending parties have been ecclesiastics. Indeed these Tibetan braves or *pa-o*, as they characteristically call themselves, are admitted, by General Macdonald, Captain Peterson, Colonel Brander, and others of our officers who have done battle with them, to have shown themselves real heroes albeit of a reckless type of the same. When fighting as soldiers such monks are said to be designated officially as *ser-makmi* "golden soldiers." An instance of the deliberate heroism and patriotism of these men came to light after the storming of the Kharu-La by the Sikh Mounted Infantry, May 5th, 1904. A document was found after the fight of a peculiar and even touching character. It purported to be an agreement in writing between three monks to band themselves in common cause against the British invaders. It was headed དཔའ་བོ་གསུམ་གྱི་ཡིག་འཛིན "Agreement of three Braves"; and ran as follows:—"The English, acting in an insolent and rapacious manner, having entered our country, we are unable to sit silent under this infliction. Soldiers must be sent to fight, and the *Dewa Zhung* (Tibetan Government) has given orders that the noble Kyi-me is to proceed as head of the army in place of the Lading Depon. With him are we three responsible Braves. We have consulted together and made this agreement, taking no account of our lives, fighting for honour only. We have bound ourselves not to quarrel with other servants, to drink no wine, not to gamble, not to lie, not to steal: if we should do any of these things we are prepared to suffer any punishment inflicted by the Master. If we do well the Master will reward us well. Each man of us will receive a yearly gratuity of 30 ounces of silver. Should we depart but little from what we have bound ourselves to do we must pay a fine of three ounces of gold." Then followed the names and seals.

The villagers of the provinces of Ui and Tsang, *i.e.*, of the central southern districts, are an ignorant, poor and not very interesting community. They dwell in quaint stone huts having walls of great thickness, well set in position, as means of defence against human enemies as well as the cold. Their character is sordid and pusillanimous, arising doubtless from their deep poverty and the oppression of the authorities. These inhabitants of the villages are (if layfolk as they usually are) all tillers of the soil. They are styled *miser* ("yellow men"); and are supposed to work on lands descending by inheritance to them, but their own really to a very limited extent. Though they have no direct rental, their liabilities to the feudal landlord are immense. This landlord may be the Tibetan Government, or some large monastery, or else a private hereditary nobleman; and the dues claimed by the over-lord are made proportionate to the produce of the land—not a fixed charge, but fluctuating according to the amount yielded each year. The payments are in butter and barley; and, in addition, the *miser* is liable to supply beasts of burden and personal service whenever Government officials pass through the district. It is this latter liability which in those districts where the chief road-tracks pass presses so heavily on the Tibetan peasant. The *ta-u* and *ulak* rights of high officials, who thereby claim free carriage not only for themselves and their personal effects but also for a vast quantity of merchandise which they seize the opportunity of transporting for other persons who have paid them to do so, has become a grinding tyranny.

The village peasantry have little patriotism or love for the rulers of their country. They look upon all the authorities-that-be naturally as only so many oppressors. Their ready submission to our advance of late into their land, when not forced to fight by the monks and the Lhása officials, shews how little they care for politics and how eagerly they would accept any *regime* which promised a yoke a little lighter than that which at present prevails.

Their whole interest is in the yield of their fields and their cattle. And in the well-cultivated and fertile valleys of the Nyang, Yarlung, Mikchhu and other rivers their labours as husbandmen are, to their limited ambitions, profitable. A Tibetan poet has depicted, with a certain dry humour, the interests and ambitions of the farmers and small-holders of these parts. In the specimen we shall here introduce we are almost taken back to the Bucolics or Georgics of Virgil:—

At the time when Spring comes, it is then you observe
The power of the ocean's warm currents increasing.
Those foot-drinkers, the trees, full of branches,
Wax arrogant with youth;
While their necks, towards the summit, gleam as with emeralds.
Such flowers as bear anthers seem about to vomit azure;
As to those with pistils, they are full of laughter.
Moreover, each one—each with its own proper colour—
When it wishes to satisfy thirst, draws forth
Nectar, pure as the soul, from its eyes.
Then, too, does the Great Earth appear overflowing with sap;
And the bluey-green of the dresma rush matches with malachite.
All rivers and streams, coming down, pour forth their chatter;
Whilst the mighty wind, though loud is the voice it utters,
Soothes the pains which the cold has engendered.
At a time such as this is husbandry prepared for.
The elders possessed of sense stand in groups:
They taste the nectar of gossiping speech;
Estimating the sun, the cold, and the warmth, which the season will bring.
"The tools required for spring must now," say they, "be collected;
"Up there, what was planted in the upland is breaking forth into name;
"Down below, on slopes above the great river, it grows very warm;
"In between, where cool and shade make things equal, one receives
"Whatsoever one wishes."
Of those three *P'u, Dá, Bar*[1] do they ever make chatter.
Then, too, in longtail, the seasons of flood in years both former and later;

[1] These are special Tibetan terms signifying the upper parts of a valley, the lower portion, and the central or medial tracts.

In the Spring could be done in old days the greater part of one's farming
And because it was in those days conspicuously fine,
It was splendid for all men.
After that, indeed, came the time when things were reversed;
The seed got frozen; and, melting, its virtue had vanished forever.
Next, minutely must be discussed the condition of yon lower valley,
Down there it lies just where the damage last year had occurred!
For there the leaves and the corn remain unswelled with the moisture.
So, thence, would they start an inquiry into all varieties of soil;
And as to the water three things—its distance, its quality, and how it
was to be carried.
Lastly indeed is set forth the features of each village in order;
While, beloved of all is this—a comparison of different manures.[1]

The houses in which the peasantry and farmers of Central Tibet and Tsang dwell are built of huge blocks of stone laid on each other with little if any mortar. The walls, as we have said, are of vast thickness, even 6 to 8 feet; and the buildings generally two or three storeys high. All rooms are small with loop-holes as windows. You mount to the different floors by rude ladders composed of one pole with irregular pegs for steps. These dwellings are dark inside and are easily defended.

THE DOKPA OR NOMADIC PEOPLE.

Besides the dwellers in settled homes in towns and villages, there exists, in all parts of Tibet, a people of nomadic proclivities living on the elevated moorlands or river-side uplands and devoting their attention almost exclusively to sheep and cattle. In Western Tibet, that is in the provinces of Rudok, Ngari Khorsum and Dok-t'ol, the whole population—with the exception of the gelongs in the monasteries and the few government officials—may be fairly classed as herdsmen. In Central Tibet, that is in the provinces of Ui and Tsang, they are found only on certain tracts where they wander around towns and villages, pitching their encampments where pasturage offers. Here their principal grounds lie to the south of Yamdok and along the lofty territory adjacent to Bhutan and in Dingtsam which borders on Eastern Nepal.[2] Again, in extensive districts to the north and north-

[1] We have made our translation from a Tibetan text which we have found included in a collection of extracts put together by Sarat Chandra Dás for use in the Bhutia Boarding School, Darjeeling.

[2] The Dokpa inhabiting the shores of the P'o-mo Jhang-t'ang lake, not a great distance from the frontier of Bhutan, are reputed to be immigrants of another day from Mongolia, and are therefore styled Sok Dokpa and Hor Dokpa. So also are the herdsmen of the Dam valley N.N.E. of Lhása, who are descended from the Koshot Mongols who were stationed there 250 years ago for the protection of the Dalai Lama of that time.

east of Lhása, beginning some 150 miles from that city, we once more meet with the nomad shepherds as sole tenants of the land.

These pastoral folk, named Dokpa in Western and Central Tibet, (after the word *abrog* which is sounded "dok" and which means "an upland pasture") wherever they wander seem governed by similar rules and traditions. They are divided into numerous tribes; and each tribe confines itself to a separate *de* or district, never intruding on the grounds belonging to neighbouring tribes. Every tribe is made up of so many "tents" or *gur*, one tent to every family, and the members of the tribe do not usually roam about in a body but divide themselves into several camps or *doks* as they are often loosely termed. The camps separate for the summer, occupying distinct pastures within the tribal confines, but re-unite in winter when they generally entrench themselves and their flocks in some natural stronghold. Each locomotive farm stays three or four months in one place, making about three moves, including the retreat to winter quarters, in the course of the year.

In Rndok and Ngari Khorsum the Dokpa are of more stationery habits than the tribes living in Dok-yul and Dok-de, the districts N.E. of Lhása. Some of them have a regular village of stone huts built round the fort of the *Jong-pon* or at the base of a large monastery, whither they retire during the five winter months. Others set up a sort of winter village of their own, excavating the ground deeply and building stone defences and walls wherein they pitch their tents to save them from the biting winds. Others again at this season have a series of galleries or compartments which have been cut in the sides of a cliff or below a plateau. At Takláá Khar in Purang, near the head-waters of the Karnali river, in the mound of the fort which is 800 feet high is quite a beehive of these subterranean dwellings. The slope is very abrupt, and one above the other are excavated as it were separate houses of one to three storeys. All the entrances into these curious dens are low and narrow, but the compartments inside are lofty and neatly cut, with steps excavated within leading to all rooms belonging to each separate dwelling. The winter residence is styled *gunsa,* and the chief summer camping-ground *yarsa,*

Throughout the length and breadth of Tibet, however, the typical residence of the Dokpa is his black tent of coarse canvas spun from yak's hair. The tent which, with its tentacle-like ropes, was compared by Huc to a huge black spider, is constructed of two pieces which when pitched are put together so as to leave an opening of 6 inches all along the top as a smoke-vent. Outside, little flags flutter from the six corners, and the poles are decorated with yaks' tails. Inside, there is room for 25 or even 30 people to sleep, so wide is the span.

In the centre a large oven and stove of clay is erected; while boxes, churns, and canvas bags are ranged round the sides where the stores and utensils are kept; but there are no compartments for separate sleeping as in the Mongol felt tent. Near the entrance stands the shrine with a rude image or two.

A Dokpa chief has often a more luxurious tent. One of these is thus described:—The tent was made of the yak's black hair and was pitched in a wide pit dug down some 7 or 8 feet below the surface of the ground, and the descent to it was by means of steps. Outside, fastened unpleasantly near the entrance at the bottom of the pit, was one of the gigantic black dogs of Lhása who with great difficulty was restrained from attacking visitors to the chief. Inside the tent were bales of shawl-wool, leather packages of tea, strings of dried beef, with a few other Tibetan luxuries such as dried apricots, raisins, &c. The poles were garnished with several matchlocks and a sword. The chief's seat was a cushion on the ground, beside a small box in which there was a drawer containing paper, ink, pens, also a couple of bowls, one for drinking tea, the other for chhang or arak. A shrine was behind his seat where were ranged on shelves images, tiny vases, brass bells, a butter lamp lighted, with a few books and pictures on cloth to the right and left of the altar. The chief was constantly smoking a silver-mounted Nepalese hookah; while tea was forthcoming at all hours.

Dokpas sleep in a most curious attitude; never on their back or sides but always with the face downwards. Drawing the knees close up to the chin, they actually pass the night resting on their knees and elbows and with every scrap of clothing they can muster huddled on their back and round their sides. Stones and earth are generally arranged so as to make a slope of the ground from the face down to the toes; and when out in the open they choose a sloping hill-side always. Those who are well-to-do have indoors a small mattress under them with a slant from the pillow-end; but adopt the same awkward attitude in sleeping. Indoors they generally strip at nights, sleeping naked with the clothing and blankets piled about them as mentioned.

Dokpa women do not work so much out of doors as the women of villages, notwithstanding their nomadic life, and consequently their faces seem fairer, though often with the ruddiest colour as well. The men are of a dusky brown colour; and take a fuller share of daily labour than husbandmen, relieving the women in many ways. Young women, however, soon wrinkle and are rarely good-looking. The dress of both sexes consists of a long robe of sheep-skin with the wool on, the skins not being tanned but rendered pliable by continual rubbing between the hands. This robe is bound at the waist by a girdle of yak-hair rope; and the outside of the robe is often covered with stout cotton-cloth or broad-cloth from Gyangtse sewn on to cover the inside of the raw skin which lies on the outer side. Women wear, besides the tunic, woollen petticoats; also a curious piebald-looking shawl made up of various-coloured strips of blanket and pinned to the tunic over the breast with large brass skewers. Their head-dress varies with the province inhabited, but is usually decorated with turquoise and coral.

As to food, the nomadic people live fairly well excepting when on journeys. Yak-beef and mutton are freely used, but are always boiled, as they assert that roasted meat impedes the breathing. They dislike fresh milk; as a rule turning all first into curds, which are dried, or into butter, and drinking the butter-milk. Parched barley meal (*tsampa*) made into soft balls with water or tea is the staple food as everywhere in Tibet. As meat in winter keeps frozen for months, several yak and sheep are always killed in November and are preserved whole for winter consumption, thus saving fodder when hard to procure.

Dokpas generally pride themselves on being superior to the ordinary Tibetan of the towns and villages; and indeed their possessions entitle them to the higher position. The flocks and herds belonging to a single tent are frequently from 1,200 to 1,500 head; while the poorest may own perhaps 25 sheep with a few *jomo* (yak-cows) and goats and a couple of bulls. Taxation is levied on the Dokpa both in the shape of cattle and ponies as draught beasts for high functionaries travelling, also a money or butter levy on their flocks, a charge sometimes repudiated by the more turbulent tribes. In Horde, north of Lhása, are four Dokpa tribes that despise sheep-keeping and devote their time to the breeding of yak, tending mighty herds said to reach as a total 20,000. In Yamdok, in Dam, and in the Tengri Nor district, the pastoral people devote many of their grazing grounds to the rearing of ponies which are taken for sale to the markets of Shigatse and Gyangtse and even to Darjeeling and Behar. These are highly prized, fetching often 600 and 700 rupees in India.[1]

However, the wealth of both nomads and semi-nomads mainly consists of sheep and goats which are valuable to the owners in a

[1] The Yamdok herdsmen also breed asses which find a ready sale at Shigatse as beasts of burden for travellers. Good animals can be bought there at 25 rupees and inferior ones cost only 18 or 20 rupees.

double way. First, there is the yield of wool. That of the sheep is of very long fleece, but is rarely exported beyond the hill districts of the Himalayas and is much used in native manufactures in Tibet. But with the inner wool of the longhaired goat it is very different; for that is all exported. This goat wool is the celebrated shawl-wool styled *pashm* in Kashmir and India, but known to Tibetans as *lena*. It is a peculiar soft down of exquisite thread, which grows at the root of the hair or coarse wool of every animal in Tibet, save the horse and the tame sheep, but chiefly, and in the best quality, beneath the outer covering of goats. In Tibet there are kept four kinds of sheep, none of which yield the fine mossy wool, but they will thrive at any height up to 18,000 feet, feeding on the poorest herbage. The yak grows *lena*, and even the ibex and *tseu* antelope, when killed, supply quantities of the down, that of the *tseu* being in special demand under the name of *tseu khut*. So universal in winter is this valuable undergrowth, that the very dogs contribute their share.

The second use the Dokpa makes of his flocks is as beasts of burden. The sheep carry the *lena* immense distances, chiefly to Le, Shigatse, and Lhása; the tall species called *jhangluk*, travelling 12 miles of mountainous pathway per diem, loaded with 40lbs. of wool. As we have already noticed, the owners of herds do not restrict their trade to realising the produce of their flocks. Some engage largely in the salt and borax traffic; whilst many Dokpa have resorted to gold washing, and in recent years colonies of the nomads have settled in the western lake district where the chief gold deposits have been found. Their sheep and yak still come in useful as carrying animals; the former carrying the borax over the Himalayas and the gold to Lhása.

Again in the Dok districts N.E. of Lhása, the nomadic people assume yet another and less commendable role, that of robbers and brigands. Not forsaking their bucolic pursuits, the members of the same tribe add to their gains by organising themselves into mounted predatory bands, which make annual excursions into distant parts and return laden with spoil. But these tribes are to be described later under a separate heading.

Dwellers in black tents are not only to be met with in the regular Dok regions of Western and Central Tibet, but exist also in the districts of Kökö Nor, especially to the east of that lake, the valleys around Sining and Kumbum monastery affording luxuriant feeding grounds for cattle. There the Dokpa, or "Kara Tangutans," as Przhevalsky clumsily styles them, devote themselves solely to peaceful pastoral pursuits; only their proximity to the dreaded Amdo robbers, whose descent is both swift and sudden, causes them to lead lives of anxiety to which the Yamdok and other tribes are generally strangers.

The Dokpa in the great districts of Khams, who form a large part of the population there, fall under another section.

THE TRIBES NORTH AND NORTH-EAST OF LHÁSA.

Any large and good map of Tibet will indicate to those who examine it that north and east of Lhása are extensive districts of country where no places with the appendix word "Jong" are to be found. In fact the major portion of Eastern Tibet has no Jong towns, and this lack at once shews that the large tracts concerned are not under the ordinary regular government of Lhása, as are the western provinces and the central parts of Tibet. We shall not yet speak of the Kongpo and Nangpo provinces east of Lhása where the Jong system prevails, nor of the great principalities of Khams where the system is re-placed by other forms of administration. The districts and people now to be described lie to the N. and N.E. of the capital, at a considerable though not very great distance from it, and are yet under a different system of government from that prevailing elsewhere in Central Tibet. The inhabitants themselves are likewise distinctive in many respects.

1. THE HORPA OR NORTHERN ROBBER TRIBES.—A number of districts will be observed in the map lying N. and N.N.E. of Lhása along the southern base of the Dang-la mountains bearing such names as Namru, Atak, Amdo, Jámar or Dzamar, Yagra, etc. These names really indicate separate tribes inhabiting those districts, who are independent one of the other and often inimical to each other. They are collectively known as the Hor De. They are not dwellers in villages but live in tents like the ordinary Dokpa of western and southern regions, and form distinct tribes or clans each ruled by an hereditary chief styled a Deba (སྡེ་པ). These tribes are, nevertheless, mostly subordinate to Lhása, though without Jongs or Jongpöns; and the distance of the capital is from 8 to 15 days' march. Taxes on pastoral products are collected periodically by emissaries from the Dewa Zhung or Tibetan Government who hold the Deba responsible for his tribesmen's deficits.

The Horpa are a bold fairly-athletic lot of people. Their ostensible and perhaps most productive means of living is the breeding and tending of yak-cattle and horses. Large quantities of butter and curds (*chura*) are yielded by their half-breed yaks and are despatched through the medium of dealers (who come to buy) into Lhása. Sheep, goats, and the larger kind of dog are also reared for sale in a less degree. These articles and animals are generally not sold to the traders for money but bartered for tea, saddlery, gay-coloured cloths, and other town-vendibles. But the better classes alone can deal thus. A number of these tent-dwellers near Tengri Nor are excessively poor. Their distorted noses, fang-like snags of teeth, deformed limbs, and stunted bodies, bear witness to their hard life amid the boulders on the ice-bound wind-stricken plains. Badly nourished, their intellects also seem of the lowest order.

However, the more popular occupation of the well-to-do tribes is not pastoral but predatory. Except in the cattle-breeding season, the men roam about in parties of from 20 to 200 bent on highway robbery. They are well-armed and thoroughly well-mounted. Their weapons consist of a long matchlock slung on the back, a sword in wooden or leathern case at the side, with generally a spear also, and sometimes even bows and arrows. As *chakpas* or marauders the tribal bands waylay travellers of all sorts, even such as are proceeding in large caravans. They also make expeditions to plunder the inhabitants of other districts. The distances to which a band will travel on these occasions seems incredible. They roam far and wide, even penetrating as far to the west as Rudok and the region north of the Manasarowar lakes, but do not enter Gart'ok or Purang. An expedition to a point sometimes six to seven hundred miles distant is occasionally planned and undertaken. Some 250 start off together and deploy in small companies. The band drive away with them whole herds of cattle and ponies as booty from villages and tents. They are rarely resisted. Travellers they strip of everything; often, however, on petition returning a few provisions, cooking-pots, and articles of clothing. They do not care to enter the more settled districts where cultivation prevails; and these northern tribes, moreover, never hardly proceed far to the N.E. or E., which parts are regarded as the field of robbery belonging to the Golok marauders. The latter claim the tracts N. of the Dang-la.

The *Chang-gi Chakpa*, as the tribes of Jámar, Yagra, Amdo, etc., are styled by Tibetans of the Central provinces, revere the Dalai Lama and have shrines in their tents, but contribute few if any of their number to the lama fraternity. They have no monasteries or temples in their districts, and rob without scruple both monks and religious pilgrims.

Their dress is usually a robe, purple or perhaps violet in colour;

and they even wear petticoats or skirts, which on horseback are pulled well up through the belt to give freedom to the legs. Their arms and horse harness are silver mounted. When they camp they heap up walls of dried dung *inside* the tents to keep out wind and rain. If away from their tents, they bivouac in the open round a fire, wrapped in their big saddle blankets. On these expeditions they carry plenty of food or else plunder it; they indulge at times in dried mutton (*shaluk*), wheat cakes, clotted milk (*pima*) and other Tibetan delicacies, but can also content themselves with tea and *tsamba* meal only.

Mr. W. W. Rockhill gives an account of a short journey made in the company of members of the Namru tribe: "To add to our discomfort, there were violent storms of rain and hail daily, drenching us and our belongings and making it most difficult to find a little fuel with which to boil our tea. The escort was worse off than we, for we had a tent while they had nothing but their big blankets in which they wrapped themselves on the approach of a storm, and supperless went to sleep. When the weather was fine they fared sumptuously. On reaching camp five or six went foraging for fuel, two others filled the kettles, and others started the fires with big goatskin bellows. The little troop was divided into two messes, each with its kettle and bellows; while every man carried his supply of tsamba, dried mutton, tea, butter, clotted cream, and wheat-cakes; also a little earthenware pot in which to boil his tea. While the tea was boiling they drank a cup or two of clotted cream; then, having well licked their wooden bowls, they fell-to; tea and tsamba as first course, tsamba and tea as second course, and buttered tea as dessert. When they had finished eating, they sat till bed-time talking, twirling their prayer-wheels, and twisting yarn—their only amusements, for games, with the exception of knuckle-bones, are, I believe, unknown among them."

As evidencing the large bands in which the Horpa go marauding and the amount of their booty, we read in the narrative of A.K. this entry: "We reached the direct road from Mane Khorchen. Here we heard that a gang of mounted robbers from the Jama district, about 300 in number, was returning by this road laden with booty obtained from the Tengri Nur district. It consisted of 100 hill ponies, 300 yâks, and 5,000 goats and sheep. To escape an attack we diverged again towards the north-west............On the 9th we left the halting-place and proceeding 6 miles we met 5 mounted robbers. On being questioned they said they were residents of the Yágra district. They followed us for two marches intending to carry off our beasts of burden, but were unsuccessful, as we gave them no opportunity."

Polyandry does not prevail among the Horpa, yet the women seem as influential and respected as in the village districts where it is so prevalent. Brides before marriage go through a form of abduction or forcible capture which in certain cases is said to have been a regularly planned carrying off of an unwilling beauty. A large fine is given to the parents of the girl on marriage. Parents when aged are often abandoned to starve, and in many instances a son murders his father without incurring punishment. It is considered a natural action when the parent becomes old and a burden to maintain.

The Horpa are estimated to number 3,500 tents or rather more. The Jāmar De (tribe) is said to be the largest of the robber clans and to comprise 1,500 tents. Not more than 3 persons, sometimes only 2, and rarely as many as 4, are reckoned to each tent. If the people of Nagchhukha are reckoned as Horpa, the estimate would be much larger; but it is questionable if the tent-dwellers of that district can be deemed nomads or robbers. There are said to be 3,000 black tents in Nagchhukha: these tents hold mostly a pacific and industrious population of herdsmen.

2. The Gyá-de tribes or Khyung-po-pa.—Our knowledge of the inhabitants of this portion of East or East Central Tibet is mainly derived from Mr. Rockhill; and he computes their number at quite 50,000. He calls the region occupied Gyá-de (རྒྱལ་སྡེ), so styled from the fact that its people are placed under the more direct rule of the Chinese Amban at Lhása. The limits of this country are given as a broad band 60 miles from north to south, stretching eastwards from East Nagchhukha in long. 92°40′ to the western confines of the principality of Chhamdo, *circa* long. 96°25′ E. By far the major proportion of the people within the region profess the Bön or Pömbo creed, a branch of Shamanism said to be the primitive religion of Tibet. It is deliberately antagonistic to Buddhism; and in these points must be post-Buddhistic; for it has incorporated in its practice ceremonies and deities imitative in their express contrariety of Buddhist analogues. The Pömbo, accordingly, circumambulate sacred objects, passing first to the right of the object and keeping the object always on their left hand—the converse of the Buddhist custom; they eat fish and pork; they have female priests; they have books expressly the counterpart of the chief Buddhist ritual books with each direction reversed. As a leading deity of the Bön faith is a *Khyung* bird flying with wings inverted, the people of the Gyá-de territory are often known as Khyung-po-pa or Khyung-mi; and three

of their tribes call themselves *Khyung-kar* the white Khyung, *Khyung-nag* the black ditto, and *Khyung-ser* the yellow ditto, respectively.

Notwithstanding the pre-eminent status given to the votaries of the Bön religion throughout these North Central districts, there are also orthodox Gelukpa monasteries in the Khyung or Gyá-de region, a fact to which Mr. Rockhill does not allude. There are eight Gelukpa lamaseries in these parts, the chief of which is the great Sok Sung-dong Gompa on the Sok Chhu. The chief Pömbo establishment is the Ting-chhen Gompa.

Gyá-de appears to be apportioned into 36 *de* or districts with a chief nominated by the Amban over each district. Nearly the whole of the country, at least so much as the mountains and ravines permit to be utilised, is occupied by pasture-lands, and there is little corn or barley grown. In the western part the people live in tents; these are generally permanent camps, each tent being surrounded by a fence or low wall. In the east we find regular villages with houses built of hewn stone. There are vast flocks of sheep and herds of *ḍjomo* or milch-yak everywhere, but very few horses are reared.

Polygamy prevails in these districts, not polyandry. A noticeable feature in the villages is the number of children playing about, so different from what is observable in West Tibet, Tsang, and Ui, where polyandry is rife and a scanty offspring the result. Little value, however, is here attached to a girl's continence either before or after marriage. Guests and even travelling lamas are sometimes pressed by a host or landlord, as a mark of good-will, to take the company of his wife for the night. In the villages travellers putting up for only a week have various offers of temporary unions from respectable girls who are said not to lose social caste or esteem by the transaction. Rockhill describes the women as good-looking when young, but disfigured by the application of a black juice (*tuija*) smeared on the face, as indeed is the custom everywhere in Tibet.

The Khyung-po people wear the full heavy robe covering the whole frame which is common throughout Tibet. It is belted up so as to make the breast part very full and capacious and useable as a receptacle for the eating-bowl, tinder-pouch, prayer-wheel and other portable articles. In colour this robe is distinctive in these districts, in that it is violet for the men and blue for the women. There is a high collar, often made of wolf or other skin; and the cuffs of the sleeves are turned back either with the same skin or with white, red, or brown cloth. This style of cuff is seen in Tsang and the Lhása district as well as here; also in Sikkim. Over this robe is worn as "best dress" a sleeved waist-coat of smart green silk with a tall red collar. Rockhill says: "The women wear their hair in a great number of little plaits, falling over the shoulders like a cloak and reaching below the waist. Down the middle of the back is fixed a broad band of red, green, and other coloured stuffs, on which they sew ornaments of silver, turquoise, coral, or any ornamental knick-knack they may own."

THE PEOPLE OF KONG-PO.

Contiguous to the metropolitan province of Ui in which Lhása is placed, there stretches to the east the extensive province of Kong-po. It lies N.E. from the town of Chethang on the Yeru Tsang-po, and south of the great caravan route between Lhása and Bathang. It is divided into Kong-tö or Upper Kong-po, and Kong-me or Lower Kongo; also Nang-po.

The men of these districts are famous throught Tibet for their athletic build and gigantic size. In the fight on the Kharú-la on May 5th, 1904, between our troops and the Tibetans, the press correspondents wrote of the latter as "a herd of giants." These giants were warriors from Kong-po, and they fought with great courage until a general panic set in. They differ from the Khampas, further east, not only in average height but also in their ready faithfulness to the Lhása Government. The latter quality arises from the fact that for many generations the large proportion of the lands have been fiefdoms of the four Ling monasteries in Lhása; and the residents have been naturally used for centuries to acknowledge fealty to their monkish over-lords. Much of this land is fruitful, lying as it does in the numerous valleys which debouch on the bed of the Tsang-po; and this character renders the lordship of the cultivators a rich possession, for Tibet at least.

The Kong-po people are not only agriculturalists. They are great hunters and horse-breeders and engage in other branches of commerce, collecting rhubarb for export to China and trading likewise in lapis-lazuli and stags' horns.

Mons. Bonvalot and Prince Henry of Orleans in their rush across Tibet met some Kong-po people engaged in transporting on yaks bags of barley-meal from Sok Gompa to Lhása. The former in his lively way thus describes the men in question:

"As they approach we are struck by the breadth of their faces and by the slant of their eyes which turn upwards at the corners. They are dressed just like our drivers, but are much taller. At first sight a new people presents a well-defined type; but, on looking more closely and examining it well, this apparent uniformity is here found to be qualified by considerable variety. We are even astonished to find a resemblance in these Tibetans to certain other nations, and even to our friends and acquaintances at home. For instance, here is one with a perfect Greek profile as shewn on the best cameos. His neighbour, on the other hand, is of the American red-skin type, with receding brow and arched nose like an eagle's beak; while he walks with head slightly thrown back. By his side is a young lad singing as he prepares some meat for sausages, cutting it on the pommel of his saddle—with his dark eyes and regular features and hair falling over his forehead, he might be an Italian.

"What we can affirm as a fact is that we are in the presence of a white race—one which has nothing in common with those of a yellow complexion but the absence of a beard. This deficiency is, however, amply compensated by the quantity of hair they have on their heads; in fact, it is not unusual to see even old men with plaits as thick as a cable."

KHAMS AND THE KHAMPAS.

The whole of East Tibet, or that huge region stretching east of long. 92° to the Chinese border, is loosely designated in Tibetan geography as Khams or Khamdo; and to Tibetans inhabiting other parts of Tibet the people of the whole of this region are classified together as Khampa. Khams, however, in reality comprises 13 principalities or sub-provinces and is inhabited by tribes of very diverse characteristics and under varying forms of government. In religion all the Khampa tribes own fealty in a general way to the Dalai Lama of Lhása; but, politically, certain of the sub-provinces accept China as suzerain; others acknowledge in a measure the jurisdiction of the *Dewa-zhung* or Lhása government.

The inhabitants of East Tibet are, however, an independent and lawless set of folk, and are very loth to admit any jurisdiction save that of their local rulers. Some of these states or principalities are governed by lay chieftains who claim the title of *gyalpo* or "king"; others have ecclesicatical princes with *debas* or deputy governors for the districts into which they are sub-divided. The two leading principalities of Khams are those of Chhamdo and Derge. Chhamdo comprises a large territory lying along the northern banks of the great river Gyama Ngul Chhu (the upper course of the Salwin) and south of the Dang-la range. Acknowledging Lhása as its suzerain, it is practically an independent state ruled jointly by two ecclesiastics, the co-lamas of Chhamdo Gompa who are known as Phagpa

Lha Yab and Phagpa Lha Shras, "his lordship Phagpa the father" and "his lordship Phagpa the son." Chhamdo, the capital of the state, occupies an important strategic position on massive rocks forming the tongue of land above the confluence of two great rivers, the Dza Chhu and the Ngom Chhu, which, after coalescence, form the upper waters of the Mekhong river. This town has been passed on their respective journeys, but not entered, by Capt. Bower, by Mons. Bonvalot and by Mr. Rockhill. These gentlemen were each begged by the authorities to avoid entering the place itself, as its denizens were described as a turbulent set very hostile to foreigners. Father Huc, nevertheless, stayed three days in peace in Chhamdo, and has left an uninviting description of the place. "Tsiamdo," he says, "presents the appearence of an ancient town in decay; its large houses constructed with frightful irregularity, are scattered confusedly over a large tract, leaving on all sides unoccupied ground or heaps of rubbish.........The numerous population you see in the town are dirty, uncombed, and wallow in profound idleness. We could not divine what were the means of existence of the inhabitants of Tsiamdo; they are without arts, industry, and we may add almost without agriculture. The environs of the town present, generally speaking, nothing but sand, unfavourable to the cultivation of corn."

Mr. Rockhill, however, informs us that the Chhamdo country further afield from the town is much less inhospitable than Mons. Huc thought. After leaving Chhamdo, his route lay, he says, at first over steep and high mountains, but then passed down a valley covered with the most beautiful pine trees, their branches draped in long cobweb-like moss of light yellow and bright orange: "There were many silver pheasants in the thick under-wood; and the yak drivers told me that bears, leopards and wolves were frequently found here. Leaving this behind we passed into another valley of great beauty in which I found nearly every variety of tree and wild fruit known to Tibet—cedars, junipers, cypress, pines and maples, plum aud apple trees, cherry and apricot, raspberries, both the orange and red varieties, strawberries, and currants."

The Khampas of the principality of Chhamdo are, as elsewhere in Tibet, properly divisable into two widely-different kinds of people. The townsfolk, lay or clerical, are a mixed race, descendant from the local tribe and from the herd of miscellaneous lamas hailing from Mongolia, Tibet and China. These are stalwart in build, but in character a blackguardly, low, dissipated and idle set. They are ever ready for a broil, in which stone-throwing is a leading feature; and when fighting at close quarters do not scruple to use their finger-nails and to hang on with their teeth.

The country-folk, some of whom are pastoral dwelling in tents and others agriculturalists living in villages, are of purer descent; they are not so tall as the natives of Kongpo, but are strong and well-built. Mons. Bonvalot in his narrative has given us some graphic pictures of the rural Khampas of the Chhamdo province. We may quote his account of a visit to a local *deba* or chief of a district, that of Seresumdo:—

We had no sooner reached the platform, which borders a river of considerable width, than we saw a number of natives who seemed to be expecting us. Several of them came forward, and, politely taking our horses by the bridles, conducted us to this great chief, who was one of the very stoutest of Thibetans that we had ever seen—quite a Vitellius. In spite of, or perhaps because of, his rotundity, he was very amiable, shaking our hands most cordially and begging us to honour him by taking a seat on his rug On each side of him was a lama, one with a head like an actor, the other with that of a faun. He himself carried on his bull-neck a splendid well-shaped head—the head of a savage monarch with hair hanging down his back. This specimen of a thick-set Goliath insisted on our tasting the contents of three iron bottles cased in tin, of Chinese make, judging by their shape; on the liquid lumps of butter were floating, having been added to the decoction out of compliment to us.........When we rose to leave, the fat chief and all his followers insisted on conducting us; so they brought him a splendid mule which, in spite of his weight, he mounted unaided; and so we started. Having crossed the river, the crowd on foot tucking up their skirts and displaying the sturdy though somewhat long legs of mountaineers, we climbed a narrow path on the edge of the chasm, pitching our tent near a clump of houses built on the mountain-side. A crowd of idlers of both sexes soon surrounded us; the women being very ugly, while a few of the young men had rather nice faces.

Here is another graphic sketch from the Chhamdo country which has the advantage of referring to the style of abode in the rural districts. We have again a corpulent *Deba*:—

We saw the ambitious chief to-day. We had, however, to wait a very long time for him in the valley, his village being perched high up like an eagle's nest and he himself being quite tipsy. As soon as he had recovered the use of his legs he descended from his eyrie. He proved to be an enormous fellow with grey eyes; but was pleasant in his cups, giving his orders with great decision and setting everybody to work. He spent his leisure moments sitting astride a bale and continuing his carouse, looking as he drank like a clumsy Silenus. Every now and then there came forth from his ponderous bosom shouts with which the whole valley rang, the outlet of his great animal spirits. We left him with mutual expressions of good will, after having bought from him a sheep for two shillings.

Hamlets and farms abound hereabouts. They are built of rough stones the walls exceedingly thick, the terraces and roofs resting on trunks of trees. We are still in a wild district, but the natives live in houses and there are signs of the early stage of civilisation. They till their land better and manure their fields; they wear stuff clothes and the women adorn themselves with trinkets. Armed men are much rarer, as if there were greater security than in the districts situated to the west.

Derge, another great state of Khams, lies N.E. of Chhamdo. It is not ruled by ecclesiastics but by a layman styled *gyalpo* or "king." The district, however, abounds with huge monasteries teeming with monks of the Urgyenpa, an heretical Buddhist sect; and Rockhill writes of these establishments that they are like so many great fortified camps, the inmates being well-armed and ever on the look-out for a fray. The chief town, known as Derge *dong-khyer*, is a famous manufacturing centre, quite the Birmingham of Eastern Tibet. Here guns, swords, metal inlaid harness, teapots, beautifully finished and often ornamented artistically with figures in beaten brass, are turned out. Doubtless many of the rifles, to which in the present British campaign the Tibetans have taken so kindly, were manufactured in Derge; while the rifle-shooters have come from Derge *gon-chhen*, the great monastic city adjoining the lay manufacturing town, the inmates of which are certainly ever "spoiling for a fight."

Immediately South of Derge and abutting the eastern limits of Chhamdo, from which it is separated by the Moto Shan mountains, is another large sub-division or state of Khams, namely Trag-yab, usually sounded Draya. Two ecclesiastics rule here, the heads of two different monasteries, one of whom is styled Chhe-tsang and the other Chhung-tsang, the former being fantastically considered the "mother" of the latter. Huc alludes to this petty state under the name of Djaya; and he describes the people as particularly independent and warlike, extremely inimicable also to the Chinese.

South of Chhamdo and East of Kongpo, occupying large tracts between the southern banks of the Gyama Ngul Chhu and the left banks of the Yeru Tsangpo, is the principality of Po-wo or Po-yul, "the land of incense." The state is partitioned into Po-me and Po-tö, both of which together are governed by a woman, an hereditary line of queens having apparently been established. Brigandage is followed by the *Debas* or chieftains in Po-tö who lead their retainers annually on pillaging campaigns. On the other hand in Po-me blanket-weaving and other industries are pursued. There are many agriculturalists also.

Other states of Khams are: Mar-kham, east of Po-yul and south of Draya; Bah, the division next east with the large and well-known town of Ba-t'ang as capital, a great grazing country with rich forests on the hills; Mili, south-west of Bah; Kham Lhari, the westernmost sub-division of Khams, lying west even of Chhamdo. Hor-chhyok or Nyagrong comprises five petty sub-states, supposed to be governed direct from Lhása by an official known as the Chikyab of Nyagrong. There is also Mönyag or Lower Nyagrong; and further south, Zayul, which district, however, does not form part of Khamyul. The Zayuli folk are slave-owners, procuring slaves from Assam through the intermediary of the Mishmis.

Taking the Khampa generally, we may follow Rockhill in dividing them into Dokpa (his *Dru-pa*) or pastoral tribes and town or village dwellers. The noble and chivalrous qualities which Father Huc observed in these Tibetans is almost confined to the former. All Khampas indeed are strong and brave; but the dwellers in the Tibetan towns near the Chinese borderland have the worst elements of the European rough and blackguard in combination, it is true, with much animal courage. The officials which the Chinese have placed as nominal representatives in all the towns and larger villages, from the rank of *Liang-tai* downwards, are on the whole a civilising influence; but the control they exercise depends mainly on the power each happens to have acquired over the fears and avarice of the head of the leading local lamasery.

THE ABORS OR ABARS.

The foremost of the tribes inhabiting the extreme S.E. of Tibet may be said to be the Abors. These people, who speak a language containing very little admixture of Tibetan words, occupy the low mountain fastnesses situated from 30 to 40 miles north of the town of Sadiya in East Assam. Their villages stand in difficult positions on the hill-sides between the debouchments from the Himalayas of the Rivers Dihang and Sessiri respectively, and also on the right or western bank of the Dihang. The gorges of the Dihang and the Sessiri are only 8 to 11 miles apart as the crow flies, so that including a breadth of about 4 miles on the west bank of the Dihang, their width of country from west to east is a restricted one. The Mishmis now occupy a large slice of land east of the Sessiri which formerly belonged to the Abors, and have even in recent years crossed the Sessiri and taken possession of much Abor land on the west of the latter river in and about the Abor settlements of Siluk and Dambuk. Northwards they do not live further than lat. 28°52′ N.

The political constitution of the Abors is peculiar. Each village seems to be independent of the others in its government and internal laws, the latter being enacted by all male adults in open meeting held at noon in the *mosup* or assembly barrack. Some few of the villagers are elected as *gam* or elders to see that these enactments are obeyed, and though these have great influence in the *mosup*, the inhabitants are alert in preserving their democratic rights. At the meetings there is much speechifying and fine oratory is applauded. In certain matters affecting the whole Abor community, deputies from different villages assemble at Membu which may be regarded as the unacknowledged capital of the country.

In the placing of their villages much care has been taken to make them strongholds. The village is perched either on a shelf in a mountain-side or on the top of some moderately-high table-peak. The approaches are rugged and stony, and various gullies are artificially made in the way and have to be crossed by single planks easily removable. Mr. J. F. Needham, the chief and almost sole authority on the subject, has described the situation of Membu. He writes "From the Siku up to Membu the distance is about two miles, and I calculated that we ascended about 800 or 1,000 feet in that distance. The village site has been marvellously well chosen. On its southern and western sides the hills rise perpendicularly from the bed of the Siku to a height of about 800 feet, and they are quite bare, while to the north and westward the hill-sides are cut up by deep ravines, and they are likewise so perpendicular that it would be impossible to ascend them. As far as I could see the only possible way of getting into the village would be by the path we were taking, *viz.*, from the southward, and there are numerous deep, though narrow, artificially-made ravines to be crossed, as well as several steep ascents to be made ere the village is reached, each of which might, if necessary, be so defended in turn by a resolute body of men as to make it an exceedingly difficult matter for any enemy to enter the village."

In the centre of each settlement stands the *mosup* or debating-house which is also especially the barrack and sleeping apartment of all unmarried men above 14 years of age belonging to the place. The building affords accommodation for from 200 to 300 residents and is constructed with many fire-places along each side. Guests and travellers are located in the *mosup*. As to the dwelling-houses, they are described as massive dignified buildings of barn-like contour from 60 to 80 feet long by 15 to 20 feet broad. In front is a long verandah covered by the overhanging roof, which roof slopes down to within two feet of the outside ground. Inside, the houses are very dark and having 4 or 5 open fire-hearths are also very warm. The population of each village is always over 1,000, and Membu has about 2000 souls.

The Abor men are savage and easily provoked; the use of poisoned spears and arrows making them formidable foes. But Mr. Needham considers them both exceedingly brave and always truthful, also readily conciliated by kind and soothing words. The men hunt but do not work in the fields which are often situated 6 or 8 miles distant from the village. Women and girls perform all the agricultural operations but are escorted to and from the fields by bands of armed men who remain on guard while they are labouring. These men bring home the heads of many wild animals they kill and the houses are ornamented both inside and outside with these trophies of the chase.

The girls are described as decidedly plain in looks but with jolly laughing faces, the unmarried ones being allowed any amount of moral latitude. All women seem to wear their hair cropped and have the breasts bare; they are clad only in a short petticoat reaching not quite to the knee. Their big heavy limbs are much exposed without any delicacy and are tatooed under the bend of the knee. Of the unmarried girls Mr. Needham remarks that they wear over the juncture of their legs, for decency's sake, five or six flat circular plates of brass, one slightly overlapping the other, called *boiop*, fixed to a platted band of thin cane under their petticoats, and while working in their fields, or in the village on a hot day, it is the only article they have to cover their nakedness; they also wear little gaiters of platted cane, coloured, about six inches wide, on each ankle, called *essong* in Abor. They are excessively fond of necklaces, earrings, and bracelets, in fact, of finery of all sorts. Their teeth are as black as a coal from continually chewing *sali*, tobacco, and *chun* (the latter the Abors make themselves out of a shell which they find in their river beds), and many of them also smoke pipes like the men. They are very fond of singing and dancing.

The Abor religion is a lower cult of the Shamán series. Demons inhabit caves, the under-soil, lakes, and trees, causing diseases and untoward events. These spirits, termed *oyu*, can be propitiated and rendered subservient by enchantments which vary with the species at issue. The Shamán priest is styled *mirü* and exorcises the *oyu* much in the same way as the Ngakpa sorcerers of Tibet proceed in such rites; as the latter menace and metaphorically transfix demons with the *phurbu* dagger, so does the Abor *mirü* vanquish them with his *yokhsha* or magic knife. There seems no Buddhist colouring in the Abor religion. According to Mr. Needham, the two most powerful deities or demons are named Apom and Nyi-pong, and dwell in india-rubber trees which are therefore considered sacred. On certain days when a *gena* or festive celebration is observed no men may pass through fields where growing crops are, else the ire of the earth gnomes is aroused.

There seem to be at least four divisions of the Abor race; the northernmost, or Abors proper, who extend as far north as lat. 29°, being styled Damlah Padam; those to the west, Siluk Abor; those in the centre and east including the Membu folk Passi Miyong; and those to the south, the Padu Abor. Among the chief strongholds are Damlah, Membu, Romkang, Padu, Gina, Mongku, Balek, Siluk and Dambuk. Our Government has lately permitted a settlement at Nizamghat near the gorge whence the Dibang river debouches.

THE MIRI TRIBES.

The Miris are a Tibetan race occupying the mountainous country to the S.W. of that claimed by the Abors. The ranges they inhabit are much higher than those in the Abor lands, being from 6,000 to 8,000 feet in general altitude. So far as can be at present ascertained the Miri country lies between lat. 27°30′ and 28°20′ N. and stretches west and east between long. 93°40′ and 94°45′ E.—in fact it comprises the valleys and hill-sides besetting the lower waters of the Subansiri river on both banks and passing N.W. to include the basin of the Kamla river. Other villages are pitched on spurs above the Seu and Sidang streams, tributaries of the Subansiri. The nearest plains station from which the Miri country can be reached from Assam is Pathalipam in North Lakhimpur.

Roughly we may divide the Miri tribes into two great sections, the Ghasi Miris occupying the lands both east and west of the lower Subansiri after the latter river has been joined by the Kamla, and the Kamla Miris who dwell in the side valleys of the Khru and Kamla rivers and inhabiting the country far to the W. and N. of the Ghasi tribes. North of lat. 28° N. in the upper valley of the Kamla are other Miri tribes of wilder and more barbarous habits. The country there is said to be much more open and the pathways easy, the villages of these more remote tribes being very numerous on the lower spurs of hills overlooking the upper Kamla.

The Miris are described as of fair complexion, and in the case of the girls and youths ruddy cheeks are a noticeable trait. Though the mouth is well cut, the face is Tartar in cast, flat in contour with snub nose, high cheek-bones, eyes far apart and slightly oblique. In both sexes the hair is allowed to grow long, though generally plaited and worn turned up and fastened with bone pins. However, moustaches and beards are seldom seen, very scanty hairs growing anywhere on the face.

As to dress, the Ghasi tribes are much better and more decently clothed than those of the N.W. districts. The males both old and young invariably wear a peculiar head-gear of wicker-work, a sort of helmet with a peak curving downwards behind on to the top of the spine; feathers and grasses decorating it above the forehead. A coarse cloth is tied crosswise over the shoulders hanging down behind, while a small waist-cloth passes between the thighs. Rude skin jackets are also worn in very cold weather or when fighting. Cane rings are always part of the body-attire, being placed one upon the other in loose order about the waist.

The female attire is only a tight petticoat fastened round the waist with, sometimes, a cloth worn cross-wise over the bosom. They have, also, a series of loose cane rings supported only by the buttocks, and always ornamentally coloured. The laté Colonel Woodthorpe, who as Captain Woodthorpe visited the Miri country in 1877-78, alluding in his *Report* to the women's dress, remarks: "Among these canes is a curious belt of leather, a couple of inches broad, studded with large and strong metal points, a most effectual safeguard against the too tender pressure of the lover's arm. When working in the fields the petticoat is frequently discarded for a thick and long fringe of grass, and in some places the men also wear a small grass apron in lieu of the waist-cloth, enabling us fully to realise the appearance of Adam and Eve when they first became alive to decency."

The Miri tribe to the N.W. in the valley of the upper Subansiri go completely naked, save that the women wear the cane-rings already mentioned about their loins.

Messrs. Woodthorpe and Robert found the Miri villages very small, containing rarely more than 9 or 10 houses; but large families dwell in each house, one visited giving shelter to 40 souls. The barrack system wherein the youths of the village live in a separate building does not prevail save in one or two of the larger villages of the Ghasi Miris N.E. of the Subansiri. The houses are built on the slope of a hill without any attempt to level a shelf on which to pitch them. They are erected on a platform supported by posts with bamboo matting for walls. There is attached to every residence a piggery also built on posts; and in each village are several large granaries with sloping floors.

The Kamla Miris are great trappers of both small animals and fish, setting snares near every path. Each man has his own hunting-ground into which others may not intrude. Moreover, a curious point is this—the various mountain-peaks take their names from those of the different owners of the hunting-ground in which each happens to stand. The Ghasi Miris and the tribes N.E. of the Subansiri, on the contrary, never set snares for animals, only for fish; but they are expert trackers of big game such as *Budorcas*, leopards, and rhinoceros, which they will follow for days through the most difficult jungle.

THE MISHMIS.

Tribes bearing the general designation of Mishmi occupy the mountainous tracts N.E. of Sadiya in Assam, from the left bank of the Sessiri river eastwards above the Brahmakund district over the Rong T'od chain into the valley of Lower Zayul. Mr. T. T. Cooper was the first traveller to have familiar dealings with them and found them less murderous than they had been described. However their bad reputaton was not without foundation, seeing that a few years previously they had barbarously slain two Jesuit missionaries (Fathers Krick and Boury) who had penetrated from Zayul. In recent years Mr. Needham has held much intercourse with the Mishmis of different districts and specially studied the dialects of the Taru and Mju tribes.

In 1899—1900 a British punitary expedition was despatched into the Mishmi country, and advantage was taken of this expedition by the Survey of India to make a reconnaissance of a portion of the territory they inhabit. As a result, a report drawn up by Lieut. G. L. S. Ward, field-intelligence officer, gives a full if tentative account of the western districts of these people. It seems that the tracts west of the Rong T'od Chhu comprise the main Mishmi country. The westernmost lands are drained by the Ithun, a big river which joins the Dibang from the east. Between the Dibang and the Ithun, north of the junction, lie the large villages belonging to the tribe known as the Mdu Mishmi. East of the Mdus are the tribe of Mthun Mishmi occupying lands east of the Ithun and north of lat. 28°18′ N. Further east and north still of this latitude are the spurs from the Atak Gangri range where stand the villages of the Taru or Digaru Mishmi. Still more to the east come the Meju or Mju Mishmi; and quite on the borders of Zayul dwells the Náhong tribe whose lands reach even up to Sama and Rima.

Each of the five Mishmi tribes mentioned is subdivided into clans, none of the members of each clan being allowed to marry save with the members of another clan. However a man must marry within his tribe; a Mdu, for example, not being permitted to marry a Mthun. The Mdu Mishmis are now in a measure civilised; while the Mthun or "outcast" Mishmi, reputed ferocious cannibals, seem to be arrant cowards and untruly accused of man-eating.

The dwellings vary in length from 40 to 200 feet, and each is boarded off into compartments. There are no houses for bachelors or debating-halls. The Mdu and Mthun tribes build stockades for defensive purposes round and below the villages. This is not the case in villages of the Mju tribe. Here each village, even each house, is quite independent of all others; and no settled form of government is in existence.

Mishmis belong to the Mongolian type, having flat noses and almond-shaped eyes. They are small in stature, very active and quick; also very dirty. Their dress comprises a woollen tunic devoid of all sleeve, having holes for the arms, with a sort of kilt or apron below. The women are fully and neatly covered both in body and limbs; the married women wearing a band of thin silver round the head. As is often the case among barbarous tribes, the men are much vainer than the women; both sexes, however, distend the lobes of their ears with enormous silver earrings. The men are armed with a short sword, and either a bow or a spear; a few have flint-lock muskets. A pouch of the skin of some wild animal is generally carried over the shoulders, and contains a pipe, tobacco, flint and steel, also some poison (aconite), to put on their arrow heads. The Mishmis exchange poison and musk-deer pods with the Tibetans (whose neighbours they are) for clothing, salt, and swords; and they barter indiarubber, ivory, beeswax, and ginger, for salt, opium, and clothing, with the inhabitants of Assam. Until very recently there was a regular slave traffic carried on by the Mishmis with the Tibetans of Zayul. They kidnapped young people, chiefly boys and youths up to 20 years of age, in Assam and brought them into Zayul where they fetched a fair price. This traffic, though curtailed by British vigilance in Assam, is not altogether extinct.

THE NATIVES OF LADAK.

As an appendix to this chapter, we venture to print some extracts from an anonymous article on the Ladaki Tibetan race, living outside the confines of Tibet Proper. This article written as a letter from Leh, the capital of Ladak, appeared in the columns of a well-known Indian newspaper, *The Statesman*, of November 26th, 1895 :—

The Ladakhis are good-tempered and cheerful, friendly and grateful, hardworking and plodding. To hear them singing and laughing over their labour, and to see them performing it with energy and good-will, is a real treat to the traveller from lower lands, where existence is so much less stern. As to their mental endowments, a short acquaintance does not qualify the observer to say much. It strikes a stranger, however, that some degree of natural aptitude for music must be one, not only because of the characteristic lama music, but also from the simple songs of the people and their apparent fondness for singing; and, again, from the way in which the Christians have picked up the German chorales taught them by the Moravian missionaries, and the pleasure with which strangers voluntarily come in and sit at the door and listen to the weekly hymn-singing practice. But as a race they have had little intellectual opportunity. Yet one cannot but be impressed with the thought that a people whose fathers, by sheer industry and hard work, turned large tracts of wilderness into a fruitful field, and won a living from the barren valleys of their native land, and who themselves exist only by keeping up the system of irrigation thus bequeathed to them, must possess great latent possibilities, if only they could be developed.

Physically the Ladakhis are a fine race, that is to say, the men are; but the women are generally small and insignificant, therein comparing most unfavourably with the neighbouring Cashmiris. They are also far inferior to the Cashmiris in beauty of feature; one rarely, if ever, sees a handsome face in either man or woman. Their features approach the Mongolian type, which to European taste is not beautiful. Some of the men even wear the pigtail, differing, however, from the Chinese in this, that the rest of the hair is not shaved off, but more or less loose hair is left at the sides. Those who do not sport the pigtail wear their hair in long loose locks. Their hair is black, and their complexions of about the same degree of fairness as that of the Cashmiris, but not of the yellow tinge characteristic of the Mongolian. The dress of the men consists of a long loose coat reaching considerably below the knees, made of undyed sheep's wool, and confined at the waist by a broad loose black or coloured cloth girdle, wound repeatedly round the body, in which are stuck a knife and a tinder-box and sundry other handy articles. On the head is a circular cloth cap, of almost any colour, lined either with red cotton or with black lambskin. It is cut long at the sides and back, and this part is usually worn turned up, making a very picturesque headdress; and the handsomer ones have a border of gold embroidery in front round the face. On the feet are woollen boots, sometimes of the whitey-grey undyed wool, sometimes of many colours; some of them reaching to the knee, some only a little way above the ankle. The women wear a decent costume—a woollen gown, generally of dark-brown or dark-claret or dark-blue, with triangular red and yellow spots—consisting of body and skirt. Round the waist is wound a dark cloth girdle similar to that worn by the men, from which on the left side hangs a sort of "chatelaine" composed of narrow strips of leather suspended from a circular shield of brass-work, and bearing sundry useful articles such as a small brass spoon, leather purse, etc., and some bunches of white shells. Their boots resemble those worn by the men. From the shoulders a sheepskin, with the wool inwards and the leather side outwards, hangs down behind; and sometimes instead of this is worn a square scarlet *chudder* or shawl with a coloured border, carried under the left arm, and fastened by its two upper corners on the right shoulder. The characteristic head-dress is the "perak," a stiff construction of scarlet cloth, pointed over the forehead, widening as it passes backward over the crown of the head, and hanging down the back.

This is coverd with turquoises in longitudinal rows—one, two, three, four, five, or even six—the number and value of the turquoises being dependent on, and indicative of, the wealth of the wearer, and the handsomest turquoise forming a centre-piece over the forehead. The value of a perak sometimes amounts to several hundred rupees, or on the other hand it may be very trifling. Under this head-dress the hair is worn in a number of small plaits on either side, beneath which are fastened some circular ear-pieces of black lambskin, coming forward on either side of the face. The plaits are collected into one central one, which hangs down the back, and is terminated by a large woollen tassel that nearly reaches the ground and is banged about by the heels as the owner walks.

* * * * * *

The lamas met in Leh and its neighbourhood are of the sect called the Red Lamas. They wear a long, loose gown, reaching nearly to the ground, and leaving the arms bare, of dark-red cloth, and a girdle of the same colour; a chudder or shawl of a lighter shade of red; and a cap of red or yellow, of the same shape as that worn by ordinary men, except that the crown instead of being flat is pointed. The chief lamas remain for the most part in their gompas; but lamas of lower degree are seen about freely, sometimes engaged in ordinary pursuits, sometimes apparently idling about and sustaining their reputation for sanctity by twirling their "prayer mills." These are small cylinders of copper or silver mounted on a handle and enclosing rolls of paper inscribed with numerous repetitions of the Buddhist prayer formula, "Om mani padma hum," which being swung round and round in the hand, as many prayers are reckoned to the credit of the bearer as the sum of the repetition of the formula multiplied by the number of rotations performed by the mill.

The large majority of the Ladakhis are Buddhists, but there is also a Mahomedan minority, who, contrary to the state of things prevailing in Cashmere, constitute the more educated and intelligent portion of the community. The official class wear a modification of the national costume, consisting of a long coat of black or dark-coloured cloth reaching nearly to the ankles, with the usual cloth girdle wound round the waist, and a white turban. Among the Buddhists prevails the custom of polyandry, and the offspring of these unions speak of their "great father" and "little father." There is besides a small Christian community of between twenty and thirty persons, including children; but Ladakhi law is stringent against Christianity, and no Christian, native or European, is allowed to possess land or house property.

But Ladakhis are not the only people who attract our interested attention in Leh nor even their congeners, the Lahoulis, Baltis, and others, from up and down the river, and over the neighbouring passes. For Leh is a great trade centre, and in its serai and bazaar representatives of many races meet, and drive their bargains, and part again. The commissioner who has this year represented British authority there, Captain Trench, established a weekly informal durbar for strangers under the shade of the Residency trees, with tea and chupatties and friendly talk by way of entertainment—for the denizens of these parts of the world have no bigoted antipathy to sharing the social board with Christians or Europeans—and his guests came together from far and wide. Russian subjects from all parts of Central Asia, Chinese subjects from as far away as Hongkong, subjects of the Shah of Persia, and subjects of the Ameer of Afghanistan, met in friendlywise to pay their respects to the British representative, and to share his hospitality In Leh during the busy months of August and September may be seen Yarkandis, Chinese, Thibetans from Lhasa, Persians, Afghans, Pathans, Hindoostanees, Punjabis, and Cashmeris,—all busy and orderly and well-behaved. You see them in the serai solemnly transacting their business; in the bazar making small bargains with the shop-keepers, or driving their laden animals into or out of the city; in the stableyards tending their patient ponies, or shoeing them in preparation for the next march northward or southward; beside the streams watering them, or applying hydropathic treatment to grievously sore backs, in the vain hope that they may soon be fit again to bear their burdens. And not only merchants, but Hadjis or Mahomedan pilgrims bound for Mecca from Central Asia pass through Leh in hundreds during the travelling season.

The Yarkandis are the most numerous and perhaps also the most picturesque figures with their round fur-bordered caps, their high brown. leather boots, and their long coats shaped something like a European dressing gown, either lined with fur or thickly wadded and covered with some dark or bright-coloured cotton stuff outside, and lined with some other bright and contrasting colour inside, and opening in front to show an inner short coat of a third colour, and this again, sometimes displaying a white undergarment. Sometimes they are accompanied by their lady-folk, who may be seen riding astride through the bazaar behind their lords and masters, dressed like them, high boots and all, except for the little white cotton veil before their faces with transparent spaces in front of the eyes to allow of their seeing the world that may not see them.

But I must not be tempted into too elaborate a description of the interesting figures to be seen in the Leh bazaar, but must close for this time, in the hope of another day concluding this series of letters with some account of Leh in its commercial and political aspects.

CHAPTER X.

LHÁSA; THE CAPITAL OF TIBET.

SITUATION AND GENERAL ASPECT.

Lhása, or "the place of the gods," stands in latitude 29° 39′ 12″ N., and in longitude 91° 5′ 30″ E.; and although in actual situation it is a degree-and-a-half *further south* than Lahore in India, it has in the summer months an average temperature just half that usually measured in the Punjab city.[1] In large measure this is due to its height above the level of the sea; the altitude varying from 11,700 ft. in the general plane of the streets to 11,986 ft. for the Grand Lama's palace on the summit of Potala. At such an elevation as that do the denizens of the place digest their food, dance, and sing, and pray, and transact commercial affairs; so that indeed they are unable to live at lower heights.

The world-renowned capital of Tibet, the Rome of the northern cults of Buddhism, is seated on a broad marshy fertile plain on the northern bank of the Kyi Chhu or "waters of happiness," a river which at this part measures some 600 yards in width. Around it lie gardens and meadows with curious walled enclosures closely packed with stunted-looking trees, the latter chiefly in the southern suburbs. There is much marsh-land on the W. and N.W. sides of the city, the great track which approaches the city from the west being beset by drain-channels, dykes, and water-courses, many of which run across the road. The marsh on this western side is termed *Dam-tsho* and on the N.W. *Kyang-thang Naga*. In the environs to the S., lying between the city and the river is also

[1] Thus on July 22nd, 1879, the thermometer in Lhása at 6 A.M. registered 48°8 exposed in shade, rising to 64° by noon. In winter, however, the cold is not so severe as might be expected. When one of our secret explorers visited the place in 1866, he took frequent readings of the thermometer throughout every day in February, and only once during that month does the temperature between 10 A.M. in a room without fire seem to have sunk below freezing point. The lowest temperature he registered was 26° at 7 A.M. on February 14th, the highest 45° at 6 P.M. on February 25th.

a tract of water-logged grounds, although here is the fashionable quarter where on embanked plots are many pleasant houses each in a a grove of trees—the suburban villas where the better class *trung-khor* or Government clerks reside. A series of canals intersects these southern lands carrying the drainage of the city to the river. There are said to be several effluent springs in the heart of Lhása which feed the canals and flush the drainage. The canals, moreover, are in request for irrigation purposes; for everywhere in the suburbs stretch long narrow fields (*shing-kha*) in which beans, wheat, barley, milled rape, and especially radishes, are cultivated.

To the N. of Lhása, some four miles distant, are the nearest hills; a low sandy range styled To-de-phu or Dog-de-phu rising up abruptly there. These are reputed to abound in silver, lapis lazuli and malachite, which however, it is said, are forbidden to be sought for. To the E. and S., much further off, loftier mountains appear; but the vicinity of the city is singularly level for Tibet, the Kyi river winding in from the E. through a series of flats the most part of which is under close cultivation.

Approaching Lhasa from the west by the main road, after the Daipung Monastery is passed, suddenly the wondrous vista of the Buddhist capital opens out. To your right, on the south, enclosed in heavy walls is a dark mass of thickly-planted trees, well-foliaged poplars, walnuts, and willows. Half hidden amidst them is a grotesque-shaped building not unrelated to the Brighton Pavilion in style. That is Norbu Linga (ནོར་བུ་གླིང་ཀ) the winter domicile of the Dalai Lama when the exposed temples on Potala become too cold for residence. More in front of you, but still to the right, and beyond Norbu Linga are two hills, Chakpo Ri and Pama Ri respectively, on the more southern of which at a height of some 250 feet stands a quaint dome-capped edifice—the Waidurya Tatshang or "Lapis-lazuli College, the central medical monastery of the kingdom. On Pama Ri is the Kesar Lha-khang, a big temple for the Chinese. To your left hand, ahead of you, within the confines of the outer portions of the city, a broad hill stands up, rising out of a basement of scattered houses interspersed with walnuts and poplars. Buildings of many tiers and extensive arcades range up and down the hill-side, and the whole is crowned by temple-like structures bearing up at intervals five low gilded domes cubical in shape and with concave sides. As the sun touches these domes they shew as if they were of pure polished gold. This hill with its temples is the famous Potala (to be described in detail hereafter) where dwells the Incarnation of the Bodhisattwa

Chenraisi, in other words the Dalai Lama or priest-emperor of Tibet. Far ahead in the midst of the city before you, start up many turrets and towers mostly with glittering head-pieces. The most prominent of these, rising above all the rest, are the gilt-plated cupolas[1] of the Jho-khang which is as it were the cathedral or metropolitan temple of Lhása.

To reach from the western road the outer or suburban city wherein are located Potala, Pama Ri and Chakpo Ri, we must first traverse a lengthy bridge which spans a big canal or affluent river (crossing the road from the north, skirting the Norbu Linga and then joining the Kyi Chhu). This bridge, the Chara Sampa, lands us on the Lingkor Road, a thoroughfare here running from north to south but which really completely girdles the metropolis, enclosing both the inner and the outer cities. The main purpose of this thoroughfare is to enable the religious to perform that essential act of Buddhistic worship—the rite of circumambulation; and to be given facilities for circling round the whole of sacred Lhása in one morning and again, perhaps, at sun-down is an advantage greatly prized and largely utilised.

Passing under Pargo Kāling, the western gateway just mentioned, and skirting a gigantic and grotesque *chhorten*,[2] built on four buttresses as if it were some four-legged monster, you soon find yourself in a broad street lined on each side with aged walnut and willow trees, mostly mere stumps, the venerableness of which is cherished.

Here at once begin rows of lofty houses, apparently exceedingly solid though built of only sun-dried bricks. They are lime-washed beautifully white and are roofed in fantastic curves covered with highly-glazed blue tiles. Every house here has windows curiously tall and narrow and deeply-recessed, the window-ledges fringed below with strips of cherry-red and amber-yellow cloth; and each house,

[1] The Tibetan name for the huge gold-plated cubes, which crown temples and other sacred buildings much as domes and lanthorns surmount cathedrals in Europe, is རྒྱལ་ཕིབས་ sounded *gye-p'i*. Neither "cube" nor any single word properly expresses the shape. It is a large hollow structure. The top is square and raised in the centre where a gold boss a foot in height protrudes. From the edges of the square top depend the sides bulging inwards in graceful crescent or concave form and reaching outwards to the edges of the bottom of the structure which is square in shape like the top but in size three times as large. The whole shape—top, sides and bottom—is constructed of copper sheathing thickly overlaid with gold. Various figures of dragons, lions and tigers cast in metal ornament the lower corners; also balls and coloured silk streamers.

[2] A masonry structure of peculiar shape holding the ashes of a lama or other relics, equivalent to the Sanskrit "chaitya."

moreover, has a turret, and across the street from turret to turret are stretched ropes strung with bits of coloured cloth inscribed with invocations. In the present thoroughfare are a number of shops; but you are not held to be in Lhása proper until an inner gateway further east in this same roadway has been passed. As you proceed eastwards approaching the inner city, or Lhása Thil as the citizens term it, you still have Potala towering up on your left, but between you and those sacred heights lies a quarter of the outer-city known as Potala Shol, or "the Sho," which is technically the lay-town or sudder bazaar appendant to Potala.

Arrived at the gate admitting to Lhása Thil, you find it a covered postern built upon a stone-bridge which spans one of the largest of the natural or deep rivulets which thread their way through the city and discharge into the River of Happiness. This canal bears the name of *Nyámo Chhu* "the stream of female fish," while the postern is known as the Turquoise-roofed Bridge (*Yu-to'k Sampa*) and is regarded as a critical rubicon by travellers; for, here is the customs station where all that enter or quit the citadel of Lhása are scrutinized by the *korchhakpa* or police guard.

The outer parts of the capital which we have been traversing is not enclosed by walls, even though it contains the Grand Lama's residence; but the Inner city is walled in portions, the space it covers being somewhat under 2½ miles in circumference and ¾ of a mile across.

THE INNER OR ENCLOSED CITY.[1]

The Turquoise Bridge having been passed, you now behold, away to your left, the massive buildings of the two chief monasteries of Lhása, the Ts'omo Ling and Tengyai Ling, and as you turn to progress along the street of shops before you, which closes the view, you notice far to your right the pent-roofed towers of the Chinese Residency—the palace where are lodged the ambans, the two puissant representatives of the mighty emperor of China whose duty it is to watch Tibet so keenly.

Then, entering the busy but rather narrow street before you, you can see at the end of it the great glittering *gye-p'i*, four in number, on the chief temple of the place now in full sight. Here in this street one notices the shops closely packed together, although they are frequently interrupted by the long front of some private dwelling. The shops comprise Chinese pastry-cooks, rug and carpet stores, second-hand clothes' dealers, cup and bowl shops, magazines of European goods

[1] Only in places does the remnant of the old walls exist.

and trifles (chiefly of Russian brand) and even small emporiums for the sale of kerosine oil, which commodity has at length reached Lhása, brought from Caspian ports by Yarkandi traders, yet too expensive to be commonly used.

In front of each store, excepting the few which belong to the Khachhe Musalmans, stands in the gutter a pedestal of dried clay. Upon this little altar are burnt, after dinner and at night-fall, oblations in the shape of remains of the food eaten. These are offered to propitiate the Drisa, aerial sprites which feed upon odours, including, it is said, the perfume of lilies, the smell of roast beef, and the stenches of the privy.

The thoroughfare we have now entered inclines from the gateway slightly to the south until it is terminated in a wide open space formed by another road which, running due north and south, cuts it almost at right angles. Here, on the opposite side of the space, rise the outer walls of the great CHO-KHANG, the principal temple of Lhása, which shall be described in detail later on. In a lane hard-by is the famous DO-RING. This is an obelisk, said to be 1,000 years' old, upon which are inscribed, in the Chinese and Tibetan languages, records of certain victories of a Tibetan general. Copies of the inscriptions, as found in an old Chinese work by Dr. Bushell, have been already published by him with a translation in the Journal of the Royal Asiatic Society.

THE CHO-KHANG SQUARE.

We are now in the very heart of the Tibetan metropolis; and this central axis takes the shape of a great wheel or circle of fairly broad roadway surrounding the Cho-khang (Jo-khang) temple and other official buildings which stand together in a block in the middle. It is in fact a sort of central square known as Par-khor-nang. Round the sides are the chief shops, whilst other shops stand clustered in the centre built up against the official edifices and against the walls of the temple itself.

On a pavement in the extreme west of this space stands a curious old tree known as *Jo-o U-tra* (ཇོ་བོ་དབུ་སྐྲ) reputed to have sprung from a hair belonging to the head of Shakya-thubpa himself. An abutment of this temple built on at the N.W. corner of the central block of buildings is styled *Kyap-gön Sim-chhung;* and it is so called because here during the Monlam season the Dalai Lama comes to reside for meditation and to take part in the various public functions. In the N.W. quarter of the great wheel or square may be seen a quaint-shaped tower or chhörten with a passage or thoroughfare beneath or passing through it in four directions; it is called *Kani Goshi.* On the south front of the temple is a space styled སྒུང་རག་ཚོས which seems to be a preaching station. The Samḍuk palace is a building on the southern outer line of the square almost opposite the preaching court.

The Nepalese shops line the northern quadrant of the Par-khor-nang; Chinese and Tibetan bazaar-sheds are erected against the central official buildings on their N.E. and S.E. walls. From the south-eastern segment of the outer circle there passes off a thoroughfare to the E.S.E. known as Thal-chhi, in the first portion of which on the northern side of the thoroughfare is the chief meat or butchers' market in Lhása—rather in close proximity to the great Buddhist fane. It is in this street there stands the largest restaurant of the city—the A-khong Săkhang. Another well-known mart full of shops and stores starts from the N.E. quarter of the Temple circle and makes to the north—this is Thom-si-gang (ཁྲོམ་གཟི་སྒང་)

LHÁSA MERCHANTS.

As we are here in the centre of the mercantile quarter, a few words may be introduced concerning the trading communities. Tibetans themselves, though leading a life of much hardness with scanty food, and therefore naturally of a grasping disposition, have little real mercantile aptitude or talent. Thus the trade of the country lies mainly in the hands of immigrant settlers and their descendants. Few of the leading merchants are pure Tibetans; and the greater part of the commerce of the capital, wholesale and retail, is wielded by Nepalese, Chinamen, and Kashmiri. The Nepalese or Palpo tradesmen stand first. The artificers in bronze and brass, the goldsmiths, chemists, jewellers, dyers and ironmongers, are all of that race. Some of their metal work is done on a large scale. The monster copper cauldrons used in Dai-pung lamasery for cooking the food of the 7,000 inmates, and reported to be 20 feet in diameter and 6 feet in depth, were cast by Nepali founders. They also turn out large bells of peculiarly rich tone which would do no discredit to Messrs. Mears and Stainbank, our Whitechapel bell founders—the size, however, rarely exceeding 21 inches in height and 13 inches in mouth-diameter. The huge concave cubes or *gye-p'i,* made of immense gold-plated sheets to adorn the roofs of Buddhist temples, are likewise constructed by these artificers. As to the Kashmiri and Chinamen, they are merchants not manufacturers. The former deal in silk, linen, and broadcloth goods; and are, moreover, the money-changers of

Lhása. There are, besides, a few Musalmans belonging to Patna in India who have opened stores in the Tibetan capital. Many of these last are birds of passage, arriving in December and leaving in March every year. Their movements, however, are strictly watched, and on returning from India each year the frontier officials seem to exact from them considerable blackmail. Both Nepalese and Kashmiri residents are allowed a local ruler in Lhása, each dwelling in an official mansion near the Chinese Ampan's embassy-house. They seem to exercise judicial as well as diplomatic jurisdiction.[1]

Here, then, in the circular space surrounding the Cho-khang, as well as in Wangdu-Shingkha market further east, are the chief shops and stores. They are, however, mostly in the cellarage of the tall houses in those areas. Steps descend to each dark workshop or goods depôt; and, if the owner be a faithful Buddhist, there will be placed the *nyi-da* mark of the sun and moon over his doorway. Women are the chief servers in the shops.

DWELLING HOUSES.

Before referring to the notable edifices of the city, mention should be made of the houses in general. They are, for the most part, very large and rambling in construction, and even the mansions of the upper classes are situated with no sort of frontage in the by-lanes and narrower streets. Those occupied by the poor and by travelling ecclesiastics and transitory merchants, accommodate many families, sometimes containing 40 or 50 rooms. An arched-way gives access to the residence, and there is generally a courtyard of circular shape beyond—the *ts'om-kor,* round which area the storeys of the house rise up. All the rooms on the ground-floor—styled the *wo-khang*—are used as stables or store-places for grain and wood, and sometimes are let out to merchants. By a side-door within the arched-entrance you can mount by a rude staircase (*kenza*) to the sets of residential apartments above.

So far most of the dwelling-houses follow one plan. Upstairs the establishments of the gentle-folk are arranged with a fair aim at comfort, but always with a greater love for tawdry ornament than of real

[1] The Kashmiri governor, who is chosen by the Tibetan Gye-po from among the Kashmiri residents of Lhása, decides all disputes between his own countrymen; whilst the Nepalese governor exercises the same powers over the Nepalese inhabitants. But when the parties are of different nationalities, the case goes before the Tibetan authorities who adjudicate upon it; and in criminal cases they assign the punishment but deliver the offender to his own governor to carry out the sentence, excepting where a Tibetan has been murdered, when the Tibetans punish the culprit by death or imprisonment

convenience or luxury. In the reception-room the ceiling will be covered with flowered satin, and bright-hued daubs of sacred edifices and of noted places of pilgrimage are hung on the walls; but there is little in the way of furniture—three or four low tables from 10 inches to 2 feet in height, a lacquered cabinet and a few stuffed mats to sit on. In fact these cushioned mats (*shu-ten*) and the quaint diminutive tables (*chogtse*) comprise the whole furniture even in better-class houses. Such dwellings, however, invariably include a worship-chamber fitted with altar and a range of shelves holding various metal effigies of deities. A modern feature in the houses of the rich, we are told, is the custom of papering the room-walls with pictures from English illustrated journals—especially coloured fashion-plates from *The Queen*, etc.—large quantities of which are imported from Darjeeling specially for this purpose.

Huc refers to the poorer dwellings, where travellers put up, thus:—"Our humble abode was at the top of the house, and to reach it we had to ascend 26 wooden stairs without railing, and so steep and narrow that in order to prevent breaking our necks we always found it prudent to use our hands as well as our feet. Our suite of apartments consisted of one great square room and one small closet. The larger room was lighted, north-east, by a narrow window provided with three thick bars, and above by a small round sky-light. To protect themselves from cold the Tibetans place in the centre of their rooms a small glazed vessel in which they burn argols (*i.e.*, dried cakes of dung). As this combustible is extremely addicted to diffuse considerably more smoke than heat, it is of infinite advantage to have this hole in the ceiling as exit for the smoke. You do, indeed, undergo the inconvenience of receiving from time to time a fall of snow or rain on your back; but such are trifles. The furniture of our room embraced two goat-skins spread right and left of the fire-dish, two saddles, our tent, two dilapidated trunks and a supply of argols in a corner. We were thus put at once on the full level of Tibetan civilisation."

The lower classes, both lay and ecclesiastic, whether visitors or residents, take their principal meals not at their homes but in social assemblages at some given house or at one of the large eating restaurants which the Chinese seem to have introduced. These *sá-khangs*, as they are termed, have in recent years become so popular that some of them, it is stated, afford room for 200 diners at one sitting. The most notable restaurant is said to be the *Ani Sa-khang* "nun's eating-house," situated at the corner of a street leading from the S.E. quarter of the Chokhang square, and adjoining the principal meat market.

DENIZENS AND VISITORS.

Dining establishments such as these as well as the large lodging-houses are specially suitable to the inhabitants of a place like Lhása. The population is principally a floating one. Everyday gelongs and lay-pilgrims from every part of Tibet, and from Ladak, Mongol, Tartary, and Southern Siberia, are arriving in the city and departing thence. Their business is perhaps to gain admission to one of the large lamaseries in the place or, if pilgrims, to visit the shrines and probably obtain a *jál-kha* or interview with the Grand Lama himself. Traders and pedlars, too, either Nepalese or Bhutanese ever come and go; and a number of native Tibetans make annual business excursions to Calcutta (where the author has frequently seen and spoken to them) travelling *viâ* Sikkim. Each nationality has its own common lodging-house, often large rambling buildings in filthy by-lanes. Some of the larger monasteries of Tibet have also town hostelries here,

As there is a considerable surplus of unmarried females in Tibet and morality is only prized theoretically, most foreign visitors, both traders and religious and particularly Chinese officials and soldiers, take temporary wives whether their stay in the capital is to endure two years or two weeks. Passing travellers find a plentiful supply of concubines. For the time being, therefore, all men appear to assume the Tibetan nationality as a result of their association with Tibetan women.[1] All would seem to form one vast social community, indulging in much joviality as well as religious festivity which like-wise includes incessant recourse to the consumption of arak and barley-beer. At the approach of the great religious celebrations in February and June, Lhása becomes very full and, in spite of pious exercises, the city is the scene of infinite disorder in which property and life find small security. The New Year festivities, wherein the government of the place is literally handed over to a lord of misrule and his myrmi-dons, brings to a climax a general madness and dissoluteness which nowhere else in the world would gain the sanction of both law and re-ligion. These practices are described in another chapter.

All our native agents who have visited Lhása agree in asserting that there are little law and order at any time in the place. Robberies of the most daring type are frequent and usually go unpunished;

[1] It is stated that a census of the lay-residents in Lhása excluding all travel-lers, temporary visitors, and the inmates of monasteries, revealed a result of 9,000 females and 6,000 males. However, those not reckoned in this calculation must generally equal in numbers the permanent populace. And if we add the 12,000 monks of Daipung and Sera, just outside the city, we might put this total at 40,000.

and the Nepalese merchants openly purchase the booty. Broils and murder are perpetually occurring, especially at festive seasons; the lamas of Daipung monastery particularly distinguishing themselves in outrages of all kinds. When Khampas visit the city, they commit much violence and theft; and these men being of althletic build, the citizens generally give way to them.

Apart from all special celebrations, however, the denizens of Lhása are much given to amusement. Dramatic representations in the open-air and feats of rope-walking are common. A general free-and-easy tone prevails. New-comers are remarked upon openly by the loungers in the streets; and, whenever the opportunity of a pause in their progress occurs, are usually accosted and cross-examined by the curious.

But what we again wish to lay stress on as the main feature of the Tibetan capital is the unceasing influx and departure of visitors. The traversers of the streets on ordinary days are chiefly of this class.

A point to be noticed, moreover, is the freedom with which women of all grades go about; in the shops, in the streets, in the vaulted entries which give access to every dwelling-house. Higher class Tibetan females are seen on small white horses, sitting astride the animal's back. They generally possess intellectual faces and in truth are often highly educated and even learned. In Lhása, women of every station, with a few exceptions—said, however, now to be on the increase—follow the custom of staining the face with blotches of mahogany-coloured dye known as *tui-ja*. This disfigurement, founded on a law enacted 280 years ago with the view of reducing the natural attractiveness of the female face to the other sex, forms almost a complete disguise to the countenance. Within doors the paint is not deemed *comme il faut*.[1]

But the principal business of the Tibetan capital is held to be religion not trade; and therefore it is high time we hastened to enlarge upon the religious edifices. Some of these are naturally the oldest and most famous in the kingdom. However, there are not so many

1 Huc was the first to explain the strange law which prescribes that women shall thus conceal their good looks. Hooker, in his *Himalayan Journals*, doubts this explanation, asserting that the real object of daubing the face is to preserve the skin which the dry cold wind would peel off. As usual Huc is here again found to be correct; but Hooker's explanation may form an element in the maintenance of the custom. Indeed all our native explorers who have visited Lhása confirm the truth of the existence of this law which is not however held to be penally binding. Urgyen Gyáts'o, in his report, remarks that every article of dress the Lhása women wear, such as the striped petticoat and the head-dress, is a reminder of the pains and penalties which once attended any lapse from the paths of virtue.

23

temples and monastic establishments within the precincts of the city as we might have expected. Small shrines and Buddhist inscriptions with figures are numerous; but the larger temples and the monasteries are few—some 10 of the latter at the utmost estimate, including only one *tsunpa* or nunnery.

The first place of sanctified repute to which the new arrival hurries is that which we have designated the Chokhang or "House of the Lord" and which is likewise the

BUDDHIST CATHEDRAL OF LHÁSA.

The huge edifice of the Jho-Khang or Chokhang which is known familiarly also as the "Jho" and "Kinkhording," is situated in an open space in the heart of the inner city; and the four gold-plated concave domes which crown the roof seem everywhere visible. However, the general look of the building is poor. A lofty flag-pole stands in front of the gateway. The portico of the main building is raised on stout pillars of wood barely 12 feet in height imparting a mean aspect to the entrance. From this porch (which is under the upper storeys of the temple and contributes to their support) a few steps bring the devotee into the presence of the presiding genius of the fane.

Here, in the *T'i-tsang-khang*—as the hall is termed—is seated on a throne a stupendous effigy of Buddha Shakhya T'ubpa. This famous image, always spoken of as *Jho-o Rimpochhe* "The most precious lord," is said to be "self-sprung" and to have been brought to Lhása by the Chinese wife of king Srong-tsan-gampo as her dowry *circa* 640 A.D. It represents the Buddha as he appeared when 12 years' old. Diamonds, emeralds, rubies, lapis lazuli, and gold have been lavished in profusion on the costume, which is not a priest's but that of a royal prince. A monster umbrella of plated gold stands hoisted like a canopy on four pillars half gold half silver. Right and left are posed images in bronze of Jhampa Gompo (the Buddha to come) and Jam-yang the Bodhisattwa dear to the Nepalese. Behind Shakya T'ubpa stands Buddha Marmedze; while to the rear of that figure is seated a being styled *Gang-chhen T'so Gyalpo*, "the king of the lake of glaciers." Shakya himself sits attended by twelve solemn embodiments of Buddha's disciples. In this same chamber is an image of Tsongkhapa with a rock and a bell beside him.

However the most remarkable-looking effigy here has yet to be indicated. It is a representation of the great Chenraisi, the being whose successive incarnations the Grand Lamas of Lhása are held to be. The reputed work of king Srong-tsan-gampo, the souls of that monarch and of his two chief queens are believed to have been absorbed within the image after death. It exhibits eleven faces and the materials composing it are thus enumerated:—A branch of the Tree of Cogitation; the soil of the mystic island of Yodan; the pith of a sandal-wood tree; the sand of the river Narainjana; and earth from the eight sacred places of India. These, together with other articles, have been pounded up into a paste with the milk of a goat and of a red cow! Hard-by, inside a small chamber guarded by iron net-work, is seen a large statue of Tsong-khapa with attendent bronze figures of Bu-ton the historian, Prince T'ogmed, Chhyakna Dorje, and two of the Sákya hierarchs. There are many other images within the *Tsang-khang* and its side-chapels. Such are T'onyerchenma (goddess of anger), Dolma, Tamdin, Otzerchen, and a curious antique figure of the Buddha-to-come nursing a sandal-wood doll supposed to be Jamyang.

In the *khyamra* or courtyard of this the main shrine, is a collection of sainted personages: Man-lha (the patron of medicine), T'angtong Gyalpo (a Tibetan engineer), Bil-wa-bas, Padma Jungnas, and Kamala Shila. Many of the effigies are very ancient, some of them being ascribed to the period anterior to the days of king Langdarma, the iconoclast, whose zeal they seem to have evaded. On festival days the courtyard is illuminated with 5,000 butter-fed lamplets.

After visiting the shrines on the ground-floor, circling round the more sacred items, and offering butter and burning scented tapers before favourite deities, the Buddhist votary climbs the wooden stair-ladders to the second storey of the Jho-khang, which is called the *bar-khang*. We need no more than enumerate the notabilities personated there: Tamdin, the horse-man deity; the goddess Lhamo Magjorma; Ser-t'ub; Nampar Zigs; Korwa Jig, etc. There is also a series of paintings pourtraying the bloody deeds of the terrific goddess Panden Lhamo, said to be over 1,000 years old.

Lastly, in the uppermost storey are found the collection of *dragshed* or wrathful deities; with a special chapel belonging to Panden Lhamo, having her gigantic effigy within, its face veiled in order to conceal the grotesque horrors of the same. Upon the walks are pointed out frescoes said to have been painted with blood that flowed twelve hundred years ago from the nose of the sainted Srong-tsan-gampo. Other chapels up here are sacred to Dolma in her terrific aspect, to Chenraisi wherein he is made with 1,000 arms, 1,000 eyes, and eleven heads, and to the sixteen Nai-ten or chief disciples of Buddha. Everywhere in these upper chambers mice are seen racing about; and, though their presence is much to the detriment of the venerable objects stored in the place, nobody is permitted to molest or destroy them. Indeed they are gazed on with reverence; for do they not hold the transmigrated essence of lamas of by-gone times, who even in their degradation haunt the chief asylum of the saints and gods in Lhása?

THE DALAI LAMA'S HOME.[1]

As already mentioned, the supreme ruler of Tibet resides in his palace on Potala hill. The proper appellation of this pontiff is Gyáts'o Rimpochhe, "the most Precious Ocean"; while the Mongols of Tartary, over whom his jurisdiction extends, style him *Dalai Lama* or "Ocean Lama." As to the present occupant of the throne, he is now 30 years of age; and it is a remarkable fact that he should have been suffered to reach an age so venerable for a Dalai Lama. He is indeed the first of all the Grand Lamas of the last 100 years who has been permitted to live beyond boyhood, his five immediate predecessors having all been poisoned, under Chinese instigation, before attaining their 18th year. At 18 years of age, it must be borne in mind, the sacred lad assumes full sway, temporal and ecclesiastical.

The buildings on the hill, which is 1¼ mile in circuit and about 300 feet in height, are piled in curious confusion up the steep sides. The whole mound, in fact, is covered with halls, chapels, colonades, and tombs, which spread in an ingenious fashion until they overhang the hill, where they are borne up by other buildings erected to a great height and starting from the base. Five gold-plated concave cubes surmount the whole mass. A large plantation encircles the base of Potala, through which are avenues leading to the various ascents, some of which are merely a series of rude ladders. At the S.E. is the chief entrance. Here is a long hall into which one can ride. Riding, also, up some shallow steps at the further end, you reach a monolith named Doring Nangma. Thence you mount by innumerable ladders through the entire height of the Red Palace, an edifice of 13 storeys.

Most pilgrims appear to find ready admission to the holy personage who is the object of their fervent adoration. As the re-incarnation of a Bodhisattwa, he receives them seated in a gold chair placed on an altar five feet in height. He is very chary of speech.

THE CITY MONASTERIES.

Every morning the denizens of Lhása—or at least the newly arrived whom custom has not yet made unconscious of the sound—are aroused

[1] A complete description of the Dalai Lama's surroundings would require an article in itself. Only a few leading points have been noted here; and the present writer would refer those interrested to a full account contributed by him to *Murray's Magazine* for October 1891, also to his paper in the *Nineteenth Century*, October 1889. When those papers were written the Dalai Lama was still only a youth.

about 5 o'clock by terrific blasts from gigantic trumpets. The blaze is emitted by the famous silver *gyáling* 8 feet in length, which are blown at that hour in the great lamaseries of Tengyai Ling and Ts'omo Ling to call the inmates to the early readings in the respective worship-halls of those establishments.

Tengyai Ling (བསྟན་རྒྱས་གླིང་) is the principal one of the great metropolitan houses known as the Four Lings of Lhása, from the four heads of which the *de facto* ruler of Tibet, the Gye-po or Regent, was up to very recent times always selected. The high position of the presiding lama of each as well as the wealth and antiquity of the institutions themselves have combined to give the Lings their pre-eminence. Otherwise, as monastic establishments, they are neither very popular, nor renowned for the learning of the inmates. Various restrictions and considerable discipline cause the number of lamas in these city houses to be few. However, it is suggested that the rich properties attached to the Lings of Lhăsa and the desire of those already in possession, who are men of influence, not to have too many to share the good things with them, are the real barriers against admission.

The heads or *khempo* of these monasteries are all of them accounted Incarnate Lamas, being each invariably imbued with the *tulku* of some particular hero of past history who becomes incarnate in the successive heads for the purpose of defending the Grand Lama and the kingdom of Tibet.

Lately, for political reasons which need not be here detailed, the circle of choice for the office of Regent has been widened and the abbots of other great lamaseries have been made eligible.

We find the Tengyai Ling in the N.W. corner of the walled city standing in its own grove of walnuts and poplars. The endowment is very large, comprising the lordship of great estates in Kongpo with the land-dues and other revenue from 5,000 householders resident there. Its abbot or *khempo* is the incarnation of Gar, the famous prime minister to Srong-tsan Gampo, and like that hero is commonly styled *Demo Rimpochhe.* In the same quarter, but nearer to Ramochhe temple, is the Ts'omoi Ling; not at all so wealthy an institution, having only 1,000 householders as tenantry, but of prestige, because the great *Desi* Regent of Tibet 250 years ago was head of this establishment. It was the *khempo* here who was accused of murdering three successive Grand Lamas just prior to the arrival at Lhása of Fathers Huc and Gabet in 1846. The incarnation of Ts'omoi Ling is known as Ts'ak-tur Nomenkhan.

At the northern base of Chakpo-Ri near the entrance to the outer city from Daipung stands the Kundu Ling, a richly-endowed foundation with 3,000 householders on its books, the head of which is possessed of the psychic essence of one *Ta-tsag Rimpochhe* and is therefore so called. He was till lately the chief executive minister, but not technically *Gyal-tsap* or Regent as the Dalai Lama had passed his majority and become full ruler of the country. Now the office seems to be vacant or suspended. As to the fourth Ling, T'se-chhok Ling, it lies away from the city, on the southern bank of the Kyi Chhu; *Yong-dzin Rimpochhe* being the incarnation there. He is lord of only 1,000 tenants.

The other chief monasteries we can only mention; the "Moru" or Meru Shi-dé, in the extreme N.E. corner of Lhása; the Tsi Namgyal Táts'ang; and the medical lamasery, the Waidurya Tá-ts'ang, on Chakpo Ri.

RAMOCHHE TEMPLE.

The street of shops on the western side of the Jho-khang runs up due north to meet the Ling-kor road. Where this intersection takes place, at the left-hand corner after you have turned into the Ling-kor road, is the entrance to a courtyard with a large and curious structure considered to be the oldest temple in Lhása. It was built originally more than 1,200 years ago by the Chinese wife of king Srong-tsan Gampo; and a crystal-palace of Lu, or serpent gods, is believed by the vulgar to exist beneath its foundations, but the temple was erected to counteract their evil influence. The present edifice is 900 years old.

The Ramochhe seems to be the only fane in Lhása where heterodox rites are permitted; and if the visitor is fortunate he may arrive when a band of *Ser-kyem-pa* sorcerers from Sera Gompa, with red instead of yellow pyramidal hats on their heads, are performing some of their necromantic jugglery.

Entering the courtyard, you find it containing many decrepit poplar trees of great age. Within to the left is a detached building known as *Ts'e-p'ag Lhakháng*. In front of you stands a line of chhortens beyond which is the antique temple of Ramochhe three storeys in height faced with an inscription in Chinese characters and surmounted by a single gold-plated *gye-ɒi* of large size. Under the temple-portico, in a room to the left with wire lattice-work before the door, are collected certain images of great antiquity. The chief treasure seems to be a huge gilt representation of Mik-kyö' Dorje, one of the Dhyani Buddhas, brought from the Rasa T'ulnang shrine in Lhása where it had been placed by Za-khri, the Nepalese spouse of Srong-tsan Gampo. Other figures here are Dolma (carved in sandal-wood), Chhakna Dorje (made of dark blue *mumen* stone), Chenraisi (two curious images, one carved out of two huge conch-shells, the other of sandal-wood), Ton-yo-dub (of jade), Ts'e-pakme (in coral), another of Dolma (cut out of a single block of turquoise), and T'o-wo Yuk-ngön-chen.

Inside the temple, eight old statues denote the disciples ot Shakya, while two monuments are pointed out which are reputed to cover the actual remains of Srong-tsan Gampo himself and his Chinese consort. Along the walls stretch strange daubs depicting in lengthy series the 1,000 Buddhas of the countless ages preceding the advent of Shakya-t'ubpa.

Before quitting the shrine we must not omit to view some famous and venerable effigies of the five queens of the khadroma fairies, otherwise styled *Mi-gyurma.* These are made in five different materials, one for each, namely, amber, turquoise, muman, conch-shell and coral. Moreover, there is an old mirror of magical capacities to be shewn, as well as a number of very ancient war-implements, Tibetan and Chinese.

No lamas reside in Ramochhe. It is a shrine referred to in all the old historical works.

WANG-TÖ-SHINGKHA MARKET.

In the heart of the city, and reached by a few lanes passing east from the Cho-khang temple, is to be found the most popular bazaar where anything, from tea to silk-robes and from radishes to a pony, can be purchased. The market or *t'om* consists of stalls over a large open space surrounded by shops of a mean appearance which, however, are capable of competing, in what they can produce for you from the depths within, with the larger emporiums further west. As with markets all the world over, the time to visit *Wang-tö-shingkha* (འོང་སྟོད་ཞིང་ཁ) is early in the morning from 8 to 11; but few Tibetans are astir in Lhása before 9 o'clock. The foreign traders lodge in Panakshol close by and spread forth their wares to lure the motley crowd which surge round the stalls and the outer square.

Here are silks and carpets from China; and, near these, the humbler native-made carpets from Kotsi near the Sikkim border. Here, from Sining in the Kökö Nor district we see gold lace, *khátá* presentation scarfs, red-leather, gold and silver ornaments, side by side with large awkward-looking saddles. Here are the ever-in-request teapots of hardware ranged in rows, red and black; and there,

Khampas and Chinamen with tables covered with beautiful bronze and copper bells and other metal work from Derge in Eastern Tibet. Amongst the latter assortment are also to be seen p'urbu daggers, dorjés, and many small effigies in brass of Tsong-khapa, Pema Jungne, Dorje P'agmo, and other popular saints. From Darchendo comes the stock of tea-bricks which that woman is wishing to sell. The tea looks like lumps of dirty Cavendish tobacco, and the woman's face with its purple-black stains looks as if it had been tinted with juice from the bricks. Musk-pods, cut from the musk deer, are often offered for sale in large quantities here by merchants from Chhamdo; but usually those goods are hidden away in lodging-houses and the dealers in them lounge about the market-place ready to begin bargaining if opportunity offers.

Meat is not usually on sale in this part of the town; there being a special *Sa-t'om* or meat-market just off the S.E. corner of the great Cho-khang square. Quantities of fish, however, are often to be seen here. Our informant mentions three kinds generally to be had; one apparently a large coarse sort of river hake sold at about 1*s.* 2*d.* a piece; another very cheap, about ten inches long, and a third kind six to eight inches. The last two are plentiful in the Kyi Chhu.

Among the more curious articles presented for sale one notices baskets heaped up with piles of long thin tapers. These are the famous *poi-rengbu* or incense sticks which when lighted fuse away with a fragrant smell and are in large demand for burning before sacred images of every degree. Vast quantities are sold, not only for use in the temples of Lhása, but also for export into Mongolia and China. Round the taper-sellers are ever gathered a knot of Mongol and Khampa pilgrims. Another queer commodity is observable at one corner of the bazaar: you may observe there a collection of fossil bones, and so they are; but not as curiosities for museums. They consist of jaws of strange animals and leg-bones, ribs, and vertebræ, evidently ancient and ready to drop to pieces. They have been dug from the low hills round Lhása where they exist in large quantities. It is as a sovereign remedy for wounds and bruises that people buy them; first crushing them into powder before applying them. Here you see this huge headpiece; it probably once belonged to a Tibetan iguanodon or an ichthyosaurus several thousand years ago. It is only a part of its skull, for the points of the long jaws are wanting, yet it measures 3 feet long and a foot and a half in breadth. It will ultimately be smashed into soft powder and the cuts and sores of several hundred lamas will be thus healed by the rotting jowl of the extinct monster.

Such fossil bones we are assured are famous remedial agents and are known as *duk rupa* or "dragon's bones."

But turn aside up this side lane. Here are the green stuff and vegetables. "*Lápu, lápuk,*" cry the female vendors lustily, and that is the one cry everywhere along the line; for it refers to the mounds of enormous radishes which all Tibetans love, and which in Lhása are made into a dish of some kind at most meals. Besides radishes, bright and clean and fresh, you have heaps of carrots, turnips, and small red potatoes, with bundles of various green leaves, some like long broad grass, others more like spinach, which are all wild herbs of sorts and much affected by the city folk.

Near the vegetable stalls and baskets, certain Kashmiri dealers sit impassive, waiting custom, but not requesting it. Beside them are ranged on ascending shelves, trays made of matting, each receptacle holding grain or dried fruit or nuts. The commonest articles are dried apricots and peaches from Ladak (called *ngári khambu*) raisins or *gundüm* and walnuts; also queer little sticks skewering numerous morsels of dried curried-meat highly spiced from China. Here, too, in small bamboo tubs is rice brought straight from Sikkim for those who care for it, but Tibetans themselves dislike rice.

Once more, look in this odd sheltered nook under the vaulted entrance to a court-yard. It seems a sort of rough-and-ready eating-house and is continuously tenanted by customers. But the most prominent and important object in the archway is the gleaming filthy face of an active woman with never-departing jollity on her broad visage. She has a large flat iron slab on the top of a big stone, and ranged on the iron are many rows of pastry puffs simmering and spluttering as she moves them about, turns them over, and every now and then tosses one into the outstretched bowl of the hungry eaters. These fried dainties are the famous *mokmo*—pastry of a heavy greasy kind stuffed with chopped meat, onions, barley-meal and sugar. Every true-born Tibetan goes into raptures over *mokmo;* so no wonder the den of Mrs. Jorzom is so popular.

It is now high time to quit the purlieus of Wangdusiga. We have no space left to notice the side market where live stock are on shew—where you see great Dumba sheep from Chhamdo, ponies from Gyangtse, valuable horses from Sining, and the trim little Lhása-bred cow styled *ba-chu,* all for sale. Neither can we pause and watch curiously those silent men whom we are told are bargaining. Each has grasped another's right hand with his, their sleeves drawn down so as to hide the signs they are making, and thus by pressing and pulling at each other's fingers they chaffer in a dumb language of their own and come to terms without letting the bystanders into the secret of their arrangements.

THE RAGYA-PA OR SCAVENGER BEGGARS.

We said it was time to leave the bazaar. But we had best have done so earlier. We shall not leave it in peace now. For here, making their way across the market square, and parting the crowd as they go, comes a squad of ruffianly-looking men, clad in filthy garments, who by their looks and gesticulations evidently have us in view as a sort of prey. They are led by a tall blackguard who wears a great yellow turban instead of the ordinary turned-up black wide-awake. We know who they must be then and try to hurry away, but it is no use. They are the villanous band who dispose of the dead at the cemeteries, carry away the garbage of the streets, and when not employed thus roam about the lanes of Lhása to beg from, insult and rob the inoffensive. They appear to believe that every new arrival in the sacred city owes them a tax, as it were in payment of his footing in the place; and thus they levy black-mail upon all fresh-comers. As these Ragya-pa or corpse-finders have set afloat a current superstition that every pilgrim who refuses tribute is destined never to regain his home but to die in Lhása and so fall eventually in their hands, they are generally successful in their demands. If not given enough, they persecute their victims every time he walks abroad.

But now the Ragyápa are upon us, and we record our interview both in English and in the Tibetan vernacular :—

An alms, an alms! Give, give:	*Sö-ra, sö-ra! nang ro nang!*
I have nothing to give you:	*Ngá khyö'la ter gyu chang me.'*
We are very poor men:	*Ngáchá wül-p'ongpa re.'*
You shall bestow some present:	*Khyö' la chá-gá shik chin go.*
Get away, you rogues, you vultures:	*Há-la gyuk! ngempa-po khyö! chá-lák khyö'!*
Give, give! you are rich:	*Chin! Chin! Khyö' chhuk-po re.'*
I shall call the watchmen:	*Ngá korchakpa-la ke tang-gyu-re.'*
Call, call! you must give four or five ṭanka:	*Rák! Rák! Khyö' la tanka shi, ngá, ter go.*
Not even one ṭanka!	*Tanka chi' lá-re me.'*
You have been a month in Lhása, yet there is nothing at all for us:	*Dá-wá chi' nai khyö' rang Lhásá-la p'ep rung, ngá-ts'o-la chang me.'*
Who cares! Who cares! I shall not give you anything:	*A'-u-se! á-u-se! Ngárang ye ter-gyu ma re.'*
Ah then! wait until we get you (*lit*: come to us):	*Chyá-ra! ngá-ts'o-la leb-pa t'uk guk-te dö' chik.*
Don't bawl like that, filthy Ragya-pa:	*Ragyá-pa ts'ichen! Tenḍe chá-cho ma gyap.*

All right; listen here! when you are a corpse, tying a rope to your neck, we will drag you like a dog outside the gates of Lhása city.	*Tik-t'ik; di-la nyön shik! Khyörang ro-ne p'o-wa-la, rang-gi ke-la t'ákpa chhing-nai, khyi tang ḍa-te khyörang Lhása t'il kyi go-mo p'enchhe' dril' yong.*
We will tear you to pieces:	*Ohhák-ṭum-la khyö'rang-le shral gyu-* [re.'

The dwelling-places of these gruesome rogues are one of the sights of Lhása. They stand in two quarters on the S.E. and E. confines of the city near the cemeteries. They are large huts built entirely of the horns of rams and oxen, the former being black and the latter white. The different colours of the horns admit of their being arranged in various queer patterns; and when the interstices are plastered up with mortar the walls are fairly solid. These horn-dwellings are the only houses in Lhása left without whitewash. A saying is quoted by S. C. Dás concerning the wealth which the Ragyapa are reputed to to amass, somewhat thus:

> Though outside their houses bristle with horns;
> Inside they are smooth and glitter with coins.[1]

THE CORPSE YARDS OF LHÁSA.

Outside the broken walls which enclose the eastern side of the inner city stands on a slight eminence an ancient chhorten of gigantic size. It is commonly believed to mark the spot where the Chinese princess on reaching Lhása made profound salutation towards the Potala hill and to her saintly husband king Srong-tsan Gampo. Around this monument is the space where the Rogyapa dispose of the bodies of the dead. On the rocky surface of this dismal mound is embedded a large flat stone said to have been brought from India, on which places have been hollowed out to accommodate the general outline of the human frame. Each body is laid here, face upwards with the arms and legs spread out to their widest extent. Troops of dogs and pigs swarm round on these occasions eager to tear and devour. However, it is considered more auspicious, and calculated to shorten the period before re-birth, to have one's remains eaten by birds instead of by quadrupeds. Accordingly, if appeased by an ade-

[1] In his report, the secret explorer U.G. mentions these men whom he styles "Ragapas." He says they are not a race but merely persons out-casted for various offences, and that, however rich they may be, they are not permitted to live anywhere but in the horn-built huts. He himself had a risky encounter with them. They hunted U.G. into the market-place of Lhása where, to his dismay, they began to denounce him as a British spy. It seemed that amongst their number was a man who had served as a *jhampani* at Darjeeling who recognised him. However he avoided exposure by bribing the Ragyapa.

quate fee, the Rogyapa will ward off the dogs and pigs until kites and vultures arrive. While the birds are at work the human ogres hack at the corpse to facilitate the process of dessication. Others prefer to have their friends buried and others are partly devoured by the pigs and then buried. Burning is not practised in this cemetery. The exact mode of disposing of each body is determined by lamas who are sent for at their death and, facing the corpse which is bound with ropes and placed erect against the wall of the room, they divine by certain auguries this point as well as the exact hour and day when the disposal ought to take place. Bodies of lay-folk who may be buried are interred anywhere in this Aceldama around the chhorten; only as the ground is rocky and hardened by continuous frost, burial is always an expensive method of disposal.

There is another *dur-toi* or cemetery further south round another chhorten; but it does not appear to be so popular as the larger place. U.G., the survey explorer, speaks of a burial-yard within the city walls near the chief temple, where only the bodies of the highest classes are done away with. We have not been able to trace this locality.

WATER SUPPLY AND CANALS.

The Lhásа anthorities are not so backward in sanitary matters as one might have supposed. Every house has its ashpit and cesspool, the contents of which are first sold and then carefully carted away for use on the fields outside the city. And, although the suburbs of the city are left in a revolting condition, those streets within the walls as well as those in the *deshol* of Potala are always well swept; certain prisoners from the jails assisting the Rogyapa in this duty.

But the plenteous water-supply furnished to the inhabitants is worthy a more advanced civilisation and more cleanly habits than Tibetans can boast. Two large conduit-like canals have been cut from the Pempo Chhu, an affluent of the Kyi river, in the mountains to the N.E.; and these bring the water a distance of 5 or 6 miles. Entering Lhása in its northern quarter, the canals are immediately subdivided into a remarkable network of by-channels which permeate every corner of the city. One large branch is carried past the base of Potala hill to meet the demands of the sacred community there. Another main artery styled the Nyamo Chhu runs down to the Yutok Sampa bridge at the entrance of the inner city. Unfortunately the customs of the citizens are strictly oriental; and, although the drinking water is nominally separated from those conduits which are contaminated with sewage, yet in the southern parts of the city the amalgamation between the two seem to be practically complete.

There, our native explorer, A.K., remarks significantly: "the water is no longer nice."

By-the-way, it appears curious to learn that each householder in Lhása is subjected to a water-rate; but it is a commendable rule, we submit, that it is restricted from exceeding the sum of 9*d.* a month!

All the canals, together with one which brings down the refuse from the cemeteries, are eventually conducted into the "River of Happiness"—the Kyi Chhu—to the south of the city. This really fine-proportioned river runs mainly ¾ mile distant from the southern walls; but to the S.W. it flows up almost to the Ling-kor road, where a massive revetment has been built to secure the city from inundation.

COUNCIL CHAMBER AND PALACE OF JUSTICE.

Lhása is possessed of its Government Offices, its treasury, its law courts, like other great cities. The Privy Council or Council of the Regent with his four colleagues, the Kalons, assembles in a chamber called the Káshak in a wing of the Chokhang, and therein they sit sometimes to cogitate over the affairs of State, sometimes as a court of justice. The present Dalai Lama has, however, this year (1904) dismissed and imprisoned all the Kalons, and chosen a council of his own composed of 4 monks; whereas the Kalons ought to be laymen, according to the Tibetan constitution.

Popularly a member of Council is known as a *shápé*, and that is the title which used to puzzle people in the newspaper reports of our operations in 1888 against the Tibetans. It means "the lotos-footed" (*Zhábs-pad*) and is likewise applied to other high functionaries besides the Kálons.

When the Shápé are deliberating on political matters, their sittings are private; but when they meet as a court of appeal, like the Judicial Committee of the Privy Council in Whitehall, respectable folk can obtain admission to the Káshak. There they squat cross-legged on square ottomans, clad in long rich yellow silk robes, and crowned with tall Mongol hats edged with scarce fur and with a large coral button on the front! They are deliberating on the fate of an unhappy prisoner who is present loaded with chains. They may order him to be drowned or strangled or beheaded, or else to be blinded; and the question is which punishment shall be recommended to the Regent as appropriate. Beside each judge is the inevetable teacup, and every now and then it is solemnly repleinshed by a stately attendant. In other rooms the *dungkhor* or clerks are seen at work. They are the civil servants of Tibet; and they, too, are imbibing tea in the same official manner.

Other Government officers are those of the Chhandzö Chhempo or Chief Treasurer of Tibet housed in a wing of the the Cho-khang istelf; another treasurer for the Dalai Lama's household is in Potala Shol at an old castle known as Dekyi Ling (commonly "Diki-ling.") These exchequer officers in all are five in number and to them the Jongpöns in the provinces send in the revenue they have collected for Government. Here are more *dungkhorpa* registering the receipts derivable from the land-tax, the traders' tax, the pig-tax, and other sources of revenue. But the clerks cannot work so freely as would be the case in England; for all accounts have to be "cooked" in Tibet, every official taking his pickings, from the Chhak-zö Chhempo in the Chokhang cathedral downwards.

THE PRISONS OF LHÁSA.

Beneath the Treasurers' offices at Dekyi Ling is one of the prisons; but it is only used for a few prisoners prior to trial. The great central jail is within the city walls, being situated next door to the grand temple, the Cho-khang; and it bears the designation of Nágtsa Shar. Adjoining the prison, and in a separate building facing T'omsi-gang, is the court where the judges of first instance sit; to wit, the chief justice the *T'impön-chyi*, and another magistrate with the suggestive title of Shal-chhe-pa "the Big-faced one." Torture is a frequent concomitant of judicial investigations in Tibet; and this court-house of the chief magistrate, as well as the adjacent prison, contains all the adjuncts for extorting confessions by the aid of physical pain. The infliction of torture is conducted in open court; and several methods of so dealing with criminals have been borrowed from the Chinese. The Chinese wooden collar, known in Tibet as *ts'o-shing*, is in common use. There is also another court-house in Lhása styled Káshak Lho.

Sarat Chandra Dás has furnished a few particulars concerning the Nágtsa Shar Jail. The most curious part of the system there is that no food is supplied to the prisoners by the authorities; but the inmates must be fed by their own nearest relatives, or in the case—which often occurs—of no relatives being available, the unfortunate culprit is solely dependant for rations on the casual charity of the kindly-disposed. Foreign traders, especially the Musalman merchants from Kashmir, are said to be the most beneficent in this way; many making a practice of sending food to the friendless prisoners starving in Nágtsa Shar. All the inmates of the jail are technically considered to be incarcerated for life; but it is always possible to obtain the release of any convict, no matter how heinous his offence, by a money payment styled *ts'e-rin* or "life-price." As a religious act, rich persons coming on pilgrimage occasionally cause one or two prisoners in the Lhása jail to regain their liberty by paying the required ransom.

Both women and men are kept in this prison. There is much association allowed not only between male convicts but also between those of opposite sex. Men and women, according to Sarat Chandra Das, are occasionally suffered to live together as husband and wife, and children are born and reared in the jail.

Executions are conducted in the open street before the people, and apparently culprits suffer not far from the temple and not outside the city, Buddhist injunctions notwithstanding. When Nain Singh visited Lhása, he saw a Chinaman beheaded in public for having endeavoured to raise a quarrel between the Sera lamas and those of Daipung, with alleged political motives.

We conclude this description of the capital of Tibet with a lengthy extract from Sarat Chandra Dás's famous "Report," in which he describes minutely a circuit he made by the road which runs completely round the city and which is known as the Ling-kor road.

"From Potala," he says, "we returned by the Ling-kor road. I have already mentioned that an extensive marsh lies to the north-west of the road leading to Lhasa from Daipung, intervening between Sera and Daipung, drained by numerous tiny outlets in summer. At the entrance of the city there was a stone bridge over an outlet of the marsh, about 40 paces long and 12 broad, with parapet walls 3 feet high on both sides. The two piers of the bridge, roughly and irregularly constructed, were about 10 feet high and 6 feet thick. The stream at this time was teeming with fish. From this bridge the road goes towards the north-east by east for a distance of 200 paces to its junction with the Ling-kor, or circular road round Lhása. From the bridge, Potala stands due east, Chagpoiri south-east, while Kunduling lies in a south-south-easternly direction, and Kesar Lhakhang, which stands midway between the Kaling Chhorten and Kunduling, bears slightly to the south-east. To the south, beyond the river Kyi, were two *lhakha* (flags placed on the tops of isolated peaks in honour of the sylvan gods) visible a great way off. Far to the north of Lhása were to be seen three lofty peaks of barren mountains without any votive flags. From the junction of the Ling-kor road with the roads coming from the bridge, at a distance of 200 paces, was a rivulet stocked with fish crossing the Ling-kor road and bridged by a culvert about 20 feet long and 9 feet broad. The grand road extends in a due easterly direction from this culvert up to Chhorten Kaling, the entrance of the city where it slightly bends northwards to join the Potala *Sho* road. At a distance of nearly half-a-mile from this culvert, in a north-easterly direction, we came to a small culvert under which flowed a tiny stream. The Ling-kor road thence runs in a north-easterly direction for a furlong, and then turning due east passes by a park on the left side, where we saw a shed for an elephant. The elephant itself was standing in a barley-field. A hundred paces further on was the gate of the temple Lukhang T'amo (house of piebald Nagas) situated exactly behind the hill of Potala. This shrine, which had a small gilt *gya-phig* (dome) on it, was about 60 feet long and 25 feet broad. Some 200 paces further along this road there branched off a lane leading into Lhása. To the right-hand side were numerous groves and gardens, and to the left suburban villages with numerous barley-fields now green with barley and pea plants (in June). The Ling-kor road runs next 300 paces and slightly bends southwards whence the monastery of Ri gyal (where the Dalai Lama resides during his infancy) is clearly seen. From this point Sera, which is about 3 miles off, bears to the north and Potala south-west by west. A road from the suburbs coming from the north joins it here. Proceeding on our road for half-a-mile we pass the gateway of the celebrated shrine of Ramochhe, and 200 paces further on this road we come to its junction with a road leading to Sera and another leading due south to the Chokhang. The latter is rather more than half-a-mile down the road thither. Our way by the circular road now bends south-east and passes for a distance of nearly 300 paces beside the filthy village of the Rogyabas (scavengers) which is distinguished from others by its huts made of horns. The road continues running in the same direction for about a furlong more, and then bends towards the south, joining a street coming S.S.W. out from Lhása. Then running still due south for about ½ a mile it skirts the walls of Lhása, here about 10 feet high and 4 feet wide, and passes by the antique chhorten which commemorates the site of the spot where the Chinese princess, on reaching Lhása, made profound salutation towards the palace of Potala and to her saintly husband king Srongtsan Gampo. Now-a-days the space round the chhorten is used as a cemetery where the dead bodies of the town people are disposed of. The pigs which feast on the dead bodies here are said to yield most delicious pork. Every day at least one dead body is considered necessary for the preservation of the honour of the cemetery, otherwise it is deemed an evil omen for Lhása. The Ling-kor road now turns towards the west, and running for about

500 paces makes another bend at a second chhorten surrounded by another cemetery. The entire land to the left of the road and the *Durtoi* (cemetery) is filled with the horn huts of Rogyabas. From this *Durtoi chhorten* at a distance of perhaps 700 yards, is the junction of 3 roads—the Ling-kor, the Ferry-ghat road coming from Ts'e-chhog-ling monastery, and a broad street coming from the interior of Lhása. The Kyi-chhu makes its appearance here. On the left side of the Ling-kor road up the bank of the Kyi-chhu the entire land is filled with gardens and groves tastefully planted with different kinds of trees and containing tanks and nicely-lined avenues. The Kyi-chhu, nearly a mile wide at this place, running due west for a distance of 300 paces, passes by the residence of the Lhading family of Lhása, the chief of whom is one of the leading dung-khors under the Government. From Lhading, the southern gate of Lhása (*Lho-go*) is only 100 paces, whence the city wall runs westward. At this gateway several helpless beggars were supplicating for alms, and many pariahs (dogs) were lying about the road. The street leading to the interior of the city from this gate is about 30 feet broad, and is irregularly lined with many old willows and other trees with large stumps. Some of these are said to be upwards of 100 years' old. At a short distance west from the gate the river bends southwards, where an extensive park comes into view. This is the famous Norpu Linga; and thence Potala bears north and Chagpoiri N.N.W. About 150 yards further on a road from the interior of the city joins the Ling-kor road and the wall (encircling the inner city) turns northward up this road to the site where stands the Doring column. There is a huge cairn which receives a stone from every passing pilgrim or traveller as a tribute of reverence to the sacred city and particularly to the grand sanctuary of Potala. At a distance of 250 paces from this cairn there lies another still larger cairn. From this latter to the Chhyag Chhe Gang (the place of offering great greetings) which contains about a dozen small cairns, the distance is 100 paces. To the right-hand side of Chhyag Chhe Gang lies a garden, the walls of which are low and adjoining the road. At the distance of 200 paces from Chhyag Chhe Gang there is an approach of a deep channel of the Kyi river, which, for a distance of another 200 paces, runs touching the Ling-kor road. Here the Tibetans, fearing further encroachments of the river towards the city, have erected a revetment wall from the very edge of the Kyi. Had it not been for this wall, the river would have ere long washed away a part of Lhása. Further on, the river recedes leaving a sandbank between it and the Ling-kor road. People come here to bathe during the summer and autumn. From beside the sandbank the road now

bends northward, and running for a distance of 500 paces stops at a culvert constructed across a deep canal teeming with fish. The culvert rests, on the road end, on a single pier and spans over to a bluff rocky ledge of Chagpoi Ri which juts over the stream. A steep passage along the southern flank of Chagpoi Ri now takes the place of, and forms the continuation of, the Ling-kor road; and in one part it traverses for some 200 paces immediately above a precipice overhanging a stagnant pool of the Kyi Chhu. This path seems very dangerous for passengers on account of its extreme narrowness as well as from the rough forky rocks projecting overhead. Here many niches are cut out in the rock-wall, within which have been carved in relief figures of Buddhas and saints. Many of these carvings, we saw, were painted blue, red and yellow. Certain monks, who are almost constantly engaged re-painting and furbishing the faded frescoes in these old niches, supplicated for alms as we passed by. This is a kind of livelihood to them. At a distance of 400 paces from the culvert was a sentry-house where the Government had stationed guards to watch the movements of strangers and travellers. The passage after this gradually becomes broader, and, running past a pair of chhorten, in about 100 paces from the guards-house joins a well-beaten road which comes from the Norpu Linga. The Ling-kor road now runs directly north for a distance of 500 feet, leaving the gateway of Kunduling to the right-hand side and that of Norpu Linga to the left. Then leaving the gateway of Norpu Linga the road travels some 300 paces trending slightly to the north-eastward, and thus meets the main thoroughfare from Daipung by which we entered Lhása on our arrival. The grand street of Lhása runs from this point in a N.E. direction, the distance between Chhorten Kaling and the Doring being 700 paces." The writer's circuit of the city ended however here at Chhorten Kaling.

CHAPTER XI.

THE MYTHOLOGY OF TIBETAN BUDDHISM.

Whatever praises modern enthusiasts may lavish on Buddhism as a pure and philosophic form of belief, they cannot long observe its practice in any country where it actually prevails without discovering that it is largely idolatrous. Certain recent writers on the subject would have us think that the Buddhism of Tibet is singular in this respect—that there only, of all Buddhistic countries, the worship of many deities and demonology are to be found. But one has merely to visit Ceylon and Burmah and examine the popular faith and practice in those lands to discover that European preconceptions and theoretic readings are far astray even in the homes of what is generally styled Primitive Buddhism. Demonology and idolatry are intrinsic parts of the religion of the common folk of Ceylon though not so tyrannical as they are with the people of Tibet.

Moreover, no impartial student can read the earliest writings of Buddhism, whether in Sanskrit, Pali, or Tibetan, and fail to confess that from the first this religion had its mythology, together with a considerable phalanx of gods and other spiritual personages. This we aver; even while we admit that as the centuries progressed a Buddhism arose much less simple and much more idolatrous and superstitious than the pristine forms. Furthermore, Tibetan phases of this creed may be said to surpass in these departments the Buddhism of the Southern School, in that they have incorporated more seriously and philosophically the fantastic mythologies which Time developed. In Tibet the exorcism of devils and mystic rites involving the invocation of deities of many orders are believed in and form part of the daily religion in the case of the learned and the upper classes. In Burmah and Ceylon, on the other hand, such ideas and ceremonials are now mainly confined to the general public. The lettered and philosophic among Burmese and Siṇhalese Buddhists, having been re-instructed in their Faith as interpreted by European theorists, have eradicated from their Buddhism even the mythology which from the earliest promulgation belonged to that religion. But their religion is no longer Primitive Buddhism, but Christianized Buddhism.

Buddhism may be said to deal in three departments of mythology:

First, may be mentioned, though they do not rank the first, the gods adopted or adapted from the Hindu pantheon. From the commencement the leading deities of Brahmanic creation were incorporated into Buddhism, forming an integral part of the scheme propounded by Gautama. The thirty-three chief gods of Hinduism, such as Indra, known in Tibetan works as Gya-jyin-wang-chhyuk,[1] Vishnu styled Kyab-jug, and Brahma known as Tsangpa, are frequently mentioned even in the earlier classical works.[2] They dwell on the top of Mount Meru—which the Buddhism of all countries agrees in locating in Tibet, and which we shall see is referred to the modern Kailas abutting on the Manasarowar Lake.[3] Representations of these primary deities are very seldom to be met with in Tibetan temples, and they are as a rule unknown by name to the general populace.

Secondly, we have the various classes of supernatural beings specially belonging to Buddhism in general and probably first originating with that cult. These comprise Buddhas and Bodhisattwas, Dhyani Buddhas and Dhyani Sattwas, together with certain orders of minor gods and demons and other nondescript spiritual creations to be enumerated later on in these pages.

Thirdly, may be ranged the many local gods and goddesses not belonging to Buddhism generally and varying with the different countries where the Faith is professed. Thus, the Buddhism of each land has its own special national deities, some of which have arisen since that religion was imported and some of which survive from anterior beliefs of the people. To these may be added the direct analogues and local variations of Indian originals, which now form distinctive deities peculiar to

1 The Mongol synonym for Indra in Mongol Buddhism is *Khormusda;* and it is not without significance that they should have imported a term from Armenian Gnostic literature, Hormusta being the Demiurge or creating deity of Gnosticism. We say *imported;* because Mongol Buddhism was long post-Christian in origin.

2 Ganesh, the elephant-faced god, is included among these and is often mentioned in early Buddhist writings as "the Remover of Obstacles."

3 Theoretically, however, in Buddhist cosmogony, Mount Meru is in the centre of the universe, the pivot or axis of a series of flat concentric rings of land and water lying one within the other. Water surrounds Mount Meru, and outside that is a circle of land, and so on land and water alternately; each land with its ring of water representing a world. Outside the last girdle is our earth consisting of 7 continents (Sansk. *dwipa*, Tib. *gling*) afloat on a huge ocean parted into seven seas. The continents are: Jambudwipa (*Dzambu-gling*), Parbatadwipa, Aparagodána, Uttarukuru, Vayudevadwipa, Yamunadwipa, and Priyangudwipa; besides which are various islands, as Lanka, Tamradwipa, etc.

the country where they have been adopted. Perhaps it is only natural that in every land we should find that the most popular objects of veneration are such as were indigenous to the soil, though now they form part and parcel of its Buddhism.

So much for the divinities of this Creed when viewed as affecting in common all varying national forms of the Faith. We now turn to the consideration in detail of the members and orders of the mythological cabinet as it exists in the Buddhism of Tibet.

BUDDHAS AND BODHISATTWAS.

These are undoubtedly the leading sanctities of Buddhism everywhere; and theoretically all the gods, however great and formidable, rank below them. Buddhas stand above Bodhisattwas, and are known in Tibet as *Sang-gye* སངས་རྒྱས, a desgination which probably may be rendered as meaning "Purity increased." The Mongol denomination is *Burkhan* or *Borhan*, an appellation which the by-gone missionaries to the Buriats at Selenginsk have unfortunately used in their translations to signify "God."

Originally we may take it there was only one Buddha or Sang-gye; that was Shakyamuni or Gautama, the founder of the religion, who is styled in Tibetan *Shakya-t'ubpa*. But he is now only one of many others of his class; and he is held in point of time not to be the first of his order. Shakya-t'ubpa, however, may be said to take precedence of all the Buddhas, in that he is the special human Buddha belonging to and presiding over the current Kalpa, that is, the Age now in progress. The successive ages which preceded the present period had each its reigning human Buddha, by whom (it is now alleged) the same doctrines were preached to the people then living as Shakya-t'ubpa taught to the sentient beings of the current age. All these Buddhas in their time, after many anterior lives under various animate forms, were at length—everyone in his respective Kalpa—born as a Bodhisattwa who after some years of earthly life suddenly developed into a perfect *Buddha on earth*, when they diligently promulgated Buddhist doctrine (or as it is technically phrased "turned the wheel of the law"—Tib. *chhos sgyurba*), and after much success were sublimated out of the world into Nirvana. Before they become Buddhas in actuality they seem to earn the title of *Bchom-ldan-adas* (Sansk. *Bhagavan*) "he who has passed through possessed of victory," or as the early German translators have rendered it, Siegreich Vollendete "the victoriously-consummated." When they quit the world they have benefited, they gain the appellation of *De-bzin-gshegspa* (Sansk. *Tathágata;* Mongol :

Tegün-zhilen-ireksen) generally rendered "he who has gone (or come) like the others."

When the present age terminates, another human Buddha, the successor of Shakya-t'ubpa, may be expected. His name will be or is —for he already resides in the Galdan heaven and has many worshippers even now on earth—Jyampa, "the loving one," the same personage as *Maitreya* of Sanskrit and Pali writings. Other Buddhas will follow Maitreya, *e.g.*, Simha, Prabhása, Muni, Pushpa, etc., to the number of 1,000.

Of the many human Sang-gye, orthodox Buddhism of the Hinayana School knows only five, and even the Mahayana School only cares to specify eight, *i.e.*, the six predecessors of Shakya-t'ubpa, Shakya-t'ubpa himself, and his immediate successor Jyampa. The Madhyamika treatises mention and give names to 1,000 terrestrial passed Buddhas. As being frequently mentioned in religious works and, to a limited extent, finding a place in the modern popular creed, the names of the seven may be set forth in order as follows:—

(1)—རྣམ་པར་གཟིགས Nampar Zi:[1] "He who saw through and through;"

(2)—གཙུག་ཏོར་ཅན Tsugtorchen:[2] "The Fire-crested;"

(3)—ཐམས་ཅད་སྐྱོབ T'amche Kyob:[3] "The Preserver of All;"

(4)—འཁོར་བ་འཇིག Korwa Jig:[4] "Golden Might;"

(5)—གསེར་ཐུབ Sert'ub:[5] "The Guardian of Light;"

(6)—འོད་སྲུང Od Srung:[6] "Dissolver of the Round of Life;"

(7)—ཤ་ཀྱ་ཐུབ་པ Shakya-t'ubpa:[7] The Mighty Shakya;"

Buddhas of this class may be said to lie beyond the pale of worship or petition; always excepting Shakya-t'ubpa who is still petitioned, it would seem. Having been sublimated within the impalpable region Nirvana, they are, in theory at least, as if they were not; and, having no longer any individuality, could hardly be considered to take

[1] Sanskrit: *Vipasya*; Pali: *Vipassi*; Mongol: *Babashi*.

[2] Sanskrit: *Sikhi*; Mongol: *Shiki*.

[3] Sanskrit: *Viswabhu*; Mongol: *Bisbabu*.

[4] Sanskrit: *Krakuchhanda* vel *Kuku-chhanda*; Pali: *Kakutsaṃdha*; Mongol *Gargasundi* otherwise *Ortshilanggi ebdekchi*.

[5] *Kanakamuni* or *Kanchana*; Pali: *Koṇdgamana*; Mongol: *Altan-chidakchi*.

[6] Sanskrit: *Kasyapa*; Mongol: *Gdshib*.

[7] Mongol: *Shigemüni*.

the slightest interest in human affairs. Thus we rarely meet with their effigies in temples. Three exceptions, however, are notable. One is that of Od-srung Buddha, who is likewise known in Tibet as ZEKSEN the "Atom-eater." Not only is this by-gone personality represented in tangible figure, but large portions of his actual corporeal substance are held to be still in existence. In fact the elements of the bodily frame of Zeksen are universally regarded as of marvellous efficacy in revivifying the expiring life of man and in imparting youth to those who are aged. Accordingly *ts'e-ril* or "life pills" composed of atoms of the Atom-eater are in great request and much traffic is done in them. Nevertheless, it seems they are not obtainable from anyone save two or three of the higher ecclesiastical dignitaries, who have apparently an inexhaustible supply of the earthly relics which once made up the carcase of the saint. Such functionaries as the abbot of Mindolling monastery and the lady at the head of Samding on Lake Yamdok have good store of the pills, which, however, they are said to bestow gratuitously and never to sell.

Another Buddha frequently represented is, naturally, Shakya-t'ubpa himself; but this is the case not so commonly as might be supposed. While in Burmah, Siam, and Ceylon every shrine has a huge image of the founder of the Faith; on the contrary, in Tibet, only the very large centres of worship find a place for the figure of the hero. Moreover, the majority of these effigies are not of great size. In the Jho-khang at Lhása is the principal representation of Shakya-t'ubpa, who there appears as a lad of twelve years. Other famous images of the *Jho-o*, or "Lord," as he is designated, are in Gyangtse chhörten and in the Kyilkhang college of Tashilhümpo monastery. The truth is that in Tibet other more sublunary personalities have displaced the Buddha from the central position in the hearts of the people Nevertheless, there is in the teaching of the books this contradiction that, notwithstanding the allegation that Shakya-t'ubpa has passed into nothingness, yet all Buddhist votaries are exhorted to cry up to him for assistance and are taught that he still concerns himself for their welfare.

THE MAITREYA CULT.

Maitreya[1] or Jyam-pa, the Buddha-to-come, is the third member of the Human Buddhas' circle, who still remains an object of devotion. Indeed his supposed position of waiting, in one of the Heavens adjacent to this world prior to his terrestrial advent, probably conveys the notion of accessibility. A considerable number of Tantras or treatises

1 Pali: *Metteyya*; Mongol: *Maidari*.

have been written giving special instruction as to the manner in which he may be brought to the aid of worshippers, and as to how his particular votaries may even get him into their own control so as to work out their own projects. Certain establishments are exclusively consecrated to the propitiation of Maitreya under his Tantrik aspects of *Jayam-kar*, the White Jyampa and *Jyam-nag*, the Black Jyampa. Other places hold some mighty figure of the coming Buddha, which is styled in that case a *Jyam-chhen*. Several of the images are truly enormous, reaching over sixty and seventy feet in height, and in fact the representations of this being are made infinitely larger than those of any other object of worship in the land. Such are the Jyamchhen at Jyampa Ling near Yamdok, at the Daipung Monastery, and at Tashilhümpo in the Thoisamling chapel. Near Leh in Ladak, a huge figure of Jyampa has been cut out, bas-relief fashion, on the face of a lofty rock. In Mongolia there is even a lama incarnation of Maitreya or Jyampa known as "the Maidari Hutuktu."

BODHISATTWAS.

The proper term in Tibet for this order of personage is *Jangchhub Sempá*, but this name is restricted to earth-born Bodhisattwa and is not to be applied to Dhyani Bodhisattwa the correct term for whom is *Ye-shes Sempá*.

A Bodhisattwa may be defined as a candidate-Buddha, and is supposed to have attained the stage in the chain of re-births immediately next to that of Buddhahood. In some cases he dies as a mortal man, though by the act of dying he becomes a Buddha. In other instances the Bodhisattwa seems to pass into the final stage while still living, and to continue the current life as a Buddha. The last was apparently the method adopted in the career of Shakya-t'ubpa. In the early years of his ministry we find in the classical treatises that he is often designated "the Bodhisattwa." However, he at length acquires Buddhahood while seated in meditation under the Bo-tree, and yet he does not die, but continues his earthly mission some years longer. In numerous instances, however, a Bodhisattwa does not after death reach the final position, but is re-incarnated as a Bodhisattwa. But when that occurs, we believe the continuance of the lower birth is at the request of the individual himself, who voluntarily defers his Buddhahood in order that, by re-incarnation, he may help the sentient creatures of the universe to emancipate themselves from the thralls of this life. In fact the special vocation of a Bodhisattwa is to convert the world from ignorance (*i.e.*, the desire to live), to point out the path to Nirvana, and thus empty the cycles of existence. His great virtue, therefore, consists in foregoing his own deliverance from the chain of birth and re-birth in order that by continuing upon earth he may be of service to others. This conception is certainly a noble one; and we should be disposed personally to rank the Bodhisattwa as occupying a higher level than the Buddha who is interested in nobody save himself.[1]

The Mahayana School—the *T'egpa chhempo* or "Greater Vehicle" as it is termed in Tibet—claims the credit of having constituted, or rather of having brought to human knowledge, the order of Bodhisattwas. Its votaries scorn the tenets of the supposed earlier School (if ever actually existent concomitantly with the Mahayana) the Hinayana or "Lesser Vehicle" system, as inculcating the rankest selfishness, Hinayana Buddhists being occupied only in attaining their own salvation. Mahayana Buddhists, on the other hand, assert that they regard the salvation or "emancipation" of others as being of greater importance than their own; and the Bodhisattwa order revealed by their system is the embodiment of that idea. So far as present-day Buddhism goes, various members of this order are still working, or supposed to be working for the good of others, and together with those who belong to the special class of Dhyani Bodhisattwas, carry on operations by repeated incarnation in the persons of certain highly-placed monastic dignitaries. Such inhabited individuals receive divine honours and are regarded as objects of worship. Nagarjuna, Atisha, and Tsong-khapa, who became or were born as Bodhisattwas when on earth, still continue as Boddhisattwas in one of the heavens concurrently with their incarnate representatives now living in the world.

Finally, the actual technical instrument whereby *ipso facto* any *Sattwa* or ordinary man is made a Bodhisattwa must come direct from one who is already a Buddha. Its usual form is that of a beam of light from the Buddha.

THE DHYANI BUDDHAS.

The Human Buddhas having gained Nirvana, and having been absorbed therein into the general ethereal nothingness, are evidently outside the pale of human tears and human prayers. But the natural instinct of mankind craves after personal deities who shall be in some sort comprehensible to his thoughts and accessible to his petitions. Consequently it was necessary for Buddhism to devise an expedient whereby the highest beings in the religious pantheon might be capable of

1 There are, besides the Buddhas who worked for all creatures' welfare and who are styled perfect (*samyaksaṃbodhi*), other more selfish Buddhas called *Pratyeka Buddha* that only worked for their own absorption into Nirvaṇa. These rank next below all Bodhisattwas.

intercourse with the world. To meet that want there came to be devised the series known as the FIVE DHYANI BUDDHAS or the Buddhas of Contemplation as distinct from the Human Buddhas who have passed away. By the Mongols these Dhyani Buddhas are styled *Titimtu Burkhan* and by Tibetans *Ye-shes Sang-gye.*

There are several accounts, not very reconcileable in detail, as to how the members of this spiritual order came into existence. It is commonly set forth, however, that the general desire to bring about happiness (which was allowable even in Nirvana so long as it took no personal form and had no definite objects of compassion), innately belonging to the Human Buddhas dissolved in Nirvana, at length took visible shape. Their conjoint quintessence evolved a ray of pure white light, which, shooting forth, entered the regions of the material universe. There the ray of light was disintegrated, as by a prism, into five rays, each of which yielded by contact with the five different Heavens a new and "self-sprung" Dhyani Buddha, each of such being correspondent, respectively, to the Five Human Buddhas from whom the white light had collectively proceeded. Thereupon these new Buddhas took up abode one in each of five heavenly kingdoms or *Bhuvana* over which he now presides though personally he is ever wrapt in mystic meditation (Tib. *Sam-tan*). The Kalachakra cult (*vide post* Chapt.—.) makes a primal uncreated Being, termed མཆོག་གི་དང་པོའི་སངས་རྒྱས in Tibetan, (familiar to English readers as "Adi-Buddha") the creator of these heavens (sometimes increased to 13 in number) and both the evolver and the president of the Dhyani Buddhas.

The names of the Five Dhyani Buddhas or Ye-shes Sang-gye are in Sanskrit, Tibetan and Mongol, as follows :—

1.—Vairochana.	Nang-pa Nang-ts'e.	Mashi-geigülün-Jokiakchi.
2.—Akshobhya.	Mi-kyö Dorje.	Ülü-küdälükchi; or *Akghorabhi.*
3.—Ratna Sambhava.	Zingsten Jungdo. (འཛིངས་རྡེན་འབྱུང་སྡོ).	Erdeni-yin Oron
4.—Amitabha.	Wö-pag-me. (འོད་དཔག་མེད)	Tsaglashi-üghe-gereltü.
5.—Amoghasiddha.	Dön-dup (དོན་གྲུབ), or Ngádra (ང་སྒྲ)	———

Of these, the first-named one, *i.e.*, Vairochana, resides in the highest Central Heaven, denominated in Tibetan GALDAN; and the others in heavens situated to the east, south, west, and north, respectively. However, the Dhyani Buddha who concerns himself mostly with the affairs of this world of ours is Wöpak-me'. He dwells in the Western Heaven, the beautiful realm of DEWACHAN; and, being as Number Four correspondent in his origin to the great Human Buddha of the present *Kalpa*, Shakya-t'ubpa, it is only natural that he should be the one who is chiefly drawn in sympathy towards the present inhabitants of the earth. Of course, he especially affects the sacred land of Tibet where he is known by several names besides Wö'pak-me' ("Immeasurable Light"), such as Ts'e-pak-me' ("Immeasurable Life") and Nang-wa T'á-ye ("Illimitable Brightness"). Moreover, in order to prove of still greater benefit to the people of Tibet, he appears continually there in human form, being incarnated in *each* successive Panchhen Rimpochhe, the head of Táshilhümpo Monastery and titular ruler of the Province of Tsang. Wö'-pak-me', the often-mentioned Amitabha or Amitayus of Sanskrit writings, seems to be the only Dhyani Buddha that undergoes a regular series of incarnations upon earth; although Mi-kyö' Dorje, otherwise Akshobhya, is a deity not unknown to the populace so far as pictures and figures in temples can make him. Moreover, the famous religious masquerade at Hemis Monastery, Ladak, and at Darjeeling, is styled the *Mi-kyö' Dorje Kyil-khor*. It is held in honour of the saint Padma Jung-nas, but is under the patronage of Akshobhya, who dwells in the Eastern Heaven.

DEWACHAN, THE HEAVEN OF WÖ'PAK-ME'.

This, the Heaven of the West (བདེ་བ་ཅན "possessed of bliss") of the Tibetans, and the Sukhávati of the Indians, is the realm that mainly concerns mortal man. Thither, when a man of virtue dies, does his spirit depart after a short period in the Buddhist purgatory, the Bardo. There, moreover, does his "astral body" continue, even after his re-incarnation, if he be a saint who engages incessantly in the *Sam-tan* form of ascetic meditation.

The delights of Dewachan are fully set forth in a Sutra of the Mdo series of the Kangyur. There, as we read, does the fourth Dhyani Buddha, Wö'pak-me' or Amitabha, preside and is ever preaching the Doctrine. It is edged all round with piles of gold, silver, glass, and topaz; has seven promenades with seven avenues of palm-trees; and is diversified with huge lotos-ponds in which grow four kinds of lotos, each of a different colour, that is to say, blue, yellow, crimson, and white. It is full, moreover, of swans, cuckoos, and peacocks; and "in that Buddha country music is always being played." Indeed a portion of this description (written in Sanskrit probably four hundred years, or rather more, after CHRIST) recalls similar descriptions in the Book of the Revelation of St. John, of which it is possibly in part an imitation. Again, for example, we have there the Sixteen Nai-ten, or chief disciples disposed in places of honour.

DHYANI SATTWAS.

In order to bring the new Order of Buddhas into closer relationship with mundane affairs, an intermediate series of spiritual entities has been devised. The members of this series rank as Bodhisattwas and bear the same position of subordination to the Dhyani Buddhas that ordinary Bodhisattwas hold to human Buddhas. While the Dhyani Buddha is, as a rule, tied to one of the heavenly paradises and does not personally communicate with beings upon earth, the Dhyani Sattwa's special vocation is to be born and re-born in mortal guise in order to lead all sensate creatures to a right understanding of the Doctrine. Thus, each member is repeatedly incarnate in the bodily frame of the successive holders of some particular ecclesiastical office, through whom he is supposed to work for the welfare of others.

The genesis of the Dhyani Sattwas or Dhyani Bodhisattwas is not dissimilar in character to that of the superior Order just dealt with. Rays of light issuing from the head of the first Dhyani Buddha were the means of producing the first Dhyani Sattwa Kun-tu Bzangpo; and from the latter were evolved, by connubial conjunction with his spiritual *yum* or *sakti* Kuntu Bzangmo, other rays which created other four Sattwas correspondent to the four other Dhyani Buddhas. There are, however, different versions of this event. A special origin, moreover, is usually assigned to the fourth Dhyani Sattwa correspondent to Wö-pak-me' and who plays an important part in Tibetan religious affairs. While in general Buddhistic lore Kuntu Bzangpo is considered to be the most important of the Five Dhyani Sattwas and is often confounded popularly with him who in the Kalachakra system is styled the "Adi-buddha," yet in the particular cults of the Faith prevailing in Tibet and in Japan it is the Fourth Sattwa that has acquired the place of pre-eminence.[1] Before, however, entering into details concerning that hero

[1] In China the fourth Dhyani Sattwa, *i.e.*, Avalokiteswara, is as popular as in Tibet; but there, by a curious development, he has been transformed into a goddess *Kuan-shi-yin* "the hear-prayer Bodhisattwa" (*Vide* Williams's Chinese-English Dictionary, p. 656). Not so, however, in Korea, where the name of the Bodhisattwa has become: *Koan Syei Yumpo Sal.*

we must first give the individual names of the series; remarking also that the number prefixed to each Dhyani Sattwa indicates the particular Buddha to whom he is appendant:—

1. Kuntu Sangpo (Sansk. *Samanta Bhadra*).
2. Dorje Chhang (Sansk. *Vajrapani*).
3. Jam-yang (also Jam-pal) (Sansk. *Manjushri*).
4. Chenraisi (Sansk. *Avalokiteswara*).
5. Dorje Sempá (Sansk. *Vajrasattwa*).

Of these beings, the most popular in Tibet are Nos. 2, 3, and 4; but No. 4 highest above all. Nevertheless we find No. 5 often set down to be equivalent to the Adi-Buddha. Dorje Chhang, who is likewise known as Chhyakna Dorje, may be found represented in metal in every temple and religious establishment of the country. He is a prime defender of the Faith, generally pourtrayed with a so-called "terrific" cast of countenance, meant to appal every would-be assailant of Buddhism. This effect is enhanced by the image being invariably painted scarlet. Thus Milaraspa invokes him as "Thou great red Dorje Chhang!" Jampal or Jam-yang, who is supposed to be endowed with a voice of magical power, becomes incarnate in endless repetition in the successive chief lamas of the once puissant Sakya Monastery. Tsongkhapa was also tenanted spiritually by an emanation of Jampal. Jampal is held, however, to have cared always less for Tibet than for Nepal, and was originally instrumental in converting the latter country to the true Doctrine. And next we come to one who claims a paragraph special to himself.

THE DHYANI SATTWA CHENRAISI, PROTECTOR OF TIBET.

Each one of the Dhyani Sattwa is deemed to be the vice-regent or deputy upon earth of the particular Dhyani Buddha to whom he owes his origin and whose spiritual son he is accounted. Chenraisi, then, has been embodied upon the world in order to second personally the designs of the great Buddha of the Western Heaven, Wö'pak-me' or *Amitabha*. In order to perform this work the more effectually, he has arranged to inhabit in perpetuity the corporeal form of every Grand Lama of Lhása that rules the destinies of Tibet. The Dalai Lama of Lhása, accordingly, is the *tulku* or apparitional form of Chenraisi and receives the homage and worship due to that benevolent being.

The full name of this, the Fourth Dhyani Sattwa, may be set forth. It is *Syan-ras-gzigs Dbang-p'yug*, in present pronunciation sounded Chanraisi Wang-Chhyuk, and signifying "the Rich Power of the Seer (clad) in a Garment of Eyes." His origin from Wö'pak-me' is thus described. A ray of pure white light streamed out from the left eye of the Dhyani Buddha and flashing on to a lake teeming with lotos buds impregnated one of them with divine progeny. This lotos blossom attained a stupendous size and beauty; and when the king of the land came to view it he descried a youth of 16 issuing out from the inner cup. Received as a divinity, the youth proved to be a Bodhisattwa, whose mission was the emancipation, of every living creature that should ever be born, from the wheel of transmigratory existence. Thus was Chenraisi first manifested. Labouring unremittingly from his place in the Dewachan Heaven under the direction of Wö'pak-me', the Dhyani Buddha, to effect the abolition of metempsychosis, he found creatures continued to be born and re-born. He was then endowed with eleven faces and eleven mouths, the better to preach the Doctrine; but still, notwithstanding much success, the wheels of life went round. Next, he developed one thousand hands and in the palm of every hand an eye; but although the thousand eyes evinced immeasureable powers of discernment, the Bodhisattwa was still disappointed—the end was not yet. So, while remaining true to his vow not to cease from his self-imposed task until the cycles of existence were emptied, he turned to more sober and slower means. He joined his spiritual essence to that of the great ruler of Tibet, King Srong-ts'an Gampo, and determined to labour upon earth through that monarch's mind and body for the general good. Thereafter he inhabited the forms of other mighty sovereigns, such as Bromston, Jenghis Khan, Kublai Khan, and various Chinese emperors. At length he has settled down to occupy the personality of the Dalai Lamas of Tibet even to the present day.

In order to further the accomplishment of his mission for the deliverance of mortals, Chenraisi devised the famous formula *Om mani padme hum* now used so widely throughout Tibet. It is composed of six magical syllables, each of which when uttered is of great effect in procuring the deliverance of one of the six classes of living creatures; the six syllables together promoting the good of all six classes. It is a petition to Chenraisi, who is animated with greater and still greater power for his work, the more human beings that repeat the sentence and the oftener they do so. Hence arose the inmeasurable methods for giving vent to the *Om ma-ni pad-me hum,* which have become prevalent in Tibet. So, whether the winds, the waters, or the human hand revolve the wheels which thus mechanically grind forth the the syllables, they are regarded by the votary as addressed, through the Dalai Lama of Lhása, to Chenraisi. Thus does everyone unite to speed his sacred work.[1]

DEIFIED SAINTS.

After the Bodhisattwas may be said to rank a large number of personages famous in the history of Buddhism or locally famous in Tibetan annals. Some of these attained the position of Bodhisattwa during life and therefore may be classed as the equal of such beings; others were emanations of Dhyani Bodhisattwa. Nevertheless these saints in themselves, independently of the *las* or *karma* carried from other personages preceding them, earned apparently a new celestial entity differentiating them permanently from such heritage and initiating a fresh lineage of their own. In this new personality, according to modern ideas in Tibet, they inhabit one of the heavens, whilst if necessary (in order to continue their labours for Buddhism) they can, in *nirmáṇa* form, be incarnated in successive generations on earth.

The highest of all such creations are the pair of pupils who were with Gautama during his early asceticism and who after their first disgust at his change eventually became his devoted followers. They died before their master's demise. This couple of disciples, Shari-i-bu or Sáriputra and Mo-u-gal-gyibu or Moggalana, are known in Tibetan mythology as ཟུང་མཆོག "the best pair." Very few images of them are to be met with in Tibet, save in the largest monastic temples and in the Lhasa Cho-khang, and then only as attendants on Shakya-t'ubpa the Buddha.

Next rank the sixteen STHAVIRAS, known as གནས་བརྟན "*Naiten*" in Tibet and as *Batu-akchi* in Mongolia. These disseminated the Doctrine in divers countries in the first 4 or 5 centuries after Shakya's death, but not in Tibet.[2] Their names in Tibetan are:—

1. མེ་སྐྱེས the fire-born.
2. མ་ཕམ་པ the unconquerable.
3. གནགས་ན་གནས forest-saint.
4. དུས་ལྡན the opportunist.
5. རྡོ་རྗེ་མོའི་བུ thunder-born.
6. བཟང་པོ the good.

[1] The six-syllabled ejaculation is both a *bija mantra* and a *dharani*. It is paralleled in Korea by the utterance of the syllables *Na-mu a-mi tah-bu*, to be heard at all times in the mouths of the religious.

[2] One tradition, however, makes Me-skyes, the first *Naiten*, preach in Ladak and Ngari Khorsum.

7. གླང་པོ་སྐྱོང protector of bulls.
8. Bhara-dwadza.
9. སྲེ་མོང the weasel.
10. སྒྲ་ཅན་འཛིན Rahula, son of Shakya.
11. ལམ་ཕྲན་བསྟན the guide in narrow paths.
12. Bharadwadza the meditator.
13. ལམ་བསྟན the path-shower.
14. ཀླུའི་སྡེ or Nagasena.
15. གོ་པ་ཀ Gopaka.
16. མི་ཕྱེད the half-human one.

There is some variation in the nomenclature of these sanctities and in the choice of the particular individuals who ought to be included among them.[1] They are usually, however, spoken of, and represented as, a sacred group not as separate personalities.

After the *Naiten* come a numerous body of saints deified and, whether regarded as sublimated into Nirvana or as in Galdan, Dawachan, or other of the heavens, still to be appealed to, coerced and conjured up, and in some instances as still taking earthly incarnation. There are certain orders or ranks in such a pantheon, naturally.

First stand those who from their splendid effect on the religious world are entitled to the prænomen of PAL-GON (དཔལ་མགོན)"splendid lord" in Sanskrit: *S'rinatha.* These are only four or five in number, including *Pal-gon Lu-ḍub* or Nagar-juna, *T'ogs-med* or Aryasanga, Tsong-khapa, and Bu-ton.

Secondly, are ranged the series of གྲུབ་ཆེན DUB-CHHEN, in Sanskrit *Maha Siddha,* said to be 84 in number. Among these are Naro and Tilo (so often mentioned in Milaraspa's *Gurbum*), Sha-wa-ri-pa, Dza-wa-ri-pa, Nya-lto-wa (*i.e.,* the Fish-bellied), Nagpo Spyodpa, Sgrom-bi-wa, and Chang-kya Rolpai Dorje, the last-named being the deified saint who still inhabits the chief Incarnate Lama at Peking,

[1] A. Grünwedel in *Mythologie des Buddhismus in Tibet* gives the names of the 16 Sthaviras substantially as above, with the names in Sanskrit of 15 out of the 16, the list running as follows: Agniya, Ayita, Vanavasa or Khadiravana, Kalika, Saraṇa Vatsaputra, Bhadra, Kanakavatsa, Kanaka-bharadvaja, Vakuḷa, Rahula, Suḍa-pant'aka, Piṇḍola-bharadvaja, Pant'aka, Nagasena, Gopaka. Nevertheless in a list occurring in the short recension of the Sukhavati Vyuha, translated from the Sanskrit by the late Professor Cowell, in the series "Sacred Books of the East," a very different list is given, manifestly incorrect in that Shariputra and Maudgalyayana with others are included as of the 16. This series runs: Shariputra, Maha Maudgalya-yana, Maha Kashyapa, Maha Kapp'ina, Maha Katya-yana, Maha Kaushthila, Revata, Suddhi Pant'aka, Nanda, Ananda, Rahula, Gavámpati, Bharadwága, Kálodáyin Wakkula, Aniruddha.

Chang-kya Hutuktu. All of the foregoing were great masters of Tantrik Meditation.

Thirdly, may be placed those entitled to the style: སྒྲུབ་པའི་དབང་ཕྱུག "Rich Power of Meditation," commonly abbreviated into སྒྲུབ་དབང་ Ḍub-wang. Of such are Milaraspa and Padma Sambhawa, the latter in his manifestation as *Humkara.*

Another rank is that of སྒྲུབ་མཆོག Ḍub-chhok, to which belong the engineer-saint T'ang-tong Gyalpo, Dampa Gya-gar, with others. Atisha, the great Indian missionary who lived for and died in Tibet, seems to stands alone, bearing the designation ཇོ་བོ་ཆེན་པོ "Great Lord." His full Tibetan style is ཇོ་བོ་ཆེན་པོ་ཕུལ་འབྱུང་ *Jowo Chhenpo P'ul Jung.*

Finally come the large band of རྗེ་བཙུན Je-tsun or "reverends." The appellation, however, belongs to many in the preceding classes as an additional title, *e.g.* to Milaraspa. This large body includes such as Zla-wa Gragspa, Sgampo-pa, Zhiwa Lha, the lots'awa or translator Marpa (Milaraspa's instructor), Zhiwa Ts'o (an Indian paṇḍit), Sangs-rgyas-bskyabs, and a host of lesser lights.

Images of most of those sacred personages are to be found in numerous temples, especially in the particular localities where they made their fame. Effigies of Padma Sambhawa, or "*Pema Jungne*" as he is known in Tibet, abound in Tsang and Sikkim as well as in the Derge province of Khams. In Eastern Tibet Tsong-khapa or "*Je Rimpochhe*" usually predominates. In Galdan Gompa, Samye and Kumbum are the finest effigies of the latter saint.

GODS AND GODDESSES.

All Buddhas and Bodhisattwas (as also many deified human beings) rank the highest of the classes of spiritual beings to whom attention is paid. All gods and goddesses, styled *lha* and *lhamo* in Tibet, take a somewhat subordinate position. Nevertheless, in the popular conception several of the latter are practically of more importance than any Buddha. However, as a matter of fact, the Buddhas and Bodhisattwas whose images are set up in temples are held to be deities and are worshipped in common with ordinary gods and goddesses. Little distinction comes from the mere class to which any of these beings belong; the favourite and most revered effigy is that which popular feeling has singled out to be the most accessible and the most powerful. The individual deity chiefly venerated in one district may be, moreover, but little regarded elsewhere.

THE MOTHER GODDESS.

Perhaps the goddesses are considered of highest account. Certainly the most widely-esteemed deity in Tibet, and the one most commonly resorted to, is a *lha-mo* or goddess. This is DOLMA (lit. *Sgrolma*, "The Deliverer") known variously, according to the pronunciation in different parts of the country, as *Rolma* (in Ladak), *Tö-ma* (in Tsang), and *Drolma* (in Khams). She is often distinguished as *Yum*, "the Mother," and asserted to be "the mother of all the Bodhisattwas." In Mongolia Dolma seems always to be called *Dara-eke* "mother Tara" or more fully: *Ketel-ghekchi eke* "the mother who rescues." She was introduced into Tibetan Buddhism as the counterpart or synonym of the Hindu goddess *Tara*. Her genesis and her after history do not wholly tally, however, with the Hindu narratives concerning Tara.

Although Dolma is supposed to have existed through many ages and to have taken many forms under the guise of which she has engaged in various enterprises, she is supposed to have been first enlisted in the cause of Buddhism through the agency of the Dhyani Buddha Wö'-pak-me.' At the moment when the white ray from his left eye brought Chenraisi into being, another ray of green light from his right eye was made to evolve the goddess whose essence had passed from distant regions into the Dewachan heaven. Being thus twin with Chenraisi, she was thenceforward ever confederate with him in his great projects for the spread of Buddhism and the emancipation of sentient creatures. So do we always observe Dolma and the eleven-faced Dhyani Sattwa coupled together in Buddhist legend.

Her earliest appearance incarnated in human form was contemporary with Chenraisi's adoption of the bodily frame of King Srong Tsan Gampo. The spiritual essence or *tulwa* of Dolma then divided itself into two; and each half became incarnate one in each of the two chief wives of that king. Dolma, having been thus split in two, continued so both in her spiritual existence—her astral body—as a goddess in Dewachan and in her manifestations upon earth. Accordingly, among the images of temples as well as in the Tantras and in Tantrik ceremonial, we meet with two principal impersonations of this goddess. We have Dol-kar or the White Dolma and Dol-jang or the Green Dolma; the King's Chinese wife being the former and his Nepalese spouse being Dol-jang. We say "principal impersonations," because two other wives of Srong Tsan Gampo were further forms of Dolma; while in more recent times the emanations from the goddess have been multiplied into as many as twenty-one, which form so many branch *tul-ku*. A Dolma *lha-khang* or "god-house," of which every larger monastery boasts one as a separate shrine, contains the complete range of those impersonations.

At the present day, as we gather from Prof. Albert Grünwedel's work, the incarnations of the goddess assume, curiously enough, male forms in Mongolia and Siberia. The Tsars of Russia successively are now deemed by the Buriat Buddhists to be the incarnation on earth of the White Dolma; while the Green Dolma, known in popular Mongol Buddhism as Nokoghan Ketelghekchi Eke "the green delivering mother," is supposed to be now corporeally manifest in a Mongol male *hubilghan* (=Tib-*tulku*) resident in Trans-Baikal.

Other branch emanations or "aspects" of Dolma are said to be the goddesses *Wöserchenma, T'onyer-chenma*, and the three-faced *Loma-gyönma*, the latter represented as dancing clad only in a girdle-band of leaves. The second-named is a wrathful form of the goddess.

PALDAN LHA-MO.

This goddess, who seems to be always of ferocious and bloodthirsty mood, is deemed to be one of the most redoubtable defenders of Buddhism. She appears to have been originally the daughter of Gya Jin or Indra. After her first period of life, she went a progress of visits to the regions of the various orders of beings dwelling on the slopes of Mount Meru, in each of which successively she was born and spent one life-time. Being naturally of a lustful disposition, she led a most abandoned career in each of those spheres. Her warlike character and physical strength, furthermore, enabled her easily to dispose of her several lovers as she grew tired of them. But, in spite of her licentious and murderous career, the goddess, because of her devotion to Buddhism, is supposed to have attained to the tenth stage in the Lam Rim Chhenpo or Mahayana road to emancipation.

This deity, whose name of Paldan Lhá-mo signifies merely "the splendid goddess," is also often termed Lhá-mo Mag-jormo "the goddess addicted to war." In mythological art she seems to be pourtrayed in two chief styles. In one she stands in rampant riotous attitude, a wreath of skulls over her shoulders and reaching to the ground, the mangled bodies of one or two of her lovers trampled under her feet; and holding aloft a skull from which she is quaffing blood. In her second attitude, or milder aspect, she is seated on a mule which she guides with a bridle of snakes, holding an umbrella of peacock's feathers over her head.

The fact that in her second aspect the goddess is riding her mule, seated side-ways as an European lady, has given currency to a curious idea which deserves to be mentioned. Many years ago certain pictures from the *Illustrated London News,* in which Queen Victoria was shown in early life sitting on horse-back to review the troops, found their way into Tibet. As the great Empress of India was commonly accounted in Tibet as a personage warlike as well as of far-reaching sway, those pictures started the notion that Queen Victoria was an incarnation of goddess Paldan Lhá-mo.[1] And so in Tibet at the present day it is always held; the mild-hearted sovereign of Great Britain embodied the blood-thirsty goddess—otherwise how could she rule over so mighty a realm of which the vast Dzambu-ling (India) forms only one fragment? Now that Queen Victoria has passed away, we do not know whether the goddess has become re-incarnate in King Edward, whose sex, as we have just seen, would not preclude the succession. It was the Empress Katharine of Russia that set going the Dolma incarnations on the Russian Throne. However, it is perhaps a pity, from the political point of view, that the British sovereigns should be held in Tibet to represent the redoubtable but blood-loving Paldan Mag-jormo; whereas the Russian royal autocrats embody the mild and motherly and popular goddess Dolma.

TAMDIN: THE GOD WITH THE HORSE'S NECK.

"A neighing was heard and then Tamdin appeared"—that is a frequent assertion in fantastic Buddhist legends; and this deity shows himself redoubtable in his power of terrifying by cries or by his uncouth appearance all demons who would molest the faithful votary of the Buddhist persuasion. Tamdin is the Tibetan analogue of the Indian *Hayagriwa,* who is also denominated Hayagriwa Mandhawa in order to distinguish him from Hayagriwa, a demon whom he fought with and overcame. The Indian deity seems to be as great a favourite in Assam as is his Tibetan brother in the land of snows; and nine miles north-west of Gauhati in Assam stands a very ancient shrine to Hayagriwa used in common both by Hindus and by Buddhists.

Tamdin is represented in images as possessed of a horse's head with streaming gilded mane and large protruding eyes, but with the remainder of his form like a man's. In Tantrik ceremonial he is addressed as *Pá-wo Tamdin!* "Brave Tamdin."

DORJE P'AGMO, THE SOW GODDESS.

The Sow with the Thunderbolt as a deity shows Buddhism in deliberate opposition to the religious susceptibilities of the professors

[1] See Ramsay's *Western Tibetan Dictionary.*

of three other chief Faiths of Asia—Judaism, Hinduism, and Muhammadanism. Buddhism claims that in past ages even that animal which is an abomination to the other religions enlisted itself to promote the spread of the new tenets. Dorje P'agmo, who was once in the flesh voluntarily as a female pig, is at the present day incarnate as a woman who presides as lady abbess over a hybrid monastery in Tibet wherein are housed both nuns and monks. She is the only woman in Tibet who is permitted to travel in a sedan chair; and she is supposed still to retain the power of transforming at will herself and the females of her community into a troop of sows. The incarnate goddess is alleged to have a goitre in the shape of a pig's head behind her right ear; and the small images of Dorje P'agmo carried as charms are always so designed. Apparently, besides the Incarnate Sow of Samding Monastery—the lady who claims the right to the sedan chair—other incarnations exist. For example, one is said to have taken form as lady principal of a convent situated on a small island on the frozen waters of the great northern lake, Tengri Nor.

GODS OF THE SOIL.

Throughout the snowy land, nevertheless, perhaps a range of comparatively inferior deities are most thought of and more earnestly striven for to be propitiated. We refer to the Sa-dag or Sa-dagpo (ས་བདག་པོ) "lord of the ground") deities which differ in every village, valley, and river-side, and which are esteemed to have jurisdiction over the earth or soil of the locality assigned to each. They appear not to be endowed with individual names, being only known as the Sa-dag or Shibdag (གཞི་བདག) of such-and-such a village or, perhaps, district.[1] To offend the Sa-dag is dreaded by all housewives, as he exercises special sway over the hearth of a house or tent. Milk or broth must not be allowed to boil or spill over on the fire, as the smell of such when burning is at once apparent to him and is most abhorrent. Butter is thrown into the fire to propitiate his anger on such accidents, but in cases he may be implacable and bring terrible ill-luck on the denizens of a tent or hut; and then Ngag-pa monks must be had in, the whole hearth dug up, and various rites of Tantrik character be nicely performed. Sometimes the *T'ab-lha* or "hearth-

[1] In Milaraspa a Shib-dag, which appears mounted on a hare and carrying a mushroom as a shield and blades of straw as weapons, is introduced as "the ruling deity of the district of Gro-t'ang."

god" is held to be not the same as the Sa-dag, but the two are generally considered identical.[1]

Chhu-lha "water-gods" and also the various river gods are likewise to be reckoned as of the class of Shib-dag or Sa-dag.[2]

Such is a general outline of the mythology belonging to the Buddhism of Tibet and Mongolia; and in its leading features, we may re-assert, it is in close agreement with the mythology which Buddhism, even in its early beginnings, gave adherence to.

At the present day in Burmah, Ceylon, Siam, as well as in Japan and Korea, the main public concerns itself not with the Eight-fold Path or the Four Noble Truths, or Nirvana; but mainly with the subjection of and ministry of demons, mountain-spirits, and the various gods of the soil. Incarnations, indeed, are more distinctively the property of the Tibetan and Mongolian creeds. Demonolatry, however, is not merely Tibetan, but is common to every indigenous form of Buddhism.

Accordingly, the inference seems irresistible. When Buddhism was introduced into all these different regions, she probably found demonology already a paramount force. Nevertheless, far from eradicating these superstitions, she incorporated many of their elements into her own system; sometimes developing them further, but giving to them all her own peculiar colouring, modelling them after one general similitude, which, under various modifications, is now found bequeathed to every Buddhistic land.

1 Among the Mongols an image of the god of the ground is placed on a small altar near the door of each tent inside. He is styled *Gājarun Edzen*, "landlord of the ground."

2 The great river-god of Amdo in N.E. Tibet is རྨ་བྱ་ཆེན་པོའི་མགོན་པོ "lord of the great peacocks" and exercises sway over the whole of the Hoang Ho.

CHAPTER XII.

THE TANTRAS AND TANTRIK RITES.

In the early centuries of the Christian era, the votaries of Buddhism seem to have become dissatisfied with the vague method for reaching wisdom, perfection, and Nirvana, prescribed by the primitive teachers. Simple as the Noble Truths and the Eightfold Path might look on paper, they were rather too general for practical and personal application. Something less etherial and more defined was called for.

The Mahayana, the Thegpa Chhenpo of the Tibetans, the greater vehicle or method of conveyance to perfection, satisfied this want in some degree. The six virtues or *paramita,* subsequently subdivided into 36, proved a more articulate monitor to right conduct than the older precepts; but the appeal to personal Bodhisattwas for assistance and the fascinating methods of scientific meditation were a stronger influence. But much was still too theoretical.

In the second century A.D., however, came Nagarjuna to the front promulgating the Madhyamika system, the Buma-pa (དབུས་མ་པ) of the Tibetans. Systems which are based on *viâ media* principles and compromise make a good bid for popularity. But there is evidence to shew that Nagarjuna made his tenets more inviting by initiating the ideas embodied afterwards in the Tantras. Later, the Yogacharya school developed the same ideas so as to apply them to all sorts of particular wants mundane as well as spiritual. Padma Sambhawa and his successors brought the system to its grossest development with machinery and purview most material.

The Tantrik system started with the profession of high perspective and lofty aims. Its goal was wisdom, perfection, and Nirvana, as much as any other Buddhist philosophy; but it made use of all the powers and resources of man's being and all the help of an enlarged pantheon of mythological personages in order to attain the end. Men's powers of memory were to be availed of to the full by the exercise of learning strings of innumerable syllables, nonsense in exterior form, but said to be replete intrinsically with mystic meaning and supernatural force. These were named *dharani*—or more expressively in Tibetan སྔགས་འཆང་ "spell-holders." Men's powers of systematic contemplation or meditation were to be definitely improved by marrying the mental to the physical. Psychical force by meditation could not only be made to animate the arterial blood but also (which was a very elemental and animal truth) make flux with the seminal or generative faculties of the body. Concentrated thought, the blood, the semen, were in some subtle manner to make an ecstatic conjuncture somewhere in the physical arteries thereby imparting miraculous powers. Thirdly, by the Tantrik system, man's dominion over deities great and small was to be asserted. He was to gain by perseverance complete control over certain divine beings as well as demons and use them to accomplish his own will and fulfil his own wants. The resources of this power of coercion—in Tibetan སྒྲུབ་པ *sgrub-pa*—to be acquired over supernatural orders of beings was enlarged by allocating to the deities the property of appearing under two or more earthly forms or aspects. These "aspects"—in Tibetan སྤྲུལ་སྐུ "*ṭul-ku*"—were classified ordinarily as ཞི་བ *shi-wa* mild or benevolent and as ཁྲོ་བོ *khro-wo* wrathful or དྲག་ཅན *drag-chan* savage. Under the first form the deity soothed and supernaturally helped; under the second aspects he terrified and took vengeance.

In process of time, as may be readily supposed, Tantrik learning and the acquirement of powers promised to votaries were sought after not for high and spiritual ends but for the mundane advantages and position they were believed to confer as well as from the love of the recondite and mystical which are innate in man's mind. The object of many Tantrik ceremonies is seen to be purely material and in order to bring about worldly sweets.

WHAT THE TANTRAS ARE.

We now come to see what the so-called Tantras are. They are the guide-books, commentaries, exposition and ritual of the system. The science and practice of Tantrik arts and magic are crystalised in the Tantras. But therein not only are particulars of the various rites and ceremonies detailed; but the history, the tenets, and the philosophy of the different schools and systems are fully expounded. To commit to memory any of the Tantra books is the vocation of the Buddhist mystic quite as much as is the endeavour to practice the arts and performances prescribed. Moreover, he who is expert in such knowledge and who has coerced to his will one or more of the Bodhi- or deities is considered well on the road to perfectness, disillusion, and Nirvana.

In Tibet the Tantras are styled བརྒྱུད *brgyud* or རྒྱུད *rgyud* a word which means literally "a string" or "that which connects;" and the method of advance upon the upward road through Tantrik learning and Tantrik ritual is known as the Dorje Theg-pa—the Dorje vehicle or method of conveyance. In the Rgyud sections of the Kah-gyur and the Tangyur may be found an immense collection of Tantras or Tantrik treatises. These set forth ceremonies of every imaginable description: to bring success to one's own projects, to do injury to one's enemies, and to thwart or to obtain the help of innumerable super-human potencies, with divers other mystic operations such as the examination of dreams. All such ceremonies are to be accompanied by many gesticulations with the small dumb-bell-like *dorje* held in the hand and with various ringings of a small *drilbu* or hand-bell. Hence we read in Milaraspa: "His *dorje* revelling in the profoundest of Tantras." Hence, also, the name of this Tantrik system, Dorje Theg-pa.

The Tantras are technically said to be divided into four classes which we need not enumerate as the classification is purely arbitrary, and similar treatises are placed indifferently in one or more of the supposed divisions. Those designated *Mula-tantra* in Sanskrit and in Tibetan བསྡུས་པའི་བརྒྱུད are of a more concentrated and subtle character gathering the forces employed into a bundle.

Doubtless the earlier treatises of the Madhyamika and the Yogacharya schools were translated into Tibetan by Bimala Mitra and others in the reign of T'i-srong Deu-tsan (680-700 A.D.). But the more eclectic rites and extravagant modes of magic based on so-called new series of Tantras are generally ascribed both in invention and in introduction to the versatile saint and sorcerer Padma Sambhawa—the Guru Pema of the modern populace of Tibet. He founded a sect with rites degenerating into mere buffoonery which still holds firm sway in certain large districts of Tibet, *i.e.*, the རྫོགས་ཆེན་པ Dzokchenpa Sect—the prevailing form of Buddhism in Sikkim and in the Derge and Jogchen districts of Eastern Tibet. This school sets forth three Theg-pa or Vehicles, to be chosen as separate methods of advance, namely, the Ati-yog, the Spyiti-yog, and the Yangti-yog.

Much Tantrik ceremonial was introduced by Atis'a, the Jo-wo P'ul Jung of Tibetans, circa 1020 A.D.

Finally Tsongkhapa, as part of his reforms, condensed and codified the Tantras in his famous work *Lam-rim Chhen-mo.* However, the usual term in Tibet for Tantrik practitioners, "Ngakpa," is derived from the cult to be next explained.

THE KALACHAKRA CULT.

In the 10th and 11th centuries, A.D., the eclectic and magical practices founded on the Tantras were still further elaborated. The system known as the Kalachakra came then into vogue. It was described as a new "vehicle" the སྔགས་ཀྱི་ཐེག་པ "Ngag-kyi Thegpa," but did not profess wholly to supersede the time-honoured Dorje Thegpa; only by its expanded mythological scheme and its fascinating and even sublime mystic conceptions it claimed to crystalise the old Tantrik methods into a regular science as complicated as it was resourceful. It was alleged to have arisen and to have been revealed in a city, probably an imaginary one, named Kalápa, situated in the country of Shambhala, a region said to be real and to have been a province of Bactria lying beyond the Jaxartes river in the plains of the Sea of Azov. The initiator and expounder of the new vehicle was one S'ri Kalachakra or, as styled in Tibetan, Pal Dus-kyi Khorlo, and the system came to be named after its originator. He is also often styled Dus-khor Páh-chig (དུས་འཁོར་དཔའ་གཅིག) Other saints who aided in its exposition and became deified thereby were Rig-den Padma Karpo, Rig-den Jampal Ḍag (རིགས་ལྡན་འཇམ་དཔལ་གྲགས) and Chhö-gyal Da-ḍag (ཆོས་རྒྱལ་ཟླ་གྲགས), the last-named of whom was king of Shambhala and a special incarnation as well.[1]

[1] The first book of the Tantra section of the Tangyur is headed with the title of the primary work of the Kalachakra cult as follows:—

རྒྱ་གར་སྐད་དུ། བི་མ་ལ་པྲབྷཱ་མཱུ་ལ་ཏནྟྲཱ་ནུ་སཱ་རི་ཎི་དྭཱ་ད་ཤ་ས་ཧ་སྲི་ཀཱ་ལ་གྷུ་ཀཱ་ལ་ཙ་ཀྲ་ཏནྟྲ་རཱ་ཛ་ཊཱི་ཀཱ།། བོད་སྐད་དུ། བསྡུས་པའི་རྒྱུད་ཀྱི་རྒྱལ་པོ་དུས་ཀྱི་འཁོར་ལོའི་འགྲེལ་བཤད་རྩ་བའི་རྒྱུད་ཀྱི་རྗེས་སུ་འཇུག་པ་སྟོང་ཕྲག་བཅུ་གཉིས་པ་དྲི་མ་མེད་པའི་འོད་ཅེས་བྱ་བ།

The first leaf is decorated with rude prints, one on each side, of དུས་འཁོར་དཔའ་གཅིག Dus-khor Pá-chig and ཆོས་རྒྱལ་ཟླ་གྲགས་ Chhö-gyal Da-ḍag, the ormer with his Yum or Sakti enfolded.

A leading feature of the Kalachakra or Dus-kyi Khorlo cult was the evolution in Buddhism for the first time of the idea of a Supreme Personal Being, most likely in rivalry of the great doctrine of both Christian and Mohammedan teaching which, in the 9th and 10th centuries A.D., was being ardently pushed by Nestorian and Musalman missionaries in Central Asia. We are introduced to a Central Arch-God or Supreme Meditative Buddha high above all other Buddhas or deities. He is denominated Adi-Buddha (or in Tibetan མཆོག་གི་དང་པོའི་སངས་རྒྱས "the first best Buddha"); and many fine and distinctively theistic characteristics of the Deity, his disposition, purity, fatherliness, benevolence and isolated power are set out in the Kalachakra treatises. It is only an effort, however, to erect a Supreme Being. He is still very like unto an ordinary Buddha and is even often spoken of as a Tathágata—in Tibetan *De-bzhin Shegs-pa* "one who has gone like those others." Indeed, by the Tibetans his personality was allocated to the place of a Buddha proper with the name of Dorje Sempa; and, later, we find the Dhyani Boddhisattwa Chhakna Dorje (ཕྱག་ན་རྡོ་རྗེ) assuming the full *rôle* of Adi-Buddha, sometimes in that aspect wherein the Bodhisattwa is regarded as Lord of the Noijin or mountain spirits (*i.e.*, as Kuvera), and sometimes under the generative or *demiurge* aspect with the designation of Dorje Chhang Yab-yum.[1] Be this as it might be, the main revelation of the Supreme Being himself was held to have been brought about by his incarnation on earth in the person of King Da-dag (ཟླ་གྲགས) or Da-wa Zang-po, the great sovereign of the country of Shambhala.[2]

The treatise opens:—

> Salutation to the sublime Dus-kyi Khor-lo!
> Possessed of Compassion itself a thousand-fold,
> Born in the three spheres and void of fear,
> A body knowing and to be known both in one;
> Salutation to Dus Khorlo the splendid!

[1] Vide *Das Pantheon des Tschangtscha Hutuktu*, by Engen Pander and Albert Grünwedel, page 59.

[2] On page 21*b* of the first of the treatises of the Tantra Section in the Tang-yur we extract the following:—

ད་ནི་འདིར་སྟོན་པ་པོ་དང་གསོལ་བ་འདེབས་པ་པོའི་འབྲེལ་པ་ཡང་བརྗོད་པར་བྱའོ། གལ་ཏེ་ན་སླ་མ་དང་ཕྱི་མར་རྒྱུད་ཀྱི་འགྲེལ་བ་ཤད་མ་ཐོས་པའི་ཚིག་འབྱུང་བར་འགྱུར་ཏེ། རྡོ་རྗེའི་ཐེག་པ་འདི་ལ་རོ་ལྷན་ན། གནས་པའི་གཏོད་

An important feature of the system was the series of Dhyani or Meditative Buddhas and their evolvements. These beings had already been in evidence in the earlier developments of the Mahayana cosmogony, but they were now brought out and properly defined. To each was assigned a separate heaven or paradise, as a realm where he dwelt and which he governed through a deputy called Dhyani Bodhisattwa.[1] With characteristic inconsistency, as we have seen, the Adi Buddha himself was one of such Bodhisattwa. He was probably thus doubly personified because of the intimate relations existing between these deputies and human beings. They were the

---

སྤྲིན་གྱི་བདག་པོ་ཆེན་པོ་བྱང་ཆུབ་སེམས་དཔའ་ཆེན་པོ་ཕྱག་ན་རྡོ་རྗེ་དེ་བཞིན་
གཤེགས་པ་ལ་གསོལ་བ་འདེབས་པ་དང་ཡང་དག་པ་སྨུད་པར་བྱེད་པ་པོ་མ་ཡིན་
ནམ། ཇི་ལྟར་ཤཱཀྱ་ལའི་ཡུལ་ཀ་ལཱ་པའི་གྲོང་གི་བདག་པོ་ཞི་མའི་འོད་ཀྱི་ལྷ་མོ་
རྣམ་པར་རྒྱལ་མའི་མངལ་ནས་བྱུང་བ་རྒྱལ་པོ་ཟླ་བ་བཟང་པོ་གསོལ་བ་འདེབས་
པ་པོར་འགྱུར། རྒྱུད་གཞན་འགའ་ཞིག་ཏུ་ཡང་མ་ཐོས་ཤིང་ལུང་བསྟན་པ་མེད་
པའི་ཕྱིར་ཕན་ཚུན་སྨོན་པ་པོ་དང་གསོལ་པ་འདེབས་པ་པོ་འགྲོལ་པ་འགལ་ཞེ་ན།
དེའི་ཕྱིར་བརྗོད་པར་བྱ་སྟེ། འདིར་སྔགས་ཀྱི་ཐེག་པ་ལ་མངལ་ནས་བྱུང་བ་དེ་
བཞིན་གཤེགས་པ་ལ་གསོལ་བ་འདེབས་པ་པོར་མི་འགྱུར་ཞེས་གང་འགའ་ཞིག
གིས་བརྗོད་པ་དེ་ནི་མ་ཡིན་ཏེ། གང་གི་ཕྱིར་བཅོམ་ལྡན་འདས་ཀྱང་མངལ་ནས་
བྱུང་བ་ཉིད་ཡིན་པའི་ཕྱིར་རོ། སྔགས་ཀྱི་ཐེག་པ་འདི་ལ་གལ་ཏེ་མངལ་ནས་བྱུང་
བ་དེ་བཞིན་གཤེགས་པ་ལ་གསོལ་བ་འདེབས་པ་པོ་དང་། སྨུད་པ་པོར་འགྱུར་ན།
དེའི་ཚེ་ཤཱཀྱའི་རིགས་མིའི་དབང་པོ་ཟས་གཙང་མའི་ལྷ་མོ་སྒྱུ་འཕྲུལ་ཆེན་པོའི་
ལྷུམས་ནས་བལྟམས་པ་ཤཱཀྱ་ཐུབ་པ་ཐམས་ཅད་མཁྱེན་པ་སྟོན་པ་པོར་མི་འགྱུར་ཏེ།
མངལ་ནས་བྱུང་བ་ཉིད་ཡིན་པའི་ཕྱིར་རོ།

[1] The particular Dhyani Buddha assigned to each heaven varies in different accounts. Amitabha always is found placed over the West seated on a red lotos, and Amoghasiddha on a bluish-green lotos in the North. Dorje Sempá or the Adi Buddha sometimes occupies a Paradise in the Zenith, but is also found in the East on a white lotos.

Powers chiefly to be conjured with under the ceremonies and meditative exercises detailed in the Kalachakra treatises.

ASPECTS AND EMANATIONS.

Both Dhyani Buddhas and Dhyani Bodhisattwas were already believed to be endowed, the former with three, the latter with two, forms of existence, having bodies palpable or impalpable (Sansk. *kaya*; Tib. སྐུ *sku*). The *ḍharmakáya* or ཆོས་སྐུ "*chhöku*" was the body of the Buddha impalpable in Nirvana; the *sambhogakáya* or ལོངས་སྤྱོད་སྐུ was the palpable form of both Buddhas and Bodhisattwas manifest in some particular heaven as Galdan (*Tushita*) or Dewachan (*Sukhávati*); and the *nirmanakáya* or སྤྲུལ་སྐུ "*ṭulku*" was the form always present on earth incarnate in some human personage. Now it was the second form the ལོངས་སྤྱོད་སྐུ the astral or heavenly body, capable of deeds and accomplishments, which had to be influenced by Tantrik ritual. This could be managed by mysticism. The heavenly form or astral existence could be made to act invisibly or, more frequently, in sensible apparitional ways; especially in being made by means of Tantrik sorcery to animate the various effigies and metal images prepared for him by the expert devotee. Such could then be effectively dealt with.

A further and ingenious expansion of the *káya* theory was this: that the Bodhisattwa or deity could in the *sambhoga* or heavenly form assume at pleasure a variety of both spiritual and earthly manifestations in order to carry out its special business of preaching the Doctrine and repressing the enemies of Buddhism. These manifestations of the *káya* or *sku* were termed སྤྲུལ་པ "*ṭul-pa*" or emanations, and often took a permanent form which almost served to differentiate them into separate personalities. This was hardly the case in the "*ṭul-pa*" of the first degree. Here, for example, the Dhyani Buddha *Amitabha* or འོད་དཔག་མེད "*Wö-pakme*" who as "immeasurable light" already appealed to the eye, was given another permanent variation of form or *ṭul-pa* as *Amitayus* or ཚེ་དཔག་མེད་ "immeasurable life," thus appealing to all the senses. Nevertheless, though mythologically represented in a style quite apart from Amitabha, the other form Amitayus is popularly deemed to be one and the same with the first.

Again *Manju-sri* or འཇམ་དཔལ Jampal took the variety form of *Manju-ghosha* or Jam-yang, appealing to the ear; but though permanent varities they are hardly considered two personages.

However, when we come to the further and more important subdivision of these emanations we find greater differentiation of personality. These further manifestations of the one deity are styled ཡང་སྤྲུལ *yang-ṭul* or Emanations of the Second Degree. Under this head we have the power whereby as *yang-ṭul* the Bodhisattwas and greater gods could assume "Aspects," these aspects or *yang-ṭul* being broadly divided into the two main sections of Mild or Soothing and Wrathful or Terrifying, the one reserved for the friends, the other for the enemies of Buddhism. The first section comprises the aspect called *santa* by Indians, ཞི་བ *shi-wa* by Tibetans, and *amurlingghui* by Mongols. It may be taken as a rule that, with one or two exceptions, the normal attitude and appearance of Buddhas, Bodhisattwas, and the greater gods and goddesses, is under the Shi-wa or Mild Aspect. This is indeed their primary *sambhoga* form, to soothe and to help. Certain such as Amitabha (Wö-pak-me) seem never to take any but the Mild Aspect. Jampal and Jam-yang also are both to be taken as generally of this the ཞི་བ aspect, though the same Bodhisattwa has his forms of the opposite disposition.

The second mode of manifestation is that of the ཁྲོ་བོ *Khro-wo* or Wrathful Aspect (Sansk. *krodha*, Mongol *kilingtü*). Under the Kalachakra system most Bodhisattwas and deities have this power of terrifying which is almost that of personating a new and wholly different creation, and under which they assume a different name. The characteristic in *Khro-wo* effigies is a figure with gnashing teeth, hair on end, three bulging rolling eyes, many arms clenching weapons or blood-filled skulls, and often trampling on victims. Of the Bodhisattwas, Dorje Chhang most frequently assumes this Aspect, having more than one variation of it. Thus, whilst as a mild deity he appears as the Green-robed Lak-na Dorje (ལག་ན་རྡོ་རྗེ་གོས་སྔོན་ཅན) and as Chhak-dor the Teacher (ཕྱག་རྡོར་ཨུ་ཙ་རྱ) on the other hand in *Khro-wo* Aspect we have him as the rageful Chhak-dor Khorchen. Jampal or Mañju-śri in the same way becomes another deity Jampal Dorje also Jampal-sgra-seng. Dolma or Mother Tara (the *Dara-eke* of the Mongols), usually so beneficent a goddess, now shews herself transformed into ཁྲོ་གཉེར་ཅན་མ "She who is wrinkled with anger." Other lesser gods are permanently wrathful and terrifying, having no mild form of apparition. Such are Tamdin (Sansk. *Haya-griva*), Shinje Gyalpo (*Yama*), and Shinjema the Death Goddess.

A third Aspect is that of the Cruel and Violent who execute vengeance on the enemies of Buddhism. This is termed in Tibetan *Tul-wa Drag-po* (སྤྲུལ་པ་དྲགས་པོ་) and the creature itself is styled *Drag-she* (དྲགས་གཤེད) "the cruel killer." The Sanskrit equivalent for both Aspect and personage is *bhairava*, the Mongol *ayolgakshi* for the former and *dokshit* for the latter. These beings seem to be properly eight in number: Tamdin in his manifestation as རྟ་མགྲིན་ལྕགས་རལ་ཅན་ ("Tamdin with the hair of whips"), Paldan Lha-mo, ཆོས་རྒྱལ་ཕྱི་སྒྲུབ, ཆོས་རྒྱལ་སྔོན་སྒྲུབ, the Six-handed Lord or མགོན་པོ་ཕྱག་དྲུག་པ, Dorje Jig-che (རྡོ་རྗེ་འཇིགས་བྱེད), Cham-shrang (ལྕམ་སྲིང་) and the lord of the five door-keepers who guard the threshold of Buddhism, namely, ཆོས་སྐྱོང་རྡོར་ལེགས་. Moreover each of the Dhyani Buddhas seems to have either a Drag-po Aspect or else a special Drag-she in his service to do his bidding.

Yet another expansion of the Emanation theory is that whereby a deity having become embodied in some great saint, henceforth a new line of what we may term Branch Emanations is started wherein the saint is differentiated as a deity from that being of whom he was an incarnation. He still carries *las* or *karma* from his primal embodier, but now in himself he has his *sambhoga* and *nirmana* bodies or forms, capable of independent aspects and of independent Earthly Incarnations. Such Branch Emanations are styled གསུམ་སྤྲུལ *sum-ṭul* or Emanations of the Third Degree. An example will do something to make this idea clearer. The founder of the Gelukpa reformation, Tsongkhapa, is held to have been emanated as an incarnation of Manjuśri or Jampal in the Second Degree. That saint (Tsongkhapa) while on earth by dint of his perfections (དངོས་སྒྲུབ) and particularly by constant meditation (བསམ་གཏན) gradually created for himself an astral counterpart or *sambhoga* form of himself in the Dewachan heaven, which became thereby an Emanation of the Third Degree of the Bodhisattwa Jampal with the name of Jampal Nying-po (འཇམ་དཔལ་སྙིང་པོ). Henceforth, as an entity separate from the Bodhisattwa, this Jampal Nying-po, the astral form or body (སྐུ) of Tsongkhapa is capable of incarnating himself in *nirmana* or earthly form in the successive abbots of the Kumbum lamassery near Tankar in Kansu. This personage the Kumbum *Ṭulku* is, accordingly, not only an incarnation of Tsongkhapa but also of Jampal in the Third Degree.

In a similar manner as a *Yang-ṭul* Emanation did Jampal in the guise of Jam-yang (*Mañjughosha*) become embodied in Sakya Pandita, of which saint the successive abbots of the great Sakya Gompa are now incarnations and at the same time Emanations in the Third Degree (*sum-ṭul*) of Jampal. So, too, did the same Bodhisattwa in his Jam-yang aspect embody Padma Sambhawa whose astral body became an Emanation in the Third Degree under the differentiated personality named འཇམ་དབྱངས་སྨྲ་སེང (Jam-yang-mra-seng), the future embodiments being the abbots of the Ri-wo-tsenga monastery (Chinese: Nu-tai-shan) in Shensi in China. Once more as འཇམ་དཔལ་མི་ཏྲ was the great pandit Bimala Mitra procreated and transmitted both in astral and earthly forms to the present day.

THE SAKTI FORMS.

Finally, when represented together with their *sakti* companions the Dhyani Bodhisattwas seem to appear as in yet another Aspect—the ཡུམ་བཅས Aspect as it styled in Tibet. Under the Kalachakra development which could assimilate Brahministic as well as Christian theories, gods and goddesses, both Indian and those local to the country where it might be introduced, could also assume the different manifestations and be generally utilised under laws like unto those asserted to belong to Buddhas and Bodhisattwas. Moreover, the *sakti* ideas of Hinduism having been adopted by developed Buddhism (even previously to the Kalachakra system) the respective goddesses soon became not merely the ནུས་མ "*nü-ma*" or female energy of a Bodhisattwa or a god, but eventually his wife or concubine. Under the Kalachakra *regime* in this aspect, the Bodhisattwa or the deity was styied the YAB or father, and the goddess his female companion the YUM or Mother. Thus the Dhyani Bodhisattwa Chenraisi (*Avalokitaswara*) has for his *Yum* the goddess Dolma Karmo ; Jampal (*Mañjusri*) is yoked to the goddess Yangchenma (དབྱངས་ཅན་མ); the Dhyani Buddha Donḍub clasps to his breast Dol-jang or the Green Dolma. The male gods such as Tamdin (*Hayagriwa*) and Dzam-bha-la had *Yum*, also, assigned to them. Images representing the deity with his female consort being among those most frequently made use of in Tantrik ceremonial are known in Tibet at the present day as *Yab-yum*, and are especially classified as སྔགས་ཀླུད "*Ngak-lü.*"

Other series of divinities included in such rites are the eight རིག་འཛིན *Rik-zin* with their leader a Wrathful Manifestation of Padma Sambhawa styled Lo-pön Hum-kara. Another Tantrik form of the latter saint when pictured sporting with the *Kha-dro-ma* fairies (Sansk. *Dakini*) is known as Pema Kha-dro Wang-dü (པདྨ་ཁ་འགྲོ་དབང་སྡུད)

The Yidam deities or tutelary manifestations of all the Dhyani Bodhisattwas, the deified saints, and the gods both general and local, make up yet a further band for Tantrik conjuration. With these may be classed the སྲིན་པོ Shrimpo (Sansk. *Rakshasa*) or rock-ogres, the གནོད་སྦྱིན Noijin (Sansk. *Yaksha*) or mountain deities, the ཀླུ Lu (Sansk. *Naga*), the གྲུལ་འབུམ Dul-bum (Sansk. *Kumbhánḍa*) or cemetery-ghouls, and the དྲི་ཟ Driza (Sansk. *Gandharva*) or musical smell-feeders. The latter as a rule are repressed or made truce with by the recital of mystic formulæ and by small offerings. Also the four འཇིག་རྟེན་སྐྱོང or Guardian Kings and the eight ཕྱོགས་སྐྱོངས or eight Protectors of the Points of the Compass.

In the older Buddhism among the more powerful tenants of Mount Meru, the centre of the universe, were these Four Kings the protectors of the four quarters of the mountains respectively. These were the *Dik Rajas* or *Lokapala* of Sanskrit terminology, འཇིག་རྟེན་གྱི

མགོན་པོ "Lords of the world" of the Tibetans. Their personal names are given usually as འཕགས་པ་སྐྱེས་པོ (Sansk. *Virudhaka*), ཡུལ་འཁོར་སྲུང (*Dhritarashtra*), སྤྱན་མི་བཟང (*Virupáksha*) and རྣམ་ཐོས་སྲས who is also Kuvera the king of Noijin or *Yakshas.* In Tantrik mythology, however, these protectors of the world have been converted into protectors of the Doctrine or defenders of the Faith, being placed among those deities known as Chhoi-kyong (ཆོས་སྐྱོང) or in Sanskrit *Dharmapala.* They are, moreover, no longer four; but have been assigned a chief or head in the person of the Shamáu god *Pe-har,* and together these have become known as སྐུ་ལྔ the Five Selfs or Personalities. The Chhoikyong kings especially guard the portals or entrances of temples and monasteries, and their figures in monstrous or terrific aspect are generally to be observed painted on or near to the chief door of the temple and that of the monastic མཛོད་ཁང or Treasury. These Chhoikyong have been, furthermore, incarnated, and the individuals whom they severally inhabit are deemed the very kings of astrologers and soothsayers; the well-known Naichhung Chhoikyong of Lhása being considered the incarnation of *Pe-har Gyal-po,* and the Karmasha Chhoikyong there personates one other of the protecting kings.

CONCOMITANTS OF TANTRIK RITES.

In the conduct of these magic rites considerable apparatus are deemed necessary. The correct robes and head-gear are first essential, the former being the full ge-long apparel, the latter either the ཞྭ་དམར (*sha-mar*) red hat or the more elaborate སྒྲོག་ཞུ a tawdry crown of five tiers—the hair, moreover, plaited with red riband. The chief apparatus may be at once enumerated with brief descriptions:—

རྡོ་རྗེ *dorje* or Indra's thunderbolt: a small open-work dumb-bell 4 or 5 inches long, with two knobs grasped in the right hand between the knobs and worked about as directed in the ritual. Sansk. *Vájra*; Mongol *otshar.*

དྲིལ་བུ *drilbu* or *tilbu*: a hand-bell usually ornamented on the handle with a triplet of mythological faces and the cup of the bell chased on the outer surface; held in the left hand. Sansk. *ghaṇṭa;* Mongol *hongkho*.

ཌ་མ་རུ *damaru:* a small drum formed of two skull crowns fastened back to back and the apertures covered with parchment or bladder; two large seeds or cowries dependent to two short cords are made to play on the drum by a quick turn of the wrist. This the Sanskrit term is generally used but ཅང་ཏེ *changte* is also heard, and ཅང་ཅང་ཏེའུ་

བུམ་པ *bum-pa* (also ཁྲུས་བུམ and མཆོད་བུམ) tea-pot-like vessels with long spouts, curled handle and inverted cover, of various forms; filled with consecrated water and often crowned with peacock feathers. Sansk. *mañgala-kalaśa;* Mongol *torkho*.

ཀང་དུང་ *kaṇg-tung* small trumpet which ought to be made out of human thigh-bone or else the tibia bone; decorated with silk tassels and pieces of skin (preferably human); blown at certain ceremonials.

ཐོད་པ *thö-pa* and ཐོད་པན *thö'pen* human skull, often an appendage to and symbol of various deities in their ཁྲོ་བོ or wrathful aspects in form of brass bowl with foaming blood in metal imitation in Tantrik rites, and when thus supposed to be full of blood it is termed ཐོད་ཁྲག; and in Pon ceremonial is even a real skull filled with animals' blood! Sansk. *kapala;* Mongol *gabola*.

མ་ནི་འཁོར་ལོ *máni-khorlo* prayer-wheel; but not often introduced in Tantrik ceremonial. Mongol *máni-kürdün*.

ཞགས་པ་ *shák-pa* sacred leash; a cord of many strands with a small dorje at each end, as supposed to be used by divine defenders of the Faith in noosing and holding-in the foes of Buddhism, and employed now in certain Tantrik rites. Sansk. *pasa;* Mongol *sür*.

ཕུར་བུ *phurbu* a bronze or bell-metal peg with three-sided unsharpened blade supposed to be useful as a dagger for exorcising demons and subjugating malevolent deities. The whole is usually about 8 inches in length, there being at the top an ornamental knob of three faces with necks running down and coalescing in the blade. In some *phurbu* the knob is further crowned with the slender neck and muzzle of the horse-headed Tamdin.

སྣ་ཚོགས་རྡོ་རྗེ *natsho-dorje* two dorjes fastened one across the other forming a Maltese cross, sometimes artificially conjoined but usually cast and made in this complex shape. Sansk. *visvavajra*.

མཆོད་ཀྱོག *chhö-kyok* is a variety of ཐོད་ཁྲག being a finely-chased metal bowl, fashioned as a skull, and used as libation bowl.

མར་མེ *mar-me* small brass cups filled with butter in which floats a tiny lighted wick, set out in large numbers.

མེ་ལོང་ *me-long* oval convex mirror, over which in forecasts holy water is poured.

The next important accessory in Ngak-pa or Tantrik ceremonial is the metal image of the particular deity dealt with. Moreover this image must be clad in the garment proper to him and to the occasion. Such clothing is styled *nabsa*, and bells, drums, *bumpa* pots, and books used in the particular rite have to wear *nabsa* corresponding in colour to that in which the deity is arrayed. The colour is the main thing and that concerns both the painting of the idol and the clothing. Red and black are employed to paint and array ཁྲོ་བོ Wrathful or དྲགས་ གཉེན Cruel Manifestations; yellow, white, and green belong to the Mild or ཞི་བ forms.

In this business the mystic circles and other geometrical figures known as *kyil-khor* in Tibet (the Sanskrit *maṇḍala*) play a conspicuous part. These are drawn with charcoal-ashes or coloured paint on the ground, or else are formed with heaps of grain usually coloured and arranged in the required lines and circles. The image of the deity or Buddha has a particular position within the *kyil-khor*! and the expression used is "to offer" a *maṇḍala* or *kyil-khor*, When deified beings are invoked in behalf of lay-folk, the *kyil-khor* is formed of coins given by the latter or even out of jewels and gold as most efficacious.

MANTRAS AND DHARANI.

Another part of the ritual and that of great importance is made up of the incantatory exclamations and magical sentences and syllables which differ according to the deity invoked and the purpose of invocation. The virtue lies in the particular verbal formulæ employed, the strings of syllables being rapidly repeated in certain prescribed order. Their variety and combinations are infinite, and whole treatises are occupied by them both in Sanskrit and Tibetan collections. The language used is always Sanskrit, though the stream of syllables has mostly no apparent meaning. These magical utterances are the famous Sanskrit *mantras* and *bija mantras*, the first being designated in Tibetan སྔགས "*ngag*" or རིག་སྔགས and the *bija mantras* or "seed mantras" being styled གསང་སྔགས. The first are usually sentences more or less translatable into some sort of significance. Thus *Om máni padme hum* and *Om vadzra sita hum* are forms of རིག་སྔགས་ *mantras;* whereas the *bija mantra* or གསང་སྔགས are sets of incoherent syllables, of which the following Romanised example may be quoted as used in the coercion of the Bodhisattwa Jampal:—

Dotsá ta na kri tám ya phăt,
Preat kri tám ta ru pa ya phăt,
Pi sha tsa ro sha na ya phăt :
Swaha !

In the foregoing will be noticed the recurrence of the syllable *Phăt.* This is an exclamation of notable virtue. Indeed, according to Milaraspa, the most powerful and comprehensive word which can be employed in such formulæ is the syllable *phăt*, which as a word has certainly no meaning at all.

'When going about you are always saying *phăt,*' remarks the philosophic daughter of a poor old woman whom the saint has effectually brought to his knees. 'What is the meaning of your *phăt?*' And then, of course, our worthy sage has his 'song' in readiness for response :—

Outwardly, *phăt* is the condensation of the items of Discriminative Perception—
Their amalgamation when those items have been too minutely subdivided and scattered;
Inwardly, *phăt* is the revival of one's sinking soul;
Rationally, *phăt* is the classification of things according to their primary nature
And the triple essence of a Naljor exists in the sphere of *phăt.*

There is, as we believe, a certain rhythm and half coherence about all mantras at least in their form; but in another class of formula even the semblance of order and swing seems to be utterly abandoned. We refer to the *ḍharani,* termed in Tibetan གཟུངས་སྔགས *"sung-ngak"* or spell-holders. These differ from mantras, in that they are not meant to be uttered but only written. They consist of sets of Tibetan words trailing off into Sanskrit syllables. Written or stamped on paper or cloth they are used to wrap up images of deities in ceremonial, and are furthermore largely employed on the cloths in which saintly corpses are enfolded. The term *ḍharani,* however, seems to have acquired likewise a much extended application. In the later works of mysticsm, after the introduction of the Kalachakra cult, we find even lengthy treatises, coherent in language but of deeply mystical character, styled *ḍharani.* These treatises are chiefly designed for the subjection to human power of demons, nagas, etc., but they are not ritual to be read or recited, and are meant to be used silently as of inherent magical virtue and of intrinsic power by mere presentation or, perhaps, requiring audible mention and allusion to be effective.[1] They are supposed, also, to contain a *snying-po,* an essence or quintessence, of that which is required for accomplishing a powerful supernatural result; the main characteristic of all *mantra* and *ḍharani* being their compendious embracive quality, that of "multum in parvissimo."

SPECIMEN CONTENTS OF BOOK OF TANTRIK TREATISES.

Tangyur: Div. རྒྱུད Vol. ཕི (44th.)

General Title at commencement of volume:—

མཚན་ཡང་དག་པར་བརྗོད་པའི་འགྲེལ་པ་མཚན་དོན་གསལ་བར་བྱེད་པའི་སྒྲོན་མེ་བཞུགས (Sansk: Náma Sangiti Brilti Námártha Prasakkár-nadipamnáma.)

Salutation: འཇམ་དཔལ་གཞོན་ནུར་གྱུར་པ་ལ་ཕྱག་འཚལ་ "Praise be unto the renewer of youth (re-juvenator) Jam-pal."

Cut on right hand of page at opening: the Lotsawa *Gnyag dznyán;* on left hand JAM-DBYANGS, with brandished gadá or mace in his right hand and dorje in his left. Blue lotus sprig clasped in bend

[1] See the titles and the character of the treatises published by Professor Laufer under the designation ཀླུ་འབུམ་བསྡུས་པའི་སྙིང་པོ in the *Journal* of the Finnish Ugrian Society.

of his left elbow. Feet with soles upturned. Head encircled with diadem. Necklet with pendent round neck. Figure sits cross-legged on large lotus flower.

Begins:—

ཟབ་ཅིང་རྒྱ་ཆེའི་སྐུ་མངའ་བའི་
འཇམ་པའི་དཔལ་ལ་ཕྱག་འཚལ་ཏེ་
སྐལ་ལྡན་རྣལ་འབྱོར་གང་ཞིག་གིས་
རྗེ་བཙུན་མཚན་བརྗོད་རྟོགས་བྱའི་ཕྱིར་
བཤད་པའི་རྒྱུད་དང་གདམས་ངག་ལ་
བརྟེན་ཏེ་འབད་པས་བཤད་པར་བྱ་
བཤད་ཚུལ་ལྔ་ཡི་སྒོ་ཕྱེ་ལ་
ཇི་སྙེད་རིགས་རྣམས་དྲུག་བསྡུས་ཏེ་
ཕན་ཡོན་བཅས་པ་བཤད་པ་ཡིན་

"When salutation has been made to Jam-pal
Possessed of profound and prodigious form,
Whosoever made holy by meditation (Yóga),
If he would cause the attributes of the Reverend one to be understood,
Exerting himself and relying on the oral precepts,
The Tantra of Exposition must be preached.
Then, when the door of the Five Modes of Exposition is set open,
And as many as six classes ranged together,
He will have both the benefit and the explanation."

This the first treatise in this volume is comprised in 41 folios and concludes with the following subscription: "Composed by the teacher Bimala Mitra at the request of his spiritual son (ཐུགས་ཀྱི་སྲས) Nyang Ting-nge-dzin. Translated at Nyeg-nyá (གཉེགས་གཉའ).

(2) འཕགས་པ་འཇམ་དཔལ་གྱི་མཚན་ཡང་དག་པར་བརྗོད་པའི་དོན་གསལ་བར་བྱེད་པ་ (Sansk: Arya Mañjus'ri Náma Sangityartha Lokaranáma).

Salutation: འཇམ་དཔལ་ཡེ་ཤེས་སེམས་དཔའ་ལ་ཕྱག་འཚལ་ལོ་

Treatise opens :—

མི་གཡོ་འགོག་མེད་དག་པའི་དང་
རང་འབྱུང་ཡེ་ཤེས་འོད་གསལ་བ་
འཇམ་དཔལ་ཞི་བའི་ཡེ་ཤེས་སེམས་
མི་རྟོག་གཟུགས་སྐུ་རང་བྱུང་བའི་
མགོན་པོ་དེ་ལ་གུས་བདུད་དེ་
རྒྱ་ཆེར་རབ་ཟབ་དག་པའི་རྒྱུད་
རིན་ཆེན་ལྟ་བུའི་དགོངས་པ་ལ་
འགྲོ་བ་ཐམས་ཅད་ཐབས་བསམ་མི་ཁྱབ་ཀྱང་
བདེ་གཤེགས་སྟོན་པའི་བྱིན་བརླབས་གདམས་པ་ཡས་
ངེས་དོན་ཕྱོགས་གཅིག་བདག་གིས་གསལ་བར་དགྲོལ་

འཇམ་དཔལ་གྱི་མཚན་ཡང་དག་པར་བརྗོད་པ་འདི་ལ་སྤྱི་དོན་རྣམ་པར་གུས་བསྟན་ཏེ།། ལེའུ་དང་པོ་ཞུས་པ་དང་། ཞུས་ལན་དུ་ཕུན་སུམ་ཚོགས་པ་ལྷ་རང་སྨྲར་ཏེ་བསྟན་པ་དང་། ལེའུ་གཉིས་པ་མི་གནས་པའི་ཡེ་ཤེས་ཆེན་པོ་དྲུག་པ་རྡོ་རྗེ་འཆང་གི་དོན་བསྟན་པ་དང་། ལེའུ་གསུམ་པ་ཤེས་བྱ་ངོ་བོས་སྟོང་པ་ཆོས་ཀྱི་དབྱིངས་ཀྱི་དོན་བསྟན་པ་དང་། ལེའུ་བཞི་པ་གཞི་འགོག་པ་མེད་པ་མེ་ལོང་ལྟ་བུའི་ཡེ་ཤེས་ཀྱི་དོན་བསྟན་པ་དང་། ལེའུ་ལྔ་པ་གཞིའི་རྩལ་སོ་སོར་དབྱེད་པ་སོ་སོར་རྟོགས་པ་ཡེ་ཤེས་ཀྱི་དོན་བསྟན་པ་དང་། ལེའུ་དྲུག་པ་གཞིའི་ངོ་བོ་སྐྱེ་འགག་མེད་པ་ན་ཉམ་པ་ཉིད་ཀྱི་ཡེ་ཤེས་དང་སྦྱར་ཏེ་བསྟན་པ་དང་། ལེའུ་བདུན་པ······དང་། ལེའུ་བརྒྱད་པ······། ལེའུ་དགུ་པ······དོན་མཐར་ཕྱིན་པར་བསྟན་པའོ། དེ་ནས་ལེའུ་དང་པོ་བཤད་དེ། དེ་ནས་ཞེས་པ་སྟོན་པ་ལ་སོགས་པ་ཕུན་སུམ་ཚོགས་པ་གནས་སོ། འདིས་དུས་ཕུན་སུམ་ཚོགས་པ་བསྟན་པའོ། དེ་ནས་དཔལ་ལྡན་རྡོ་རྗེ་འཆང་།

ཐལ་བས་ལུས་བྱུགས་ཁྲག་འཛག་པའོ་

མཚམས་རྣམས་སུ་ནི་མེ་ཏོག་མ་དང་མཛེས་ལྡན་

དང་ནི་འོད་ཟེར་འཁྲིག་དང་མདངས་འཁྲིག་མའོ་

གཡས་ན་ལྷུགས་ཀྱུ་གྲི་གུག་མི་མགོ་རྒྱུ་མའི་ཞགས་

གཡོན་ན་ཐོད་པ་ཁྲག་གིས་བཀང་བའོ་

སྨུག་ནག་མཐིང་ནག་དམར་ནག་ལྗང་ནག་

འཇིགས་པའི་གཟུགས་ཅན་བདུད་མོ་བཞིའོ་

ཐུགས་ཀའི་རེ་ཕའི་ཧཱུྃ་ལ་སྤྱན་དྲངས་

བསྐྱིམ་སོགས་རྫོགས་བྱས་ནས་

གསང་བའི་སྔགས་ནི་རབ་ཏུ་བཟླས་

ཨོཾ་ཀུརྨ་ཊ་བི་ཧྲ་ར་ཡ་ཧཱུྃ་ཕཊ་

ཊོ་བྷྲ་ཏ་ན་ཀྲོ་ཧྲ་ཡ་ཧཱུྃ་ཕཊ་

པྲེ་ཏ་བི་ས་ན་ཡ་ཕཊ་

པི་ཎྜ་ཙ་ཧ་ཏ་བ་ལ་ཕཊ་སྭཱ་ཧཱ་

ཀུརྨ་ཊ་ཀ་མ་ཡ་ཕཊ་

ཊོ་སྟ་ཏ་ན་ཀྲི་ཊཱ་ཡ་ཕཊ་

པྲེ་ཏ་ཀྲི་ཊཱ་ཏ་ཧྲུ་པ་ཡ་ཕཊ་

ཞེས་པ་བཟླས་ཏེ་

སྔོན་དུ་བསྙེན་པས་བསྒྲུབ་བྱའི་རྟགས་ནི་རིམ་པ་དྲུག་པར་བཏག་

རྟགས་བྱུང་བ་སྐད་པའི་ལས་བརྩམ་མོ་

ཨོཾ་ལས་རླུང་བསམས་སྙིང་དུ་བསྐྱེད་

དགུག་ཅིང་ཨུཙྪ་ཥ་ཡས་བསྐྲད་

ལས་བཅོལ་འཕྲིན་ལས་གཞན་ཡང་བརྩམ་

རབས་ཆད་ནག་པོའི་གྲོད་པར་ནི་

གཟུགས་བཞག་བསད་པས་དུར་ཁྲོད་སྒྲ་

ཧཱུྃ་མེ་དཔུང་འབར་བ་བརྗིད་པའི་སྐུ་

གང་རྒྱངས་བཞད་མཛད་ཐལ་མོ་རྡེབས་

རྒྱ་མཚོར་ཞབས་ནུབ་དབང་པོ་མནན་

སྐུ་གསུམ་དོན་ལྡན་ཞལ་འཇུམ་བཞད་

ཕྱག་དྲུག་བདུད་འདུལ་མཚོན་ཆ་འཛིན་

རྡོ་རྗེ་ཅན་ལ་ཕྱག་འཚལ་བསྟོད་

. . . . . གསོལ་ནས་བསྒྲུ་བའོ་།

བདག་གིས་གཞན་ལ་ཕན་ཕྱིར་བརྩམས་

དགེ་བ་དེ་ཡིས་འགྲོ་བ་ཀུན་

བླ་མེད་བྱང་ཆུབ་ཐོབ་པར་ཤོག་

ནམ་མཁའི་རིགས་ལས་ བྱུང་བའི་ཛཱ་བ་རི་ བས་མཛད་པའི་བདུད་བཟློག་པའི་ཆོ་ག་རྫོགས་སོ།།

(3) *f.* 48. *a.* ངོ་བོ་སྟོང་པ་ཉིད་ཀྱི་དོན་འཆད་དེ། སངས་རྒྱས་རྣམ་པར་སྣང་མཛད་ཆེ Has no Sanskrit title. When Buddha gives complete enlightenment, to define the Very Void (*Sunyatá*) in its essence.

(4) *f.* 52. *a.* གཞི་འགགས་པ་མེད་པའི་མེ་ལོང་ཤེ་ཤེས་ཀྱི་དོན་བསྟན་པའོ No Sanskrit title. A Mirror, which is free from both origin and cessation, for instruction in the meanings of Wisdom.

(5) *f.* 54. *b.* སྲིད་པའི་རི་བོ་ཆེན་པོ་འཇོམས། Subduing the great mountain of the world, *i.e.*, Mt. Meru.

(6) *f.* 59. *b.* Title illegible.

(7) Apparently omitted.

(8) *f.* 65. *a.* ཆེ་བ་བརྗོད་པ་སྔགས་ཀྱི་སྒྲ་དང་བཅས་པ་བསྟན་པར་བྱའོ་ The Enumeration of the great things which ought to be taught with a mystical voice.

(9) *f.* 67. *a.* མཚན་ཡང་དག་པར་བརྗོད་པའི་ཉེ་བར་བསྡུས་པའི་རྣམ་པར་རྟོག་གི། (Sanskrit title illegible). A thorough method for epitomizing the enumeration of actual characteristics (of Bodhisattwas and deities).

Salutation to Jampal the renewer of Youth! A lengthy ritual subdivided into 10 sections.

(10) *f.* 91. *b.* ཉེ་བར་བསྡུས་པའི་རྣམ་པར་རྟོག་གི་དང་སྦྱར་བའི་བསྡུས་དོན་མཚན་གྱི་སྒྲོན་མེ། "The lantern of signs and their meanings, collecting as in a handful all which can be brought together."

Opens as follows :—

བླ་རིགས་མཆོག་ཏུ་སངས་རྒྱས་ཀྱང་
ཀུན་ཏུ་གཟིགས་པས་འདོད་བྱིན་པ་
སངས་རྒྱས་ཀུན་བསྐྱེད་ཡབ་འགྱུར་ཞེས་
མཚན་གསོལ་འཇམ་དབྱངས་དེར་བཏུད་ནས་
རྙེད་ལ་གདུད་སོགས་ད་མིན་གྱི་
མ་དྲིས་མཚན་ལ་དད་སེམས་ཀྱིས་
བདག་དྲན་ཕྱིར་བྱས་འགལ་བ་མེད་
གཞན་དུ་གྱུར་ན་འང་དེ་མི་འགལ་
སངས་རྒྱས་ཀུན་གྱི་ཡེ་ཤེས་སྐུ་
གཙུག་ཏོར་ཆེན་པོ་ཚིག་བདག་གི་

མཚན་རྣམས་ཡང་དག་བརྗོད་པ་ལ་

སྤྱི་དོན་བཅུ་བཞི་དེར་བསྡུས་བཅི་

(11) *f.* 99. *b.* འཕགས་པ་འཇམ་དཔལ་གྱི་མཚན་ཡང་དག་པར་བརྗོད་པའི་འགྲེལ་པ་སྙིང་པོ་མངོན་པར་རྟོགས་ པ་སློབ་དཔོན་ཆེན་པོ་དཔལ་ གཉིས་མེད་རྡོ་རྗེས་མཛད་པ

A lengthy treatise subscribed as having been translated into Tibetan by the great *yogi* Prajnya Shri Dza-na Kirti.

(12) *f.* 138. *b.* འཕགས་པ་འཇམ་དཔལ་ཡེ་ཤེས་སེམས་དཔའི་མངོན་པར་རྟོགས་པ (Sans: Arya Dznya-na Sattwa Mañjus'ri Nopikanáma) Translated by Prajnya Shri Dzana Kirti.

(13) *f.* 140. *a.* འཇམ་དཔལ་ཡེ་ཤེས་སེམས་དཔའི་རིན་པོ་ཆེའི་ཕྱག་རྒྱ་དྲི་མ་མེད་པའི་ཆོ་ག Ritual of the stainless precious gestures of the Dhyani Sattwa Jampal.

(14) fol. 141. *a.* འཕགས་པ་འཇམ་དཔལ་ཡེ་ཤེས་སེམས་དཔའི་མངོན་རྟོགས་པ (Sans: Arya Dzñana-Sattwa Mañjus'ri Nipakanáma) Examination of the Bodhisattwa Jampal.

(15) fol. 142. *a.* "Ceremony of the most precious stainless gestures of the Dhyani-sattwa Jampal."

(16) fol. 143 *b.* རང་བཞིན་དུ་གནས་པའི་ སྔགས་ཀྱི་སྦྱོར་བཅུ་པ་

(17) fol. 144. *a.* རྨི་ལམ་བརྟག་པ (Sans: *Swapneksha*) The Examination or Scrutiny of Dreams.

(18) *f.* 145. *a.* སངས་རྒྱས་ཀྱི་བྱང་ཆུབ་བསམ་གཏན་དུག་སེལ་བར་བྱེད་པའི་མར་མེ A lamp which cleanses from poison the *bodhi* meditation of a Buddha.

(19) *f.* 146. *a.* The Wheel of Meditation which enters the mind of the Dhyani-sattwa Jampal.

(20) *f.* 149. *a.* ཐིག་ལེ་གཅིག་པ (Sans. *Tila-kaukanám*) "The first method of Seminal Contemplation."

(21) *f.* 150 *a.* "Coercion of the heart of the Dhyani-sattwa Jampal."

(22) *f.* 151. *a.* འཕགས་པ་འཇམ་དཔལ་གྱི་ཟབ་ཅིང་རྒྱ་ཆེ་བའི་འགྲོལ་བ་སློབ་དཔོན་དྲིལ་བུ་པས་མཛད་པ

(23) *f.* 159. *a.* "Method of Verbal Coercion of the actual bodily tokens or characteristics of Jampal."

(24) fo. 191. *a.* དཔལ་བཅོམ་ལྡན་འདས་རལ་པ་གཅིག་པའི་སྒྲུབ་ཐབས་སློབ་དཔོན་ཆེན་པོ་མི་ཕཾ་སྦས་བས་མཛད་པ་ The Coercion of the sublime Bhagawan Ralpachigpa, as performed in secret by the great teacher Mip'am.

(25) fo. 191. *b.* དཔལ་བཅོམ་ལྡན་འདས་རལ་པ་གཅིག་མའི་སྒྲུབ་ཐབས་

Salutation: "To the Sanctified (རྗེ་བཙུན་) Ralpagchigma!"

(26) fo. 192. *a.* དཔལ་བཅོཾས་རལ་པ་གཅིག་བའི་སྒྲུབ་ཐབས་ "The Coercion of the Glorious Chomdendé Ralpachig-wa."

(27) fo. 193. *a.* དཔལ་རལ་པ་གཅིག་མའི་སྒྲུབ་ཐབས་ "Coercion of the Glorious Ralpachig-ma."

Salutation: To the Blessed Mistress!

(རྗེ་མོ་བྱིན་བརླབས་ཅན་)

Concludes:—

དཔལ་རལ་པ་གཅིག་མའི་བསྒྲུབ་ཐབས་འཁོར་གཏོར་སྦྱིན་དང་བཅས་པ་
རྫོགས་སོ༎ རྗེ་གྲུབ་ཐོབ་ཆེན་པོའི་ཐུགས་དམ། གཉུབས་ལོ་ཙཱ་བས་བསྒྱུར་བའོ༎

(28) fo. 194. *b.* བསྐོ་ག་ནོར་བུའི་སྒྲོན་མ་

The whole follows:—"The Lamp of the Jewel Devotion," or "Lamp of Precious Ritual."

དཔལ་རྡོ་རྗེ་སེམས་དཔའ་ལ་ཕྱག་འཚལ་ལོ་
ཀྱེ་ཀྱེ་རྡོ་རྗེ་འཛིན་སོགས་བདག་དགོངས་གསོལ་
དཔའ་ཆེན་ཁྱོད་རྣམས་ཚད་མེད་ཀྱིས་

བདག་བཅག་ཉོན་མོངས་དགྲ་ལས་རྒྱལ་
ལེགས་སོ་མགོན་པོ་ཁྱོད་ལེགས་སོ་
ཨེ་མ་ཧོ་རྡོ་རྗེའི་ཐུགས་སངས་རྒྱས་
ཨེ་མ་ཧོ་ཨེ་པཾ་རྡོ་རྗེའི་ཆོས་
ཨེ་མ་ར་སྒྲུབ་དགེ་འདུན་ཚོགས་
སྐྱབས་གསུམ་རྡོ་རྗེ་གཅིག་ཁྱོད་འདུད་
ས་གསུམ་མཁས་སྤྱོད་གནས་གསུམ་དང་
སྒོ་གསུམ་རྡོ་རྗེའི་སྐུ་གསུང་ཐུགས་
མངོན་གསུམ་ཟབ་ཞི་དྲི་བྲལ་དུ་
སྟོན་པ་ཁྱོད་ལ་བདག་དགའོ་
དེ་ཕྱིར་བདག་དང་འགྲོ་ཀུན་གྱིས་
བགྱིས་དང་བགྱིད་འགྱུར་དགེ་ཆེན་འདི་
འོད་གསལ་བདེ་ཆེན་རྣམ་མི་རྟོག་
སྐུ་གསུམ་རྣམ་དག་མཐར་ཕྱིན་ཤོག་
སྐྱེ་ཞིང་སྐྱེ་བ་ཀུན་དུ་ཡང་
རིགས་སུ་སྐྱེ་དང་དམ་ཚིག་ཅན་
ལག་ན་རྡོ་རྗེ་དྲིལ་འཛིན་ཅིང་
ཟག་མེད་བདུད་རྩི་འཐུང་བར་ཤོག་
དྲི་མེད་རང་འབྱུང་སྐྱོབ་བདེ་དང་
དགའ་བདེ་འདུས་མ་བྱས་སྔགས་ཟབ་
དཀྱིལ་འཁོར་མཆོག་ཚོགས་མི་སླུ་བའི་
བདེན་པས་དངོས་གྲུབ་མཆོག་ཐོབ་ཤོག་

ཇོ་ཛྫེ་ཐོགས་པའི་བསྟོ་ག་ཉོར་བྲུའི་སྒྲོན་མ་

སློབ་དཔོན་མི་ཕམ་ཟླ་བས་མཛད་པ་རྫོགས ||

End of treatise.

(29) fo. 194. *b.* དཔལ་བཅོམ་ལྡན་འདས་རལ་པ་གཅིག་པ་ལ་བསྟོད་པ་

Praises to the Sublime Bhagawan Ralpachigpa.

(30) fo. 197. *a.* རང་གི་སེམས་དལ་སོས་པར་བྱེད་པའི་མན་ངག་ཚིགས་སུ་བཅད་པ་ཉི་ཤུ་རྩ་ལྔ་པ་ "Twenty-five directions in verse for soothing one's own mind."

(31) fo. 198. *a.* རྟོགས་པ་བརྗོད་པ་སུམ་ཅུ་པ་ "The Thirty Aphorisms of Perception."

Salutation : To the Rich Power of Chenresi!"

Last verse (quartette) :—

སྒྱུ་མར་རྟོགས་པས་བདེན་རྟོགས་འཛོམས་
རྟོག་མེད་སྒྱུ་མ་ལ་མི་གནས་
མི་གནས་འགྲོ་ལ་ཕན་བརྩོན་པས་
ཨེ་མ་ནོར་བུ་རིན་ཆེན་རྙེད་

"He who perceiveth the nature of Illusion
Hath acquired knowledge of the truth.
He abideth not in ignorant delusion,
But presseth on beyond mere goings and stayings;
And findeth indeed jewels most precious."

Subscription :—

རྣལ་འབྱོར་གྱི་དབང་ཕྱུག་ཆེན་པོ་མི་ཏྲ་ཛོ་ཀི་དེ་ཉིད་ཀྱི་སྤྱན་སྔར།
གནུབས་ལོ་ཙཱ་བ་བྱམས་པའི་དཔལ་གྱིས་བསྒྱུར་བའོ་

(32) fo. 199. *b.* དཔལ་ཁ་སརྤ་ཎི་ཡབ་ཡུམ་གྱི་སྒྲུབ་ཐབས་

Translated by Nubs the Lotsa-wa.
Salutation : To P'ags-pa Chenresi.

(33) fo. 200. *a.* གནོད་སྦྱིན་སྤུན་གཉིས་ཀྱི་སྒྲུབ་ཐབས་ "Coercion of the two Nö'jin brothers."

Salutation : To Pal Dorje Dzin.
Opens : —

གང་གིས་བཀའ་སྟོད་འཇིགས་པའི་གཟུགས་
གཞོན་ནུ་ཁྲིས་པ་ཇམ་པའི་ཚུལ་
གདོད་སྤྲིན་རྒྱལ་པོ་ནོར་སྤྲིན་དང་
གྲགས་ཆེན་འཇིགས་པ་མཁས་པས་བསྒྲུབས་
དུར་ཁྲོད་ལ་སོགས་ཡང་བར་བར་
འཇིག་རྟེན་མཆན་པོའི་ལྷས་མཐོང་བས་
དེ་ཉིད་རིག་པ་དྲན་བྱས་ལ་
ཚར་གཅོད་རྗེས་སུ་འཛིན་པ་ཡིས་
བྱང་ཆུབ་སེམས་གཉིས་ཡང་དག་བསྒོམ་

(34) fo. 201. *a.* རིགས་ཀྱི་འཇིག་རྟེན་མགོན་པོའི་སྒྲུབ་ཐབས་ཀྱི་སྣང་བ་རྗེ་བཙུན་མ་ཧི་མས་མཛད་པ་ "The enlightenment made by the Reverend Mahima for the coercion of Rigs-kyi Jig-ten Gompo."

(35) fo. 204. *a.* ལྔ་བཅུ་པའི་བཤད་པ་ "The Explanation of Fifty Acts."

Or, more fully : རིགས་ཀྱི་འཇིག་རྟེན་མགོན་པོའི་ལྔ་བཅུ་པ་ལས་ལྔའི་དེ་ཁོན་ཉིད་རིམ་པར་ཕྱེ་བ་

A lengthy treatise in Three Sections : translated by Yarlungs-pa Shud-kye Grags-pa Mts'an, as uttered by the great man Lha-je Megaling in the monastery of Pal Sá-kyá.

(36) fo. 220. *b.* ཀུ་ལ་ལོ་ཀ་ནྣ་ཐའི་བྱིན་རླབས་དང་རྗེས་གནང་བྱ་བའི་རིམ་པ་ཁ་ཆེའི་པཎྜིཏ་བི་མ་ལ་ཤྲཱིའི་ཞལ་སྔ་ནས་མཛད་པ་

(37) fo. 221. *b.* ཀུ་ལ་ལོ་ཀ་ནཱ་ཐཱ་ཡ། འཕགས་པ་སྤྱན་རས་གཟིགས་རིགས་ཀྱི་འཇིག་རྟེན་མགོན་པོའི་རྗེས་གནང་གི་ཚོ་ག "Kula-loka-nát'aya ;

Ritual for committal into the charge of P'ags-pa Chenresi, Protector of the World of Races" (*i.e.*, "the inhabited world.")

Translated by the Lotsa-wa Lobten (བློ་བརྟན་)

(38) fo. 222. *b.* རིགས་ཀྱི་འཇིག་རྟེན་དབང་ཕྱུག་སྒྲུབ་ཐབས་

(39) fo. 224. *a.* འཕགས་པ་སྤྱན་རས་གཟིགས་དབང་ཕྱུག་ཡི་གེ་བདུན་པའི་སྒྲུབ་ཐབས་ Method of Coercion by means of the seven initial letters of Phaps-pa Sypan-ras-gzigs-dwang-phyug.

Subscription :—

གནུབས་ལོ་ཙཱ་བ་བྱམས་པའི་དཔལ་གྱིས་བསྒྱུར་བའོ་

(40) fo. 226. *a.* ཚེ་དང་ཡེ་ཤེས་དཔག་ཏུ་མེད་པའི་སྒྲུབ་ཐབས་

(Sansk : Aparimitàyur Dzñana Sàdha Nam) Method of Coercion which is immeasurably wise and is everlasting.

(41) fo. 229. *b.* བཅོམ་ལྡན་འདས་མགོན་པོ་ཚེ་དང་ཡེ་ཤེས་དཔག་ཏུ་མེད་པའི་དཀྱིལ་འཁོར་གྱི་ཆོ་ག་

"Ritual for the Mandal of Bhagavan Gon-po whose life and wisdom are immeasurable."

Subscription: Ye-shes-kyi Mká-agro-ma grub-pai rgyalmos mdzad-pa—"composed by the queen of such as have become contemplative fairies."

(42) fo. 239. *b.* ཚེ་དཔག་མེད་ཀྱི་སྒྲུབ་ཐབས་ "Coercion of Ts'epag-me."

Subscription: བོད་ཀྱི་ལོ་ཙཱ་བ་གླན་དར་མ་ཚུལ་ཁྲིམས་ཀྱིས་བསྒྱུར་བའོ་

(43) fo. 242. *b.* ཚེ་དང་ཡེ་ཤེས་དཔག་ཏུ་མེད་པའི་དཀྱིལ་འཁོར་གྱི་ཆོ་ག་

Salutation: To Chomdende Ts'e-pag-me.'!

Same translation as preceding treatise.

(44) fo. 249. *b.* ཚེ་དཔག་ཏུ་མེད་པའི་སྦྱིན་སྲེག་གི་ཆོ་ག་ "Burnt-offerings to T'se-pag-me'."

(45) fo. 251. *a.* རྟ་མགྲིན་གྱི་སྒྲུབ་ཐབས་ (Sansk: Haya-griwa Sádhana)

"The mode of Coercing Tamḍin."

Salutation: To Padma Sung-gi Lha (Lotus God of Speech)! The whole treatise is given below :—

ཡིད་འོད་གནས་སུ་ཉེར་འདུག་ནས་
བདེ་བའི་སྟན་ལ་གནས་པ་དང་
བྱང་ཆུབ་མཆོག་ཏུ་སེམས་བསྐྱེད་ནས་
ཀླ་ཁམ་སྨུག་ནག་དཀྱིལ་འཁོར་དུ་
པཾ་ལས་ཚུ་སྐྱེས་འདབ་མ་བརྒྱད་
མཾ་ལས་ཉི་མའི་གདན་སྟེངས་སུ་
ཧྲཱིཿདམར་རྒྱུའི་ས་བོན་ལས་
ཡེ་ཤེས་བསྐལ་བའི་མེ་ལྟར་འབར་
གདུག་པ་ཅན་རྣམས་མ་ལུས་བསྲེག་
མེ་དཔུང་འབར་བའི་དཀྱིལ་འཁོར་དུ་
ཧྲཱིཿལས་བསྐྱེད་པའི་རྟ་མཆོག་ནི་
ཞལ་གཅིག་ཕྱག་གཉིས་སྐུ་མདོག་དམར་
སྟེང་ཞལ་རྟ་མཆོག་ལྗང་ཁུ་ནི་
དྲག་པོ་རྟ་སྐད་རབ་ཏུ་བཞད་
ཁམས་གསུམ་མ་ལུས་དབང་དུ་སྡོད་
ཕྱག་གཡས་ཐོད་དབྱུག་དཀར་པོ་བསྣམས་
བགེགས་དང་འབྱུང་པོ་མ་ལུས་འཇོམས་
གཡོན་པ་སྡིགས་མཛུབ་མེ་ལྟར་འབར་
གནོད་བྱེད་མ་ལུས་སྲེག་པར་བྱེད་
གཡས་སྐུམ་གཡོན་བརྐྱང་བདུད་བཞི་མནན་

སྤྱན་གསུམ་སྨྱང་མིག་ཁྲོ་གཉེར་བསྡུས་

ལྡུགས་འདྲིལ་ཆེ་བ་མེ་སྟག་འཕྲོ་

སྐྲ་སེར་དབུ་རྒྱན་ཐོད་སྐམ་ཅན་

ཁྲག་འཛག་བརྒྱ་ཕྲེང་དོ་ཤལ་བྱས་

སྟག་གི་པགས་པའི་ཤམ་ཐབས་ཅན་

ཀླུ་ཆེན་བརྒྱད་ཀྱིས་ཉེ་བར་བརྒྱན་

འཇིགས་བྱེད་གཤིན་རྗེའི་གཟུགས་འཆང་བ་

གང་གིས་མི་ཚུགས་རྡོ་རྗེའི་སྐུ་

ཐུགས་ཁར་ཉི་མའི་དཀྱིལ་འཁོར་དུ་

ཧཱུྃཿཡིག་སྔགས་ཀྱིས་བསྐོར་བ་ལས་

འོད་འཕྲོས་ཡེ་ཤེས་དགུག་གཞུག་བྱ་

སངས་རྒྱས་རྣམས་ཀྱིས་དབང་བསྐུར་རོ་

དེ་ནས་སྔགས་ཀྱིས་བཟླས་པ་ནི

ཨོཾ་བཛྲ་ཀྲོ་དྷ་ཧ་ཡ་གྲཱི་བ་ཧུ་ལུ་ཧུ་ལུ་ཧཱུྃ་ཕཊ་

འབུམ་དུ་བཟླས་ནས་ལས་རྣམས་འགྲུབ་

དེ་ནས་གཏོར་མ་དབུལ་བ་ནི་

ཡཾ་དང་རླུང་དང་རཾ་ལས་མེ་

ཨ་ལས་ཐོད་པཡ་ངས་པ་ཏུ་

ཤ་ལྔ་བདུད་རྩི་ལྔ་ཡིས་གང་

ཡེ་ཤེས་བདུད་རྩི་གཉིས་སུ་མེད་

ཨོཾ་ཨཱཿཧཱུྃ།

ཨི་དཾ་བ་ལི་ཨམྲི་ཏ་ཁ་ཁ་

ཁཱ་ཧི་ཁཱ་ཧི་ཙ་སྤོས་བདགས་ལ་ལན་གསུམ་གྱིས་

ཕྱུལ་ནས་བསྟོད་དང་གསོལ་བ་གདབ་

ཧཱིཿལས་བསྐྱེད་པའི་རྟ་མཆོག་སྐུ་

ཉི་མའི་འོད་མཆུངས་ཉོན་མོངས་བསྲེག་

བདུད་བཞི་མ་ལུས་འཇོམས་མཛད་པའི་

དཔའ་བོ་རྟ་མགྲིན་ཕྱག་འཚལ་ལོ་

སློབ་མའི་བར་ཆད་བསྲུང་བའི་ཕྱིར་

གཏོར་མ་བྱིན་གྱིས་བརླབ་པ་ནི་

ཨོཾ་ཨཱཿཧཱུྃ།

སྐུ་གསུང་ཐུགས་རྣམས་བསྒྲིམ་པའོ་

ལྷ་དང་སྔགས་ཀྱི་རྫས་གནང་བ་

སློབ་མས་ཕྱག་འཚལ་ཡོན་འབུལ་ལོ།

དཔའ་བོ་རྟ་མགྲིན་སྒྲུབ་པའི་ཐབས་

འོད་དཔག་མེད་ཀྱིས་ལུང་བསྟན་པའི་

མཁའ་འགྲོ་གྲུབ་པའི་རྒྱལ་མོས་བརྩམས།། དགེ་བས་རྟ་མཆོག་སྐུ་ཐོབ་ཤོག།།

པཎྜ་ཟླ་བ་བཟང་པོ་དང་བློན་ཚུང་དར་མ་ཚུལ་ཁྲིམས་ཀྱིས་བསྒྱུར་ཅིང་ཞུས་ངག་གོ། ।། ༄༅།

(46) fo. 251. *b.* འཕགས་པ་ལག་ན་རྡོ་རྗེ་གོས་སྔོན་པོ་ཅན་དྲག་པོ་གསུམ་འདུལ་བ་

Salutation: To Chomdendas Jampai Dorje!

(47) fo. 264. *a.* གནོད་སྦྱིན་གྱི་སྡེ་དཔོན་ཆེན་པོ་ལག་ན་རྡོ་རྗེ་གོས་སྔོན་པོ་

ཅན་གྱི་སྒྲུབ་པའི་ཐབས་འཁོར་ལོ་ཆེན་པོ་ "The Great Wheel Method for the Coercion of the Green-Robed Lag-na Dorje, the Mighty Ruler of the Nö'jin."

Salutation: To Pal Chhak-na Dorje!

Concludes:—"The Great Wheel Method for Coercion made by the Great Teacher Dza-wa Ri-pa is ended."

(48) fo. 267. *a.* གནོད་སྦྱིན་གྱི་སྡེ་དཔོན་ཆེན་པོ་ལག་ན་རྡོ་རྗེ་གོས་སྔོན་པོ་ཅན་གྱི་གཟུངས་ཀྱི་སྒྲུབ་ཐབས་བདུད་རྩི་ཐིགས་པ་ "The Drops of Nectar Method of Coercion of the Strength of the Green-Robed Lag-na Dorje, the Mighty Chief of the Nö'jin."

(49) fo. 269. *a.* ལག་ན་རྡོ་རྗེ་གོས་སྔོན་པོ་ཅན་གྱི་སྒྲུབ་པའི་ཐབས་མདོར་བསྡུས་པ་ "Abridgement of Method of Coercion of the Green-Robed Lag-na Dorje."

(50) fo. 270. *a.* ཀླུ་རིགས་བཞིའི་སྒྲུབ་ཐབས་ "The Mode of Coercion of the Four kinds of Lu (Nágas)."

Salutation: To Pal Chhak-na Dorje!

Concludes:—"The Mode for Coercion of Lu made by the Teacher Dza-wa Ri-pa is finished."

(51) fo. 272. *b.* གནོད་སྦྱིན་གྱི་སྡེ་རྣམས་སྦྱོང་ཞིང་སེལ་བ་ཞེས་བྱ་བའི་སྒྲུབ་ཐབས་ "The Method of Coercion which is styled the Purging and Cleansing of the chiefs of the Nö'jin."

(52) fo. 274. *a.* ཡི་དགས་དང་ཤ་ཟ་དང་གྲུལ་བུམ་དང་སྲུལ་པོ་རྣམས་རྣམ་པར་སྦྱོང་ཞིང་སེལ་བའི་སྒྲུབ་ཐབས་ "The Mode of Coercion which completely purges and cleanses away Yidags and Shá-zá and Ḍul-bum and Shrulpo."

(Sansk: Kushmanḍodsádha Preta Pisháṭsa Yewishodha Yahara Sádha Nám.)

The whole treatise is here transcribed:—

སྐུ་གསུམ་ཕ་རོལ་ཕྱུག་དྲུག་ལྡན
སྡུག་བསྔལ་རྒྱ་མཚོ་ལས་སྒྲོལ་བའི་

རྡོ་རྗེ་ཅན་ལ་གུས་བཏུད་དེ་
སེམས་ཅན་རྣམས་ལ་ཕན་ཕྱིར་བྲི་
སྔོན་དུ་བསྙེན་པ་རབ་རྫོགས་པས་
ཡན་ལག་ཚོན་སྣམ་རབ་བཅིངས་ནས་
ལྷ་ཡི་རྣམ་པ་གསལ་བསྒོམས་དེ་
རྟགས་ནི་རབ་དུ་གསལ་བ་བརྟགས་
བརྟགས་ཟིན་ནས་ནི་སྒྲུབ་པ་བརྩམ་
ས་ཡི་ཆོ་ག་རྫོགས་བྱས་ལ་
སྟ་གོན་ལེགས་པར་རྫོགས་ནས་ནི་
དཀྱིལ་འཁོར་ཐིག་སྐུར་བྱིན་བརླབ་གདབ
ཡེ་ཤེས་ཐིག་གདབ་ས་ཐིག་ནི་
ཚངས་ཐིག་ནས་བཟུང་སྒོ་རྒྱན་བར་
ལེགས་ཤིང་རྫོགས་པར་གདབ་པར་བྱ་
དེ་ནས་ཚོན་དགེ་དབུས་ཀྱི་དཀྱིལ་
པདྨ་འདབ་བརྒྱད་གེ་སར་བཅས་
ཁ་དོག་སོ་སོ་གྲུ་ཚད་ལྡང་
རྡོ་རྗེ་ར་བ་ལྷ་སྣམ་རིགས་
མཚན་མ་ས་བོན་རབ་དུ་དགོད་
ཤར་ནས་བརྩམས་དེ་འཁོར་ལོ་རལ་གྲི་དང་
དགྲ་སྟ་རྡོ་རྗེ་ཁ་དོག་སོ་སོར་བྲི་
ཤར་སྒོ་ནས་བཟུང་ལྕགས་ཀྱུ་གྲི་གུག་དང་
མི་མགོ་དང་ནི་རྒྱུ་མའི་ཞགས་པ་བྲི་

མཚམས་སུ་གཏོར་མ་ཕྱོགས་སུ་མཆོད་

པ་དབུས་སུ་སྐུ་གདུང་བཅས་

གུར་དང་བླ་རེ་ལྷ་སྣམ་ཕྱོགས་སྐྱོང་གཏོར་མ་སོ་སོར་དགྲམ་

བུམ་པ་ཕྱོགས་བཞིར་ལས་ཀྱི་བུམ་པ་ཤར་སྒོར་བཞག་

མདུན་དུ་བླ་མ་ཡི་དམ་སྤྱན་དྲངས་མཆོད་ནས་སྟོང་ཉིད་བསྒོམ་

དེ་ནས་ཧཱུྃ་ལས་ས་གཞིར་བ་གུར་དུ་གྱུར་པའི་རྡོ་རྗེ་མ་འོད་བཅས་

དེ་ལས་ཧྲཱུྃ་ལས་གྲུ་བཞི་སྒོ་བཞི་རྟ་བབས་བཅས་ཤིང་དབང་པོ་ཉི་ཟླའི་གདན་

དེ་སྟེང་བདག་ཉིད་གསུམ་གྱིས་ཞལ་གསུམ་ཕྱག་དྲུག་བསྐྱེད་

ཐལ་དཀར་མདོག་དང་གནག་དང་སྔོ་དང་ཤིན་ཏུ་གནག་

གཡས་ན་འཁོར་ལོ་རལ་གྲི་དགྲ་སྟ་རྡོ་རྗེ་དང་

གཡོན་ན་སྡིགས་པའི་སྡིགས་མཛུབ་པོ་

ཤིན་ཏུ་འཇིགས་པའི་བདག་ཉིད་ཅན་

བལ་པོའི་བླ་མ་དེ་བ་པུཎྜ་མ་ཏི་དང་།

ལོ་ཙཱ་བ་ཆོས་ཀྱི་བཟང་པོས་བསྒྱུར་བའོ། ॥ ॥

(53) fo. 275. *a.* དཔལ་ཕྱག་ན་རྡོ་རྗེ་གོས་སྔོན་པོ་ཅན་གྱི་གཟུངས་ཀྱི་གཏོར་མའི་ཆོ་ག "Torma Ceremonial for the Support of the Green-Robed Pal Chhak-na Dorje."

(54) fo. 276. *a.* རིམ་པ་དྲུག་པ "The Six Grades."

(55) fo. 278. *b.* གསད་པ་བདུད་རྩི་གསོ "The Nectar which nourishes those who have been killed."

(56) fo. 280. *a.* བདུད་རྩི་འོ་མའི་མཆོད་པ "The Offering of Milk-Nectar."

Salutation: To Dorje Snams!

(57) fo. 280. *b.* ཀླུ་ཁྲོ་བོས་གསད་པའི་ཕྲིན་ལས། "The Deeds which are destroyed by Fierce Lu," or "by Lu in an angry condition."

(58) fo. 282. *a.* ཀླུ་རིགས་བཞི་མནན་པའི་ཆོ་ག "Ceremonial for keeping under the Four Species of Lu."

(59) fo. 282. *b.* ཕྱག་ན་རྡོ་རྗེ་གོས་སྔོན་པོ་ཅན་གྱི་སྦྱིན་སྲེག་གི་ཆོ་ག "Burnt-offering Ceremonial to the Green-Robed Chhak-na Dorje."

(60) fo. 283 *b.* Treatise with name precisely same as the preceding one.

(61) fo. 285. *a.* གནོད་སྦྱིན་གྱི་སྡེ་དཔོན་ཆེན་པོ་ལག་ན་རྡོ་རྗེ་གོས་སྔོན་པོ་ཅན་གྱི་དཀྱིལ་འཁོར་གྱི་ཆོ་ག "Ceremonial for the adjustment and arrangement of the Green-Robed Lag-na Dorje, the Great Chief of the Nö'jin."

(62) fo. 296. *a.* མཛེ་ནང་ཀྱི་མཚན་ཉིད "The Characteristics of Cancer (Inner Leprosy)."

(63) fo. 298. *a.* གནོད་སྦྱིན་གྱི་སྡེ་དཔོན་ཆེན་པོ་ལག་ན་རྡོ་རྗེ་གོས་སྔོན་པོ་ཅན་འཁོར་ལོ་ཆེན་པོའི་ལྷ་ཚོགས་ལ་བསྟོད་པ "The offering of Praise to the pantheon of the Great Wheel of the Green-Robed Lag-na Dorje, Great Ruler of the Nö'jin."

(64) fo. 299. *b.* རྟེན་ཅིང་འབྲེལ་པར་འབྱུང་བའི་བསྲུང་བ "The amulet which produces the connection between Cause and Effect."

(65) fo. 300. *b.* ཕྱག་ན་རྡོ་རྗེ་གོས་སྔོན་པོ་ཅན་གནོད་སྦྱིན་དྲག་པོ་ཆེན་པོ་རྡོ་རྗེ་གནོད་སྦྱིན་མེ་ལྕེའི་རྒྱུད་ཀྱི་འགྲེལ་པ

The foregoing is a lengthy work in 12 chapters or ལེའུ་

(66) fo. 344. *a.* འཕགས་པ་ཕྱག་ན་རྡོ་རྗེ་གོས་སྔོན་ཅན་གྱི་སྒྲུབ་ཐབས "Coercion of the Green-Robed Chhak-na Dorje."

(67) fo. 349. *b.* གནོད་སྦྱིན་གྱི་སྡེ་དཔོན་ཆེན་པོ་ལག་ན་རྡོ་རྗེ་གོས་སྔོན་པོ་ཅན་གྱི་སྒྲུབ་ཐབས "Coercion of the Green-Robed Lag-na Dorje, Great Ruler of the Nö'jin."

(68) fo. 358. *a*: Treatise with same title as foregoing one. Salutation: To the Three Most Precious Ones (དཀོན་མཆོག་གསུམ་)

(69) fo. 360. *a*. གནོད་སྦྱིན་གྱི་སྡེ་དཔོན་ཆེན་པོ་ལག་ན་རྡོ་རྗེ་གོས་སྔོན་པོ་ཅན་གྱི་དཀྱིལ་འཁོར་གྱི་ཆོ་ག་ "Ceremonial for the arrangement of the Green-Robed Lag-na Dorje, Great Ruler of the Noijin."

(70) fo. 367. *a*. ལུང་བསྟན་སྒྱུར་བའི་མན་ངག་སློབ་དཔོན་ཆེན་པོ་ཀླུ་བས་མཛད་པ་

(71) fo. 370. *b*. རྡོ་རྗེ་ལས་ཀྱི་ཚོགས་རིམ་པར་ཕྱེ་བའི་ཆོ་ག་ "Ceremonial for arranging in rows collections of Precious Works."

This treatise concludes the volume which comprises 386 folios in all.

CHAPTER XIII.

THE POET MILARASPA.

Everywhere throughout Tibet and Mongolia are the writings ascribed to this poet and mystic read and quoted. Composed in language differing considerably from the stilted artificial style of the Kangyur treatises and much akin both in vocabulary and in construction to the vernacular of the present day, the works of Milaraspa can be listened to by the people with comprehension. Thus they are perused not merely as a formal religious deed of merit—as is the case with the older standard books—but because of the real interest of the matter they contain. In Mongolia they are met with translated into the Mongol-Tartar tongue as well as in the Tibetan originals, which fact is a certain indication of a popularity not only conventional.

The Reverend Milaraspa (རྗེ་བཙུན་མི་ལ་རས་པ་) is said to have been born 1038 A.D. in Gung-t'ang on the borders of Nepal, a little to the east of the modern Kirong and only a few miles to the west of the peaks abutting Mount Everest. His father was one Mila Shesrab Gyal-ts'an and his mother bore the name of Myang-ts'a Kar-gyan. At an early age both parents died and he was brought up by an aunt and uncle who treated him with great harshness. Quitting their protection, eventually, he attached himself to religious studies and became the pupil of a famous *lo-tsa-wa,* or translator of Sanskrit works, named Marpa. Having taken the fullest vows, he began to qualify himself by systematic ascetic meditation to attain the position of a Nal-jor (རྣལ་འབྱོར་) the Tibetan form of *Yogi.* When his spiritual father, Marpa, had quitted this sphere, Milaraspa forthwith took to a calling which he adopted as his especial function, that of a peripatetic missionary. In that character he traversed all the mountain ranges along the Tibeto-Nepal frontier, visiting Purang, Dengri, Kirong, Lake Manasarowar, etc. His plan of operations varied. Sometimes he abode near villages expounding, both in prose and verse, Buddhist doctrine to many hearers. At other times he withdrew to caves in inaccessible spots and remained in persistent mental absorption for months and even years. The result of such a line of life was natural in a country where learning and lonely mystic contemplation are held in the highest repute. He obtained a large following who were known by the designation of *Ras-chhung-wa* or "the little cotton clad ones." These disciples appear to have usually wandered about with their master, and to have shared in a much less measure in his austerities; but, according to the narrative, they were also often absent from him.

As his name indicates, one of the principles of Milaraspa was to be clothed merely in cotton, eschewing the customary wearing material of Tibetans which is invariably of wool. In that respect his votaries were expected to imitate him. In spite of the icy temperature of his haunts, the ascetic went about clad only in one thin vestment. He thus describes himself in one of his exordia:

I am Milaraspa great in fame,
The direct offspring of Memory and Wisdom.
Yet an old man am I, forlorn and naked;
From my lips springs forth a little song,
For all nature at which I look
Serves me for a book.
The iron staff that my hands hold
Guides me o'er the ocean of changing life.
Master am I of Mind and Light,
And in showing feats and miracles,
Depend not on earthly deities.

The particular Buddhist sect to which Milaraspa belonged was a hybrid one, formed of the Ká-dampa school, and the Ká-gyüd-pa school, which had been started in rivalry to each other. A powerful deity, Lag-na Dorje, prince of the Noi-jin or gods of the mountains, was held to preside over the sect, and was, in fact, the tutelary deity of Milaraspa. The leading theories set forth in the sage's songs are those of the universal illusiveness of all thoughts and possible conceptions as well as of all material things, and the advantages of various mechanical methods of meditation principally induced by suppressing one's breath, and so forcing it to enter certain specified bloodvessels of the body. To these processes we shall refer more particularly later on; but it was, he averred, by the artificial warmth, which the *Tum-mo* or meditative ecstasy induced, that he was enabled to withstand the extremest cold.

We are about to examine at considerable length the productions which are assigned to Milaraspa. But we should first mention that these are only two in number, although certain reference is made to a third work which, however, if ever current, is not in circulation at the present day.

The chief work is that which is known familiarly as the GURBUM or "One Hundred Thousand Songs." It embraces a sort of fitful narrative of a portion of the worthy man's wanderings which in places are described with considerable topographical detail. This account is plentifully interspersed with his ditties and metrical expositions of doctrine. The "songs," nevertheless, number only some 200 instead of 100,000 as stated in the metaphorical title—the full designation being རྗེ་བཙུན་མི་ལ་རས་པའི་རྣམ་ཐར་རྒྱས་པར་ཕྱེ་བ་མགུར་འབུམ་[1] In the course of the narrative Milaraspa instructs his votaries, preaches to those whom he chances upon, works spells and miracles and falls in with divers adventures. His practice, when asked a question or when relating past experiences, was to drop at once into verse. Thus the Gurbum takes the form of a record of travel in which metrical digressions—which by the way have no particular metre whatever—are perpetually recurring. It should be noted, however, that the whole recital is not supposed to be told by the hero himself but by some third person unnamed who relates the doings and sayings of Milaraspa.

The other book is less in bulk than the Gurbum and differs from it in form, in that it runs in the first person; Milaraspa himself being personally the narrator throughout. Accordingly, we have this work generally distinguished as the NAM-T'AR, although that designation occurs in the title of the first mentioned work also. Nam-t'ar, which means literally "the full deliverance," is the usual term in the Buddhist sense for biography or even autobiography and in the present case carries the latter signification. The complete title of the book

[1] The title of this Gurbum seems to vary in different copies. We have two specimens of that work in our possession. One bears the title as given above and is a block-print of 264 leaves printed on both sides. The other copy has the imprint on the outer leaf as follows: རྣལ་འབྱོར་གྱི་དབང་ཕྱུག་ཆེན་པོ་རྗེ་བཙུན་གཞད་པ་རྡོ་རྗེའི་རྣམ་ཐར་རྒྱས་པར་ཕྱེ་བ་མགུར་འབུམ་ It will be observed, then, that in this edition the name *Milaraspa* is omitted from the title, the appellation *Gzhad-pa Dorje* (*i.e.*, "the Laughing Dorje") being substituted. This last is a fine issue, very clearly printed and comprising 324 leaves. The St. Petersburg example has, we see, 342 leaves; and is therefore another edition still. Our copy of the Nam-t'ar or ཀ volume is a well-printed specimen consisting of 144 folios, double-sided.

stands as རྣལ་འབྱོར་གྱི་དབང་ཕྱུག་དམ་པ་ཆེན་པོ་རྗེ་བཙུན་མི་ལ་རས་པའི་རྣམ་ཐར་ཐར་པ་དང་ཐམས་ཅད་མཁྱེན་པའི་ལམ་སྟོན་ "The All-famous Stages in the Course of Life of the Great Holy Rich Power of Meditation, the Reverend Milaraspa."

Both compilations are frequently found between the same pair of boards as if they were two volumes of one and the same work. In this arrangement the Nam-t'ar always comes first, being labelled as ཀ་ first letter of the alphabet, and the Gurbum follows as ཁ་

The vocabulary and linguistic forms of these narratives make it a moot question as to whether or not Milaraspa, who lived 800 years ago, actually himself composed them or not. Much of the phraseology agrees with the current speech. Whoever may have been the author, there can be no question that he possessed the faculties of a true poet. Assuming that he may have been Milaraspa himself, we can plainly assert that the quaint old sage had not only an eye for the beauties of nature but also words at his command wherewith to record the feelings with which such beauties inspired him—all nature, as he avers, was to him "a book." Therein he carries the poet's credentials.

Tibet is a land abounding in the more fantastic phases of geology —everything there on a stupendous scale; and weird, forbidding, mysterious. And the influence which mountains, great snows, darksome glaciers and unfathomable gorges, exercised over the writer of Milaraspa's memoirs is evidenced in almost every page. So, it is this sense of the romance of God's handiwork in its wildest developments which justifies the claim we have placed on a previous page—that the Tibetans are a people by no means devoid of poetical tastes.

Milaraspa is full of interest and novelty not only for the frequent depth of feeling displayed, but also as setting forth the recondite philosophy and mysticism of the northern cult of Buddhism. That fact causes his writings to be of some importance to the student. It is our purpose in the ensuing pages to confine ourselves to one work, the Gurbum; but we shall introduce lengthy quotations from our author supplementing the extracts by such commentary as shall best serve the purposes of elucidation. The amount of particular information into which we shall thus be led derives its chief interest in that it concerns the more advanced school of Buddhistic thought.

Plunging forthwith *in medias res*, our first translation may appropriately be taken from the opening pages of the Gurbum to which our remarks are to be confined. The narrative begins in this way :—

Hail Teacher! That rich power of Meditation, the Reverend Milaraspa himself, under the influence of the Great Translucent Charm, was sojourning in the district of Chhong-lung-jung. It happened one night he rose up to prepare his food; but there was not even a piece of wood in the out-house—not to mention, no flour, salt, water, or herbs. There being neither water nor fire on the hearth, he reflected: 'It is indeed too much for me to have suffered my thoughts to slip to a degree so great as this; and it will now be necessary to go and find room for some faggots in my coat-skirt.' So departing; when he had lighted on as much wood as he could manage, a high wind sprung up. While he carried the wood, the wind seized on his garments, and whensoever he clutched hold of his garments, it seized on the wood. Then the thought arose in his mind:

'Though I have been sitting in times past so lengthy a space on that ridge of hills, yet was I mentally absorbed in attachment to self. I may have indeed succeeded with the doctrine of mental absorption within my very self, but what do I now propose to do? Then let me say—If the garment be pleasing to me, let the garment be taken away; or, if the wood be pleasing, let the wood be taken.' Having seated himself, he lost consciousness from the effects of poor living and the cold. When he roused himself the wind had lulled and his garment was fluttering from the top of a tree-stem. In the depth of the mental weariness which succeeded, he placed himself flat against the perpendicular surface of a boulder of the size of the body of a sheep. Just then there floated up from out a reddish-grey valley on the eastern side a white cloud. Below the white cloud in the reddish-grey valley was a gompa (*i.e.*, monastery). He revolved: There did my lama, the interpreter Marpa, sit translating. In the midst of the group of my father, mother, and fellow-disciples—the brethren of the Dorje—was he." And recalling the substance and style of his precepts, together with his powerful expositions of the Tantras, he thought: "If only he were seated there now, whatever might intervene, I would go to salute him." Being carried beyond bounds with despondency at these vivid memories of his teacher, many tears were shed, and he uttered this ode—a song of yearning grief—in his keen remembrance of the lama:—

Recalling my father, and following the steps of Marpa—
He who was the remover of longings—
Yearning dirges should vanish away.
O Marpa the Master, on the red rock to the east of the valley of Chhong!
Ah, that rock beneath yon holder of water,
The white cloud soaring upwards,
The floating white cloud!
On a rock backed by a hill beside which huge elephants are despicable;
On one which is faced by a hill beside which great lions seem but pigmies.
In the Gompa of the red-grey valley, a mighty residence,
On a stone prodigious, the throne of Amolika—
A divan covered with the skins of lions' ears,
On which to be seated is not to sit—
It was there sate Marpa the translator;
Oh, if now he were sitting, how would I rejoice!
Of small consequence though I be,

Yet from my heart should I wish to do homage
Though undue yearnings should be little.
I remember this lama possessed of mental and bodily graces,
I remember Marpa the lo-tsá-wa and his meditations,
Flames more holy than a mother's couch.
Oh, if now he were sitting, how would I rejoice!
Though far distant and inaccessible were his seat
I should wish to do homage.
Comely and thoughful is the lama I recollect;
Marpa the lo-tsá-wa I recall as he meditates,
His *dorje* revelling in the profoundest of Tantras.
Oh, if now he were speaking, how would I rejoice!
Though poor be my powers of mind,
From my heart should I crave to rehearse what he said;
Remembering the lama, his mental and bodily graces,
Recollecting Marpa the lo-tsá-wa as he sits meditating
Tantras, mighty in gesture and sound.

It would seem that his spiritual instructor, this Marpa, over whom our poet thus utters lamentation, had once enjoined his pupil to proceed to the summit of a lofty mountain which may be certainly identified as Mount Everest, for the purpose of ascetic meditation. Thus, the earlier peregrinations of Milaraspa are in the region of this the highest peak of the Himalayas and of the world, which is known to modern Tibetans by the name of Lap-chhyi-gang, and which is mentioned by Milaraspa under that appellation. We find in the Gurbum some curious information concerning the famous mountain; and, as no European has ever penetrated within 50 miles of Mount Everest, such information is worth noticing. It is described as a lofty pinnacle of snow and ice on a desolate and uninhabited chain of mountains, and on the top of it reside five fairies named Ts'e-ringts'e (or "life, long life") who became deeply attached to the poet. The glaciers of Lap-chhyi-gang produce five lakes, situated on the northern flanks, the waters of each differing in colour one from the other; and these lakes were dedicated by Milaraspa, one to each of the five fairies aforesaid. Further north of the Everest range mention is made of a vast lake named Kyema Ts'o, and of a mighty snow-capped peak styled Jomo Gang-karmo.

In his ascent of the hills which buttress the main summits of this range, Milaraspa has several adventures. One of these may be here introduced:

Then roving upward to fulfil the command of his lama, he reached the outworks of Lap-chhyi-gang. On the approach to Lap-chhyi, when he came to Nyánam, he found the people of the neighbourhood celebrating a great beer-drinking revel. Now in the beer-house gossip, there was babbling of this sort: 'Well! as to him who is called Milaraspa, he seems to be leading a penitential life. Is it possible that he is that devout hermit who has located himself on this very range of hills, where no man dwells?'

As they were talking thus praisingly of the Reverend one, he presented himself at their doorway. Whereupon a young woman, adorned round the face with goodly ornaments, came forth making numerous exclamations of welcome.

'O Naljor!' she cried, 'whence are you?'

Said his Reverence: 'He who is now speaking to you is one Milaraspa, a great meditator, who has been abiding on a mountain the whereabouts of which I am not sure of. You, hostess, must bestow as alms some fragments of victuals.'

She returned: 'Sufficient to feed on shall be brought forth. But are you indeed that very one who is called Milaraspa?'

Quoth he: 'It would be without sense to tell a lie about it.'

The woman ran in brimming over with joy, and said to the revellers: 'A delightful monk is here who says he has just now come from a distance, and he has cast himself down this moment at this very door.' All rushed forth, some welcoming him, others inquiring his history; and when they were certain it was his Reverence, they invited him indoors, and offered him distinguished attention. Then the young woman, a rich householder and a Bön priestess, who was at the head of the revellers, said: There has taken up his abode in the hollow of our valley a goblin, and you must therefore by blessing purge the ground. We will then afford you all the service in our power.' The other folk added: 'Splendid indeed! For our pastures are most pleasant lands, but we are so dreadfully afraid of bodily injuries from this goblin that we no longer wish to occupy the same. Pray come quickly now.' All assembled beseeching him, his Reverence retorted: 'I am indeed going quickly, but it is not on account of your pasture-lands that I go. Because of the command I have from my lama I am going, to meditate.' They replied: 'That is quite sufficient for us. We will grant you servants, together with good food.' The Reverend One rejoined: 'Being a man who relies upon himself, there is no need to me of companions and good provisions. I am going quite alone to the uppermost regions. We will see afterwards about these marvellous services you are going to render.'

So saying, his Reverence set out by himself for Lap-chhyi-gang. Arrived at the pass-top, terrific apparitions of those who were not human appeared. As soon as he reached the cairn on the pass the sky was convulsed, the thunder rolled savagely, and the lightning darted gleamingly, whilst the mountains in the valleys far and near seemed to shift! The mountain-torrents, whirling together, grew into a huge lake whose billows boiled violently. His Reverence cast a mystic look, and plunging his staff into the waters, the lake, though deep, disappeared, and was resolved into mist and pools. Then, coming up for an instant from below, supernatural monsters puffed forth their breath and broke down crags far and near. Numerous boulders sprang out, clashing and fighting one another in a turmoil of billows. Thereupon the sky-walking witches opened a path in between the valleys like a mountain-serpent running downwards; and, standing on the path when the rolling of rocks was abated, he shouted at the hill. Thereat the demons of the feebler kind became quiet; whilst the larger species, though they could not find any opportunity, sought for another chance just where the hill-path of the witches terminated. Accordingly, the Reverend One cast a magic glance which drove them back subdued. All being quietened by enchantment, a footprint arose on the stone in the place where he had sat; and after a little while both earth and sky resumed their joyous aspect. Then, seated on the hill-spur, he meditated lovingly on living creatures, and with such profit that he named the place the Spur of Love. Afterwards, reaching some pleasant waters, his mind in meditation entered into union in its very essence with the flowing of the stream. And thus closed the tenth day of the first autumnal month of the year of the Male Fire Tiger.

Our next extract is introduced with a view to justify the assertion already put forward, that the author of these memoirs is certainly more than a poet in name. We have many passages to choose from; but here may be given as a specimen the description of a wooded mountain-slope, prefaced by the following quaint incident:—

The Reverend Milaraspa himself had come from Ragma to the fortress of the skies, Kyang-p'an. One night, at the time of seating himself (for meditation), there appeared a monkey riding upon a hare, bearing a fungus as a shield, and carrying arrows and a bow made of straw just as if looking for an opportunity to use them. Thereupon a laugh slipped forth from his Reverence.

The other (*i.e.*, the monkey) exclaimed: 'I have come hoping to frighten you; but, if you are not afraid, I shall depart.'

On the other saying this, his Reverence remarked: 'Having come to the conclusion that all things that have appearance are imaginary, and believing the imagination itself to be only as the body of the Doctrine (*i.e.*, impalpable), whatever feats of jugglery a goblin like you may exhibit, it will be an occasion to laughter to a Naljor like myself.'

Thus he spoke. Whereupon the other, who was the ruling deity of Grot'ang, made verbal engagement to render him fealty, and departed with speech and countenance as of the rainbow. Then the householders of Grot'ang, who had arrived for the purpose of saluting his Reverence, enquired: 'What are the good points about this locality?' So, replying to their question, he uttered these verses:—

Let salutations be thrown up to the venerable lamas!
Know you, or know you not, the virtues of this place?
If not; let me describe them:
Kyang-p'an, the fortress of the skies, is a lonely spot;
The fortress of the skies is, as it were, in a palace.
Above it, to the south, lie clouds filmy and purple;
Below, fall down waters transparent and green;
Behind, are red rocks and the expanse of the heavens
In front, are meadows piebald with flowers;
On the borders, the roaring of beasts issues forth
In the air insects like finest rain are descending,
The bees keeping up a perpetual song.

Deer and wild asses—mothers and their young—frolic and stamp;
Apes and monkeys are gambolling on the sward;
Young larks interchanging notes in many voices;
That divine bird, the Gongmo, pouring out its lay.
The clayey streams chatter softly and harmoniously below: [rated.
Their voice is the voice of Time—of friends whose friendship has degene-
Yea! the virtues of the place cannot be penetrated by one's thoughts;
But the joyous soul leads them captive into song,
And speeches sage are driven forth into the mouth.
Ye fathers and mothers of households here assembled
Do as I do, and regain your name;
Renounce your deeds of sin and attain to happiness.

Occasionally, however, our friend seems not to have been received by the denizens of the places he visited in the amicable spirit he deemed his due. Such slights he meets with unruffled composure, apparently; but then, forthwith, as we shall find, he shows himself to be a past-master in the art of ingenious abuse, and rapidly succeeds in reducing the most churlish to abject docility. Let us see his method with an old woman who accused him of coming after her daughter:—

The Reverend Milaraspa resolved to proceed for meditative purposes to Jáng-tagoi Gang ('the Glacier of the Northern Horse Gate'). Arriving one night in the autumnal month, he presently went to greet the people with three basketsful of gourds. The country-folk were all busy reaping the corn. In the upper part of one large field in particular a young woman about twenty-three years of age was superintending. She was possessed of all the tokens and marks of a wise Khádoma (fairy), and was placed over a band of reapers composed of many men. 'Good people,' said he, 'pray bestow some victuals upon me, a Naljor.' Said the girl: 'O Naljor! go ye and enter in at the gate of yonder castle. I shall be coming there immediately.' Thereupon the Reverend One proceeded to the castle-gate, and, having given a push with his hands to the door, had entered some distance within the gateway. At that very moment, however, an old woman of unprepossessing appearance came from indoors. She was meanly clad, and was carrying her hands full of ashes.

'What beggars you Naljor are!' she exclaimed. 'In the summer-time you ask alms of white food, and in the winter you come begging for sour things. There is never for you any season of sitting still. You fancy you are going to get my daughter as a bride, and steal her goods as a dowry. Have you come from the East just at this time, when there are no men about?' As she spoke her body trembled with passion, and she made ready to fling the ashes and to brawl much more.

'Old woman,' cried out his Reverence, 'there will be plenty of time afterwards to throw your ashes; but listen a little while first to this song of Milaraspa.' And he proceeded to set forth some verses containing conundrums for the old dame:—

My first is the bliss of those who escape to the heavens above;
My second, the woe of the three classes of the damned below;

My third, the loss of all power of those who may be in the intermediate worlds:
In course of time these three will meet three.
Black-hearted old granny, bearing spite against religion,
See that you consider this closely in your heart.
In your doings, perform the doctrine of the holy gods;
In relying, depend on some accredited lama;
When you return to your home, first reflect—
Has such an one appeared?
My first is she who gets up the earliest in the morning;
My second, she who lies down the last at night;
My third is the labour which is never finished:
Some day these three will coalesce in one.
Skinny old woman, servant of servants and void of a stomach,
See you revolve that carefully in your heart.
In your doings, perform the doctrine of the holy gods;
In your relying, lean on some orthodox lama;
Reflect—Has such an one appeared?

. . . .

My first is the lifting action of one drawing tent-pegs from the ground;
My second, the walking action of one creeping after fowls;
My third, the crouching action of one breaking stones and clods:
Some day these three actions will be combined.
Old woman, dejected in mind and decayed in the intestines,
See that you revolve, &c., &c.
My first are the wrinkles puckering the skin without;
My second, the flesh, blood, and decaying bones left within;
My third, the dull, dumb, deaf, blind, dazed, crippled being between:
Some day those three will be united in one person.
Old granny, ugly in appearance and wrinkled with wrath,
See that you take this to heart, &c., &c.

. . . .

Rarer than stars in the day-time
Are they who're set free in the heavens above;
More plenteous than tiny chips of gravel
Are those doomed to woe in the spheres down below.
Just now, when body and soul must part company,
The mind feels dejected.
Old woman, conscious of guilt, hopeless, and without appetite for death,
See you take to heart and consider this!
In your doings, perform the divine precepts;
In your relying, lean upon some orthodox lama.

Having given ear to the song poured forth in condescension by the Reverend One, faith devoid of self-reliance was born in the ancient dame. Allowing the ashes in her hand to drop through her fingers, the old woman called to mind the actions committed by her in past times, and repented.

Thereafter Milaraspa endeavours to instruct this old soul and her daughter—who, coming in, and finding her mother in tears, is near picking a quarrel with the Saint—in the rudiments of his doctrinal theories. As is invariably the case in Buddhist philosophical statements, were we to quote here (as we do later on) these enunciations, they would be found to contain no real recondite wisdom, nor even any scheme of metaphysics and morality which could be dignified with the title of an ethical system. They are mostly mere pretentious phrases which have little consistency, and the profundity is only apparent, and will not bear analysis. There is nothing ennobling to the individual, or calculated to make the world the better; or, even in the Buddhist sense, less steeped in misery, in the doctrines of sublime vacuity and indifference to all earthly claims, with which Buddhism, whether Indian or Tibetan, occupies itself. It is essentially the religion of phraseological forms and onomatopoetical positions. Even the universal philanthropy preached becomes degenerate when it would condescend to practical individual exercise.

There is, nevertheless, one great principle in which the Christian and the seeker after the highest happiness in any Faith might acquire improvement at certain junctures of life from the Buddhist, and that is the principle which expresses the unimportance and indeed nothingness of the good things offered by the world as compared with the consolations and changeless attitude which Religion presents to him who yields himself up to its sway alone. This, of course, is no new doctrine. Solomon in Hebrew ethics had preached it long prior to Buddhism. But the Buddhist, that is the Buddhist who may really endeavour to fulfil what he professes, accepts no compromise with the material world on the subject. The greatness and happiness of human life are, at least in theory, not even to be reckoned as considerations in the question. Of course the reason assigned is that all visible and physical advantages are not only merely temporary but are in themselves complete illusions. While such a motive may indeed appear inferior in its moral sanction to that which can animate the Christian to any like attitude or similar sentiments, nevertheless as an impulsive force as observable in Buddhist practice it seems stronger than the Christian motive. Christianity, however, is infinitely superior when it teaches the nobility of this present life, its joys and its possibilites.

Now we find in Milaraspa many expositions of this Buddhistic high principle, and firm and fine is the position which he personally assumes in the matter. But we shall make a lengthy quotation from the Gurbum dealing fully with the Buddhist point of view:—

Hail to the Teacher! The reverend Milaraspa himself was dwelling in the cave of Nyi-shang Giri Katya in the South Himalayan country and sitting in mystic contemplation of the current of the river. At such a time it happened that certain huntsmen coming to Nyi-shang observed his reverence seated and with mystic look composing verses. They were consumed with perplexity and afraid; and one and all fled. However, coming back again, they planted their bows upright and exclaimed :

'You are either a man or a demon; and if you are a man you seem much as if you were taking count of something.'

But the reverend one sate on giving no reply, wrapt in his mystic expression. Whereupon those men, stationing themselves above, shot down many arrows, but did not aim straight. Then, desisting, they were about to cast their weapons aside, but found themselves incapable of stirring their bodies. At length flames of fire broke the spell, scorching yet not consuming them. So they hurled themselves down into a ravine at the base of a rock where a large river was tumbling. Writhing and twirling they did not so much as rest on the surface of the water, but were tossed back upwards from the midst of the river, flying aloft again and arriving at their former station.

Yet the other, uttering not a word, sate on enthralled. Then, all of them brought back, filled with amazement, cried out: 'Did ever such a man as this sit in a mountain cavern?'

One of the cotton-clad (*ras-chhungpa*) of the men of that place, overhearing the huntsmen, remarked to them :

'That is my lama, a good and genuine Nal-jor of Tibet. He has the tokens of one who has reached the final fulfilment of such things as can be gained and accomplished. He can throw the spell of his meditations even over the beasts, and thus has even fastened his own meditative powers upon both dogs and deer.'

Such accounts of what his doctrine had brought about having been set forth to them, all were turned humbly to the Faith, and the fame of the reverend one filled the whole country of Nepal. Thereafter, he who happened at the time to be king of Yerang and Kho-khom heard the reports of his reverence; and he, too, marvelling, humbled himself and believed.

Then spake Dolma (the goddess) to this king of Kho-khom: "There is in your treasury a piece of Benares cloth, also some of the ever-victorious Arura fruit. Now he who is abiding in the cave of Nyi-sbang Katya in the mountains of the southern district is a Tibetan Naljor, a great Bodhisattwa of the Ten Continents—offer those to him; and he will foretell what should be done to bring to you the greatest benefits in this world and the next.

Thereupon that king despatched a man acquainted with the Tibetan tongue to search for him. He, meeting with his reverence, observed all that had been attained to by entirely abandoning this life; and he was filled with wonder and converted. Then did he reflect: This man seems from every point of view to be Milaraspa; yet it is necessary to make sure.'

'O Teacher,' he inquired, 'what are you called? Also, being entirely destitute of food and drink, have you not come hither for relief in your want? What is it then that you desire in order to supply such necessaries of life as you may lack.'

In reply to questionings of this sort, his Reverence made answer:—

'I am a Naljor of Tibet, Milaraspa so-called. And to lack of necessaries forsooth is due my being entirely free from wretchedness; and what that is equivalent to let me duly describe in a song:

To the lords lamas, let salutations go up!
I am Milaraspa so to be styled.
At present I am free from desire of wealth,
I wish not to heap up earthly pelf;
So, firstly, am I without the misery of getting,
And next, I am free from the misery of guarding,
While lastly, I am without all misery of coveting more;
Thus that lack of having nothing at all is good.
Again, at present I am free from desire for relatives;
I wish not to be encompassed by love and cheerfulness;
So, firstly, I am separated from attachments of mind,
And next I am free from bickerings and retorts,
Lastly I am subject to no separations;
Thus deprivation of the pleasures of love and cheer is well.
At present I desire not to be full of news,
I wish not to listen to rumours and reports;
So, first, I am free from the trouble of making enquiries,
And next I escape the perplexity of hoisted signals,
Lastly I am without any fears of injury;
In being set apart from gossip and news I am happy.
At present I am devoid of the desire for one's country,
I wish not any special land to dwell in.
So, first, I am rid of the misery of partizanship;
And next am I free from the thraldom of government;
Lastly, do I escape the trouble of watching faces (or "opportunities;")
The want of any certain dwelling-place is good.

The emissary having come before the king, related in full the account of his adventures, adding: "Such as this is Milaraspa."

Thereupon the king, confident in faith and humility, rejoined: 'See if you can entice this Milaraspa hither; but, if he will not be persuaded, offer him both these things.'

So he despatched the Benares cloth and the infallible Arura fruit to influence him; and (the messenger), having met with the reverend one, said: 'I have been deputed by the pious king who resides in Kho-khom and Yerang to summon the Naljor of Tibet; it is necessary that you attend.'

From the mouth of his Reverence: 'In general when I arrive at towns and villages I make not the acquaintance of men, and in particular I make not the acquaintance of kings. I have no wish for delicacies of food and drink; and as an individual practising religion I am without any relation or story about dying from hunger or cold. The man who adheres to a king will cast aside a lama. As for me, as I am carrying out the precepts of Marpa of Lhobrag I shall not come. You yourself go back again.'

The other replied: 'When a mighty king summons a mere man who is a *yogi* is it not seemly that that one man should set ont and come to do homage at his feet?'

Quoth his Reverence: 'I am also a mighty king of the wheel that re-revolves; and a king who abounds in riches is by no means happier or mightier than I.'

The other retorted: 'You king of the revolving wheel, where, pray, are your seven kingdoms? As you are going to be a great and rich king, if those exist, point them out."

From the mouth of the Reverend One:—

'Ye circle of officers of the kingdoms of the world, if you but followed a kingdom such as mine is, you would yourselves be changed into the greatest of monarchs; while the power and the wealth belonging to everything would spring forth (for you). And thus let me express this in a song:—

Ye courtiers desirous of joy and happiness!
Such as this is the kingdom of Milaraspa:
In its sway it is blest to everybody both here and hereafter.
Mila's government is like this:
There is Faith, the most precious of things that revolve,
Which unites itself with deeds of virtue night and day;
There is Wisdom, the most precious of jewels,
Which fulfils the hopes of all for themselves and others;
There is Religious Duty, the most precious of queens, which is adorned with ornaments of surpassing beauty;
There is Complete Abstraction, the most precious of officers,
Which amasses both integrity and wisdom;
There is Chastity, the most precious of draught beasts,
Which carries mighty loads of the teachings of Sang-gyas;
There is Diligence, the most precious of horses,
Which bears you into a land where Pain itself is not;
There is Attention, the most precious of generals,
Which routs the armies of the enemy Wrong Perception.
If you gain possession of a realm like this,
You will acquire the glory and fame of a sovereign;
Perpetually will you triumph over that which is hostile;
Vassals will become feudatory to the works of the Ten Virtues;
Sensate creatures without exception will become as mothers.
Come, then! Be a king according to my plan!'

Thus did he speak; and thereupon the other exclaimed:—'Most wonderful must it be to be moulded in such faith as that a *yogi* should be unmoved by anything. However, the king bestows on you these two gifts.'

So saying, he presented into his hands the Benares raiment and the infallible Arara fruit. The other, taking them, blest them; and offering up prayers, he accepted them.

* * * * *

We cannot attempt to follow this peripatetic saint systematically in his wanderings, but must content ourselves and seek to interest the reader by picking out the more characteristic pieces. The next quotation is a lengthy one, and may be regarded, in a sense, as valuable archæologically, inasmuch as it includes elaborate descriptions of certain articles of ordinary use. Our narrative being several centuries old, this means that we have minute accounts of these everyday things as they then were known :—

That rich power of meditation, Milaraspa himself, had been engaged during the summer-time in contemplation, seated on the southern slopes of the Shri mountain. It being now autumn, when harvest-time had arrived, one evening when tired he set forth in quest of food-alms. On the way, in a hidden nook in the desert, he fell asleep. Then there appeared to him a woman with both eyebrows and beard gleaming yellow in the clear blue of the night. She was leading her son, a small youth, as much as twenty years of age. 'Milaraspa,' she said, 'you possess eight hearts in a bunch, and one of them really belongs to this lad; therefore bestow it upon him.' Having thus spoken, he dreamt that she vanished. Thereupon Milaraspa, arousing himself, began to revolve the matter.

'Evidently,' he mused' 'that woman must have been a khádoma' (*i.e.* aerial female sprite), 'and there will come to me eight pupils ripe for *karma* —human beings, or, as it were, hearts sifted unto the uttermost. Only this very day shall I meet one human being whose fate must be determined by his actions; and I must set myself to be really useful to him.'

Proceeding upward to the side of the rugged road into Tibet, he sat him down and slept for a while hard-by the River of One Hundred Thousand Silver Eyes. After which there came up a stripling riding on a black horse.

'O Naljor! he exclaimed, 'what are you doing lying down there? Then, said his Reverence: 'O citizen layman, whither are you going?' He replied that when he had got across the river he would pursue a way straight forward into the midst of the Ding-ri mountains.

Thereat the aged Naljor remarked that he, too, was going over the river, and requested that he might mount on the back of the citizen's horse.

Said the youth: 'I am hastening away to see sights and to obtain knowledge in the East. If you get up, too, my horse will be injured.' Having thus spoken, he went on ahead, not wishing to keep company with the Naljor.

Then the Reverend One, mystically drawing in his breath in the very ecstasy of a saintly lama's meditation, started off, and walked onwards up and down upon the surface of the river. Yet he did not sink in the waters. 'Look with one eye behind,' he cried; for he who a little time ago went on ahead was now being tossed and turned by the frothy waves in the midst of the waters. Looking back, the youth beheld the Reverend One walking forward, and not sinking in the water. Is it an illusion of my eye?' he thought, 'for he is actually not sinking in the water.' When he had reached the farther side of the river, he approached right in front of where the lama had taken up his position, and gazed at his feet. 'The water has not risen even above the soles of his feet!' he exclaimed. Thence belief and love were bred within him, and to the lama who had attained to such accomplishments he said: 'I beseech you to credit that I was ignorant, and to pardon me for not mounting you just now on my horse.'

Moreover, taking the ends of the bridle of his black horse, and placing them in the hands of his Reverence, he besought him in a song as follows :—

Here is a saint who beholds everything beforehand;
A being who has escaped from human life;
A Buddha whom it is rare to encounter face to face;
An emanation whom it is difficult to speak and listen to.
As to his name—now I hear it, now I don't;
As to his person—now I recognise it, now I don't;
As to his hands—now I grasp them, now I don't;
As to his health—now I inquire after it, now I don't.
Overwhelmed by your graciousness, I crave forgiveness.
My black horse is able to cleave through the winds,
Its neck ornaments waving as if lifting up praise;
The harness is of choicest quality,
The saddlecloth of the softest strips,
As firmly stretched as the saddle of Ped-kar the Master,
With an apron in front and stirrups suspended;
A crupper tied with red ribands and magical knots;
A bridle which would pass for a jewelled collar;
Eyebrows swept as with smiles by tassels of tiger-skin,
Above each a mirror embossed like the great northern star.
The bit, like an officer, governs the mouth,
And a white whip lets fall its instructions.
I, who am marked strongly as a worldly man,
Would offer the horse to my reverend father,
And beg you not, as a magician, to deliver me into hell.

Thus humbly speaking, he offered the horse; but his Reverence would not accept it. 'I have,' he said,' 'a horse superior to that of yours'; and then, at the other's request, he poured forth this ditty:—

Hearken here, O son! to what may be useful:
I have a stallion of the wind—even perfect knowledge;
My flag, though folded up, lifts up praise;
My harness is the entrails of him subsisting on snatches of food between meditation;
The saddle I stride, the clearest self-knowledge;
The stirrups I press are mental objects—the nails of concentration!
My bridle is Rlung, which I draw in as my breath;
That which flits before my eyebrows are three knobs on my nose;
That which embosses my head are waves of tranquility within;
And to govern my mouth there is the life of illusion without.
The switch I strike with is the beating current of thought;
Whilst the Uma vein is that which capers and heads and leaps upon the plain.
Such is the steed the Naljor has beneath him.
If it flees, he escapes from the mire of the cycle of life;
If it pursues, he arrives on the dry ground of Perfection.
Thus I do not desire the charger of you, a mere man;
Therefore, young fellow, hasten to depart yourself.

The Reverend One having thus delivered himself, again the other thought: 'Though he has declined my horse, nevertheless, as his feet are bare, he may be able to make use of my boots'; wherefore, pulling off his best boots, which were an ornamental pair, he made a proffer of them in rhyme :—

O Naljor, accomplished and precious!
As you are attached to no country yourself,
But through the realm you roam aimless,
Perchance some angry dog may snap your toes,
Or jaggéd thorns may wound your feet,
Or walking barefoot may bring fatigue.
These boots are fine, with green-hued tags:
They have laces made of silk most costly;
In front they are worked with handsome braid,
Whilst projecting brass nails are beaten into the caps.
The fur of the *Káshá* deer is let into the middle of the upper parts,
The hide of the wild yák forms both the soles,
And a cunning workman has stitched the whole together;
The overflaps guard the toe-nails from mischance,
And cling firmly, so to speak, as the water-leech to a lion's head.
These are the patrimony of me, a young man,
And I place them at the feet of your Reverence.

But the Reverend One refused acceptance, remarking: 'I have boots of my own surpassing any of yours;' and then, at the other's request, he spoke these lines :—

Listen faithfully, little man, my son!
Here in my fatherland, the circle of the Three Kingdoms,
The dense darkness of Ignorance has beshrouded;
The meadows are filled with the swamps and mire of Lust;
The moss-lands bristle with the thorns of Envy;
The wild dogs of Anger bark and bite;
The mountains and rocks of Arrogance are lofty and steep.
I, having picked my way across the four rivers,
Have sought to flee to the plains of mighty Bliss.
There Ká-shá fur is illusive and perishable stuff,
Your two leather soles are the perverted longings for existence,
And are stitched together by belief in the fruits of *karma*;
The green tags are, as it were, the pleasures and property in the land;
The silk laces give freedom of attachment to one's own ideas;
Memnonic verses to induce meditation are the beaten brass bosses,
While the buckles compressing them are the three physicial fetters restraining meditation.
The best boots of the Naljor are not such as that
I do not desire your adornments;
Depart, O citizen, to the home to which you were going.

Quoth the youth: 'Be it so, your Reverence; but if you decline the boots, is there not any single article of clothing you would like, as you will feel the cold? Here, indeed, is a red and green overcoat for a bed-covering.' And with the view to his taking it he sang as follows :—

Precious lama and finished saint!
As you bind not yourself to any place,

But rove about void of store and provision—
At one time you wander to the top of a mountain,
At another you sleep in the street of a town—
As you are without a single cotton cloth for raiment;
Your body, being in nakedness, must needs be cold.
This, which has been worn by me, a youth,
Is dyed red and green with the juice of the *mendi* plant and the water
of clouds;
A skilful worker has cut it out and put it together;
Inside it is finished with fleecy lining white as the clouds;
Above it is satin-trimmed with marmot's fur;
Round the lower part are fastened flounces of lynx skin;
The border below is turned in with otter-skin;
On the shoulders silk ribbon-streamers are knotted.
Now, by wearing this, not only will it look dashing and lustrous,
But also you will not dread the cold piercing wind.
On the whole, it is a robe for an envoy or a Brahmin.

The Buddhism of Milaraspa is almost identical with the philosophic Buddhism most popular in Tibet at the present day. Although Milaraspa lived some 350 years previous to the period of Ts'ongkhapa (the reformer of Tibetan Buddhism), he is supposed to have professed similar principles. His creed maintains the utter illusiveness of all material things, the world itself only existing in the imagination of its inhabitants. All mental reasonings and earthly knowledge (*Rtoks-pa*) are despised, as obscurations of higher perception (*rig-pa*), intuitive learning (*shes-rab*), and the perfect wisdom of a saint (*ngos-grubs*). Compassion for the physical sufferings of men and animals must be swallowed up in an impersonal and unimaginative pity, prompted solely by the fact of their being still the subjects of ignorance and mistakes. Divers difficulties and foes stand in the way of attainment to this effulgent state: not only the allurements of the appetites and passions, and the seductions of science, but also the many supernatural beings of Buddhist mythology—demons, goblins, gnomes, etc. On the other hand, there are spiritual agents who, on propitiation, can aid the aspirant, such as the *Noi-jin*, or mountain-gods, and the *Lu*, or snake-gods, dwelling in the numerous lakes of Tibet. But demons, gnomes, and gods have more than a spiritual influence. They have the control of diseases, and are the cause of most temporal and bodily ills; they have the disposal of earthly abundance, are the arbiters of good and bad fortune, and can make a man impervious against the schemings, and even the physical attacks, of his human enemies. The Naljor or the Buddhist sage, according to the extent of his ascetic and magical attainments, possesses more or less power of coercion of deities and devils for those mundane purposes; and the populace in general value the expert ascetic chiefly as a guide to earthly acuteness and as a medium in dealing with invisible protectors and foes. The Ngag-pa sorcerer is now, however, the miracle-worker in modern Tibet; and he is altogether a more mundane personage than the Naljor of the older days.

Now, it is a cardinal doctrine of Buddhism, both ancient and modern, that none can hope to gain perfect wisdom and the miraculous powers of a saint unless they practise continuous and systematic meditation. Meditation consequently assumes the position of a science; and its methods and stages have been studied and shaped to such a nicety as to form the science into an abstruse art, the rules varying, however, in different schools of philosophic Buddhism. Milaraspa, who belonged to a sect of the Madhyamika school of thought, itself a sub-division of the great Maháyana branch of Buddhism, lays down the stages of systematic meditation as four:—

ལྟ་བ་ *Tá-wa.*—Contemplation or concentration.

སྒོམ་པ་ *Gom-pa.*—Complete abstraction.

སྤྱོད་པ་ *Chyö'pa.*—Consummation, and the Very Self seen.

བྲས་བུ་ *Dai-bu.*—Fruition, with new faculties under one's will.

Such meditation, before it ripens, must often be continued for years, and with only the most necessary relaxations and the scantiest diet. The majority of the hermits found dwelling in caverns throughout Tibet never reach further than the *Gom-pa* stage; but, properly or theoretically, a Naljor-pa, who is also a miracle-worker, is one who has gained the third stage. As to the curious artificial means employed to induce meditation, and the weird fancies connected therewith, they have been described in another chapter. So far, enough has been said to enable the reader to follow more intelligently further extracts from our author:—

The people begging to be given the opportunity of learning and bringing into easy comprehension the arts of contemplation, meditative abstraction, and consummation, in reply thereto he sang to them this ditty:—

May the lama's benediction enter your souls!
Blessed is it to perceive the Very Void!
In returning thanks to you householders who believe,
Accept a song which my tutelar gods delight in.
That which is apparent, that which is void, that which is liberated from discernment of distinctions—
Three are these;

And these three sum up the rules of Contemplation.
That which is plain, that which is unrecognisable, that which disturbs not either way—
Three are these;
And these three make up the sum of Abstraction.
That which is free from all attachment, that which is without any cravings, that which bears one on to the end—
Three are these;
And these three make up the sum of Consummation.
Freedom from hope, freedom from fear, freedom from mistakes—
Three are these;
And these three make the sum of one's Final Recompense.
Freedom from maintaining appearances, freedom from secrecy, freedom from craft—
Three are these;
And these three make the sum of what one vows.

Having thus spoken, those people went away believing, and for some days many inquirers came to meet him. They who had been before would then ask: 'Is your Reverence well and comfortable in bodily health'? In response to those inquiring after his ailments he delivered these verses:—

I bow to the feet of the holy lamas
In the forest-glades of places lonely and void of man;
In the manner of his meditation Milaraspa feels happy.
He is well in his illusive body when it is free from disease and heat;
He is well in being free from sleep;
He is well in such meditation as is devoid of effort;
He is well in the meditative warmth that escapes any chill;
In penitential exercises void of despondency he is well;
In husbandry requiring no exertion he feels well;
In solitary places, while undisturbed, he feels well—
And such are the comforts of the body.
In the vehicle of skill and knowledge combined he is happy;
When the mind compasses Arterial Absorption,
At both the generation and the expiration of the process he is happy.
When his consciousness regards not the ebb and flow of *rlung* he is happy
In severance from conversation, being freed from babbling comrades, he is happy—
And such are the comforts connected with speech.
In pure enlightenment, changeless and unpremeditated, he is well;
In felicity, whether in its elements or in bulk, he is well;
In the ceaseless undulation of ideas he feels well.
Thus is the region small where much joy can exist.
In a song the soul's gladness has been now poured forth;
Contemplation and Consummation have been harmonised.
They in the future who strive for perfection,
Let them retain things such as these in their minds.

At these words the listeners remarked: 'Great and most astounding are the methods of happiness belonging to the carriage of body, speech, and mind in a lama. But whence do they originate? 'They arise,' replied he, 'from the understanding of one's own soul.'

If the essentials of systematic meditation, both spiritual and artificial, are continuously persevered in for years, then rapid and assured advance through the stages of ascetic rank proceeds. From the grade of *Trub-t'op* (གྲུབ་ཐོབ) that of *Gomchhen* (སྒོམ་ཆེན) is attained; and when the subsequent stage of *Naljor* is at last reached, miracles such as those described in our next and concluding extracts are rendered possible.

Due north of the Kumaon portion of the Himalayas, and just within Tibet, is a region famous both mythologically and geographically. Here are situated the cluster of peaks known as Mount Kailas and the pair of lakes named in our maps Manasarowar. Geographically the lakes, which bear in Tibet the names of Ts'o Má-pang and Ts'o Lang-gak, are of importance. From the latter issues forth the Sutlej river; while three other mighty rivers—the Indus, the Karnali, and the Yeru Tsangpo—are bred from monster glaciers on the surrounding mountains. Kailas, styled Gang Tisé by Tibetans, continues absolutely unexplored; but it has a central summit measured trigonometrically at 21,830 feet. Desolate, even for Tibet, though the locality is, eight monasteries stand on the shores of Lake Má-pang and four others on the slopes of Gang Tisé.

In the course of his travels, Milaraspa with a band of his pupils reached the great snowy mass of Mount Kailas or Tisé. He found the sacred mountain in possession of a priest of the Bön religion—the aboriginal cult of Tibet previous to the introduction of Buddhism, and which has a considerable following still in the remoter districts of the country. On Milaraspa's arrival he claims Tisé as the inheritance of the Buddhists. This claim the Bön chief repudiates, and comparing Milaraspa and the sacred mount as being both of them nothing close at hand, but famous only at a distance, he proposes that they should compete in feats of jugglery, the winner to hold sway over Tisé. The heretic begins by straddling over Lake Má-pang, placing one foot on either shore, and opens thus:—

Great is the fame of white, frosty Tisé,
Yet for helmet has the mountain only snow.
Great, too, is the talk about Má-pang, the turquoise-lake,
Yet, being merely water, by water is it torn apart.
Big, likewise, by report is Milaraspa,
Yet is he but an old man bound to lie naked;
From his mouth a puny song flows forth,

And in his hand he grasps an iron staff.

. . . .

If miracles be wrought, like this should they be shown.

Because the Bön thus spoke his Reverence proceeded to sit down, and, though his body did not become larger, and Lake Má-p'ang did not grow smaller, he covered the entire surface. Then this song did he utter:—

Ho! ho! then hearken, gods and men?
On the hill of the Vulture's Peak
The victor, Shákya T'ubpa, sits.
There, too, the Sixth Buddha, Dorje Chhang;
While the mighty mother, his other self,
Born together with him, revels in his essence.
Mila, with name all famous, am I;
And, fulfilling the commands of Marpa of Lhobrag,
I come to meditate here on the snows of Tisé.
As to you, you heretical Bönpo,
I will measure in my verse answers to your dicta.
Great is the fame of Tisé white and frosty,
Snow is the covering of that mountain's crest:
Snow-white also are the teachings of Buddha.
Great indeed is the talk about Má-pang,
The lake so like unto the turquoise;
Being water itself, by water is it rended:
So do existing things pass into the ground and are consumed.
Great, too, is the repute of me, Milaraspa;
That old man, bound to lie naked,
Has issued forth from the overthrow of all his tastes.
From his mouth proceeds a little song,
And all he sees takes form as in a book;
In his hand an iron staff is poised,
Which has steered him o'er life's ocean.
Ye Bönpo, embrace the Doctrine, and be useful to all!
Not doing so—conquered by my mystic arts—
Depart ye to other lands and countries;
And look, moreover, on this feat.

Thus speaking, he held forthwith Lake Má-pang on the tip of his thumb; and this he did without injuring the living creatures which dwelt in the waters.

. . . .

The Reverend One enunciated: 'Though the stars in a body compete with the sun and moon to give light, nevertheless it is the sun and moon only that dispel the darkness of the Four Continents. So also, though you and I make trial of our skill, you cannot match yourself with me. Tisé is my property. However, as much for your own immediate satisfaction, as well as in order that all may behold the might of the Tantrik achievements possible in my religion, the exhibition of magic performances is allowable.'

Having spoken, his Reverence all at once transferred himself to the Lotos Cave in the valley on the western side of Tisé, where he seated himself; and whilst the Bönpo remained on the east of the mount, his Reverence stretched forth his legs from the west, right round on to a rock in the religious cell of the Bönpo, and left his footprints there. 'You do like that!' he cried.

The other stretched out his legs towards the west, but they did not even reach down to the margin of the water. Thereat the demons which were in he sky set up a peal of chuckling laughter.

Although the Bönpo was confused and ashamed, nevertheless, 'Once again,' he exclaimed, 'let us test our magic.' So the Bönpo started out on his Bön circuit round the mount (*i.e.*, from right to left), while the Reverend One went forth on the strictly orthodox round. Once more meeting, this time on the southern side of Tisé, a shower of rain began to fall. As it seemed needful to make some shelter from the rain, his Reverence asked: 'Will you build the walls below, or will you construct the roof for the top?'

'You build the walls; I shall put on the roof,' was the reply. Then his Reverence beckoned to a huge boulder as big as three men to ascend upwards. 'Oh now, pass over to the farther side,' he said. 'I do so,' it said, and went. Looking at the back of the walls, he noticed that as much in height as the body of a child of eight years was required to finish them, and that just such a piece had been rent from the boulder. Casting at it a magic glance and lifting his index-finger, he cried: 'Let that stone be cleft in the middle and brought to me!'

'That piece is mine which you have broken,' said the Bönpo.

'If you vie with me in miracles, then you can cause that it be unbroken. You cannot make the magic glance that broke it. However, break it, and fetch it if you can.'

Then the Bönpo—able to break a piece like the first—attempted to lift it up; but the other with his magic glance made it incapable of being raised, and the Bönpo stood with averted eyes.

CHAPTER XIV.

THE PRACTISE OF MAGIC AND SORCERY IN TIBET.

Amongst the Buddhist fraternity the highest ambition in real life is not the attainment of Nirvana, but the acquirement of magical powers. This is believed by all Buddhists of every land,—whether of Burmah, Ceylon, or Tibet,—to be actually possible to any man with sufficient learning and earnestness of purpose. It is considered, also perfectly legitimate, in that the possession of such skill is in itself a sure sign of the sublimest sanctity.

The general works of classical Buddhism teem with examples of Buddhas and saints who acquired supernatural capabilities of this sort. Unlike the miracles of the Christian Scriptures, which in every case were executed evidently from motives of the highest philanthropy, the Buddhist miracle appears rarely as a deed of direct benevolence. It is rather intended to startle, a marvel to strike awe in the hearts of beholders and to testify the holiness of the performer. Thus Shakyat'ubpa is related to have requested that a thousand lampwicks might be inserted in holes made all over his body. This having been done, they were lighted and fed upon the fat of his frame without causing him any practical inconvenience. Again, Milaraspa, the Tibetan ascetic (as we have seen) displays his power by holding up on the tip of his thumb the Manasarowar lake, and it is characteristically mentioned that he did this so carefully that *none of the living creatures in the lake were injured!* Sometimes, indeed, the wonder is worked with a result which is productive of benevolence of a certain type, but the good object seems generally of secondary importance. In this way we find Atisha, the Indian sage, washing in a lake, and causing a stream of water to issue from the back of his head. A number of *yidak* or *preta*, observing the spouting stream, drink thereof and obtain some release from the torments of hell.

Buddhist miracles are nearly always of this fantastic nature. Very different both in intention and in mode of performance they appear to those wrought with such self-restraint, such deep meaning, and infinite compassion, by the Founder of Christianity.

In Tibet the arts of occult mystery (which include all departments of magic, ramifying into necromancy, astrology, demoniac agency, and into every branch of sorcery) are studied with different purposes by two different classes of persons. The larger body are those who apparently devote themselves to the pursuit with the object of gaining wealth, power, and influence. And these, we must admit, are intensely practical. Consciously or unconsciously, they indulge in many forms of trickery which are sheer charlatanry and imposture. Nevertheless, there can be little doubt that in the efficacy of certain of their magic rites they are as frank believers as those who pay them for their services. Indeed there is often considerable *boná-fides* on the part of the sorcerer; and some of the results brought about are not always to be explained by "common sense" investigation. As to the other and numerically smaller class of occultists, they seem to follow their profession rather from an honest desire for the possession of mystic knowledge and miraculous powers than from any mercenary motives. They submit eagerly to privation, solitude, and systematic meditation with a single-mindedness which in the abstract is certainly to be admired. One might compare these, perhaps, with the astrologers of the middle and early ages in Europe; only the intelligence and the partially true science of the latter are here replaced by gross stupidity and a routine which never seeks to pass to new methods or dreams of fresh discoveries.

Between the two classes we have mentioned, moreover, there are of course other shades and orders partaking more or less of the characteristics of either class. Mixed motives prevail here as everywhere. The magician, who works for a mundane recompense, is not always devoid of ambitions which concern his own sanctification; while there are certain ascetics who intermingle with their ghostly meditations considerable efforts after the earthly offerings of the faithful. But we shall now venture to describe the practical dabblers in magic, together with their methods and the uses to which their arts are put. Moreover, as a matter of convenience, we shall, for our purpose, divide the magicians into two general classes, namely, (1) the Practical Sorcerers to whom the public resort, and (2) the Philosophical Ascetics whose aim, ostensible or real, is to compass their own sanctity and increase their own magical powers.

I.—PRACTICAL SORCERERS.

In Tibet the public workers of magical ceremonial are usually known as སྔགས་པ་ Ngakpa. In their neophyte days many of these have belonged to the school of Tantric learning or *Ngakpa Ta-ts'ang* in one of the great monastic establishments where instruction in the philosophy and the ritual of occult rites is regularly given. One of the most noted and frequented of these schools of magic is the Thoi-samling Táts'ang in Tashilhümpo monastery.

There is a general impression among Tibetan lay-folk that members of the Gelukpa institutions are not versed in Tantrik arts and that it is always best to resort to monks of some Nying-ma or unreformed monastery or even to the Bönpo priests who possess many Buddhist treatises garbled or doctored so as to suit the Bön shibboleths. Tsong-khapa, however, was a great Tantrik teacher and one of his chief works for the reformed or Gelukpa Buddhists was one dealing with these rites and their intelligent performance. Still, except in Lhása itself, the fashion is to prefer a Nyingma monk; and in the districts a graduate of the Mindol Ling [1] སྨིན་སྒྲོལ་གླིང་ can carry all before him, being also consulted by Gelukpa priests themselves. The more learned men of any very large establishment are known as *Ge-she* དགེ་བ་བཤེས་ and these have often a considerable "practice."

For special prognostics, as to the right day for starting on a journey, the best day to commence harvest, the interpretation of a dream, particular prescription of ceremonial in the case of severe illness—in such business it is usual to resort to a *Ge-she* or man of reputed learning or else to the head of a monastery, particularly if the latter should be a *ṭulku* or incarnate lama. But for ordinary rites of *kurim*, cases of sickness, services for a safe journey, child-birth conjurations, etc., etc., sets of Ngakpa readers and Gelongs are employed. In Lhása those ritual reciters belonging to the guild of Serkyempa or dealers in the golden drink—especially the band attached to the Ramochhe Temple—are in general request. In the same city, the common folk go for consultation to such popular sorcerers as the hermit of Tala-luguk cave near Chakpo Ri; [2] while the rich may betake themselves to the State Astrologer the Nai-chhung Chhoi-Kyong.[3] But in

1 Mindol Ling is the chief Nying-ma, or red-cap, monastery in Central Tibet, and is considered the head-quarters of the Dukpa sect. It is built on a hill ten miles south of the Yeru Tsang-po and not more than 15 miles from the famous Gelukpa establishment of Samye.

2 Also styled *Tak-la-lu-bup* བྲག་ལ་ཀླུ་སྦུབ་ "the hole of the nágas in the rock."

3 Besides being the State Oracle the Naichhung Chhoikyong is also open to private consultations by the general public. His ordinary fee is stated to be 10 *srang*

Daipung and Sera monasteries there are many consulting lamas of reputed learning, each of whom have their votaries; and thus Lhása people have a wide choice.

2.—PHILOSOPHICAL ASCETICS.

Persons of this class devote themselves, with at least a certain amount of solitude and privation, to systematic meditation of a settled and peculiar quality. Moreover, by dint of such meditation, they arrive at, or are supposed to arrive at, certain defined stages in the art which bring with them accompanying degrees of spiritual perfection as well as of physical adroitness.

Before describing the character and the stages of this ascetic pursuit, the individuals who practise it should be briefly denoted. Some of them are among the regular dwellers in monasteries. In nearly all such cases, if a personage devotes himself to any marked extent to the art, he is a man of learning and position. Occasionally he may be a Tulku or Incarnate Lama, but one of that order—though he is always supposed to engage in systematic meditative functions—has rarely the privacy or the leisure for anything prolonged of this nature. His public duties, and sometimes his private business avocations, where he is permitted to manage the monastic revenues, would probably preclude the due concentration of one's whole being which is believed to be indispensable to any perfection in the pursuit. Generally, however, where any resident in a gompa devotes himself to exercises of this abstract quality, he is the head of some mystic school such as the Ngag-pa Tá-ts'ang in the place. Such a man has usually considerable knowledge of technical doctrines and occult rites as set forth in the books. Others who are *Ká-ram,* or members of any school established for philosophical study, often like to pose as *gom-chhen* or systematic meditators. In these cases it is the custom for the devotees to withdraw for lengthy periods to certain sets of caverns or to artificially-constructed cells, a series of which are available in the rocky heights adjacent to all the larger monasteries. These cells are styled *ḍub-khang.* When the spell of mental concentration is over, they return to the community and

After consultation he bestows a scarf stamped with *sung-ngak* or *dharaṇi* sentences in colour either red or white according to whether the man is married or a celbate. A great deal of outward reverence seems to be offered to the Naichhung Chhoikyong, as the incarnation of the god Pe-har. No one, for instance, may look at him when he proceeds into Lhása. Incense is then burnt before him and he is attended by a retinue of 70 *trápa* or religious. Even high state officials have been fined for looking on him while passing. Members of the recent "Mission" to Lhása who visited his oracle-chamber describe it as fitted up in most exquisite taste and as being different from all other shrines they saw in its superlative cleanliness.

resume with ardour their studies. For there in the treatises, which we have already alluded to at some length, they will find everything that is calculated to render them experts in the mystic profession they have adopted.

In villages and country-places, the lama or head of the local gompa will occasionally retire for mystic contemplation. There is generally to be found for such purposes, on the slope hard-by, a rude circular hut of rough stones, well lime-washed outside, with no aperture save at the top in the roof. Sometimes this cell stands even in the centre of a village. Wherever it is placed, hither the lama shuts himself up for several days or longer; he holds no communication with anyone during his incarceration, and the little food he allows himself is shut up with him. While there, he is said to be *tsham-la* མཚམས་ལ་ "You cannot have a *jalkha* or interview with the *kusho* or holy one," is often the rejoinder. *Karé chhir-la,* "wherefore," you demand. *Tsham-la shuk,* "he sits in the mystic enclosure," is the conclusive reply.

In certain parts of Tibet, particularly in the eastern districts east of Kong-po, and in localities of special sanctity everywhere, the *gom-chhen* are usually hermits who have broken connection with monastic life and who dwell apart from their fellows in a solitary cavern or built hut perched on an inaccessible mountain-ledge, or else form one of a colony of such ascetics in a series of caves or cells. In this case the *gom-chhen* is generally designated a *rit'oi-pa* like any ordinary hermit (or simply a *rit'oi*) and his abode a *tak-p'uk rit'oi.* However, if he is known to be a profound meditator his particular cave is dignified by the appellation of *ḍub-p'uk.*

The inimitable Huc has given us, as might be expected, a graphic account of these abodes of the Ri-t'oi-pa :—

> "The rocky and rugged mountain which backs the lamasery, serves as an abode for five contemplative monks who like eagles have selected as the site of their aeries the most elevated points. Some have hollowed out their retreat in the living rock; others dwell in wooden cells stuck against the mountain like enormous swallows' nests; a few pieces of wood driven into the rock forming the staircase by which they ascend or descend. One of these Buddhist hermits, indeed, who has entirely renounced the world has voluntarily deprived himself of these means of communication with his fellows; a bag, tied to a long string, serves as the medium for conveying to him the alms of the lamas and shepherds."

Certainly it is a fact—as Huc goes on to assert—that many of the dwellers in such places have embraced the life merely because they have read of holy lamas doing so. These pass, as he states, their waking hours in prayer, and when they are tired of praying, relax in sleep.

Moreover, they personally collect alms from the neighbouring hamlets and monasteries.

But if the recluse aspires to become a *gom-chhen,* or perhaps eventually to attain the sanctity of a *nal-jor-pa,* such as was the great Milaraspa, solitude of a complete nature is imperative and he must for lengthy terms renounce intercourse with outsiders. Philosophical ascetics of this type, accordingly, make their habitations on the loftiest ledges without leaving access from below; but the bags which they let down the face of the cliff and which remain permanently suspended are always sufficiently filled with food and fuel by villages living hard-by.

Certain anchorites of this class located near Tse-t'ang, at a place named Yarlung Shos on the Yeru Tsang-po, do not dwell in caverns or high up; but pass their existence in small stone hovels by the roadside built without doors or windows. They hold no communication with the outer world except by means of one hole in each hut through which offerings are received from the public, and on such they entirely depend for subsistence. The sanitary state of these abodes must be truly awful; yet the occupants are asserted to attain to a great age.

THE SCHEME OF MEDITATION.

And now for the employment to which the genuine *gomchhen* adapts himself. This is, as we have said, systematic Meditation. The mode of operation appears to be something thus: An object is first selected upon which to concentrate the thoughts. For a beginner it must be something of tangible shape and mystic import. It may be a small metal image of a deity or a saint; or it may be a *dorje* or other sacred priestly implement set up in a corner of the cave; or an iron nail or a peacock's feather. However, the best outward object on which to fix the mind and the eyes is considered to be the Tibetan letter ཨ which is the last character in the alphabet and is in shape of particularly subtle import.

Having set the *gom-ten* or visible focus of meditation at a convenient distance, and having abstracted his thoughts from all other subjects, the devotee seats himself in a prescribed attitude in front of it. Sitting thus he gazes at it intently measuring with his eyes its colour, size, shape; at first abstaining from thinking of its inner meaning or symbolism, merely contemplating its outward aspect from every possible point of view. As he looks thus, he must strain his gaze by degrees more and more, until the object wavers and swims before his eyes, and until at length his whole mind becomes absorbed in it. He will then find that he loses all visual sight of the outward figure; but his eyes are not shut. However, the figure itself has been transferred to his brain where it is seen as a black outline edged with crimson and floating in a sea of pale-yellow light. That at least is the description given by commencing ascetic meditators. Older practitioners profess to behold nothing either outwardly or mentally.

This portion of the course when successfully carried out brings the votary to the first stage in the meditative art. He is said, then, to have accomplished TÁ-WA or CONTEMPLATION. He must, however, persist in repetitions of the process, practising it daily and for several hours together until expertness becomes so great that little effort is required to throw him into the half-trance-like state which is stated to supervene. The main requisites of Contemplation are laid down as abstinence from food not only during, but for three hours previous to starting off, and also freedom from all outward objects of distraction, which therefore means solitude and an unfurnished and completely empty cell.

The second step in systematic meditation is considered infinitely harder to perform than the first, and he who acquires any degree of success in effectuating it is far on the path to sainthood. This stage which is styled GOM-PA or COMPLETE ABSTRACTION takes rank as being a real part of downright Meditation; compared with which *Tá-wa* or Contemplation can scarcely be named beside it.

Except when he wishes to co-erce or acquire power over some particular deity (a business already explained fully) the devotee who attempts the Gompa stage of the art, dispenses with any outward figure to steady his mind. He has grown adroit enough to disdain the helps which novices demand. He requires, to begin the process, some mental object indeed, but it is carried entirely in the mind's eye. Moreover it must not be any idea which shall call for intellectual experience—*tog-pa* or mental knowledge, as commonly understood, being a positive failing in a saint—or for any worry or excitement. It is therefore always some suppositious thing, not an abstract train of intelligent thought even, but a fanciful object which could never really exist.

Accordingly, among the favourite *mig-te'* or mental concentrators we find *Mo-sam kyi Bu* or the Child of a Barren Woman, and *Ribong-gi Go-la Ru* or the Horn on a Hare's Head. Says the ascetic Milaraspa:—

> My sons, wander not, wander not, in the midst of a lesson!
> For if you wander in the midst of instruction,
> Sometimes there cometh up the appearance of food

Whensoever the semblance of food shall arise,
Instead of food, swallow untainted Contemplation;
Know all the sweetest flavours to be illusions.
Sometimes there cometh up the appearance of raiment;
Whensoever the aspect of raiment shall arise,
Instead of clothing, be clad in the blessed warmth of the Tum-mo;
Learn that all softness and finery are illusions.
Sometimes there cometh up the semblance of wealth;
Whensoever the semblance of money shall arise,
Instead of money, seize on the Seven Jewels of the Saints;
Learn that all things costly are illusions.
Sometimes there cometh up the appearance of Friends;
Whensoever the semblance of friends shall arise,
Instead of friends, confide in the Wisdom that is Self-sprung;
Know all comrades and acquaintance to be illusions.

* * * * * * *

Nevertheless, knowing everything to be illusive,
That which is profound may arise—THE HARE WITH A HORN.
That Horn is as a King seated on the divan;
Behind, it is like a white flag uplifted on a hill;
In front, it resembles a mound heaped with precious things;
At the summit, it is like a jewelled cock's-comb;
It is as officers bending low on seven mountains;
It resembles a maṇḍal of gold in a wooded meadow.
Those destined for conversion are on such a hill as that;
And you, when you have gone thither, accomplish their conversion!

Having devised some such imaginary *mig-te'* as the above, the Meditator must assume the prescribed pose of the body. In order to take this attitude the limbs and facial organs should be disposed in accordance with the following seven conditions known as the *Nedün*:—

1. ཕྱག་གཉིས་མཉམ་བཞག་ཏུ་བཞག་སོང་ Hands loosely united over the stomach, the fingers enfolded but the thumbs extended apart.

2. སྐུ་རྡོ་རྗེ་སྐྱིལ་ཀྲུང་བཞུགས་སོང་ The body seated, with the legs folded inwards and crossed, with the top of each foot turned over resting the toes on the thigh opposite and the soles of the feet turned uppermost.

3. རྒྱལ་ཚིགས་མདའ་ལྟར་སྲུང་སོང་ The backbone on the alert straight as an arrow.

4. དཔུང་པ་རྒོད་ཤོག་པ་ལྟར་སྲུང་པ་ལ་ The shoulders slightly rounded but on the watch as the wings of a hovering eagle.

5. མིག་སྣ་རྩེར་འབེབས་པ་ལ་ The eyes looking down on the tip of the nose.

6. མཆུ་དང་འབབ་ཏུ་བཞག་པ་ལ་ The lips adjusted one upon the other.

7. ལྕེ་རྩེ་ཡ་དཀན་ལ་སྦྱར་བ་ལ་ The tip of the tongue adhering to the roof of the mouth.

In order to pass beyond the second or *Gompa* stage and so to reach the third and supreme position, that of སྒྲུབ་པ་ *Sgrubpa* CONSUMMATION, the devotee must acquire and become a complete expert in a certain physical process connected with the breath. This process is known as Arterial Absorption.

It is part of Buddhist Tantrik science to believe and teach that the breath may be drawn in by numerous successive inspirations, with as little expiration as possible, so as to be forced into the main arteries of the body. Practice, they allege, produces great expertness in holding in the breath and pumping it into the blood, where it causes a magical warmth and an ecstatic giddiness in the head. Three conduits are supposed to proceed from the heart, and by this process the airy humour in the body known as *Rlung* is said to be drawn from two of these—the *ro-ma* and the *kyang-ma*—and forced into the centre one—the *u-ma*. The Tibetan letter ཨ་ is said to be a diagram of these conduits and passages. It is when the *Rlung* is in the *u-ma* that a mystic heat is promoted throughout the whole frame, necessitating the gradual casting aside of every garment in the coldest weather. With this, meditation waxes hot likewise, and at length the intense mental concentration causes *Sem*—a vital elixir which nourishes the soul during its residence in the body—to pass also into the *u-ma*, where it at once unites with the *Rlung* present. That is the zenith of the process, and at this stage the devotee is believed to be emancipated from the laws of gravity, and to be able to expand and to contract his body to an indefinite extent, causing monstrous illusions to by-standers. The fit of *Tum-mo*, as it is termed, then subsides; but the meditative glow or *de-tö* continues, enhancing the power of contemplation for days, and advancing him along the path to *ngoi-dup* or transcendental wisdom.

CHAPTER XV.

MAMMALIA OF TIBET.

The fauna of Tibet is, like all else connected with this land, singular and set apart from that prevailing in other countries. It may be said to possess two remarkable characteristics. First, the extraordinary abundance of animal life, both wild and domestic; secondly, the unique nature of nearly all the species found.

I. For regions so elevated, the quantity and variety of quadrupeds are certainly phenomenal. In a country of great fertility and with temperate or tropical climate, one might expect to find in the sparsely inhabited districts a surplusage of wild animals. But in a land such as Tibet, notable for its scanty vegetation and the rigour of its seasons, with an altitude of unparalleled loftiness, such profusion as really exists is somewhat startling. Especially on the great northern tracts, where the elevation ranges from 15,500 to 17,500 feet above the sea, does this plethora of mammalian life prevail. During the summer season the Jhang-t'ang (as those parts are styled) teems with all kinds of game. Herds, numerically immense, of the herbivorous species such as yak, antelope, wild ass, goat, and wild sheep, roam everywhere over the open, shallow valleys. Nor are the carnivora wanting; for wolves, lynx, and bears haunt in large numbers the same realms, preying on the grass-feeders, while, again, a multitude of smaller rodents, as the hare, the marmot, and the lagomys—each in several varieties—are never absent from the same wondrous grounds. Neither in the depths of winter are these tracts altogether destitute. The brave travellers, who in recent years have crossed the upper regions of the north when valleys were snow-fields and rivers lay ice-bound, report the presence of yaks and hares and antelopes which they have observed scratching below the snow for the possibly-surviving herbage in January and February.

However, the southern districts of Tibet are hardly as prolific as the northern steppes. The elevation is generally of much lower average—the upland pastures and lake-side fens varying from 13,000 to

15,000 feet, the river-valleys from 11,000 to 13,000 feet. But here, too, exist large quantities of mammals—wild ass, ovis ammon, gazelle and ibex on the mountain crags; stags on the scrub-yielding plains; musk-deer and *napo* in the lower valleys—while, to the S.E., the fauna, though different, seems quite equally abundant.

It may be interesting at this point to supplement these general statements by quoting from the reports of recent travellers particular instances of the vast concourse of various animals observable everywhere in Tibet.

Mr. Rockhill, passing through the country some 90 miles S.S.W. of Kökö Nor at an average altitude of 14,000 feet, towards the close of April, remarks: "The country was everywhere literally alive with game; yak and wild asses were particularly plentiful, but *orungo* and *tsérin* antelopes, wild goats, bears, wolves, hares, ducks, geese, sheldrakes, sand grouse, and partridges, were also met in vast numbers."

A. K. brought back extraordinary accounts of the herds of wild creatures encountered by him on the plains just north of the Dang La range, circa long. 92°—93° E. in October 1879. He speaks of the country being over-run with enormous numbers of *dong* (wild yak), *cho* (a deer), *goa* (chamois), *na* (wild goat), *nyen* (ovis ammon), *changku* (wolf), *yi* (lynx), *kyang* (wild ass), *chipi* (marmot), and so forth. The elevation here averaged 14,700 feet.

Dr. Thorold, summing up the animals seen during his journey across Tibet, keeping between lat. 33° and 34° N. and thereabouts in the height of summer, writes: "The high central plateau of Tibet appears to be densely stocked with animal life. Yak, Hodgson's antelope, ravine deer, kiang, barhal, ovis ammon, wild dog, gray wolf, were the larger well-known animals met with in suitable ground, often in immense numbers. Herds of 40 to 80 yak—bulls, cows, and calves together—were seen grazing in sheltered valleys on the hill-sides. As many as 300 kiang, 700 or 800 antelope, and 80 or 100 ravine deer, were sometimes viewed on the same day."

Then, in quite a different district a few miles east of the easternmost upper waters of the Indus, one of the Survey pundits—when crossing the Nagts'al range 60 miles N.E. of Manasarowar Lake—saw: "a very large herd of wild yak; his party counting over 300 before the herd ran off. Those yaks, called "dong," were mostly seen between Majin Kinglo and the Manasarowar lake. Great herds of wild asses were observed throughout, some 200 in sight at the same time. The Hodgsonian antelope, wild goats, and sheep (the latter including the gigantic ovis ammon) were all seen in numbers. Large grey wolves were constantly noticed, but never more than two or three at a time; and packs of wild dogs were heard yelling at night. Numbers of reddish hares and a kind of fox were seen on every march."

Finally may be quoted an extract from the report on the lofty plateau separating the two branches of the early Indus in the Gartok district of Ngari Khorsum: "In spite of the desolate aspect of the mountains traversed, the number of wild animals was remarkable—quantities of Tibetan antelopes, wild asses, yaks, yellow wolves, hares, and marmots. Wild fowls swarmed on some of the small lakes, and ravens used to visit the camp in pairs."

From statements of this sort it may be assumed, we imagine, that any sportsman lucky enough to be admitted on a leisurely trip through Tibet would most probably be able to rival the bags of large game once possible to a Gordon Cumming in South Africa. But, personally, we shall be truly overjoyed if the mere slaughterer of animals be forever excluded, lest this land also become one day as bereft of magnificent herds as is the greater part of the Africa of present times.

Now, we do not at all consider it to be either necessary or possible to discover set causes for every remarkable fact in the physical world. The vagaries of nature, particularly when they prove inexplicable to modern science, are a delight to us. Yet, in the present case, it may be owned, that reasons apparently sound can be assigned in part explanation of the phenomenon of the crowded state of animated nature in these regions.

Accordingly, first, let it be observed, that explorers of the territory under review, such as Przhevalsky, A.K., Captain Bower Obruchev, and Mr. St. George Littledale, unanimously agree in noting the abundance of coarse grasses which for some four months cover valley-bottom and undulating hillside through the major extent of North Tibet. The curious rapidity of its maturation combined with a certain uncouth luxuriance are features of these vast stretches of pasturage. Much herbivorous food for a certain short space of the year is accordingly provided for the troops of living creatures existing there. During those months, at least for animals, the food supply is practically inexhaustible; and the fact that they increase prodigiously and appear well-fattened, indicates that the herbage, though of coarse quality, must be exceedingly nutrient. One other fact, moreover, should not pass unmentioned. While the beasts flourish on the yield of grass, so does the grass in its turn derive rich sustenance from the feeders in the shape of ample supplies of manure. Thus the pendulum of inter-dependence once set swinging, the source of mutual support becomes ceaseless. Such is the reciprocity which the Creator has made inherent throughout nature.

But there is a fact unexplainable in the existence of animal life on a scale so enormous in these inhospitable heights. How do the countless thousands find the barest sufficiency during the winter—in many parts for at least seven months in the year? Grubbing beneath the snow would appear hardly likely to afford any sustenance for the majority. Great numbers miserably perish, as their skeletons fully testify. Whence, however, so considerable a portion draw their winter supply of food is still not evident.

Secondly, in seeking to account for the vast army of wild quadrupeds in Tibet, another plain reason can be reckoned. With the Buddhist population of Tibet there is ever the strongest repugnance to the slaughter of game. Although their doctrine of transmigration does not seem to hinder them from being mighty feeders on the flesh of domestic animals which they have certain methods of slaying satisfactory to their religious sense, yet the killing of wild animals is greatly disapproved of. Carnivorous beasts are rarely shot by Tibetans; while near monasteries no wild creatures whatever are permitted to be molested. Such localities as the Yamdok peninsula, the banks of the Yeru Tsangpo between Shigatse and Tse-t'ang, and the beautiful valleys of Riwochhe, are described by travellers as magnificent game-preserves, stocked with pheasants, hare, and deer, of many kinds, which are never disturbed or shot over.

Although we have thus endeavoured to point out that at certain seasons of the year there is an ample provision of food for the sustenance of vast numbers of animals, we do not pretend to account for their actual presence in the country in such force or to have solved the problem of their support throughout the year. No one can term the vegetation of Tibet in any sense luxuriant, yet the fact remains that animals of the larger kinds flourish there in astonishing profusion.

Tibet is not, however, the only region of the earth where conditions of this apparently contradictory nature prevail or at least once prevailed. South Africa is or was a case in point. Dr. Charles Darwin, in his fascinating *Journal of the Voyage of H.M.S. Beagle*, draws special attention to the case of Africa. He places in contrast the wide plains of that country with their wretched poverty of vegetation and the swarms of wild animals, mostly of great bulk, inhabiting and multiplying on those plains. He does not profess, moreover, to account for the puzzling fact. He only concludes that no close relation, therefore, exists between the number of animals or their large size, and the quantity of vegetation in the countries they inhabit. Thence, also, he deduces his desired point, that the fact of many large quadrupeds found fossilized in the strata of the tertiary epochs does not necessarily prove the existence at those periods of a luxuriant vegetation to sustain them.

II.—Passing, next, to the second feature of the Tibetan fauna, let the unique quality of the species be considered. Mr. W. T. Blanford, the most discerning of modern naturalists, has in his zoological papers more than once pointed out what he terms "the remarkable specialization of the mammalian fauna inhabiting the Tibetan plateau."

Mr. Blanford gives a list of 46 different mammals known to inhabit the tracts north of the Himalayas and south of the Kuen-lün and Nan-shan ranges at elevations exceeding 12,000 feet. Out of these 46, he distinguishes no fewer than 31 as animals not known to exist beyond the confines of Tibet; and among these 31 he notes that in addition to so many species peculiar to the country there are five new genera of which no representatives occur elsewhere.

We should hardly venture to avow any difference of opinion from so high a zoological authority as Mr. Blandford, nevertheless we should like to point out that his list might be legitimately extended. For example, if he includes *Budorcas taxicolor*, he can hardly with justice omit *Nemorhædus Edwardsii*, *Moschus Sifanicus*, *Kemas cinerea*, and *Sus Moupinensis*, all of which were met with first and are still found in approximately the same quarter of Eastern Tibet. Then we should like to see the yellow wolf and the black wolf differentiated as species. Can they be local variations of the same wolf, as they both occur in one district and side by side? Moreover, the natives regard them as distinct kinds; they have different names for them, and aver that they never interbreed. General Kinloch, also, has noted several radical contrasts in their structure as well as in their colouring. Again, from information supplied us from Tibetan sources, there seems little room to doubt that other species of fox, besides *flavescens* and *ferrilatus*, exist in the country. Tibetans themselves count four different kinds which are styled *wámo, wátse, wátrotro,* and *wánák* respectively. Next, must be put forward the claims of both the tiger and the leopard. The thick-furred, broad-headed, Chinese variety of the former is frequently seen between Litang and Darchendo, at heights approaching 12,000 feet; while both the tiger and the leopard were reported to Père Armand David as occurring between his "Moupin" and the Derge territory to the west, *i.e.*, still further within Tibet. Also two leopard-cats hail from these districts, and another cat has been described by the various Russian travellers who have explored the southern or Tibetan base of the Kuen Lün range.[1] Furthermore, with regard

[1] Mr. Blanford has included *Paradoxurus laniger* in his list; but perhaps this mythical creature should now be omitted from zoological enumerations.

to the smaller insectivora and rodentia the principle of selection for inclusion in Mr. Blanford's list is not clearly apparent. Where, for example, are "the musky mole" '*Scaptocheiros moschatus*' and that nondescript outcast from the genus Talpa '*Scaptonyx fuscicaudatus*,' together with *Uropsilus soricipes*, all of which frequent the Tsaidam region south of the Altan Tag range near the head-waters of the Hoang-ho? Where, likewise, are many items of Lepus, Arvicola, Mus, and Hystrix? Finally, Mr. Blanford has entirely barred out all Quadrumana and, with the exception of Eupetaurus, all the Pteromyidæ.

On the whole, we think, it is undesirable in compiling any catalogue of Tibetan mammals to fix any limit of altitude as a condition of admission thereto. Many writers are unaware of the variability in the range of elevation occurring in every part of the regions in question. Thus Mr. Blanford names the geographical boundaries of what is commonly designated "the Tibetan plateau"—though plateau it is not—and takes the lowest limit of altitude within those boundaries at 12,000 feet. As a matter of fact, no river-valley of Central Tibet east of longitude 90° E. and south of the latitude of Lhásа attains that height. The extensive valley of the Yeru Tsangpo east of Shigatse and west of Tse-t'ang (both towns in the heart of Tibet) averages 11,000 feet; and east of Tse-t'ang (lat. 29, 15. N. long. 91° 43'E), it rapidly drops towards 10,000 feet. But in estimating the fauna of Tibet it would be ridiculous to exclude from our purview the river-valleys, to which, moreover, such characteristic items as the musk-deer, otter, and hedgehog are confined. Down to the south, towards one portion of the Nepal frontier, Tibetan territory sinks still lower; and Kirong, an important Tibetan town with small district attached, registers only 9,075 feet above the level of the sea. Again to the far S.E., still in regions legitimately assigned to Tibet, the descent to lower levels becomes truly extraordinary, and the extreme point is reached in Zayul, where the chief town Shikha is marked at only 4,650 feet in altitude.

Avoiding, however, the inferior elevations in the southern parts of the country and proceeding due east only, towards the confines of China, we come down to 9,200 feet without leaving Tibetan soil. This is the altitude of "Moupin," and that district—although it is nearly 3,000 feet under his 12,000 feet limit—is undoubtedly not excluded from the jurisdiction of Mr. Blanford's list. Moreover, it is in these eastern extremes that some of the most curious and distinctive of the quadrupeds occur. Thus both *Aeluropus melanoleucus* and *Budorcas* do not seem to prevail at higher altitudes than 10,000 feet; but injustice would be done to the peculiarities of the Tibetan fauna if we fail to reckon these and others as within its sphere. However, on a later page, we shall venture to present a list of wider scope than Mr. Blanford's and one which will afford, as we believe, a fairer view of the variety and specialisation of the mammals of Tibet. All forms occurring between the southern and northern barriers of the country and between Ladak and the Szechuan-Yunnan frontier-line, at whatever altitude, have a plain right to be classed as Tibetan animals. Our list, however, is in a measure a speculative and therefore an unscientific one, several items being discriminated as species solely on native evidence and native opinion.

In examining the leading characteristics of the genera of mammalia found in Tibet, we cannot fail to notice the large number of herbivorous animals and small rodents. Of the deer and antelope kind, no fewer than 25 different species are met with; while as akin to these might be added thereto the wild yak and four wild sheep, together with two species of wild pig. Then the little creatures of the marmot class are an especial feature. Everywhere throughout the length and breadth of the land do their warrens extend. So perforated is all ground, save that on the steepest hill-sides, with holes and burrows, that riding is beset with continual peril. As many as four species of marmot are already known; whilst of the *lagomys* or "tailless rabbit" at least six kinds have been discriminated. With these might be linked the large variety of rats, mice, voles, and shrews, some of them of considerable size, notably *Mus flavipectus,* a huge fellow measuring 15 inches from nose to tail-tip. Of these smaller rodents and insectivora about 34 species have been recorded within the confines of Tibet.

In truth Tibet appears to be the land of burrowing animals. Numerous are the kinds of every class which resort to such methods of habitation or shelter. And that it should be so is most reasonable, considering the intense cold and the poverty of scrub and underwood in this barren-looking territory. Great numbers of quadrupeds live thus beneath the ground. We find for example the foxes with holes hardly larger than those of the marmots; and that the 15 kinds of martin, weasel, and badger—not to mention the otters, the porcupines, and hares—dwell down below goes without saying.

Glancing over the members of the fauna, still in a general manner, another observable point is that while several of the animals distinctively Tibetan, and found nowhere else, have a very wide range, being met with in every quarter of the prescribed regions, on the other hand a much larger number are extremely local. The wild yak, the wild ass or kyang, the Tibetan wolf, the Ovis nahura, the musk-deer, the Goa, and Hodgson's antelope, although known only to Tibet, nevertheless occur everywhere throughout that country. Again, in one quarter particularly, down to the far east and south-east, is found a bevy of curious mammals distinct not merely in species but even in family from animals belonging to any other land, and which are not seen elsewhere in Tibet. And under this head a few remarks should be made specially in the following paragraph.

That part of Tibet lying to the east and, more peculiarly so, to the south-east has certain unique characteristics. In its greater portion it is of considerable altitude—not indeed so lofty as further to the west, but much loftier than the outside countries immediately adjacent to it, *i.e.*, than the contiguous districts of China and Burmah. But in addition to its great general elevation, ranging in its average plane from 8,000 to 12,000 feet—the lower height along the eastern and south-eastern fringes—in addition, we say, there occurs this exceptional quality, that the country is mostly well-wooded and subjected to exceeding moisture. Moreover, for dampness of climate, we need not travel so far to the S.E. as Darchendo or the Yunnan frontier. Much further north, as far north indeed as Latitude 33° N., heavy rains in summer and deep snows in winter seem the normal conditions on the eastern borders. And the result of such unique circumstances—a position on the Earth's surface not greatly removed from the tropics, considerable altitude, and excessive rainfall—appears to have promoted a richness and peculiarity of animal life comparable to Sikkim or Malaysia. In the south-eastern corner of Tibet, in the wooded heights and deep river-beds abutting Yunnan, we have indeed the greatest variety of novel species to be met with anywhere out of Madagascar. Semi-tropical forms congregate here with others almost of palæarctic type, but all unique in actual species, sometimes even in their genera. Carnivora, large and small; quadrumana, simial and lemuroid; rodentia, arboreal and terrestrial, present a wealth of curious fauna which affords some half-dozen new items to every naturalist fortunate enough to penetrate these localities. If one form of deer, or leopard cat, or bear, or porcupine, or monkey, or civet, be found either in Nepal to the south of the Himalayas or in Tibet to the north, you are fairly sure to obtain related forms but of distinct species in the triangle of country between the three points Bat'ang, Darchendo, and Torong—all technically within Tibet. Our remarks are necessarily restricted to the mammalian fauna, but it may be mentioned that both the reptilian and the residential bird life are of a character equally distinctive and novel.

This district, which is watered by the upperportions of the Mekhong and Yang-tse-kiang, includes the S.E. part of the sub-prefecture of Bat'ang and the whole of the Tibeto-Chinese chieftainry known as Chien-chang T'ing. Forest, luxuriant thicket, river-gorge, and lofty mountain-ridge scaling up to 15,000 feet, are the physical features, with a general elevation not often under 8,000 feet. The region has been explored only in places by travellers such as Gill, Baber, and Prince Henry of Orleans and by naturalists such as Pratt and John Anderson, and by native collectors whose spoils have been assorted and appraised by Milne-Edwards, W. T. Blanford, G. Dobson, etc. So far as we know, the following are the species occurring in this region and nowhere else, save perhaps in contiguous districts :—

Macacus cyclopis.	*Capra Heurdii.*	*Pteromys caniceps.*
	Kemas griseas.	*Mus Yunnanensis.*
Felis tristis.	*Nemorhædus Sumatrensis.*	*Mus griseipectus.*
Prionodon pardicolor.	*Budorcas taxicolor.*	*Mus viculorum.*
Aelurus ochraceus (*var.*)	*Pteromys Yunnanensis.*	*Hystrix Yunnanensis.*
Lutra Salwinensis.	*Pteromys alborufus.*	*Manis aurita.*

Another portion of the eastern border-land of Tibet which has had some measure of exploration from the zoological purview lies further north, about 150 miles or so E.N.E. of Darchendo. It is often referred to in works of Natural History as Moupin, and always as having yielded some rare finds brought home by the Roman father Mons. David and described by Mons. Milne-Edwards. But where and what is Moupin? The name is given with such grave pronouncement by zoological and botanical writers that one would fancy it was as certainly known and well-established a locality as Assam or Yunnan. We verily believe that scarcely one of the writers who mention it so freely have anything but the vaguest notions of either its situation or physical circumstances.

As this Moupin affords a fair specimen of the country and products of the "no-man's land" running down from the Huang-ho due south towards Darchendo along the Tibetan fringe of the Chinese provinces of Shensi and Szechuan, we have taken some trouble to make out its exact whereabouts. It is a district or sub-prefecture lying between Latitude 31° 30′ and 32° N., and between Long. 102° 30′ and Long. 102° 50′ E., and is so small a tract that to write, "this species inhabits Moupin" would be paralleled by stating as the general habitat of the English weasel "it is found in Gloucestershire." The name Moupin occurs in no map, the fact being that the Abbé David has told us the Frenchified form of the Chinese name of a Tibetan district. Moupin, which should be "Muping-sze," is a Chinese designation for Nang-chhen Sbring-wa, commonly known to Tibetans as Drumba or Jumba. This Drumba, otherwise "Moupin," is occupied by a Sifan tribe and is shut off from China by a lofty snow-capped range styled by Tibetans Gyalmo Mordo. The average elevation may be set at circa 9,000 feet, and the climate is exceedingly damp, *rain or snow falling, it seems, nearly evrey day.* Though the Chinese are fast immigrating and burning the timber up in wasteful fashion, the country is still well-wooded and encradled amid lofty heights covered with trees and thicket.

We have made so lengthy a digression as this, because a full knowledge of the exact situation and physical features of the locality in question supplies us with a ready explanation as to why the animal-life there prevailing should be in any way specialised as it is from the rest of Tibet. On the whole, too, the country there, in quality and in its natural history, may stand as a sample of the entire mountainous region which separates Eastern Tibet from China. We shall not, however, here specify the considerable number of quaint mammals which were collected by Mons. David in Drumba or Muping-sze and made public by Mons. Milne-Edwards, as sufficient enumeration occurs in the general list of Tibetan quadrupeds to be introduced presently, and sufficient description of certain items is given subsequently. It may be as well to mention that a Mr. Kricheldorff, a German in the employ of Mr. A. E. Pratt, the naturalist, visited this district in 1891, but did not add much to the previously-ascertained information.

Reverting to the animals belonging to the main territory of Tibet, passing reference may be made to the curious under-growth of delicate down or soft silky wool which is a characteristic feature of the greater number of these quadrupeds. This pashm—or *lena,* as it termed by Tibetans—grows beneath and at the root of the outer hair which forms the ordinary coat of the animal. Hardly a single species of mammal appears to be unfurnished with such accessory covering. The goat is provided with it in its thickest and most perfect form; but in fact every tame animal, save the sheep and the horse, and among wild animals all except the marmot, hare, and lagomys, are supplied more or less with this warm under-clothing. Even the dog and the wild ass, the wolf and the yak, rejoice in their down of softest growth and finest texture.

We now proceed to display our speculative and tentative catalogue of Tibetan quadrupeds, which relates to all animals found at any height within the prescribed limits, and including also a few domestic animals. However, in common with Mr. Blanford, the entire series of Cheiroptera has been omitted by us from the list, as forming an anomalous section entitled to separate classification. Comparing, then, our list with Mr. Blanford's and on that account excluding the domestic items of it, we find there are 146 different species of mammalia occurring somewhere or other within Tibetan territory while he has reckoned only 46, exactly 100 less! Of these, 70 are, species peculiar to Tibet, in which number we do not include several kinds so far found only in the Kökö Nur tracts but which may be reasonably supposed to extend into Mongolia and Western China. As to unique genera confined to Tibetan regions, they may be estimated at five, or, with the peculiar insectivora of Kökö Nur, at nine. We are fully conscious that many items deserve to be erased by the new school of zoologists who prefer the word "variety" to that of "species," but we leave erasure to them.

The Tibetan native synonyms are in many cases here first published. In other cases a more accurate version of the name than those quoted in zoological works have been given.

A SUGGESTED LIST OF TIBETAN MAMMALS.

(Being such as occur between Ladak and the Szechuan-Yunnan frontier and between Northern Tsaidam and the Indian Himalayas.)

Scientific Name.	*Tibetan Name.*	*Locality frequented.*
	QUADRUMANA.	
Macacus Assamensis:	སྤྲེའུ་ *Teu*	Kirong, Lhobrak, Dza yul.
Macacus cyclopis:	ཨན་བོ་ *An-wo*	Darchendo, Da-yul.
Macacus Tibetanus:[1]	སྤྲེ་ཁོ་ *Shtre-khö*	Chhamdo, Derge, Zok-chhen.
Semnopithecus schistaceus:	སྐུ་བྲུབ་ *Ku-bup*	Lhobrak, Subansiri upper waters.

[1] Mons. Bonvalot brought home a species of monkey alive from Eastern Tibet, which was placed in the Jardin des Plantes at Paris. This was a female and was procured by him near Chhamdo. I am unable to trace any description or scientific identification of this monkey. Probably it proved to be *M. Tibetanus.* Kozlov also found monkeys in that region.

FELIDÆ.

Felis tigris (*var.* Chinensis):	སྟག་ *Ták*	Darchendo, Mouping, Huang-ho basin.
Felis leopardus:	གཟིག་ *Sik*	Bat'ang and to south thence.
Felis irbis:	གསའ་ *Sa* (in Ngari: *Shan*)	Ubique.
Felis macrocelis:	དཔུང་དམར་ *Pung-már*	Kirong, Chhumbi.
Felis malun[1]:	*Málor* (Mongol name)	Kuen Lün ravines.
Felis pallida:	*Getü*	Tsaidam, Amdo.
Felis scripta:	གུང་ *Gung*	Mouping, Tsárong.
Felis domestica[2] (*var.* Tibetica):	ཞུམ་བུ་ *Shumbu*	Ubique
Felis manul:	དབྱི་དཀར་ *Yi-kar*	Ubique.
Felis isabellina:	དབྱི་ *Yi*	Southern Tibet.

VIVERRIDÆ.

Viverra civettoides:	གསའ་ཕྱུང་ *Sá-chhong*	Dengri, Lhobrak.
Viverra————:	གླ་ལྡན་གསའ་ *Lá-den-Sá*	Lhása, East Tibet.
Prionodon pardicolor:	གཟིག་བཙོམ་ *Sik-chom*	Darchendo, Dzá-yul.

CANIDÆ.

Canis laniger:	སྤྱང་ཀུ་ *Chang-ku*	Ubique.
Canis lycaon (*var.*)[3]	སྤྱང་རོག་ *Chang-rok*	Western Tibet.

[1] Captain Roborovski lately sent to St. Petersburg several skins of this wild cat which he shot in the defiles of the southern base of the Kuen Lün.

[2] The domestic cat of Tibet is a most peculiar animal certainly entitled to varietal distinction. It is clothed not with hair but with close thick curly wool like a young lamb. In colour it is a dirty ochre; and Tibetans aver that it is invariably deaf. Mr. Paul, when at Darjeeling, had a specimen of this cat given him It came from Lhása, and was undoubtedly stone deaf.

[3] On the analogy of Gray's *Canis chanco* as the name for *C. laniger*, I would suggest *C. chang-rok* as the appropriate designation for the black wolf of

Cuon alpinus:	ཕར་སྤྱང་	*P'ar-chang*	N.E. Tibet.
Cuon primævus:	ཕར་བ་	*P'ar-á*	Ubique.
Vulpes flavescens:	ཝ་ཙེ་	*Wátse*	S. Tibet.
Vulpes ferrilatus:	ཝ་གྲོ་གྲོ་	*Wá-tro-tro*	Central Tibet.
Vulpes montana:	ཝ་མོ་	*Wámo*	Kirong, Purang.
Vulpes Tibetana:	ཝ་ནག་	*Wánák*	Central Tibet.
	MUSTELIDÆ.		
Martes flavigula:	རྡོའུ་ལོ་	*Toulo*	Ubique.
Martes toufæus:	རྡོའུ་ཕྱི་	*Tou-p'i*	Dengri, &c.
Putorius Tibetanus:	ག་ཤུལ་བྱི་	*Shül-jhi*	Ubique.
Putorius zibellina:	བཀའ་བློན་སྲམ་	*Kálön-sham*	N.W. Tibet.
Putorius auriventer:	སྦུ་ལ་ཁ་	*Bulaka*	Tsang, Dok-'tol.
Mustela erminea:	ཁ་བ་སྲམ་	*Khau-sham*	Dang La range.
Mustela temon:	སྲེ་མོང་	*Ṭemong*	South Tibet.
Mustela canigula:	ལ་ཁྱི་མོ་	*Lákyimo*	Western Tibet.
Mustela Moupinensis:	སྲེ་མོང་	*Stre-mong*	Eastern Tibet.
Mustela astutus:	*Sémong*		Dza Chhu valley, E. of Derge.
Mustela Davidianus:	དབུ་རྗེང་	*Ujeng*	Kökö Nur, Tsaidam.
Helictis monticola:	སྐག་དཀར་	*Wok-kar*	Dengri; Gandak sources.
Meles leucura:	གྲུམ་པ་	*Tumpa*	S. Tibet.

Tibet, should it be accorded specific dignity. The black wolf has been encountered not far from the Manasarowar lakes by three Europeans on separate occasions: Colonel Kinloch, Capt. Biddulph, and Mr. H. Savage Landor.

Meles Kumbumensis :	རྡོར་སྒོ་ *Dorgo*	Kökö Nur district.
Arctonyx albogularis :	གྲུམ་ཕུ་སེ་ *Tum-puse*	Ubique.
Lutra aureobrunnea :	བྲག་སྲམ་ *Ṭak-sham*	Ngari Khorsum.
Lutra leptonyx :	ཆུ་སྲམ་ *Chhu-sham*	Lho-yul, P'o-yul.
Lutra Salwinensis : [1]	ཆུ་སྲམ་ *Chhu-stram*	Ba-t'ang district.
Aelurus ochraceus :	ཝོག་གདོང་དཀར་ *Wokdongkar*	Zayul ; Subansiri valley.

URSIDÆ.

Ursus pruinosus :	དོམ་ *Tom*	Central Tibet.
Ursus lagomyarius :	དྲེད་མོང་ *Tre' mong*	N.E. Tibet, Amdo.
Aeluropus melanoleucus :	སྒྲིག་དོམ་པ་ *Dik-tompa*	Derge, Chhamdo, Szechuan frontier.

TUPAIIDÆ.

Tupaia Chinensis :	ཤིང་དིང་གླིང་ *Shing Ting-zhing*	Nyagrong, Mákham.

ERINACIDÆ.

Erinaceus auritus :	རྒང་གཟེར་མ་ *Gang-serma*	N.W. & N.E. Tibet.
Erinaceus Amurensis :	ཛ་ར་ *Zará*	Kökö Nur, Amdo.
Erinaceus———— : [2]	ཛ་བྲ་ *Zabra*	Central Tibet.

[1] This is a purely tentative name which I have ventured to introduce in order to designate a species of otter noted by the French missionaries as occurring on tributaries of the Upper Salwin. From their information it is clearly to be differentiated as a species peculiar to S.E. Tibet and Yunnan.

[2] A hedgehog occurs in the Lhása district, and I think it most improbable that it should prove of any known species when its isolated habitat is borne in mind. I have only general allusions to the animal.

TALPIDÆ.

Talpa macrura :	བྱུ་ལོང་ *Byu-long*	Yeru valleys.
Scaptonyx fuscicaudatus :	*Surâman*	Kökö Nur district.
Uropsilus soricipes :	བྲ་ལི་ *Práli*	Tsaidam, Amdo.

SORICIDÆ.

Sorex nigrescens :	ཕུ་སེ་ *P'use*	———
Sorex murina :	བྱི་ཆུང་ *Pichhung*	———
Sorex myoides :	སྟག་ལྷུང་ཅན་ *Tak-lung-chen*	Kirong, Lhobrak.
Anurosorex squamipes :	*Nomon*	Tsaidam.
Nectogale elegans :	*Chhu-jhitse*	Ubique.
Scaptocheiros moschatus :	གླ་རྩི་བྱུ་ལོང་ *Látsi-byu-long*	N.E. Tibet.

BOVIDÆ.

Bos Tibeticus :	*Báchu*	Lhása district.
Poephagus grunniens : [1]	*Wild male :* འབྲོང་ *Dong* *Wild female :* འབྲི་མོ་ *Dimo* *Domestic :* གཡག་ *Yak*	Ubique.

OVIDÆ.

Ovis dalai lama : [2]	*Argali* or *Kocha*	Kuen Lün and Dungbura ranges.

[1] Russian naturalists seem fond of discriminating two species of yak, to one of which they apply the name *P. mutus*. As we all know, the commonest form of domestic yak in Tibet is the cross-breed, the male of which is styled *zo-p'o* and the female *zo-mo*.

[2] The *Ovis ammon* of Northern Tibet is clearly to be differentiated from the widely-spread *O. Hodgsoni*.

Ovis Hodgsoni:	གཉན་	*Nyen*	Ubique.[1]
Ovis nahura:	གནའ་པོ་	*Nápo* or *Ná-o*	Ubique.
Ovis vignei:	ཤ་པོ་	*Shápo*	N.W. Tibet only.
Ovis aries (*var.*)	བྱང་ལུག་	*Jhang-luk*	Ubique.

CAPRIDÆ.

Capra Kashmirensis:	ར་བཙུ་	*Ráchu*	W. Tibet (Changchhenmo).
Capra megaceros:	ར་ཕོ་ཆེ་	*Rap'ochhe*	W. Tibet (Guge, &c.)
Capra Heurdii:	ར་ཆེ་	*Ráchhe*	Eastern Tibet.
Capra sakeen:	སྐྱིན་	*Kyin*	Ubique.
Capra sibirica:	*Ogáltsa*		Kuen Lün, Tsaidam.
Hemitragus jemlaicus:	ཇོ་ལགས་	*Jhola*	Kirong, Chhumbi.
Kemas goral:	ར་གོད་	*Rágö*	Dengri, Chhumbi.
Kemas cinerea:	*Yangir Yaman*		Eastern Tibet.
Kemas grisea:			Bát'ang, Dayul.
Nemorhædus bubalinus[2]	བསེ་རུ་	*Seru*	Southern Tibet.
Nemorhædus Edwardsii:	ཤང་ལི་	*Shangli*	Derge, Kökö Nur. Dárchendo, Mákham.
Budorcas taxicolor:	ཏ་སྐྱིན་	*Tákyin*	Dzá-yul, Dá-yul, Derge.
Procapra picticaudata:	གོ་བ་	*Goá*	Ubique.

[1] Of the *Ovis Hodgsoni* and *Ovis nahura* Mr. Littledale reported: "After leaving Tengri Nor on our return journey, we never saw but one lot of Tibetan antelope the whole way to Leh, but we passed through a grand Ovis Ammon and Burral country." He was travelling westward from Tengri Nor mainly between the 32nd and 33rd parallels of latitude, making for Rudok through the lake country.

[2] The Serow is frequently referred to under the more correct name of *seru* in Tibetan vernacular literature. Milaraspa several times alludes to it, and one of his favourite similes is: "lonely as a seru."

Procapra gutturosa:	རྒྱ་ར་ *Gyára*	Kökö Nur district Amdo.
Procapra subgutturosa:	འཛེག་རན་ *Dzéren*	Kuen Lün west range.
Pantholops Hodgsoni:[1]	གཙོད་ *Tsot;* also གཙོ *Tso* or *Cho;* also གཅིག་རུ་ *Chi-ru*	Ubique.

CERVIDÆ.

Cervus affinis:[2]	ཤ་བ་ *Shau*	Purang, Tsang, Chhumbi.
Cervus Thoroldi:	ཤ་བ་རུ་བཅུ་ *Shá-a-ruchu*	Eastern Tibet.
Cervus eustephanus:	*Bugu*	Kuen Lün terai; Amdo.
Cervulus lacrymans:		South-East Tibet.
Elaphodus cephalophus:	གནའ་ཕྱི་ *Náp'i*	Muping, Lit'ang, Ba-t'ang.
Moschus Sifanicus:	སྐུ་བདེ་རིགས་ *Kuderi*	Khams province and Z'ayul.
Moschus moschiferus:[3]	གླ་བ་ *Lá-á*	West Tibet, Nepal.
Moschus Saturatus (*Hodg.*)	གླ་ཕོ་ *Lá-p'o*	Central Tibet.

CAMELIDÆ.

Camelus bactrianus:	ང་མོང་ *Ngámong* (wild camel: *Ngá-gö'*)	N.E. Tibet, Tsaidam.

[1] This antelope was observed by Mr. Littledale as far north as the neighbourhood of Cherchen, some 60 miles north of the Akka Tag, the Tibetan boundary (*Geog. Journal*, May 1896).

[2] Three specimens of this fine stag were shot by the officers of the recent Tibetan campaign in the Chhumbi valley; and one was captured alive by Captain Ottley on the Lingma-thang in the same district.

[3] H. B. Hodgson differentiated no fewer than three species of musk-deer as inhabiting the Nepal and Sikkim Himalaya, namely: *Moschus chrysogaster*, *M. leucogaster*, and *M. saturatus* (see *Journ. Asiat. Soc. Bengal*, 1839, p. 202).

Equidæ.

Equus caballus *var.* Tibeticus:	རྟ་ངན་ *Tángan*	Tsang and north of Lhása.
Equus asinus *var.* Tibeticus:	བོང་གུ་ *Bong-gu*	Ubique.
Equus kiang:	རྐྱང་ *Kyang*	Ubique.

Suidæ.

Sus Moupinensis:	ཕག་རྒོད་ *P'ak-gö'*	Derge, Muping, Tsárong.
Sus scrofa:	*Bodong Gáhai*	Tsaidam, Shang, &c.

Sciuridæ.

Sciurus castaneoventris:	ཤིང་སྲམ་ *Shingsham*	East Tibet.
Sciurus Sladeni:	འཇག་མོང་ *Jakmong*	Kirong, Chhumbi.
Sciurus McClellandi:	གང་སྡིང་ *Gang-ding*	P'o-yul, Makham.
Sciurus Nipalensis:	ཐལ་བྱི་ *T'alyi*	Yeru Valley, Kirong.
Eupetaurus cinereus:	སྟག་སྲམ་ *Taksham*	Shigatse, Kyi Chhu.
Pteromys Yunnanensis:		Zayul, Darchendo.
Pteromys melanopterus:		Muping, Derge.
Pteromys alborufus:		Hor-chhok, Bat'ang.
Pteromys Montgomerii:		Lit'ang, Darchendo.
Pteromys magnificus:	*Jhiyum Chhempo.*	Yarlung, Subansiri Valley.
Pteromys albiventer:		Ngari Khorsum.
Pteromys caniceps:	བྱི་ཡུམ་ཆེན་པོ་ *Biyum-chhempo*	Bat'ang.
Pteromys alboniger:	སྦྲམ་བྱུ་ *Drembyu*	———
Pteromys villosus:		Lower Yeru and Subansiri banks.
Arctomys Himalayanus:	དཀར་འབྲིས་བྱུ་ *Kardripyu*	Chhumbi, Kirong.

Arctomys caudatus:	ཕྱི་བ་	*Chhip'i*	Ubique.
Arctomys aureus:		*P'iyá*	W. Tibet.
Arctomys robustus:[1]		*Chhip'i*	Mouping, Derge, N. E. Tibet.

LAGOMYIDÆ.

Lagomys Roylei:	རང་རོང་	*Rang-rong*	Sutlej Valley.
Lagomys Curzoniæ:	ཨ་བྲ་	*Abra*	Tsang; Lhása.
Lagomys auritus:	བྲ་སྤུ་ཙེ་	*Brápuse*	Rudok district.
Lagomys griseus:		*Práli*	North and Cent. Tibet.
Lagomys Ladakensis:		*P'itsi kyaring*	Changchenmo.
Lagomys ogotona:	འོ་གོད་ནོ་	*Wokhö'ṇo*	Tsaidam, Amdo.

FAMILY LEPORIDÆ.

Lepus pallipes:[2]	རི་གོང་	*Ri-kong* or *Ri-bong*	Cent. and East Tibet.
Lepus hypsibius:		*Ri-ong*	Lingzhi-t'ang; N.W. Tibet.
Lepus Tibetanus:	ཙན་འདའ་ག	*Chan-dága*	West and Cent. Tibet.
Lepus Yarkandensis:		*Tabshagá*	Base of Kuen Lün.
Lepus oiostolus:	རི་བོང་	*Ri-bong*	Dengri, Jong-nga.
Lepus tolai:	ཏུ་ལ་	*Tula*	Kökö Nur district.

[1] Captain Wellby noted the immense size of Tibetan marmots: "I happened to be taking shelter under a rock from a storm of sleet, when I saw sitting up below me some huge marmots. They were of an enormous size, as large as men." Again he once mistook a marmot with its young for a man with a dog (*Through Unknown Tibet*, pp. 169 and 186-87). These marmots occurred in N.E. Tibet near the early waters of the Di Chhu north of the Dang La range.

[2] Tibetans rarely if ever will eat hares. They assign as a reason that they belong to the same family of animals as the domestic ass! Moreover they give the ass and hare similar names, the former being called *bong-gu*, the latter *re-bong*, or "ass of the mountains." *Lepus hypsibius* is found in W. Tibet at elevations even over 18,000 ft.

Muridæ.

Gerbillus unguiculatus :		Kökö Nur district.
Cricetus songarus :		Garhwal frontier.
Nesokia Scullyi :	དསྨུ་གི་ *Muki*	(?)
Leggada Jerdoni :	*T'ang-gi tsi-tsi*	Purang (11–13,000 ft.).
Mus nitidus :	བྱི་ཙི་ *Jhitsi*	Ubique.
Mus caudatior :	*Jhi-nak*	Ubique.
Mus Yunnanensis :		Darchendo.
Mus flavipectus :	བྱི་དམར་ཆེ་ *Bimár-chhe*	Riwochhe, Ba-t'ang.
Mus Wang-Thomæ :	དབང་འདུ་མི་ *Wang-dumi*	Zayul, Dayul.
Mus griseipectus :		Darchendo.
Mus chevrieri :	ཙི་ཙི་ *Tsi-tsi*	Eastern Tibet.
Mus viculorum :	*Bitsi*	S.E. Tibet.
Mus sublimis :	ས་བྱི་ལིག་ *Sábilik*	Ngari Khorsum.
Mus pygmæus :	ཙི་གི་ *Tsi-ki*	Lhása, Khams.
Mus confucianus :		Hor-chhok, Derge, &c.
Arvicola Roylei :		Ngari Khorsum.
Arvicola Stracheyi :		Rudok, Pangkong.
Arvicola Blythii :		Pangkong, Chang-chenmo.
Arvicola Sikkimensis :	ཤིང་སྤུ་ཙེ་ *Shing-putse*	Tsang, Sikkim frontier.
Arvicola mandarinus :		Tsaidam, Sining.
Arvicola melanogaster :		Muping, Zokchhen.
Arvicola Przhevalskii :		Hu-ang-ho sources.

Hystricidæ.

Hystrix leucura :

Hystrix Yunnanensis :

Hystrix alophus :

MANIDÆ.

Manis aurita:	གྲོ་མ་ཟ་མཁན་ *Toma-zákhen*	Darchendo,[1] Ba-t'ang.

THE YAK.

NOMENCLATURE.—The scientific name *Poephagus grunniens* Lin. is by Russian naturalists and some German writers restricted to the tame variety, while the wild yak is discriminated as *Poephagus mutus* Przhev.—Mongol: *bukha,* wild yak, *sarlok,* domestic yak; East Turki: *Kutaz;* Chinese: *changmao niu;* Hindustani; *ban-chowr.*—Tibetan: *ḍong* (spelt འབྲོང་ *abrong*) wild yak; *ḍong-dri,* female wild yak; *yag* གཡག་ tame male yak, *dri-mo* འབྲི་མོ་ tame female; *drimdzo,* cross between common Indian ox and *dri-mo; dzo* or *jo* cross between yak-bull and common Indian cow, *jomo* (or *dzomo*) female of this breed and the most widely-used domestic animal in Tibet; *garpo* and *garmo* (sometimes *karwa*) male and female resulting from further crossing of *jo* or *jomo* with Indian cattle; *tolmo* further cross, back towards the yak, by interbreeding *garmo* with pure-bred yak-bull. The *dzomo* or *jomo* is styled *pien niu* by the Chinese and *ünye* by Mongols.

GEOGRAPHICAL RANGE.—The yak cannot in ordinary life exist below an altitude of 8,000 feet; and in the wild state it rarely wanders below 14,000 feet in summer or 11,000 feet in winter. It lives with ease at elevations of 19,000 feet; though, occasionally, numbers succumb to the extreme cold of great altitudes in wind-swept regions. The habitat of the yak in its wild state is the whole of Tibet save the South-East extremity. It occurs nearly everywhere from the Depsang plains near the Karakorums in the far North-West to the vicinity of the Atag Gang La in South-East Tibet and from the Sutlej and Indus valleys in South-West Tibet to the borders of Kökö Nor in the North-East. In the direction of Amdo the wild breed probably penetrates, in places, over the Chinese frontier, but keeps always to the south of the course of the Hoang Ho. In the bounding ranges of Northern Tibet the wild yak is often shot, being systematically hunted by Taghliks of Lob Nor and Cherchen on the Akka Tag range as well as on the Chimen Tag, which is a direct

[1] Mr. Pratt reported seeing in the market at Darchendo skins of "a species of armadillo." In all probability they were skins of the above-named pangolin.

western continuation of the South Kökö Nor mountains. A.K. mentions the Sait'ang plains north of the latter range and lying between lat. 38° and 39° N. as visited by wild yak; but, at any rate, it never crosses the Altan Tag range, though said to resort to the southern slopes of those mountains. On the Ladak side a few are found on the northern spurs of the Karakorums and a certain number annually visit the Chang Chhenmo Valley, specially in the Kyobrung offshoot; also the southern shores of the Pangkong Lake. In Ngari Khorsum at the present day none of these animals are seen west of the Sutlej, but one of the Survey Explorers reported a herd in the upland country North-East of the Manasarowar Lakes. Mr. Webber, forest officer, has also shot several in Purang beyond Taklakhar.

Passing to the domestic yak and the cross-breeds, those naturally have a wider sphere of habitation. Besides a widespread distribution in Tibet itself, they are common as beasts of burden and farm animals much further to the west than is generally supposed. They are in everyday use by the Kirghiz of the higher districts of Ili and Kuldja, and are met with in most of the Kirghiz villages of the Pamirs. Sven Hedin states that the inhabitants of the Eastern Pamirs live chiefly on yak's milk and on mutton; whilst it was on the back of a yak that he made his famous ascents of the Mus-tag-ata, and reached on this yak a point 20,660 feet in altitude. Again, in the Indian hill-states of the Himalayas, the domestic animal is reared in plenty. In the higher valleys of Bhutan, Sikkim, Nepal, Kanawar, Kulu, Lahul, Spiti, Rupshu, and Ladak, droves of yak form the most coveted possession of the people. In the Chinese province of Kansu, the slopes of the Nan Shan afford pasturage to vast numbers of the tame variety, and between the towns amid these mountains the traffic is carried on chiefly by yak-labour. East of Sining-fu, however, this animal is hardly seen, being replaced as a beast of burden by the mule. The domestic yak cannot live in Mongolia Proper or north of the Nan Shan.

PHYSICAL CHARACTERISTICS.—The *ḍong* in general outline is not unlike the American bison. It carries its shoulders very high, the neck sloping sharply downwards to the head, which is large and heavy and borne hardly a foot from the ground. Again from the shoulders backwards there is a slope, though not so steep, to the tail. The appearance of massiveness arises from the enormous masses of long woolly hair which adorn in an extraordinary manner the sides and flanks and hang in thick festoons to the hoofs, insomuch that viewing it sideways no daylight is visible between the fore and hind-legs. Nevertheless, the belly itself is really destitute of this drapery. The bull yak is naturally much larger than the female wild yak, many specimens of the former measuring 11 feet from nose-tip to tail-root, while the average cow does not exceed 8 feet. But the wild yak, though of great girth and considerable length, is not a tall animal, the male at the shoulders rarely, if ever, exceeding 5 feet and the female standing under 4½ feet high. The horns curve beautifully and present the points forwards. In the bull, their length is 30 to 33 inches; in the cow about 18 inches. In the domestic kind the horns are shorter and much more slender.

In the wild yak, its great peculiarities are the tail, the tongue, and the hoofs. The tail is a huge and singular appendage expanding in a cascade of bushy hair towards the tip, often measuring nearly 4 feet in length and 4½ feet in circumference. Tibetans designate it *Jukmai yab*, "the father of tails," and regard it as sacred. In the wild animal the colour of the tail is jet black, now and then speckled with silver; in the tame and cross-breeds it is pure white or else dun and sometimes a beautiful buff, generally one colour throughout. A pure black wild yak's tail of enormous bulk and spread fetches a large price as a *chowry* for importation to India or China. As the *ḍong* is an expert climber of mountains, the hoofs are adapted to that end. They are often as large as a camel's, even 18 inches in circumference. There are two toes, and these are of a prehensile nature enabling them to cling to rough and rocky points. Behind the toes are, as it were, large secondary hoofs generally carried off the ground but capable of expanding downwards to give a hold on glaciers and steep slippery rocks. The yak's tongue is a formidable object. It is armed with veritable hooks of horn, the barbs curving backwards down the throat. These are necessary to help to tear out and triturate the coarse wiry herbage, the camel's thorn, lichens, mosses, and rough *astragali* which it delights in; for, curiously enough, the yak will not eat corn, barley, or gram, though fond of a truss of hay or soft grass when available.

The tame breeds and *jomo* are much smaller in size than the *ḍong*. Miss Gordon Cumming alludes expressly to the former as "the little ox." Their general outline is the same, though in the domestic animal the arch of the shoulders is less dome-like than in the other. While the wild yak is pure black throughout, save for a few grey streaks on the neck, the tame beast grows large patches of white, yellow, and brown hair, and presents in general a variegated appearance. In July 1903 we saw in the Antwerp Zoological Gardens a herd of 19 yak, but they were all colours and small in size.

HABITS.—Stony valleys and the roughest mountain-sides are the yak's delight. Such desolate regions as those in the far North-West corner of Tibet enclosed between the Linzhi-t'ang plains and the Kuen Lün mountains do not repel it. Moreover, it takes a pleasure in clambering up perpendicular mountain-sides to protruding ledges which seem inaccessible to anything which is without wings. In summer-time, when the rolling shallow valleys of the Jhang-t'ang are clothed with their luxuriant and miraculous grass-crops, then the yak in vast herds roams with the wild asses and antelopes over the comparatively flatter grounds. But when the weather becomes too warm, the herd will suddenly retreat up some mountain-side even to heights above the snow-line. In winter it climbs to any altitude, rooting up the snow with its barbed tongue in search of yellow herbage, *saussurea,* and mosses hidden below. The snows of winter, however, often drive the animals to lower grazing grounds. Thus, to the Chang Chhenmo valley and to the Pankong Lake district, considerable numbers descend from higher regions in the winter, roaming there plentifully from October to March; luckily for their preservation, just at the season when want of leave shuts out the panting subaltern from these his happy hunting grounds. In the summer only a few stragglers come so near civilised territory. Small herds of from seven to sixteen animals are usually met with in the southern and western parts of West Tibet; but in the lake district of North-West Tibet the herds run to 40 and 60. In Central and North-East Tibet yaks roam in large troops numbering often 200 and 300. Captain Wellby, when travelling along the base of the Kokoshili mountains in North-East Tibet, notes: "On one green hill we could see hundreds upon hundreds of yak grazing; there was, I believe, more yak visible than hill." Mr. Rockhill, also, remarks upon the countless herds in the vicinity of the Dungbura Range, and estimated at "thousands" those which he observed, much further East, in and about the Tsulme-t'ang and Karma-t'ang—plains lying just East of the sources of the Hoang Ho. The natives of North-East Tibet and of Tsaidam make a regular profession of yak-hunting, sending the products to Sining and Sa-chu; while Taglik hunters from the Lob Nor region take back their spoils for sale in Cherchen and Khotan.

Bull-yak when hard-pressed in chase will readily charge, and native huntsmen regard the animal as ferocious at all times. On the contrary, however, Captain Wellby ridicules the allegations of Przhevalsky as to the perils of yak-stalking. Mongol and Taglik hunters, however, will never stalk the beast except in couples.

The skin, the flesh, the horns, and the hair of the wild yak are all prized. Leather of exceeding toughness and durability is made from the skin of the back, which the *Kowa Nye-khen* of Derge and Lhasa manufacture into saddles and harness of great repute. Boats, for transport purposes on the great rivers, are made from the untanned hide. When cleaned and combed, the long hair forms the staple of the famous black felt tents of the Dokpa nomads of Tibet and of the Tanguts of Kökö Nor. Felt and a rough unyielding canvas are both woven from the hair, which is of a coarse silky quality, and blankets styled *chháli* from the soft wool growing at the root of the hair. The fat is considered a sustaining and portable comestible. Captain Wellby notes: "The fat of the yak was so precious to us that we used to boil down every ounce of it and put it into our old cocoa tins. These cakes of yak's fat were very much appreciated by all. We used to knock off bits of it and eat it as if it were Everton toffee."

Uses of the Domestic Yak.—As beasts of burden in the mountains the domestic breeds are in request all over Tibet as well as in the adjacent Himalayan states wherever the elevation does not run below 8,000 feet. The trading caravans comprise many hundreds, that proceeding annually between Lhasa and Sining often consisting of 1,500 yak. Their rate of progress on comparatively level paths when loaded, is a steady 3 to 3½ miles per hour. Their agility and hardiness in surmounting passes deeply embedded in snow renders them invaluable for draught purposes. Though loaded, they will leap down sheer depths of 6 to 8 feet, alighting, heavy beasts as they are, without shock on their feet. They will climb ice-encrusted rocks and hard snow-banks, scraping out with their fore-hoofs lodgment for their steps as they advance. Again if the animal fall through a treacherous surface of snow into a crevasse of a glacier, it will, if not sunk too deep, carefully adjust its chin on the opposite edge and heave itself out on the other side by a superlative effort of leverage. So sensible is the brute that on suddenly dropping into some bottomless crevasse it will sometimes manage to root its body across the depths just in time and hold itself as still as death until the drivers loop a rope round it and cause the other yaks thus to haul it out. Father Huc, moreover, described long ago how yak are often driven on ahead over newly-fallen impassable snows in order to trample a passage for men and horses. Yak are likewise safe though disagreeable riding-beasts. Dr. Sven Hedin's experience of the Mustagh-ata mountain on this kind of steed is worth quotation: "You require some practice before you can feel at home in the saddle.

One moment the heavy animal balances himself on the sharp edge of a rock; the next he jumps incontinently over a yawning chasm, and somehow manages to secure a foot-hold on the opposite side. Sometimes, again, he pulls himself together and, with rigid immovable legs, proceeds to glissade down a precipitous gravel slope, where a two-legged being would inevitably come to grief. Riding a yak, however, is a trial of patience, by reason of his absolute sluggishness of temperament. He often comes to a dead stop, and has to be reminded of his duties with a cudgel. To any application of the whip he is absolutely insensible, whilst he looks upon a moderate blow as a sort of caress, and answers it with a cheerful grunt."

As a dairy animal the *jomo* or hybrid animal is pre-eminent. The milk is singularly rich in cream, notwithstanding the pasturage is of the poorest. When on a long march their nourishment is often mere scrub and picked up where they can find it. Girls tend the yak and accompany them, in parties of three or four, quite unprotected by male escort, to lonely and distant valleys for pasturage. Butter, which forms such a staple article of food throughout Tibet, is obtained in double quantity from a given amount of yak's milk as compared with that derived from an equal measure of cow's milk. Butter, made from the two kinds of milk mixed, keeps the longest. Placed in sheep's stomachs it will remain good in the elevated regions of Tibet for many years. On great occasions this butter, 35 to 45 years old, is brought out as a delicacy with the same pride that a British connoisseur shows in producing his rare old port. Tibetan physicians prescribe this ancient butter, *mar-nying* by name, as a remedy for epilepsy and madness.

WOLVES.

Nomenclature.—Russian: *volk* and *biryuk;* Turkish: *boré;* Eastern Turki (Kashgar); *buru;* Persian: *gürg;* Armenian: *kahl;* Thian Shan Kirghiz: *bürü;* Siberian Yakuts: *börö;* Mongol: *chono* (spelt: *chinoi*); Buriat: *shono;* Nepalese: *bowángso;* Tibetan: *changku* the grey wolf (*Lupus laniger*) and *changku nagpo* the black wolf (*Lupus niger*); in Lahul and Spiti *changku* becomes *shangku.* In parts of Tibet as well as in Mongolia there is a prejudice against using the proper term for the wolf in common conversation, and to use it is thought to portend the destruction of flocks by wolves. Accordingly a paraphrase is employed, *khyi-gö* "wild dog" and sometimes *jukma tülpo* or *juk-tül* "blunt backside." The Siberian Tatars have a similar superstition and style the wolf by an epithet almost identical with the second Tibetan expression, namely *sodan kuzuruk* "stumpy tail." Mongols use the paraphrase *görösön nahoi*, "wild dog," when talking of the wolf.

GEOGRAPHICAL RANGE.—General Kinloch's reasons for differentiating the black and the grey wolf of Tibet as distinct species are so well put, that we can only refer the reader to his remarks on the subject. The black wolf, there is the best evidence to believe, is restricted to the westernmost districts of West Tibet. It has been seen, or shot, or captured alive, near Hanle, Lanak La, the Pangkong Lake, and about the Sutlej tributaries in Guge. Mr. Savage Landor records having seen a black wolf on the southern shore of Ts'o Langgak (Rakas Tal) as he was gazing at mount Kailas across the lake; and, indeed, the Manasarowar Lakes are known by natives as a haunt of this rare animal. General Kinloch procured two cubs in the Indus valley, and these eventually reached the Zoological Gardens, London, where they lived 8 or 9 years and bred together, the cubs in each of these litters being all pitch black in colour. The grey wolf of Tibet is found plentifully in every part.

THE MUSK DEER.

The species found so extensively throughout Central Tibet and in the eastern sub-provinces of Kong-po, Kyung-po, and Chamdo, as well as in Tsang, is the type *Moschus moschiferus*. Skins and dead animals brought into Darjeeling vary considerably in certain points from this type. In parts of Tibet other species occur.

This deer is as an adult male about 3 feet 3 inches in length from nose to the root of the tail; rather less in the female. It stands much lower on the fore-legs than on the hind, being about 33 inches from the shoulder to the ground but 37 inches to the top of the rump. It has several rather curious points.

First, as to the hair, which is of singularly spiky texture. In adults this is of a dark umber colour, glossy, and of a close deep pile like a bed of soft pliable thorns packed together, the hairs almost rattling when sharply rubbed over. Secondly, the scrotum is in colour of a vivid scarlet, very peculiar in appearance. Thirdly, as to the two foremost canine teeth in the upper jaw. These protrude downwards out of the mouth, one on each side of the muzzle, from beneath the upper lip, imparting the appearance of tusks. They are employed by the animal in digging and scraping up scanty herbage on steep rocks and often beneath snow. During the rutting season the males when fighting are said to inflict downward blows with these fangs.

However, even when extracted, the length of the tusks rarely exceeds 4¼ inches.

The third and greatest peculiarity of the musk deer is the small hair-covered pendant pouch attached to the abdomen of the male animal and yielding the curious intensely-scented substance known as musk. The musk-bag hangs by a very short valve or stalk close in front of the genitals of the male, and in size is not often larger, in the Tibetan species, than a big hen's egg. In the Siberian animal the pouch is about half as large again. The bag of *Moschus altaicus* is smaller than that of any other species, and is perfectly ball-like and covered with hairs of yellowish hue. In the very young animal the bag is quite empty, while in the old and feeble the musk is small in quantity and poor in strength. At most, the best bag yields barely half an ounce, the usual amount in a good mature animal being one-third of an ounce of pure musk. In one of his voyages to Patna, the old traveller Tavernier mentions buying 1,663 musk-bags which weighed 1,557½ oz., while the musk taken out of the bags produced only 452 oz. This allusion, moreover, shows the immense slaughter of these deer which then prevailed. The musk is said to be secreted stronger and in greatest abundance in the rutting season. The secretion has a much stronger odour in the animal which inhabits Tibet and China than in that which frequents the more northern districts of Siberia. In the fresh state the musk has an extract-like consistence, and a reddish-brown colour, with an odour so powerful that the huntsmen can scarcely endure it. By drying this odour diminishes, and the musk acquires a friable granular state, and a dark-brownish colour. In Siberia the chase occurs in spring and summer. In Tibet the pursuit is restricted by the government to certain periods, and the bags which are obtained are stamped with the Government signet.

By careful removal of the bag, there remains the musk, which is solid, in grains of different sizes, adhering to each other, soft, and unctuous to the feel, of a reddish-brown colour, like a clot of blood dried, having frequently a number of hairs intermixed, derived from the inner side of the orifice already described. The taste is bitterish, acrid, disagreeable, and somewhat astringent. The odour is strong, peculiar (musky), penetrating, very lasting, and extraordinarily diffusible. It is stated that a single grain can constantly fill the air of a large apartment with a sensible impregnation for many years, without its weight being perceptibly diminished; and one part can communicate its odour to 3,000 parts of an inodorous powder.

It should be kept in glass-bottles, very closely stopped, and preserved in a place neither very dry nor too damp.

By the analysis of Geizar and Reiman it appears to consist of: 1, a peculiar volatile principle (which can exist in a free state); 2, ammonia; 3, a peculiar, fixed, uncrystallizable acid (these three are in undeterminable quantity); 4, stearine and oleine; 5, cholesterine; 6, a peculiar bitter resin; 7, osmazome, with several salts; 8, a mouldy-like substance, in part combined with ammonia, and numerous salts; 9, sand; 10, water, acid, &c., with some volatile odorous matter.

It has been hardly ascertained upon what musk depends for its peculiar properties beyond ammonia and some animal oils. Taken in the dose of a few grains, musk rouses the energy of the digestive organs; and it soon afterwards produces sympathetic phenomena, the powers of the whole animal system appearing suddenly increased. By repeating the doses till half a drachm or a drachm is consumed, the active principles penetrate the whole frame, influencing all the tissues, and exciting effects demonstrative of its stimulating property; the blood circulates with more force, accompanied sometimes with bleeding from the nose: the perspiration and other secretions are perceptibly increased.

It also acts strongly on the brain, spinal chord, and nerve centres, producing by large doses strangely severe spasmodic actions. Accordingly, on homœopathic principles unacknowledged by those employing it in their practice, it was formerly in vogue both for hysteria and epilepsy, administered in small doses. It has been similarly tried both in typhus fever and in Asiatic cholera; and in the latter disease it ought from its "provings" to be useful. In old days musk was said to exercise a powerful effect in cases of hydrophobia in the human subject; and in Tibet and Mongolia, where hydrophobia is often prevalent through the number of rabid dogs, it is now highly valued as an alleviative of the tetanus and as a professed cure. So, too, in Arabia.

The demands in Europe for this curious product has greatly decreased for the last 30 years or more. Its use in England both medicinally and as a perfume is now almost in abeyance. In Poland and parts of Germany musk is still employed for both purposes. In China and Eastern countries, including North Africa and Egypt, a considerable demand continues.

In commerce the "pods," as the musk receptacles are termed, are discriminated as of three varieties, which may be thus described:—

1. The Tonquin or Tibet musk, received from China, also imported direct into Kashmir and India, is made up in small oblong-rectangular boxes, lined with lead, and covered with paper or silk. Each bag, or pod, as it is termed, is wrapped in thin blue or red paper, on which are marked some Chinese characters. Sometimes the bags

are enveloped in a deep yellow-brownish nearly transparent paper, which becomes brittle by time. The most distinctive mark of this sort of musk is, that it is slightly flattened, nearly round and very rarely pear-shaped. The yellow or yellowish-brown hairs, chiefly at the sides, are often cut, while those which remain in the centre are darker coloured, finer, and less bristly. Generally the hairs converge or point towards a small natural opening. The pods are mostly about two and a half inches long, and one and three-quarters broad. The weight of different specimens varies considerably, some being merely three drachms thirty grains, others nine drachms forty-seven and a half grains; the average is six drachms twelve grains. The average quantity of musk contained in the sacks is about two and a half drachms.

2. Kabardin, Russian, or Siberian musk, is either received through St. Petersburg, or, it is said, sent to China, and laid for some time among the bags of genuine Tonquin musk, to acquire the odour of the latter, and then forwarded to Europe. The pods of this sort are in general larger, more oval, more compressed, and the margins often have large portions of the skin of the abdomen attached to them. The colour of the hairs is a dirty milk-white. The musk exhibits a more homogeneous and less granular appearance, having a much fainter odour and taste than the preceding kind. The odour is augmented by moisture, but is somewhat nauseous and disagreeable. Musk is more soluble in water than in alcohol. Of 100 parts of genuine Tonquin musk, boiling water dissolves 90 parts, alcohol only 50. Of Kabardin musk, water dissolves only 50 per cent. It is likewise soluble in ether, acetic acid, and yolk of egg.

3. A very small kind of pod is sometimes met with, which is not flattened, but perfectly round, the hairs of a yellowish-brown colour. This is probably the musk bag of the Moschus Altaicus.

It is safest to purchase the musk out of the pod, as there is then less opportunity of adulteration. Infusion of genuine musk is not precipitated by a solution of bichloride of mercury (corrosive sublimate); but genuine musk is precipitated by nitric and other strong acids, by acetate of lead (sugar of lead), and infusion of galls. The musk bags are used by perfumers to prepare 'essence of musk.' An artificial musk is sometimes made with nitric acid and oil of amber.

In spite of its general disuse in England, we still observe it quoted in drug prices current; and it still stands at a high price. Thus in the List of the London "Army and Navy Stores" for 1905, pure musk is priced at £1 1*s.* 6*d.* the dram; that is, £8 12*s.* per ounce. Per grain it is put at 5d.

CHAPTER XV.

THE FLORA OF TIBET.

In considering the botanical characteristics of Tibet, it might be deemed impossible to treat so large an area as a whole. Moreover, the general altitude of one portion of the territory is so much above that of other portions, which also in their turn vary in elevation, that the vegetable productions could not conveniently—one would suppose—be estimated on any common footing. However in the case of Tibet the difficulty of such general treatment is curiously small. Strange to say, notwithstanding the variety of range in the height above sea-level in different districts, the flora throughout these regions is with certain limitations remarkably uniform. Thus the main body of plants occurring in the lofty valleys of North-Western Tibet is analogous, at least in genera, to those found in the central provinces of Ui and Tsang, where the average elevation is some 4,000 feet lower; while, again, we do not meet with a dissimilar flora far to the N.E. and E., in the Kökö Nur region and on the borders of Northern Szechuen, although the main level of the territory there is from 2,000 to 3,000 feet under that of the central provinces. When it is borne in mind for example that the ordinary elevation of the country around the lakes visited by Captain Bower and by Major Deasy in N.W. Tibet scales some 17,000 feet, yet the lands abutting the head-waters of the Hoang-ho average only 11,000 feet or less, the kindred quality of the botany of the two areas is a little inexplicable. Nevertheless, it must be noted that the similarity only extends to genera and but rarely to individual species. But on this last point we shall enlarge later on.

In remarking the uniformity of the flora in its leading members throughout the regions under review, certain important exceptions have to be named. As you enter the south-eastern parts to the east of longitude 92° E. and to the south of latitude 30° N., the analogy to the other districts of Tibet becomes less noticeable. Going further S.E. (and approaching the confines of the southern portion of the Chinese province of Szechuen), even where the altitude maintains a level above 11,000 feet, a vegetation arises radically different in many points to that prevailing on the lofty ground west of long. 92° E. Again, the flora of the lower reaches of the Yeru Tsang-po, having an elevation ranging from 7,000 to 8,500 feet, although occupying a position north of latitude 29° N., cannot be classified with those of either of the spheres just mentioned. Still more distinctive is the botany of Zayul, lying between the 97th and 98th meridians and between the latitudinal parallels of 28° and 29° N. in the furthermost south-eastern angle of Tibet, but still within Tibetan territory. The flora of this district, together with that of the district further to the east just south of Bat'ang, resembles very closely in fact that belonging to Yunnan. Indeed we have noticed that certain items brought from those parts are wrongly accredited to Yunnan alone in botanical descriptions, perhaps through misconception as to the exact situation of the localities named.

Accordingly, in dealing with the present subject, it will be found on the whole that, ABOVE THE ALTITUDE OF 11,000 FEET, THE FLORA OF TIBET IS GOVERNED LESS BY THE DIFFERENT ELEVATION OF THE VARIOUS DISTRICTS THAN BY THEIR LONGITUDINAL POSITION. In fact, so much does longitudinal position seem to influence vegetation that plants found at 17,000 feet in Western Tibet occur at 11,000 to 12,000 feet in the North-East; and such occurrence is rendered more anomalous and unaccountable when it is remembered that the eastern parts of this territory experience a considerable annual rainfall and are therefore in climate much damper and probably much warmer than the elevated districts to the west.

There can be little doubt that in surveying the vegetable phenomena of the country in question, one portion of these regions must be of dominant interest. Tibet is mainly a territory of singular loftiness. Accordingly the character and details of the botanical yield of the higher tracts must form the central object of our investigation. We shall consequently limit the present account in its particulars to the country lying west of the 92nd meridian, which embraces all the most elevated districts, although at the same time it includes the valleys of some of the larger rivers and those valleys, even so far to the west as this, sink in a few places to a level rather under 11,000 feet above the sea.

For the purposes of any exact enquiry, which ours is not, it would be proper, as we think, to divide the regions west of long. 92° E. into three separate areas dependent chiefly on the leading physical characteristics of each. To apportion these areas, first we should split the prescribed territory horizontally into two great stretches of country, one lying to the north and the other to the south. The two belts may be taken to be demarcated by a southernly dipping line from west to east—dipping from about latitude 34° in the extreme west down to latitude 31° just beyond the meridian of Lhása; long. 92° being our eastern limit. Such a division is in some respects purely arbitrary and as a distinctive botanical line will not carry throughout. However, we may take the area north of this line as embracing a botanical zone fairly consistent in its products in every part, the general altitude, apart from the traversing mountain ranges, being from 15,500 to 17,500 feet. The southern belt of country, nevertheless, ought to require further subdivision, and cannot be viewed as a single botanical zone. The western parts of this southern portion are much higher than those to the east; and the latter, moreover, are everywhere cut up by ramifying river-valleys. Irrespective of the uniformity in genera which, as we have stated, governs the flora of the whole Tibetan plateau, there is in particulars a decided change noticeable in the southern zone as we proceed east beyond the 85th degree of longitude. Unfortunately we can only speak of the difference here in general terms. So, while we indeed imagine two botanical areas to the south, this meridian forming the boundary between them, nevertheless we shall treat of these hypothetical areas of the south under one heading only.

Our three areas might, however, be thus summarised :—

(1) The Northern; comprising the north-western districts north of lat. 34° N., and the north-central districts north of lat. 31° N., bounded to the east by long. 92° E. Geographically this area includes the Jhang-t'ang with the stony deserts along the base of the so-called Kuen Lün range; also the Salt-lake tracts lying N.W. of Lhása.

(2) The South-Western; comprising the country bounded by Ladak and Rupchu on the west, by the Indian Himalayas on the S.W. and S., and by long. 85° E. on the east; the northern barrier being a south-easternly dipping line from Lu-Kong at the head of Pang-kong lake to the point of intersection between long. 85° and the latitudinal parallel 31° 35′ N.

(3) The South-Central; comprising all territory between the 85th and 92nd meridians, south of lat. 31° N. and

north of the frontier line of Nipal, Sikkim, and Bhutan. Geographically this area includes the great valley of the Yeru Tsang-po along the central portion of its course through Tibet, together with the valleys of its many affluents; also the whole of the two central provinces of Ui and Tsang with the savannah-like valleys lying N.W. of Lhása to Nam Ts'o Chyidmo (Tengri Nor).

In examining these portions of country the main difference observable in each is said to be *the change in species* of the plants represented. With a certain number of important exceptions where the genera of one area are not found to intrude within other areas, we shall usually find a particular species belonging to one area disappearing in another but still replaced inevitably by another member of the same genus. This is especially noticeable in the case of genera so distinctively Tibetan in habitat as Meconopsis, Delphinium, Arenaria, and Pedicularis. Indeed the species of Pedicularis seem to vary with every district of the country, two or three species being peculiar to each district. So, too, with the many kinds of Astragalus and Oxytropis, plants conspicuously characteristic of the flora of Tibet. But instances of these and other genera with regard to the replacement of correspondent species will be particularised under the respective areas. Our leading keys to the botany of the southern belt are the results of the researches of the late Dr. Thomson and of Sir J. D. Hooker, supplemented by the information and specimens furnished by Strachey, Royle, and H. A. Jaeschke, as well as by Dr. Prain's native collectors. Dr. W. G. Thorold and one or two of the companions of Pevstov are for present purposes the sole direct reporters upon the northern flora; besides which we now have the collections made by Messrs. Wellby, Littledale and Deasy, sent to Kew to be adjudicated upon by Professor Hemsley. We regret that this chapter has been written before Professor Hemsley has reported.

The existence of any vegetable products whatever at the heights where they are found in Tibet seems almost beyond belief. We have in N.W. Tibet a vast series of broad shallow valleys generally of little concavity and developing almost into plains. These are often of great extent and bounded by low undulating hills not of any considerable elevation above the far-reaching bottoms. When occasionally the bounding ridge rises steep and rugged from one open valley, it falls away in gentle slopes into the level of the next on the other side. This contour is a common feature both in the northern and southern belts of the territory we are co nsidering.

But in the northern parts the general altitude of these shallow valleys is 16,000 feet and over. Nevertheless vegetation is by no means absent. Where the ground is formed of dry biscuit-like flakes of black calcareous soil, not a blade of grass will be probably found.[1] But the usual constituent of the valleys is a loose sandy gravel. In fact almost everywhere it is gravelly; and, when July has fairly begun, a coarse yellowish-green grass covers the whole of these steppes in innumerable isolated knotty tufts. The grass between 16,000 and 18,000 feet above sea-level is nearly universally various species of Poa, chiefly *Poa alpina,* but seven varieties or species have been noted. Also *Glyceria* and *Festuca* grasses have been found plentifully up to 16,500 feet. It is on these *Gramineae,* which spring up, mature, and ripen with incredible rapidity, that the mighty herds of antelope, wild asses and yak of these regions and the myriads of marmot and lagomys chiefly feed. Poor enough herbage it looks, and of miserable fructification and seeding power; nevertheless vast is the amount of animal life it sustains.

East of longitude 81° these extensive valley-plains of the north are known as the *Jhang* or *Jhang-t'ang ;* and except when the deposits of nitre and soda are in surplusage—for a certain saline taint lies everywhere in this region—the abundance of grass on the *Jhang* for 3 months of the year is proverbial throughout Tibet. Yet such pastures here in the north range from 15,500 to 17,000 feet in general altitude! And up there in summer the great herds are nourished and multiply. Moreover, Captain Bower writes of "long grassy plains" at an elevation of 17,600.

However, where Nature is less grudging in her inducements to vegetable life, grateful indeed is the response. Brown and yellow, purple and ochreous-red are these hills you are mounting; but now you look down from the top of the ridge, and lo! at the roots of the spurs, close below you, the brightest emerald green skirts in fringes right and left and thus marches forth into the plain. The truth is, amongst the gravel down there, a secret stream exudes; not indeed a gushing running brook, only a sort of watery suppuration. But it is

1 Moreover extensive plains exist in these northern tracts where no grass or vegetation of any kind is possible. Such are those parts where the chief deposits of borax are found; for example the vast desert country known as P'a-yul Bul-yul lying east of the T'abchhab Gangri mountains and north of lat. 33°. Soda and borax occur in such plenty in that district that the whole plain, which takes several days to cross, is a glistening dazzling white, so trying to the eyes that all Tibetans journeying there wear spectacles of yak-hair. Similar districts stretch E. S. E. of Rudok and near the Lingzhi T'ang in the far N. W.

sufficient, and in the damp and spongy beds it makes the yellow wiry *Poa nemoralis* become soft and verdant and luxuriant; whilst amid the muddy stones sprout up such small reeds as *calamagrostis holciformis* and *Trisetum subspicatum* with the feathery *Stipa pennata* and perhaps the glaucous-looking *Elymus Sibiricus* with its stiff spike and long creeping roots netted among the stones. Hard by are sure to be patches of that grass-like sedge so widely distributed throughout Tibet which was first discovered by the ill-fated Moorcroft and named after him *Carex Moorcroftii.* This sedge grows on sandy gravelly soil even up to 17,600 feet, at which height it was gathered by Dr. Thorold, and is greedily eaten by many graminivorous animals. Indeed this carex in certain districts forms the greatest part of the pasture.[1]

Happily in these lofty regions there is water provided beyond mere dribbling mountain rills and stony puddles. Travellers have recently revealed to us the existence of extensive lakes even at the greatest altitudes in Northern Tibet. In the N.W., amidst the long transverse mountain ranges and the broad-breasted valleys mentioned above, lie the large lakes visited by Captain Bower and Dr. Thorold in 1892. This group is distinct from the series along the central axis of Tibet made known by Nain Singh, and those of the group more to the west are not so saline in their waters as the central series. These sheets of water are the highest-placed in the world; nevertheless, such stupendous elevation does not prevent them proving a source of life to the country around their shores.

So far as we have spoken only of grasses, reeds, and sedges; but now, besides greater plenty of herbage of that kind, we shall also hear of small shrubs and flowers.

One of the lakes discovered in the N.W. by Messrs. Bower and Thorold was that styled Horpa Ts'o. It is no paltry pool, but a fine sheet of water some 18 miles by 15, and lies at a height of 17,930 feet above the level of the sea. Not only was pasturage found bordering this lake, but even flowers—dwarfed and stunted, it may be, but still flowers. They, moreover, were not all of them the mere stemless ground-buttons met with on the higher Tibetan pass-tops, but regularly-stalked blossoms. Those collected here were:—*Ranunculus*

1 Among the grasses of this elevated region, specimens of which were brought home by the Bower Expedition, was a new Agropyrum gathered at 16,500 feet. This new species has been described by Professor Daniel Oliver and named by him *A. Thoroldianum* after the discoverer. For description see "Icones Plantarum" for May 1893 (*Dulau & Co.*).

cymbalariæ and *Cochlearia scapiflora* on streams running into the lake; *Parrya lanuginosa* with small purple flower, the blue *Tretocarya pratensis* and the humble yellow-blossomed *Cremanthodium humile* growing among muddy stones; also a new *Braya*, and finally a *Crepis*, probably *Sibirica*. We particularise these as they are evidently prominent members among the loftiest-blossoming flowers known, namely those growing at heights closely approaching 18,000 feet.

Again, a little further east, on the borders of the Tsarol Chhe Ts'o (Bower's "Lake Aru Cho") at an altitude of 17,200, the adventurous captain records how they travelled "up the west side of the lake over a plain lying between the water and the mountains *covered with grass and flowers*." From Dr. Thorold's notes we find that these included *Adonis cærulea, Tanacetum Tibeticum, Erysimum funiculosum, Saussurea subulata, Saussurea sorocephala, Crepis glauca, Taraxacum leucanthus, Nepeta longebracteata,* and a new species of Saxifraga as yet undescribed. This seems a goodly list from an altitude of over 17,000 feet. But more occur than those. Amongst other plants met with on the more fertile high-level plains and valleys, the following occurring above 17,000 feet deserve to be mentioned: *Ranunculus pulchellus, Corydalis Tibetica, Sisymbrium humile, Braya uniflora*[1] (at 17,600 by Dr. Thorold), *Draba alpina, Capsella Thomsoni, Arenaria musciformis, Taraxacum officinale* (up to 18,000 ft.), *Senecio arnicoides, Potentilla pumila,* and *Gentiana squarrosa*.

Naturally one must ascend to the passes to ascertain what are the highest-growing plants on the Tibetan plateaux. Even on the pass-tops of the dark ranges separating the valleys of Northern Tibet, vegetation of a kind occurs. But the plants are mostly of tufted habit, nearly all stalkless and clinging closely and desperately to the ground as if to derive all the warmth and nourishment possible from the sterile soil. A small number only are woolly or hairy ones growing in matted tufts; and, strangely perhaps, the majority are bare and unclothed species. The chief exception is the *Saussurea gossypina*, known to Tibetans as *Yákyima*, which assumes the form of clubs of the softest

[1] Of this curious little plant which was first found by Dr. Thomson in Nubra (Ladak), and subsequently specimens brought home by Henderson from Yarkand and by Thorold from near Mangtsa Ts'o in N.W. Tibet, Professor Oliver writes: "It is the only member of the large and familiar Order Cruciferæ—so far as my experience goes—in which we have true cohesion of the sepals....It is singular that in an Order of considerably over 1,000 species, in a very large number of which the sepals are erect and closely applied in their imbricate aestivation, a tendency to a gamosepalous calyx should not be more frequent."

white wool; its flowers and leaves, as Sir J. D. Hooker quaintly remarks, being uniformly clothed with the warmest fur that nature could devise.

One of the most curious growths to be found on passes, up to an altitude of over 18,000 feet, is a sort of sandwort of monstrous development, which forms great hemispherical balls on the ground eight to ten inches in diameter. This is *Arenaria holosteoides*, and is termed by Tibetans *chiki* or "furry rabbit," who eat it cooked as a vegetable. Hooker states that it greatly resembles the Balsam-bog found only in the Falkland Islands and which grows amid very similar scenes.

Perhaps the plants met with at a higher altitude than any others are the two *Delphinia*, namely *D. Brunonianum* and *D. glaciale*, which are found on passes up to 19,000 feet, the first in Western Tibet, the latter in the neighbourhood of Lhása. The flowers are small but beautiful, of two or three colours; but they exhale a musky scent of a rank and penetrating character. Tibetans style both of them *láskar* or "star of musk." *Glaciale* is also called *ládára*. Two other species of Delphinium not growing at such extreme heights seem to have been collected by Dr. Thorold in the heart of Tibet, N.W. of Lhása. Next to *Delphinium* and probably occurring equally high up are several *Artemisia, Sedum, Astragalus, Saussurea*. Some to be specially mentioned are *Saussurea tridactyla* found at 19,000 feet, *Saussurea glandulipera, Microula Benthami, Dracocephalum heterophyllum* (which also grows on passes in Ladak, where it is commonly designated *shang-ku* "the wolf"), *Sedum Stracheyi, Arenaria Roylea, Thermopsis inflata* (found by Dr. Thorold at 18,500, with yellow flowers in bloom). On passes up to 18,000 feet are many others such as, *Potentilla polychrista, Corydalis Tibetica, Pedicularis tubiflora*, and including several species of a genus, *Oxytropis*, which seems particularly to affect the Tibetan plateau; six different kinds, three of which were at least new varieties, having been obtained by Dr. Thorold. Some species, as *O. chiliophylla* and *O. physocarpae*, form great circles on the ground; for, being perennials and the centre annually decaying, the new shoots grow outwards and are constantly enlarging the circle.

It must not, however, be assumed that only hardy and tufted vegetation with inconspicuous flowers can be seen at the climax of Tibetan passes, even though the altitude be considerable. Some most delicate and fragile-looking plants with large and beautiful flowers are occasionally found withstanding the keenest winds and, though the season is summer, having to undergo at night-time a temperature little above freezing-point. The stalks are under 5 inches or less, and they crouch to the lee of sheltering rocks if possible, but still they are there. One of these is the Tibetan blue horned-poppy (*Meconopsis aculeata*), which occurs up to at least 16,000 feet. So likewise grows that specimen in Dr. Thorold's collection described by Mr. W. B. Hemsley as *Meconopsis horridula*, but which possibly is not quite the same. Miss Isabella Bird refers thus graphically to this flower: "In the midst of general desolation grew in the shelter of rocks poppies blue as the Tibetan skies, their centres filled with a cluster of golden-yellow stamens—a most charming sight. Ten or twelve of these exquisite blossoms grow on one stalk; and stalk, leaf, and seed-vessels are guarded by very stiff thorns." Other slender and pretty flowers are a purple Aster, (*A. Tibeticus*) found up to 17,800 feet, the strong-smelling spikenard *Nardostachys Jatamansi* up to 18,200 feet, and a new species of yellow Iris gathered by Dr. Thorold on the top of a pass of 17,670 feet in lat. 32° 28′ N. long. 85°52′ E. To these should be added the Tibetan forget-me-not, *Myosotis alpestris* (affinis), with clear blue flowers much larger in expanse than its English relative; also *Androsace chamæjasme.*

And now we might introduce the trees and shrubs of these regions. Unfortunately in the northern tracts of Tibet, trees are utterly unknown; though in the river-valleys of the south, to which we are to refer later, the case is otherwise. Very few also are the plants in these more elevated parts which can be described as shrubs; and such as may be so specified are exceedingly low, trailing, and decumbent.

Perhaps the commonest shrub, and one familiar to all travellers in Ladak and Tibet from its universal employment as fuel, is the *Eurotia* known everywhere as *burtse.* It developes above ground an extensive meshwork of woody roots which can often be collected in large quantities; and being exceedingly dry they ignite readily and maintain heat a long while. It grows up to 18,000 feet and is rarely absent where the country is broken up into crags and ravines; but in the great savannahs of the salt country between long. 82° and 88° E. it becomes very scarce. There it is frequently replaced by a low bush bearing red berries known to travellers as "camel's thorn" and which is met with in the most barren and salt-encrusted deserts throughout Central Tibet, the Kökö Nur district, and Mongolia. Camels readily devour the whole shrub, thorns and all; the men relish the berries, which are dried and are said to resemble raisins in flavour. The scientific name is *Nitraria Schoberi*, and in Tibet it is called *taru*, the Mongols styling it *harmū.* Then there is the yellow-flowered Tibetan furze, *Caragana pygmæa*, the "dáma" of the natives, differing slightly from the European in not being quite so thorny. Its bushy growth affords excellent fuel; but it is less abundant in the Northern tracts than in Southern Tibet, where it is very plentiful. It lies in patches on hillsides, however; and often the more sheltered valleys even up to 16,800 feet have their gravelly bottoms covered with a luxuriant underwood of furze, perhaps swarming with hares which get up as you approach on all sides.[1]

Other woody shrubs are *Myricaria Germanica,* akin to tamarisk, called "ombu," growing thickly on the alluvial fans of rivers; *Lonicera glauca* ("shedo") up to 16,000 feet; *Ephedra Gerardiana,* up to 17,000 feet; and another miserable stunted species of honeysuckle with brittle twigs (*Lonicera quinquelocularis*). None of these stands more than 6 inches from the ground in the higher altitudes.

We have now apparently set forth a lengthy list of the shrubs and flowering plants of the Northern zones of Tibet; and indeed these names might be considerably added to. The collection brought home by Dr. Thorold numbered 115 species, all of which were obtained at latitudes north of the 34th parallel and at heights varying from 15,000 to 19,000 feet. However, 17 of these were sedges and grasses. Mr. W. B. Hemsley of Kew described and classified the whole. Nevertheless, although Dr. Thorold avers he gathered laboriously specimens of every scrap of vegetation he could find, his collection is not considered an exhaustive one even for these starved and frost-bitten tracts. For example, his list does not include all the species occurring in the herbaria amassed from the various Russian expeditions made to the south of the Kuen Lün mountains.

Taking the whole flora of Northern Tibet and separating from these all such plants as have been found at an altitude higher than 17,000 feet, we ascertain the remarkable fact that over 200 species occur above this height. Large though such a number, which does not include mosses, may appear for a region so elevated and exposed, we must put away all conception of anything like luxuriance or profusion. Beyond the growth of abundant grass, which from 15,000 to over 17,000 feet is certainly phenomenal, the character of the general vegetation in these tracts is as miserable as it might well be expected to prove.

On the whole, we shall be sufficiently impressed with the real

1 Although the Myricaria, Eurotia bushes and Tibetan furze are so dwarfed in the lofty parts of the North as to rarely exceed 6 or 8 inches in actual height from the ground, yet in the less elevated regions they present a very different appearance. Thus in N.E. Tibet, in the country lying between the Altan Tag range and the upper Di Chhu and in Southern Tsaidam, extensive thickets and almost woods of such shrubs occur where *Nitraria* ("camel's-thorn"), Myricaria, and Eurotia flourish as small trees 7 and 8 feet high. The elevation there is about 8,700 feet.

character of the botanic productions of the northern districts if one fact is borne in mind. Of all the plants brought home by Dr. Thorold and gathered at heights exceeding 15,500 feet, not a single species even in the middle of the summer season grew more than six inches above ground, while the majority rose out of the soil only from ¾ of an inch to 2½ inches.[1] Densely tufted and with leaves and blossoms closely packed on the ground is the prevailing habit. These often form sub-globose and hemispheric cushions, as we have seen is the case with the several *Arenaria* and is especially so for instance in *Thylacospermum rupifragum*. Both the scanty rainfall and the continuous violence of the daily wind have probably as much to do with the peculiar and restricted growth of the flora as has the excessive cold.

Another curious characteristic of all these Tibetan plants has yet to be mentioned. Their contracted and scanty appearance above ground is to some extent compensated by the extraordinary size of their roots below. To the meagre and often minute leafage and flowering apparatus seen on the surface, there is attached in nearly every example some enormous tuber or a long fleshy tap-root or an extensive system of underground runners, or in the case of the so-called shrubby plants a mass of woody fibres which eventually become exposed and dry up into a wiry tangle on the surface. In the Astragali and Oxytropes of Tibet, though the show above is so trivial, large fleshy appendages penetrate deeply in the soil. Sometimes the rootstock of the tiny plant is ridiculously long and creeping, bearing in its course many small fleshy tubers, as may be observed in one or two species of Cardamine. Moreover, in those cases where the rootstock is woody with a stout and heavy crown it is generally thickly clothed with the withered petioles and leaf-sheaths of past seasons. The Tibetan species of Anemone and Corydalis are quaint examples of the persistent manner in which the remains of old growths cling to the ancestral stock. Other types of the Tibetan style of root are to be met with in the underground developments belonging to Braya, Megacarpœa,

1 The self-restraint in growth exhibited by Tibetan plants is strikingly exemplified in the genus Meconopsis, which is all the more remarkable because that genus is essentially sub-alpine and alpine in its natural distribution, being confined to cold and inclement climates. Thus we find these species of Meconopsis which actually occur in Tibet either stemless or nearly so, while the scapes from the root which bear the flowers are extremely short, *i.e.*, from 3 to 6 inches in *M. horridula* and 2½ to 6 inches in *M. primulina* (Prain). By contrast, however, the members of the genus growing just outside Tibetan limits have tall and even branching stems with lengthy scapes, rachss and petioles. So *M. Nipalensis*, found in Nipal at altitudes between 10,000 to 12,000 feet, has stems 4 to 6 feet high; as also, *M. robusta* which bears floral cymes 2 feet long and leaves of 14 inches.

Chorispora, and Meconopsis—the appendage in the two last-named genera being spindle-shaped.

As one might well expect from the substantial nature of the roots, Tibetan plants are almost without any exceptions perennials. Such genera as Artemisia and Arenaria, which in other regions number many annuals among their species, are here strictly perennial plants, although the Tibetan species are comparatively numerous. Perhaps the only annual in Tibet is an Erodium; and it is said to be usually biennial in actual growth.

The curious amplification of the subterranean parts of the members of the Tibetan flora cannot be regarded otherwise than as a provision of the Creator for the preservation of life to vegetation in so rigorous a climate, where the extreme cold is generally unaccompanied by the preservative palliation of heavy falls of snow.

The inhabitants of these desolate steppes are not slow to avail themselves of this excellent subterranean supplement to the scanty productions of the surface of the earth. Several roots of plants are favourite articles of diet in Tibet. One kind is particularly so; namely, the large knotty tubers of *Codonopsis ovata,* which are eaten either boiled or else are roasted and grated into flour. Natives term these roots *Lu-dü* "knots of the Lu,"—the Lu being the nága or serpent god. Another root much prized is that of *Potentilla anserina,* a little fern-like plant called *Choma.* When in the month of June the first tokens of germination appear above ground, then the soil is scratched up to the depth of a couple of inches and quantities of creeping roots are found. To these, which are long and thin like dog-grass, innumerable little tubercles are attached, filled with a very sweet juice. Washed carefully and fried in butter the rootlets make a tasty dish, as good Father Huc long ago testified.

Another point of great interest connected with vegetation in the higher valleys of Tibet is the remarkable celerity with which it rushes to maturity when once it has appeared on the surface. The necessity for such haste is evident. In the upper tracts of 16,000 feet or so altitude, brief indeed is the period during which blade and leaf and blossom can remain exposed. Three to four months only elapse from the first sprouting above ground to the death and decay on the surface. The small buds begin to show on the plants as July opens, and in September everything with sufficient fertility has turned into seed. Dr. Thorold's last flowers at 15,000 feet were plucked early in September.

But, although the process of maturation is thus hurried, there is —especially in the all-important grasses, the Poas, the hardy fescue, and the universal Carex Moorcroftii—a fullness of growth and a sufficient luxuriance. Though the time is cut short, each stage of growth is complete.

Both Dr. Thomson and Sir Joseph Hooker explain the rapidity with which, in the greater altitudes of Tibet, vegetation proceeds to fructification by the additional power which the sun possesses in the clear untrammelled atmosphere of such upper regions during the summer months. But it is not only the greater vitalising influence of the sun (which up there is also tempered from burning and scorching when thus employed). Another force has been previously at work as well; and that is the anterior tonic influence of the intense cold on the roots and the early germination. This, as Dr. Thomson has hinted, causes primarily a checking of the vegetative organs below, resulting in a secret, pent-up stimulus to extraordinary activity afterwards above-ground, in which activity the unaccustomed clear warmth of the sun is of course a powerful factor.[1]

No agricultural operations are carried on in that portion of Tibet which for the purposes of this enquiry we have denominated the Northern Belt; *i.e.*, nothing is planted or reaped by the hand of man west of the meridian of Lhása in all the territory north of a diagonal line descending from lat. 34° in the extreme west to lat. 31° in the meridian of Lhása.

SOUTHERN BELT OF TIBET.

As we have already pointed out, some of the conditions affecting the vegetable world in Northern Tibet prevail equally in the south where, as in certain localities is the case, the plane of general elevation exceeds 15,000 feet. Moreover, as the passes of Southern Tibet are fully as ofty as those in the north, and indeed much higher above the surrounding country than the northern ones, we shall find practically the same Pass-flora in both zones. As a fact the difference of flora on Tibetan Passes is rather varied according to the situation west or east than

[1] Sir J. D. Hooker makes the following interesting observations on this subject in his "Himalayan Journals" "From May till August the vegetation at each elevation is (in ascending order) a month behind that below it; 4,000 feet being about equal to a month of summer weather in one sense. I mean by this, that the genera and natural orders (and sometimes the species), which flower at 8,000 feet in May, are not so forward as that at 12,000 feet till June, nor at 16,000 feet till July. *After August, however, the reverse holds good.* Then the vegetation is as forward at 16,000 feet as at 8,000 feet. By the end of September most of the natural orders and genera have ripened their fruit in the upper zone, although they have flowered as late as July; whereas October is the fruiting month at 12,000, and November below 10,000."

governed by the position in the Northern or the Southern Belt. Thus in Eastern longitudes we find *Parrya platycarpa* substituted for *P. macrocarpa* of the west. *Delphinium Brunonianum,* so frequent on lofty Passes in northern and southern districts of the west, yet is wholly absent on Passes of the same height in Central and Eastern Tibet, where it is replaced by *D. glaciale.* Again *Arenaria musciformis* found in W. and N.W. Tibet is ousted for *Arenaria pulvinata* on the Passes of Tsang.

Although the vegetation on the Passes in both Belts is in many respects identical, this is not the rule with the general flora. The main level of the southern districts west of the 91st meridian varies from 13,000 to 15,000 feet, the beds and valleys of the larger rivers being considerably lower, descending almost to 11,000 feet. Moreover as the same characteristics extend further east in the southern zone we have expanded our botanical area east to long. 92°.

The contour of the country now under review differs essentially from that in the north and middle axis of Tibet. Plains and high-level shallow valleys are no longer the feature. Numerous large rivers cause deep and lengthy depressions, and although there are many upland pastures and sloping hill-sides, the ranges separating river-basins are loftier and more abrupt. Again the bases of the mountains as they abut upon the great river-valleys are split up into deep ravines. Indeed ravines, long alluvial flats and steep, many-peaked mountain ranges constitute the leading qualities of Southern Tibet.

Summer being rather longer and winter less inclement at, say, 14,000 feet and under, we have more continuous pasturage, and even in winter, except when snow is lying, considerable grazing remains for cattle. And this is a main feature to be noticed, namely that the grass is not as in the north given up to innumerable wild animals, but is to a very large extent monopolised by domestic flocks and herds. Every place of importance on the map in the south-west has its double locality with its summer and winter pasture-grounds attached. The same name is used for both situations, which may be far apart, the summer quarters having *yarsa,* the winter *gunsa,* appended. Thus Gar Gunsa is the winter retreat of the shepherds and flock-owners of Gart'ok or Gar Yarsa, which is 30 miles distant and holds the fort and monastery. The main constituents of the grazing herbage seem to be *Poa trivialis,* a rough-stalked grass, and *Festuca duriuscula,* which are everywhere largely intermingled with the ubiquitous Carex Moorcroftii. Under 13,000 ft. Meadow Fox-tail prevails in many places.

The plants clothing the mountain-sides on the lower spurs, at thirteen and fourteen thousand feet, cannot be conveniently enumerated here. They include several varieties of Melilotus, Taraxacum, Aconitum, Polygonum, Potentilla, Tanacetum, Pedicularis, Oxytropis, and notably Iris Kumaonensis. Long patches of rose-red primulas are frequently to be seen at 14,500 feet bordering fields of snow. Saussureas and Astragali grow higher up; but in Tsang in South Central Tibet are such species as *Chelidonium dicranostigma, Aconitum luridum, Papaver nudicaule,* all found under 14,000 feet altitude.

Of course the vegetation of the river-valleys is of a different character to that we have hitherto referred to. Not only do we have another range of flowering plants; but we are now introduced to the larger shrubs and even to the trees of Tibet. In this lofty bed of the Indus and in that of the upper course of the Sutlej (where the altitude is over 13,000 feet) are lengthy alluvial flats and the fans of affluent streams, upon which grow only the coarser type of brushwood. Great thickets of the thorny *Hippophaæ rhamnoides* and of Tibetan furze occur there. These attain several feet in height—very different from the "shrubs" of the northern area—and, if villages or grazing grounds adjoin, are a special haunt of wolves, of both the golden and the black species.

But if we pass further east to the many rivers which flow into the Yeru Tsangpo, we shall soon find better things. On the alluvial terraces and lower cliffs of the rivers of Dokt'ol, north-west of long. 88°, occur numerous small willows and poplars. We have three species of willow—*Salix alba* or the "mál-chang," *S. daphnoides*, and *S. tetrasperma*—and three species of poplar—*Populus nigra, P. balsamifera,* and *P. euphratica.* Further east still and following the Yeru the appendant river-valleys become more and more fertile, until in the Penam-nyang Chhu (the river of Shigatse), the Yarlung Chhu, the Kyi Chhu, and the Holkha valley we meet with the climax of such fruitfulness as Tibet Proper can offer us. Not only do the willows and poplars continue and grow larger, but other trees, generally cultivated qualities, namely walnut, apricot, peach, and pear are common also. Near Lhása are to be seen junipers, large yews (*Taxus baccata*) and ilex in plenty. Those who took part in the recent expedition to Lhása (in 1904) speak of that city as appearing to lie amid a circuit of greenery, this appearance arising from the large quantity of trees with which the suburbs and the western quarters are planted. Trees there are most carefully preserved, and those in the city precincts are all numbered and registered, though two to three thousand in the aggregate. Another feature noticed on this occasion was the number of common English flowers cultivated in private and monastic gardens.

Among these, hollyhocks, marigolds, stocks of various colours, wall-flowers, nasturtiums, asters and large ranunculi were especial favourites.

And this at length brings us to an important branch of our subject—the interference of man with Nature and the extent to which the cultivation of crops is carried on. This branch belongs essentially to the southern districts.

Now, wherever the Tibetan can do so, he resorts to husbandry. He is a born farmer by instinct. In the northern parts of the country west of the meridian of Lhása, neither sheep-raising nor agriculture seem possible. But in the Southern Belt the conditions are different. In the extreme west indeed, outside the confines of Ladak, no cultivation of crops is attempted; and the inhabitants devote their energies to sheep, goats, and hybrid yak. It is said that nothing cereal is grown in Tibet itself west of long. 87°; and the inhabitants there depend for their grain supplies on importations from Ladak, Lahul, Garhwal, Kanawar and Nepal. East of Ralung monastery near the Yeru Tsangpo, the cultivation of the soil is first to be met with; and thence along the great river eastwards and up the valleys of its tributaries every available spot on terrace or alluvial flat is turned to account. Especially near and on the rivers of the central provinces of Ui and Tsang is agriculture pursued. Here the valleys yield long flats of rich soil, and numerous streams of rapid current debouching from the uplands render irrigation comparatively simple. Terrace above terrace is cultivated, and great ingenuity—akin to that of the denizens of the hills below Simla and in the Kulu Sutlej valley—is shewn in conducting water from below to the higher spaces.

On the Kyi Chhu or Lhása river, which flows down to the great Yeru from the N.E., there is as much grain grown as anywhere else in Central Tibet. Just about Lhása the valley of the river expands into a wide plain which is irrigated profusely by canals chiefly cut from a branch of the Kyi—the Pempo Chhu—coming down from the north. These are led from the Pempo a long distance into the Kyi and by a minute system of subdivision an enormous range of open country is artificially watered. As the general level here is only about 11,500 feet, every cereal and vegetable possible to Tibet is thus raised where there is naturally the largest demand, in the immediate vicinity of the chief city. This cultivation continues along up both the Pempo and Kyi rivers for a considerable distance. The fields are very small and separated by low walls of massive stones.

The highest latitude, west of 92°, where crops are produced in Tibet (not including Ladak or Nubra) is 31°15′ in the lake district and 30°20′ N. in the neighbourhood of Lhása. Rading, in elevation about 13,800 feet, is the most northern place in the Lhása district where fields are seen. However, in Eastern Tibet cultivation is prosecuted much further to the north than in the central and western provinces.

The most popular of the cereals are barley and buckwheat; of the pulses, peas (both Indian and Chinese) and a bean known as *taichung*. The barley is of two leading kinds : *soá* or *so-wa*, a thick-shelled sort mostly given to cattle as fodder, and *ne*, the beardless loose-grained variety (known commercially as *grim*) which needs little manure or depth of soil and ripens at greater altitudes than any other grain. The last-named prolific species can be readily grown up to 14,500 feet, and in a few spots it is produced even above 15,000 feet, Mr. Frederick Drew mentioning an instance at that altitude where 12 acres were sown with *ne* and yielded harvest. But at Ombu on the N.W. shore of Dangra Yum Lake in Central Tibet is the highest place where this barley is regularly grown; it is 15,240 feet in altitude. On the Re Chhu and Raka Tsangpo in Tsang province whole villages are dependent for food on the produce of this grain grown at 13,800 to 14,000 feet. It is from *ne* that the staple food of the country, namely *tsampa*, is prepared, as well as *chhang* the favourite beer. However, *ne* barley has three different varieties, all of which are cultivated. These are distinguished by Tibetans as *yangma* or *tukchu ne*, the early kind which springs up and completely ripens within two months after sowing; *chhe-ne*, a middling sort; and *sermo*- the best kind, which matures later than any other.

Buckwheat is largely consumed in certain districts, and is known as *dao* or *brau*. There seem to be two forms of it : *Fagopyrum emargi*, *natum*, a coarse hardy plant, and *F. esculentum*, a better kind cultivated only in sheltered spots near Lhása and in the Yarlung valley. Wheat (*tro*) is always raised where possible, but often fails to ripen above 11, 500 feet, though grown up to 12,650 feet. It is consumed only by the richer classes, and the peasantry profess to dislike it. Two kinds of oats are also cultivated, called *kátsam* and *yu-ku*, the former of which ranks above buckwheat in general estimation and is sown wherever possible. Rice grows nowhere in Tibet, but is imported from Sikkim and Tawang. Other grains raised where feasible are millet (*chhitse*), maize (*mámoipe loto*) and rape (*nyungkar*). Mustard is grown everywhere in several varieties, but is more plentiful in Khams and South East Tibet. Sometimes in the lower valleys millet can be raised as a second crop after the early barley (*tukchu ne*).

However, the favourite crops are root-vegetables. Radishes are the first choice, and are allotted as much space as barley. Turnips (*nyungma*) and carrots (*lapu-serpo*) are considered somewhat luxuries only obtainable in the lower valleys; and potatoes of two sorts—*sho-ko* white, and *to-ma* small, sweet, red ones—are largely planted near Lhása, though on the Chinese borders all potatoes are a commoner vegetable. Onions (*tsong*) seem to be widely cultivated; also garlic.

Agriculture on any considerable scale can be carried on only in the long wide valleys wherein the larger rivers take their course. Many of the rivers flow through valleys of fine open aspect, which, however, are walled in by mountainous sides, rising tier above tier in receding series, to varying, but always lofty heights. Along the banks of the river, which generally lies in a deep channel, are stretched broad tracts of land eminently fitted, with the aid of irrigation, for cultivation. These spacious flats have been formed of rich alluvial soil which the waters have deposited on either side, and which ages of such a process have lifted to a considerable elevation. In-flowing tributary streams, which run down from the bounding ranges at frequent intervals, contribute materially to the process. The valleys of this quality are always thickly studded with villages, whose inhabitants are ardent agriculturists. Every available yard of ground is utilised, the affluent streams, as we have said, affording valuable facilities for irrigation.

The most fruitful valleys in Central Tibet are those of the Nyang Chhu, the Rong Nag Chhu, the Lhon Chhu, the Yarlung Chhu, the Kyi Chhu or Lhása river, the Shang Chhu or Penam-nyang, the Zing-chhyi Chhu, and the Tsemong Chhu, all of which flow into the mighty Yeru Tsang-po. However the Nyang and Yarlung rivers bear away the palm for the fertility of the lands they water. For the last 65 miles of its course, the valley through which the Nyang runs keeps an average breadth of 10 miles, every yard of which is cultivated. The produce of wheat, oats, millet, peas, and various pulses is enormous, although the altitude averages 12,650 feet. Along the banks are numerous flour-mills worked by water-power provided by the ever-recurring tributaries from the hills on either side of the Nyang. Where the hill-streams are absent the mills are worked by artificial irrigating canals. In places where the slope to the river is too steep for cultivation, the banks are rendered attractive to the eye by a perfect clothing of Tibetan furze bushes (Caragana versicolor), which, though less handsome than English gorse, impart in summer the gayest of colouring. The only trees are

[1] In the Eastern districts turnips are by no means scarce, cattle being fed on a mash made from them. Horses are often fed on this turnip pap by force, a horn funnel being put down their throats for the purpose.

42

willows and poplar on the flats, and dense thickets of *pa-ma* (Juniperus squamosa) and fir (*som-shing*), interspersed with a few walnuts (*targha*), covering the lower terraces of the bounding heights. But so fruitful is this whole valley that it has received the name of Nyang Chhu, or "river of delicacies"—delicacies, at least, to the poor Tibetan.

However, the Yarlung Valley and the lower parts of Lhobrak have perhaps the greatest reputation for fruitfulness in Central Tibet Unfortunately, although explored by the Survey agent Urgyan Gyats'o and also earlier by Nain Singh, apparently no specimens of the flora of those districts or particulars of their produce were brought back. Their fertility, which is always spoken of as something unusual for Tibet, is probably owing not only to the comparatively lower elevation (Yarlung valley: 11,350–11,600 feet; Upper Lhobrak valley 10,800 –11,200 feet); but also to the considerable rains and snow they experience. Apparently the Yarlung district comes in for a share of the abundant rainfall which Western Yunnan and South-Eastern Tibet are favoured with—due to currents brought up from the ocean *viâ* the Yangtse-kiang and Salwin river. These moist discharges do not seem to reach to the Nyang Chhu or to Lhása. Nevertheless the Tsang province, where the Nyang occurs, receives some slight effects from higher currents of the Indian monsoon, the superflux of which passes in over the lower summits of the Bhutan Himalayas. The Lhobrak district, moreover, enjoys the moisture driven up from Bengal through the defiles of the Lhobrak Tsangpo and the Manas river.

KHAMS AND EASTERN TIBET.

We can hardly close these imperfect remarks on Tibetan vegetation without a few words on the Eastern Provinces. In the northern parts of Eastern Tibet, when the altitude of the plains north of the long Dang La range and south of Koko Nur runs between 10,500 and 11,800 feet, the flora which has been revealed somewhat meagrely by Przhevalski's collections approximates to that of Western Tibet, Lahul, and Phari at higher altitudes. In the Tsaidam salty steppes and the region at the base of the Altán Tag range, we have likewise a related flora, even though the general level is more than 2,000 feet lower.[1] The collections of the Russian explorer Obruchev, made from

[1] In a letter to the author dated May 1895, Dr. David Prain of the Royal Botanic Gardens, Calcutta, alluding to this matter, says: "The point you raise is indeed a very pertinent one, and it is one that has often puzzled me. Why do species occur at lower levels as we go progressively further east? I find it true

1893 to 1895, and Major Wellby's of 1896, have not yet, however, been assimilated, so far as published reports reveal.

South of the Dang La range in the many districts of the province of Khams, that is, south of lat. 33° and east of long. 92°, we have few materials for any detailed description of the plants and trees of Eastern Tibet.

Travellers in those parts assure us that the whole aspect of the country, with its vegetation, is different to the general condition in the west. For example, in portions of the Khams territory lying so far north as lat. 31°25′ and a few miles west of Chhamdo, where the elevation ranges between 10,800 and 11,500 feet, we are told of picturesque gorges and lovely bits of forest scenery; and there amidst rocks flourish large rhododendrons, coccinea, and junipers, with groves of fir trees. Pine woods of considerable growth, probably of *Abies Webbiana,* skirt thickly the banks of the Dzi Chhu, only a little further south, affording timber of large girth used as roof-beams for the houses. Again in the Riwochhe district, a few miles still further south (*circa* lat. 31°12′ N., long. 96°15′E.) along the northern bank of the Gyáma Ngul Chhu, we find one of the most beautiful valleys conceivable, rivalling the best in Kashmir. Forests of rhododendron (probably *R. Hodgsoni* or *R. campylocarpum*) and fir overhang the river, with here and there open grassy vales with trees scattered park-like about. The abundance of wood-fuel allows of iron-smelting operations being carried on. Moreover the fields of barley are here separated by palisading of fir branches instead of with stone walls. Yet the observed altitude of the Riwochhe valley is put down at quite 12,000 feet. There can be no doubt that considerable supplies of ocean moisture penetrate even so far as this up the Gyama Ngul Chhu by way of the Salwin River, into which the other river developes.

However, in certain narrow and sheltered valleys much further to the north than the latitude of Chhamdo, an unexpected luxuriance of vegetation may be met with. Thus, the Russian traveller Kozlov writes in glowing terms of what he styles "the warm-wooded valley of one of the tributaries of the Upper Mekong, the Ra Chu," where his party wintered in 1900–01. This valley would be as far north as

of *all* the Himalayan genera that I have studied so far. When the same species does extend so far I find that plants of 12,000 ft. in the N.W. Himalaya occur at from 9–10,000 ft. in Sikkim and at 7–8,000 ft. in Yunnan and Szechuen. What is odder still, occasionally we find species, that occur up to these levels in the Himalaya, still present in the Khasia Hills and at times even in the Shan Hills, where they can't go above 6,000 ft., as there is no possibility of their extending higher for *want of elevation.*"

lat. 32° N. and in about long. 97°45′E. Kozlov says: "The expedition found here large forests of fir, and of a tree-like *Juniperus Pseudo-Sabina*, intermingled with birches, willows, wild apricots, wild apples, and a great variety of bushes. The rugged crags, covered with a rich vegetation of trees, bushes, and grasses, presented a beautiful harmony of colours. In the thickly tree-clad gorges we found quantities of the white-eared pheasants (*Crossoptilon thibetanum*), the green *Ithaginis geoffroyi*, the *Tetraophasis obscurus*, the *Tetrastes sewertzowi*, several species of woodpeckers, and a great quantity of smaller Passerine birds. During warm and bright days the naturalist, and in fact every person not insensible to the beauties of nature, could reap enjoyment both with eyes and ears. Flocks of pheasants walked about the little meadows, the eagles described their curves on the blue sky, and from the thickest of bushes, richly coloured by sun's rays, the songs of thousands of small birds could be heard. Of mammals which we did not see previously, we found monkeys, which were living in large and small colonies—very often in close neighbourhood to the Tibetans."

Further north still, in Eastern Tibet, in the valley of the Di Chhu (the upper waters of the Chinese Yangtse-kiang), almost as far N. as lat. 33°, the same traveller found in March a surprising degree of warmth and of advance in vegetation. "Here on the banks of the Blue river, which flows at an altitude of about 10,500 feet above sea-level, it was also very warm, and we saw already the first appearance of spring vegetation; the *Gentiana squarrosa* was in bloom, as also the buttercups, the dandelions, and so on. All sorts of insects and butterflies flew about. We also noticed the bank swallow (*Cotile riparia*). The Tibetans were busy in tilling the soil, and some of them had already begun sowing wheat and barley, while on the best fields we saw the first seedlings of wheat piercing the ground."

The principal trees of Eastern Tibet, S.E. of Chhamdo, appear to be various species of pine, evergreen oak, holly, and rhododendron, which quite take the place of the miserable willows and poplars of Central and Western Tibet. *Juniperus excelsa* forms the common scrub on the hillsides from 10,000 to 13,500 feet; and, wherever it is, there do the lovely *Crossoptilon* pheasants abound, feeding on its berries. On the mountain spurs below 10,000 feet *Ribes* shrubs with several sorts of *Rubus* bramble supersede the juniper.

As you approach the region lying just west of Batang and you descend to an elevation between eight and nine thousand feet above the sea, the whole vegetation changes; and you journey among clematis, syringas, jessamine, eglantine, and scandent species of *Colquhounia*. Past Batang, though the general level ascends to 10,000 feet, and along hill and valley between that place and Darchendo, you arrive in the region of the regular flora of the southern borders of Szechuen. Here are orchids (*Dendrobium* chiefly), hydrangeas, varied azaleas of all sizes, purple ipomoea, crimson gloxinia, primulas, and wild roses of the deepest red. The richness of the flowers even at considerable heights in this part of Tibet rivals those of the valleys of Sikkim. One might say this especially of the various species of large rhododendron with magnificent blossoms of every colour. Near Darchendo rhododendrons grow in wanton luxuriance up the neighbouring hills to a limit of about 12,000 feet.[1] Another feature of the country between Litang and Darchendo is the profusion of wild gooseberry, black currant, and raspberry bushes. The black currant (*Ribes nigrum*) here developes into a tree 18 feet in height and bearing bunches of fruit 12 to 16 inches long. Apples, peaches and nectarines are also abundant, while in the gorges and deeper valleys the vegetation becomes distinctly sub-tropical.

However, the wealth of flora here on the utmost confines of Tibet is due as much to the plenteous rainfall of these parts as to the decided decrease in altitude.

[1] Mr. A. E. Pratt, camping at 13,000 ft. near Darchendo, writes: "The tent was pitched at the head of a valley, the sides of which could be seen for miles down covered with rhododendrons in blossom of all shades of white, pink, and red—a perfect sea of bloom" Surely this is a scene unknown even in the Sikkim of Hooker's time?